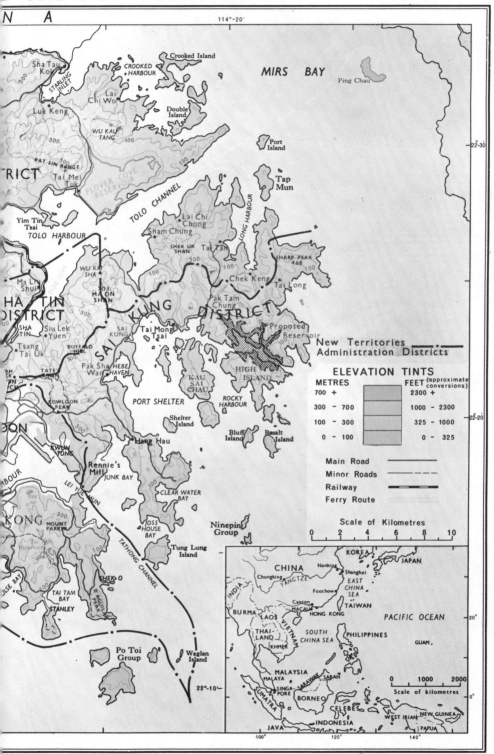

N A

114°-20'

Crooked Island

MIRS BAY

Ping Chau

Sha Tau Kok

CROOKED HARBOUR

STARLING INLET

Lai Chi Wo

Double Island

Luk Keng

WU KAU TANG

100

Port Island

22-30

300

PAT SIN RANGE

500

Tai Mei Tuk

PLOVER COVE RESERVOIR

TOLO CHANNEL

Tap Mun

RICT

Yim Tin Tsai

TOLO HARBOUR

300

Lai Chi Chong

Sham Chung

SHEK UK SHAN

Tai Tan

200

KONG HARBOUR

SHARP PEAK 468

100

Ma Liu Shui

WU KAI SHA

303

MA ON SHAN

Chek Keng

100

Tai Long

HA TIN DISTRICT

SHA TIN

Siu Lek Yuen

160

SAI KUNG DISTRICT

Pak Tam Chung

Tai Mong Tsai

Proposed Reservoir

New Territories Administration Districts

Tsang Tai Uk

BUFFALO HILL

SAI KUNG

ELEVATION TINTS

TATE

Pak Sha Wan

HEBE HAVEN

KAU SAI CHAU

HIGH ISLAND

METRES

FEET (approximate conversions)

ON

KOWLOON PEAK

PORT SHELTER

ROCKY HARBOUR

700 +

2300 +

300 - 700

1000 - 2300

Shelter Island

100 - 300

325 - 1000

Hang Hau

Bluff Island

Basalt Island

0 - 100

0 - 325

Rennie's MHL

JUNK BAY

Main Road

BOUR

KWUN TONG

LEI YUE MUN

CLEAR WATER BAY

Minor Roads

Railway

300

Ferry Route

KONG

MOUNT PARKER

100

JOSS HOUSE BAY

Ninepin Group

Scale of Kilometres

0   2   4   6   8   10

Reservoir

TATHONG CHANNEL

Tung Lung Island

KOREA

JAPAN

CHINA

Nanking

Shanghai

ULSE BAY

TAI TAM BAY

STANLEY

SHEK O

D'AGUILAR PEAK

Chungking

YANGTZE

EAST CHINA SEA

INDIA

Foochow

TAIWAN

BURMA

Canton

MACAU

HONG KONG

PACIFIC OCEAN

20°

Po Toi Group

Waglan Island

LAOS

VIETNAM

SOUTH CHINA SEA

PHILIPPINES

GUAM

22°-10'

THAILAND

KHMER

22°-10'

MALAYSIA

MALAYA

SARAWAK

SABAH

SUMATRA

SINGAPORE

BORNEO

0   1000   2000

Scale of kilometres

CELEBES

WEST IRIAN

NEW GUINEA

JAVA

INDONESIA

PAPUA

0°

100°

120°

140°

THE GOVERNMENT AND POLITICS OF HONG KONG

NORMAN MINERS

Senior Lecturer
Department of Political Science
University of Hong Kong

HONG KONG
OXFORD UNIVERSITY PRESS
LONDON NEW YORK MELBOURNE
1975

Oxford University Press

OXFORD LONDON GLASGOW NEW YORK
TORONTO MELBOURNE WELLINGTON CAPE TOWN
DELHI BOMBAY CALCUTTA MADRAS KARACHI LAHORE DACCA
KUALA LUMPUR SINGAPORE JAKARTA HONG KONG TOKYO
NAIROBI DAR ES SALAAM LUSAKA ADDIS ABABA
IBADAN ZARIA ACCRA BEIRUT

© *Oxford University Press 1975*

Filmset by T.P. Graphic Arts Services, Hong Kong
Printed by Everbest Printing Co. Ltd.
Published by Oxford University Press, News Building, North Point, Hong Kong

To my wife, Wilma

Preface

THIS book is not written to prove a thesis or to test an hypothesis; it is not an historical treatise, though a certain amount of historical detail has had to be included. It is intended simply to be a description of the way the crown colony of Hong Kong is run in the year 1975, within the constraints imposed upon it by its international position and its economy. This system of government is in many respects very different from the position as defined in the colony's constitutional documents. In practice the Governor is much more circumscribed in the changes he can effect than the listing of his powers in the *Letters Patent* and *Royal Instructions* would indicate; and the unofficial members of the Legislative Council, far from being an impotent minority, are normally able to get their own way if they can agree among themselves on what should be done. But this contrast between legal theory and day-to-day political practice is frequently not appreciated by students, who sometimes seem to think that the present Governor, Sir Murray MacLehose, can act in ways which even his nineteenth century predecessors seldom aspired to.

The problem is that it is much easier to discover what the Executive Council, the Public Service Commission or the Heung Yee Kuk are legally entitled to do than to investigate the actual extent of their influence over particular decisions. The annual reports of government departments have grown thicker with facts as the years go by, but the earlier post-war reports were often more idiosyncratic and informative, before the public relations aspect of this exercise took priority. Debates in the Legislative Council likewise often conceal more than they reveal; but occasionally when controversy becomes intense they disclose something of the processes of government decision-making. Unfortunately there is a dearth of memoirs and autobiographies by the chief actors in Hong Kong since the war; the only exception is Six Alexander Grantham's candid account of his colonial career ending as Governor from 1947 to 1957. For the rest I have had to rely on what an outsider can pick up while working in Hong Kong for the past five years. It is particularly difficult for a foreigner to give an account of the attitudes of the Chinese population to their British overlords; for this aspect I am heavily indebted to discussions with students at the university and the comments of Chinese friends and colleagues, supplemented by what little survey evidence is available.

The plan of this book took its original inspiration from a paragraph in a speech in 1971 by Mr. Dennis Bray, then District Commissioner for the

New Territories, in which he spoke of the stability of Hong Kong as resting on a tripod of consents—the local people, China and Britain—none of which could be tampered with without imperilling the whole structure. (see p. 225) In a sense the following work is an extended commentary on this text, though I have added the economy as a further limiting factor of equal importance with the other three.

The manuscript was delivered to the publishers in May 1974; more recent developments have been incorporated where possible. But it is a hazardous business to attempt to describe a continuing governmental system; what formerly seemed like rocks in the political landscape can suddenly prove to be nothing but sand castles and disappear without trace at the next high tide. More prosaically, the observant reader will notice instances where the fine cutting edge of a paragraph's argument is blunted by the note at the end of the chapter which brings the story up to date; though there are other notes which have the opposite effect.

Where this seemed helpful I have compared the workings of the institutions of government in Hong Kong with those in Britain, from which many of them were originally derived. In view of the absence of meaningful elections in the colony it might be thought more appropriate to compare the Legislative Council with such nominated assemblies as the People's Consultative Congress of Indonesia under Sukarno, or the legislatures of the few other remaining colonies. Unfortunately these political systems have been little studied and their environments are very different from Hong Kong; so it seemed more useful to stress the similarities to and differences from the system of government in Britain, with which readers of this book are most likely to be familiar.

As far as possible I have tried to avoid the technical vocabulary favoured by some political scientists, believing that the argument would gain nothing by its use. In accordance with local practice the Hong Kong administration is generally referred to as 'government' without any article.

A number of government officers, unofficial members and others have been generous with their time in answering my questions and commenting on particular points. I would have liked to thank them all individually by name, though this might have given a spurious authority to the work; but since several have insisted on civil service anonymity it seems best to encompass them all in one omnibus but very sincere acknowledgement. However, I must record my special thanks to my colleague, Gordon Lawrie, who read through each chapter as it was written and saved me from many errors of fact and syntax. His restraining hand may be detected wherever a fine sweeping generalization is qualified by an intrusive 'perhaps', 'probably' or 'to some extent'. I am also most grateful to Miss Anita Ng who deciphered and typed successive drafts with uncomplaining efficiency. The responsibility for any remaining flaws, errors and omissions is mine alone.

Department of Political Science,   N.J. MINERS
University of Hong Kong,
March 1975

Contents

Preface   vii
Acknowledgements   xii
INTRODUCTION   xiii

PART I: THE SOCIAL AND ECONOMIC CONTEXT

1. BRITISH COLONIAL RULE   3
   The Strategic Argument   3
   The Moral Argument   5
   The Economic Argument   6

2. THE PRESENCE OF CHINA   15
   The Economic Balance Sheet   17
   Diplomatic and Strategic Considerations   22
   China and Democracy in Hong Kong   24

3. CHINESE ATTITUDES AND BRITISH RULE   29

4. ECONOMIC CONSTRAINTS AND GOVERNMENT'S IDEOLOGY   40
   The Ideology of Government   43

PART II: THE INSTITUTIONS OF GOVERNMENT

5. HONG KONG'S CONSTITUTION: THE LETTERS PATENT
   AND ROYAL INSTRUCTIONS   49
   Constitutions in General   49
   The Constitution of Hong Kong   50
   Constitutional Conventions   53

6. THE GOVERNOR AND THE EXECUTIVE COUNCIL   58
   The Executive Council   62

7. THE PUBLIC SERVICE   71
   The Colonial Secretariat and the Departments   71
   Administrators and Specialists   76
   Recruitment and the Public Service Commission   78
   The Progress of Localization   80
   Boards and Committees   84

8. THE LEGISLATIVE COUNCIL: COMPOSITION AND
   THE PASSING OF ORDINANCES   90

Membership 90
Voting 92
The Process of Legislation 95
Delegated Legislation 100

9. THE LEGISLATIVE COUNCIL: FINANCIAL CONTROL 104
Financial Control in Britain and Hong Kong 104
The Finance Committee 107
The Annual Financial Cycle 112
The Audit Department 114
Financial Control from London 115

10. THE LEGISLATIVE COUNCIL: CONTROLLING THE
ADMINISTRATION 119
Debates 120
Questions 121
The UMELCO system 123

11. THE ROLE OF THE UNOFFICIAL MEMBERS 128
The 'Unrepresentativeness' of the Unofficials 128
The Unofficials as Part-time Legislators 129
The Lack of a Vigorous, Open Opposition 132
The Illiberality of the Unofficials 134
The Power of the Unofficials 135

12. LOCAL GOVERNMENT: THE NEW TERRITORIES 139
Their Acquisition: Problem of the Walled City
of Kowloon 139
The Administration of the New Territories 140
Village Representatives, Rural Committees and the
Heung Yee Kuk 143
The Future Pattern of Administration 146

13. LOCAL GOVERNMENT: THE CITY DISTRICT OFFICES 148

14. LOCAL GOVERNMENT: THE URBAN COUNCIL 155
Composition and Elections 156
Functions and Powers 160
Finance 162
Non-statutory Functions 163

15. THE REFORM OF LOCAL GOVERNMENT: 1946–1973 168
The Young Plan 168
1966–1973 169
The Case for Elected Local Authorities 171
The Practical Difficulties of setting up Local Authorities 174

PART III: PRESSURES AND INFLUENCES

16. NOT DEMOCRACY, BUT POLITICS 181

17. PRESSURE GROUPS 185
Why Pressure Groups are encouraged by Government 186

How Pressure Groups influence Government 188
An Assessment of the Pressure Group System 191

18. PUBLIC OPINION 195
The Sources of Public Opinion 197
Government's Efforts to influence Public Opinion 200

19. THE ROLE OF THE BRITISH GOVERNMENT 203
The Framework of Powers and Conventions 203
The Actors: Ministers versus the Hong Kong Administration 207
Channels of Communication: The Foreign and Commonwealth Office and the Hong Kong London Office 210

20. PRESSURES FROM CHINA 215

21. CONCLUSION 221

Appendixes 226
Bibliography 283
Index 289

Acknowledgements

The author and publisher wish to make grateful acknowledgement to the following for permission to reproduce copyright material:

Curtis Brown Ltd., Cassell & Co. Ltd., Hong Kong University Press, Houghton Mifflin Company.

Quotations from Crown-copyright records on the Public Record Office appear by permission of the Controller of Her Majesty's Stationery office.

Extracts from Hong Kong Hansard reproduced by kind permission from the Hong Kong Government.

Quotations from *The Times* reproduced by permission.

Introduction

IN the last thirty years most countries in East and South-East Asia have suffered major political upheavals. Regimes have been overthrown and constitutions rewritten following defeat in war, the withdrawal of the colonial powers, communist revolutions or military *coups d'etat*. Throughout all these convulsions Hong Kong has continued to run its affairs in accordance with a constitution which is basically and formally the same as it was in the nineteenth century. Indeed, if the first British governor of Hong Kong, Sir Henry Pottinger, were to return to the colony today practically the only things he would recognize would be the outlines of the Peak and the system of government, which has hardly changed in 130 years: power is concentrated in the hands of a royal governor, advised by a nominated executive council whose advice he can ignore, and laws are still passed by a nominated legislative council in which he commands a majority of the votes, just as was the case in 1843. Such continuity of governmental institutions is not unique; similar stability may be found in the isolated mountain kingdom of Bhutan in the Himalayas, which has not yet been touched by the pressures of the twentieth century, and in the Portuguese colony of Macau. But Hong Kong is not a remote backwater; it is a flourishing manufacturing city with a national income per head third to Japan and Singapore in Asia,[1] and a total export trade greater than that of India. The remarkable advance made by the colony in mastering modern techniques in the industrial and commercial sphere only serves to highlight the contrast with its apparent lack of progress in the realm of government and administration.

Why has this living fossil of early imperial government managed to survive and prosper when its larger neighbours have undergone such far-reaching changes? The short answer is that the colony continues to exist only because it suits the interests of Britain, China and its own citizens that this should be so. Any one of these three could initiate or force a change in the *status quo*, but each refrains from making any move, for fear that the results would be more detrimental to it than the present equilibrium. So long as this consensus continues, the colony is safe, provided only that it remains able to earn its living by successful trading in the world's markets; for an economic slump would put its separate existence in jeopardy as surely as any conscious act by Britain, China or its own population.

This extraordinary congruence of interest between a decayed imperial power, the self-proclaimed leader of the coming world revolution and the local Chinese is commonly too much taken for granted. British policy since 1967 has been to withdraw from all her military bases east of Suez and concentrate her declining strength in the European theatre. Why then does she retain Hong Kong with its garrison of 8,000 men, though the rest of her colonial empire is nothing more than a few scattered islands whose total population is less than a fifth of that of Hong Kong? Mao Tse-tung has not hesitated to reestablish direct Chinese rule over Tibet, a province that slipped from Chinese control in the nineteenth century. Why then has he not moved to recover Hong Kong which was annexed by the British after defeating China in the first and second opium wars? As for the attitudes of the local population, it is easy to explain the support given to the British administration by the leading businessmen who have made handsome profits in the past twenty years, and by the middle classes who fled from the chaos of the Communist takeover. But why have the poorer Chinese remained so politically apathetic? Hong Kong offers the ordinary labourer a higher standard of living and a wider choice of consumer goods than is available in the People's Republic; more nebulously the success of a few self-made millionaires nourishes the hope of the poorest hawker that he can rise to wealth by diligence or by good luck on the stock exchange. But these advantages must be balanced against the greater insecurity of livelihood under a free economy with a minimal system of social welfare. Elsewhere in Asia and Africa nationalist leaders have been able to convince the masses that poverty in freedom is preferable to affluent slavery under foreign rule. Why have such appeals, which have made colonial rule impossible in the most backward parts of Africa, been unsuccessful among the proudest race in the world?

Before we look at the formal structure of government it is necessary to try to provide an answer to these questions, since the continued presence of the British, and the continued restraint of the local population and the Chinese government can never be taken for granted. The possible reactions of London, Peking and its own citizens enter into every decision of the colonial government and severely limit the scope for possible changes in the administrative or constitutional structure of the colony. We must also look at the state of the economy, since unless this continues to grow and satisfy the rising demands of Hong Kong's expanding population all political manoeuvres designed to preserve the colony's future are likely to prove futile. If the colony were bankrupt and its people were starving Britain would not long retain its sovereignty, nor would China have any reason to hold back from absorbing it once more into the motherland.

1. In 1972 Singapore's G.N.P. per head was approximately US$1,170; Hong Kong's was US$1,050.

PART I

The Social and Economic Context

1 British Colonial Rule

'Her Majesty's Government remain unchanged in their determination to
maintain their authority in the Colony and to discharge their full responsibilities towards Hong Kong and its people.'

House of Commons, 17 January 1968

SINCE the end of the second world war it has been British policy to guide
the colonial territories to self-government within the Commonwealth, and
to grant independence when the inhabitants of a territory are ready for it.
'Readiness' is notoriously difficult to define; in practice the main consideration was the strength of the local pressures on the British to hand
over and a calculation of the relative costs, in cash and goodwill, of
attempting to postpone or accelerate the inevitable end of empire.
Compared to most of the territories that have gained self-determination
in the last twenty years Hong Kong is more ready for the burdens and
opportunities of independence. It is rich by the standards of colonial
territories, it has no problem of inter-racial tension such as exists in the
plural societies of Africa, and it has a large cadre of efficient Chinese
administrators, the heirs of a tradition of civilized government far older
than that of their temporary colonial overlords. The missing factor is any
demand on the part of most articulate opinion in the colony that the
British should leave. In itself this is no reason for the British to remain.
Elsewhere, for example in Ceylon in 1947, the British handed over power
when there was very little popular demand for independence.

Britain's unqualified reaffirmation of her determination to maintain
her authority in Hong Kong, expressed on a number of occasions by
British Ministers during and after the 1967 confrontation with the
communists,[1] has been explained in terms of its strategic importance, of
Britain's moral obligation to the colony's inhabitants and of the economic
advantages derived from it.

THE STRATEGIC ARGUMENT

At the time of the original seizure of Hong Kong the colony's role, in
addition to its commercial importance, was envisaged as being one of
the string of British naval stations round the world which provided
bunkering and repair facilities for the Royal Navy. During the nineteenth
century it served as a base for British operations in China and the Far

East. The last time that Hong Kong was used in this way was in 1950 when troops from the garrison were sent to defend South Korea against attack from the North as part of the United Nations force.

But this era is now passed. The naval dockyard has been closed down. There is no British fleet in the Far East and the visits of the American Seventh Fleet are purely for shore leave and recreational purposes; their bases are elsewhere, in the Philippines or Hawaii. The British base in Singapore has been run down and Hong Kong is now an isolated outpost to which reinforcements would have to be sent by air from England in an emergency. Possibly, if the situation in Hong Kong was quiet, troops from the garrison could be spared to reinforce the Gurkha battalion in the British protected state of Brunei.[2] But that would be the limit of Hong Kong's capabilities.

The tasks of the British garrison, as officially stated by the Minister of Defence, are to assist in the internal security and external defence of the colony. In 1956, 1966 and 1967 British troops were called out to assist the Police and the locally raised Hong Kong Regiment. They were mainly used for cordoning operations and to enforce curfews and on no occasion did they need to open fire.[3] As far as external security is concerned the normal British garrison of about 8,000 men[4] is obviously too small on its own to defend Hong Kong against a full-scale attack by the People's Liberation Army. The swift fall of the colony in 1941 showed how exposed it was and is to invasion from the mainland, particularly when lacking adequate air support.[5] When there were real fears of such an attack in 1949 the garrison was reinforced to 30,000 men. At most the present forces might be able to delay the invaders for a few days to enable diplomatic pressure to be brought to bear on Peking. In the 1950s, the then Governor, Sir Alexander Grantham, argued that the United States Forces in Taiwan and the Seventh Fleet might then be used to force China to withdraw.[6] Clearly no such assistance would be available in the state of China-U.S.A. relations in the 1970s.

On a realistic view the present task of the army units near the frontier is to patrol the border so as to deter any attempt by the People's Liberation Army or the local militia to make a foray across.[7] Such an incursion might be in pursuit of an escaping refugee, or an initiative launched by a local commander without the authorization of Peking (as perhaps occurred at Sha Tau Kok in 1967 during the chaos of the Cultural Revolution). The army presence also stops any moves by China to nibble away at the border by advancing her frontier posts to take in an extra field here or a strip of land there.[8] Moreover, if it were not for the security provided by these troops the inhabitants living close to the frontier would lack the confidence to obey the laws of Hong Kong rather than instructions sent from the People's Republic of China.

It is hardly likely that China would ever have to fight to conquer Hong Kong. A demand from Peking, coupled by a credible threat of the use of force if the ultimatum were not accepted, would doubtless be sufficient to persuade Britain to negotiate the cession of the colony. But if there ever were to be an invasion the army could at most hope to fight a limited holding action which would give time for the evacuation of the European population and those Chinese who would be compromised by the services they had rendered to the colonial regime.[9]

THE MORAL ARGUMENT

When the British garrison was reinforced in 1949 the arriving troops were told that in defending Hong Kong Britain was fulfilling a moral obligation, which could not be honourably overlooked or renounced, to those who had fled to the colony for protection.[10] The same argument was also given a prominent place by speakers in the British Parliament in the debates in 1967.

This argument needs to be examined with a certain scepticism. Britain has had moral obligations to many faithful supporters of her rule whom she found it necessary to abandon in the course of divesting herself of her Empire. The treaties guaranteeing everlasting British protection to the Indian princes were unilaterally abrogated when India became independent in 1947; and so were many similar agreements with local chiefs and tribal potentates in Africa who had loyally served as the instruments of Indirect Rule on behalf of the colonial power. The European settlers and the Asian traders of East Africa relied on Britain's continued protection only to find, in the case of the latter group, that their promised access to Britain was delayed and curtailed because the politicians at Westminister were afraid of losing votes at the next election.[11] It may well be that the British had no real choice, given the realities of power at the time in question. But these examples underline the fact that governments do not allow themselves to be bound by the same standards of morality which apply to private individuals.

In the case of Hong Kong, no one suggests that Britain is under an obligation to defend her colony in an heroic but ultimately futile last ditch stand against a full-scale Chinese invasion. It would not be in the interests of the inhabitants if the communists took over a heap of burning rubble. But suppose some future British government, without any prompting from China, considered that on balance Britain's economic interests would best be served by abandoning Hong Kong, would any residual feeling of imperial responsibility for the colony's inhabitants carry any weight when the matter was argued out in the corridors of Whitehall? On past form one might think not, but moral obligations and sentimental or emotional ties cannot be ignored quite so easily as this. British governments always have to take public opinion into account and this may prove decisive when the arguments for and against a particular policy are fairly evenly balanced. One reason why massive reinforcements were sent to Hong Kong in 1949 was the fear felt by the Labour Government that the loss of the colony would redound to their disadvantage in the approaching general election.[12] If it was decided to return Hong Kong to China, efforts would certainly be made to rouse a storm of protest at such a betrayal and to persuade the opposition in parliament to denounce the plans. Such an outcry would be led by those who have connexions with the colony and in particular would be orchestrated by those businessmen whose interests would suffer if it were abandoned; but because of the moral issue and the emotion that would be engendered, the agitation would involve a broader spectrum of opinion. Occasionally such campaigns can be effective in inducing the British government to modify its plans: for example in 1968 tentative negotiations with Argentina over its claims to the small British colony of the Falkland Islands proved abortive because the passionate refusal of the small British community there to consider any diminution of its link with the United Kingdom was taken up by the Conservative opposition.

However, it is unlikely that British public opinion would feel so strongly about the fate of 4 million Chinese. In the past twenty years almost all sentimental attachment to the imperial idea has been eroded away, and the British public would probably welcome any proposal to hand over the colony to China without a qualm, and only express surprise that this had not been done earlier.

The policy accepted by the Labour Party when in office from 1964 to 1970 was that Britain should not hold back any territory that wished to become independent, but on the other hand should not seek to push any territory faster than it wished to go. A minister speaking for the Conservative government in 1971 confirmed that this policy remained unchanged.[13] However, this statement leaves vague how the extent of the 'wish for independence' is to be assessed. This is easy in the case of most of the remaining colonies such as Gibraltar or the Seychelles where there is a parliament chosen by a general election, which can pass a motion asking for the end of British rule. But this method is not available in Hong Kong. In Palestine in 1948 and Aden in 1968 the British government regarded the persistence and success of small groups of terrorists as sufficient excuse to justify an imperial retreat, whatever the wishes of the majority of the populations there may have been. Presumably the same criterion would be applied in Hong Kong.

THE ECONOMIC ARGUMENT

The main reason why Britain continues to retain its hold on Hong Kong is clearly the economic advantages she gains from her imperial position. But these benefits are rather difficult to quantify, and there are also certain countervailing costs to be considered.

The main disadvantage is the cost of the garrison. This comes to about £28 million a year in foreign exchange and only £8 million of this is reimbursed by the Hong Kong government. The amount of this defence contribution is renegotiated every five years.[14] Thus Hong Kong has its armed forces provided very cheaply and in addition gains the appreciable economic advantage of the money spent by the army on local goods and services. Most of the troops in the colony are Gurkhas, who serve only in the Far East, but the garrison also includes two British battalions and supporting services, and also naval and air force units amounting to about 1,000 men. When the British Army is overstretched, as it is at present with its large commitment in Northern Ireland, finding troops to send to Hong

Kong can be inconvenient; but in normal circumstances this presents no difficulty, and service in the colony is a popular overseas posting.

Britain runs an adverse balance on visible trade with Hong Kong and this deficit is increasing, as shown by the following figures:[15]

	1969	1970	1971	1972	1973
British Imports (c.i.f.)	£125.5m	£128.4m	£164.8m	£184.7m	£264 m
British Exports (f.o.b.)	£89 m	£99.5m	£104.3m	£100.9m	£127.2m

Hong Kong has always been a free port and almost all British goods have to compete on equal terms with those of other countries in the open market. There are only a few exceptions to this, and none of importance: Commonwealth tobacco and liquor pay a slightly reduced rate of excise duty; motor vehicles not manufactured in the Commonwealth have to pay an additional tax when first licensed in the colony, and the two franchised public transport companies (the Kowloon Motor Bus Company and the China Motor Bus Company) are required by the terms of their ordinances to buy Commonwealth vehicles unless a specific exemption is granted by the Governor in Council.[16] British exports also benefit marginally from the natural preference of government officials to buy British goods when price and quality are comparable with those from elsewhere. But apart from this Hong Kong does not in any sense provide a captive market for British goods as was the case with certain other colonial powers, such as France.

On the contrary, Hong Kong has been able to take advantage of the Commonwealth preferences granted by Britain to develop a flourishing export trade to the mother country, particularly in textiles. These have been so successful that Britain has been obliged to ask Hong Kong to impose quotas on her exports in order to protect Britain's own textile industry in Lancashire. The British Textile Confederation would like to see even more severe restrictions imposed on Hong Kong imports, but because Hong Kong is her colony the British government feels inhibited from taking such action.[17]

However these disadvantages are small compared with the economic benefits which Britain obtains. Though statistical evidence is not available it is very likely that Britain's adverse balance on visible trade with the colony is compensated for by a surplus on invisible transactions, including such items as the pensions paid to retired Hong Kong civil servants in Britain, dividend remittances to British shareholders in Hong Kong enterprises, and payments for insurance, shipping and other commercial facilities arranged through the city of London.[18]

There are also other trading advantages for Britain. It has been claimed that Hong Kong provides a very useful shop-window and local base for British exporters selling in Asia.[19] In particular, the colony is a unique point of entry for trade with China. The old British firms here have developed very good relationships with the buying missions from the People's Republic stationed in Hong Kong, and also with their principals in Peking. The Chinese authorities generally seem to prefer to deal with trading partners that they know, and this gives an initial advantage to

British salesmen by providing them with commercial intelligence on what China is likely to need, and advice on how best to promote their products and the terms to offer. Whether they finally make any sales will of course depend on the quality of the goods they have to offer. In fact British trade with China has not done well over the past few years, but there was an improvement in 1973 as seen in the figures below:[20]

	1969	1970	1971	1972	1973
British Exports (f.o.b.)	£54.7m	£44.6m	£28.3m	£31.6m	£84.7m
British Imports (c.i.f.)	£37.7m	£33.5m	£31.6m	£35.6m	£47.8m

No one can say how much help is given by agencies in the colony, but the expertise available must help to smooth the path of British exporters.

However, Hong Kong can sometimes hinder rather than help the harmonious development of Sino-British trade relations. The colonial administration may occasionally feel obliged to take some action for internal reasons which gives offence to Peking, for example, the closing of a Communist school. As a result the Chinese might decide to place a contract elsewhere in order to demonstrate their displeasure or to induce the British government to put pressure on the local administration to alter its decision. In contrast, French or German firms are not liable to find themselves embarrassed in this way.

The most obvious benefit to Britain from her imperial position is the large sterling balances which Hong Kong maintains in London. In September 1973 these amounted to £736 million, which were partly invested in British government and local authority bonds and partly in short term loans and cash.[21] This money came from three main sources: the accumulated budget surpluses of the Hong Kong government; sterling assets held by the government's Exchange Fund as backing for the colony's currency and banknotes; and the reserves owned by Hong Kong's commercial banks.[22] In September 1973 Hong Kong's sterling balances represented about 12 per cent of Britain total foreign liabilities, and accounted for about 27 per cent of the total gold and foreign exchange reserves held by the Bank of England. In previous years the proportion was even higher; in March 1969 Hong Kong's balances represented 35 per cent of the Bank's assets. By keeping her reserves in London Hong Kong is in effect making a long-term loan to Britain, for which the colony receives a substantial rate of interest and also (from 1968 to 1974), a guarantee of their value in case the rate of exchange of sterling declined in international money markets.

From 1941 to 1972 Hong Kong was obliged to keep her external reserves in sterling because the colony had been compulsorily enrolled as a member of the sterling area by Britain. The sterling area was a grouping consisting mainly of the Commonwealth and a few other countries which had agreed to pool their reserves in London, to impose broadly similar controls on their residents to limit their use of foreign exchange, but to allow free movement of money within the sterling area. The advantage of this arrangement was that the currencies of member countries were backed by a far larger reserve held in London than any of them would call on individually as a defence against speculative pressures, and this reserve was also available to help members in temporary balance of payments difficulties, since not all members were likely to run into such difficulties at the same time. However, as time went on, the independent countries of the Commonwealth became increasingly unwilling to hold all their reserves in sterling and so made agreements with Britain to diversify part of their holdings into gold or foreign exchange. But because Hong Kong was a colony the British Treasury was in a position to forbid it to do the same.[23]

The whole sterling area system was effectively wound up in June 1972 when Britain unilaterally decided to allow the pound sterling to 'float' in foreign exchange markets and to impose exchange control on the transfer of capital to the rest of the sterling area. But this did not mean that Hong Kong was then free to move her external reserves out of sterling. When Britain had devalued her currency in 1967, sterling area countries had suffered heavy losses in the value of their reserves as measured in other currencies. In the case of Hong Kong this loss, in terms of the Hong Kong dollar, amounted to HK$450 million. Naturally all these countries then wished to diversify their reserves still further out of sterling, to avoid the possibility of this happening again. To prevent this threatened liquidation of sterling balances Britain offered all sterling area countries a guarantee of compensation for 90 per cent of any future losses sustained on their external sterling reserves, if Britain should devalue her currency again. The loss was to be measured in terms of U.S. dollars, since this was then the world's strongest currency and also the standard unit of the International Monetary Fund. This guarantee (known as the Basle arrangement) was only on condition that sterling area countries maintained the same proportion of their reserves in sterling as before. In the case of Hong Kong this proportion was 99 per cent, though it was subsequently reduced to 89.1 per cent in 1971. This guarantee was offered by Britain and accepted by Hong Kong for a period of five years from September 1968; so Hong Kong was not free to diversify her reserves, even though the sterling area system had been abolished, until September 1973, unless it was prepared to break this contract and forgo the guarantee.[24]

In September 1973, without any negotiations, Britain offered Hong Kong and the other sterling holders a renewal of this guarantee for a further six months at a slightly higher rate, but again only on condition that their balances held in London were not diminished. The Hong Kong government had been asking for some time that any renewal of the guarantee should be on terms which would allow the colony to diversify its reserves into other stronger currencies such as the Japanese yen, the German mark or the Swiss franc. This was because Hong Kong had a higher proportion of her external reserves in sterling than any other country, and also because the U.S. dollar itself had twice been devalued since 1968 (in December 1971 and February 1973), making the guarantee worth much less than had appeared in 1968. But the British government ungenerously refused to allow any such diversification, and assumed that

Hong Kong could not afford to reject her unilateral offer, since it was thought that the colony would be likely to incur greater losses by attempting to dispose of her sterling reserves in the prevailing state of the international money market, than if she accepted Britain's unsatisfactory terms.

In fact, the British government miscalculated. The Hong Kong government delayed notifying her agreement to Britain's unilateral offer from 6 September until 15 December. During this time the Hong Kong banks diversified their reserves out of sterling, a process which they had already begun some months earlier, by 'selling sterling forward'—that is, making contracts to buy foreign currencies at a fixed price in sterling on a date in the future.[25] Once this was done and about a third of the reserves had been moved out of sterling, Hong Kong indicated to London that it was ready to accept the September offer, but only on the understanding that the reserves of the banking system were not to be included. This was quite contrary to the September terms, since these applied only on condition that Hong Kong sterling assets remained undiminished; but by December Britain was suffering from the effects of the world oil crisis, coupled with the threat of a national coal miners' strike, and was in no position to quibble. So the guarantee was amended to cover only the Hong Kong government's sterling assets.

In March 1974 Hong Kong received compensation of about HK$44 million under this guarantee. It was then extended to the end of 1974, but it was no longer based on a fixed rate of exchange to the U.S. dollar. Instead, the value of the Hong Kong's reserves was to be calculated relative to the movements in a weighted average of a number of major world currencies, and Hong Kong was to receive compensation if the value of sterling dropped below a fixed point on this scale.[26]

In fact the pound sterling suffered only a slight depreciation during 1974, and by the end of the year Britain's reserves were in a comparatively healthy state, reaching $3,364 million in November, compared with £2,237 million in 1973 and £1,009 million in 1968. This was not because the decrepit British economy had suddenly revived but was solely the result of the quadrupling of the price of oil during the year, bringing a massive increase in the wealth of the Arab oil producers. Much of this money was banked in London to take advantage of the high interest rates available on short term loans there, in spite of the fact that these new deposits were not covered by any guarantee against currency fluctuations. This influx of funds brought substantial benefit to the reserves (estimated by The Economist at £1½ billion), which more than offset Britain's increased oil bill. This windfall enabled the Chancellor of the Exchequer to announce in November 1974 that the guarantee to the former members of the sterling area would not be renewed after the end of the year.[27] So from January 1975 Hong Kong is at last completely free to diversify her reserves as she pleases. However, this liberty is unlikely to be carried too far, since heavy losses would be suffered if the colony's holdings of British government securities were sold off at prevailing prices instead of waiting until the loans are repaid in full at the end of their term. The cost which would be incurred by immediately liquidating the portfolio will probably continue to keep a substantial portion of Hong Kong's reserves in sterling for some time to come.

Not unnaturally there has been much local criticism of the fact that until recently almost all the external assets of the Hong Kong government remained locked into sterling. It is argued that the money would be better used to pay for government building projects in Hong Kong, rather than acting as a prop for the ailing British economy, particularly since the real value of the reserves has been steadily eroded over the years by inflation. However, the slow growth rate of the British economy over the past twenty-five years, punctuated by periodic crises, meant that until the latter part of 1974 Britain's reserves were never large enough to allow Hong Kong's sterling balances to be substantially reduced, because of the fear that this would precipitate international speculation against the pound, forcing Britain either to deflate the economy or to devalue. Even a rumour in September 1973 that Hong Kong would refuse to accept the terms of the renewed guarantee was enough to set off a flurry on the foreign exchange markets.[28] At the end of 1974 Britain was for the moment less dependent on Hong Kong's sterling reserves than at any time in the previous twenty years. But if the oil states should decide to shift their money elsewhere, the colony's reserves may once again be needed to help buttress the value of sterling. Since 1968 this support has been secured more by financial bargaining between London and Hong Kong than by the exercise of Britain's prerogative powers over the colony. But the fact that Hong Kong is a dependency gives Britain an advantage in negotiations that she does not have when dealing with an independent country.

This support is likely to continue even if China seized the colony. Should this happen Britain would immediately take powers to freeze Hong Kong's sterling balances pending negotiations with China on compensation for British property and the payment of pensions and compensation for loss of career to British officials. Such talks could be protracted, and Britain would be in a strong bargaining position to ensure that any balances left after all claims had been settled would be liquidated only over a long period of time.

Britain has used this tactic once already. In 1939 the Soviet Union annexed the small Baltic states of Estonia, Lithuania and Latvia, which had been independent since 1918. The gold reserves of these countries had been deposited for safety in London, and so the Soviet Union demanded that these reserves should be handed over to her. Britain refused until agreement had been reached on the repayment of certain loans which had been entered into by these states. Agreement was not reached till 1967, twenty-seven years later, after three previous rounds of Anglo-Soviet talks on the issue had broken down. Meanwhile the reserves stayed locked in the Bank of England. So, on this analogy, Britain might think Hong Kong's reserves would be just as securely under her control if China seized the colony as they are under present arrangements.[29]

The British government indirectly gains one further economic benefit from Hong Kong in the profits earned by the nationalized British Airways Corporation. Since Britain manages all the colony's external affairs foreign airlines which wish to use Kai Tak airport must negotiate with the British authorities in London. Hong Kong is a very desirable stopping point for the world's airlines. Besides being one of the most efficiently run airports in Asia it is a very convenient landfall for airlines flying across the Pacific and a crossroads for passengers wishing to fly on to other destinations in Asia. This gives Britain a very useful bargaining counter. The profitability of an airline is directly related to the number of desirable routes on which it is allowed to operate, and so normally landing rights at Kai Tak are only granted if in return British Airways is allowed to fly a foreign route which the applicant airline would prefer to monopolize for itself. An airline which has no such return benefit to offer is likely to have its application refused. Compared to most world airlines BOAC (the forerunner of British Airways) had a good record of profitability and one of the main reasons for this was the negotiating strength it derived from the colonial status and geographical location of Hong Kong.

This may be advantageous for British Airways, but it is not equally advantageous for Hong Kong. The interest of Hong Kong is the maximum utilization of Kai Tak by as many airlines as possible, and in the past applications by foreign airlines such as SAS have been supported by the Hong Kong government, the Hong Kong Tourist Association and the Trade Development Council, but have been turned down by London out of consideration for narrowly British interests.[30] Quite apart from the revenue from landing fees, the more travellers who pass through Kai Tak or change planes there, the more opportunity there is to persuade them to spend a few days sightseeing in Hong Kong to increase the tourist trade. But the interest of Britain is to limit access by foreign airlines as much as possible, so that those who wish to fly to or from Hong Kong are obliged to use British Airways. In recognition of its value to Britain the British government gave an interest free loan of £3 million for the extension of Kai Tak runway in 1955, but ungratefully declined to give the colony any help when a further extension of the runway was required in 1970.[31]

For the moment there is no sign that Britain intends to abandon her largest remaining colony. Though statistics are not available it is highly probable that the profits made by British firms, the benefits to British Airways and the ultimate power to control Hong Kong's sterling balances far outweigh the only direct cost incurred by the British taxpayer, the colony's defence bill. Her Majesty's Government may occasionally suffer embarrassment from its colonial connection—in its relations with Peking, in attacks on colonialism in the United Nations, and particularly when under pressure from textile manufacturers at home. But these do not add up to very much. Ministers are normally kept too preoccupied with more immediate crises to consider taking any initiative in the affairs of the colony so long as it remains prosperous and peaceful. But this situation might alter if Hong Kong suffered a prolonged economic recession, or there were serious rioting which made it necessary to send troop reinforcements. The 'nation of shopkeepers' would soon cut its losses and move out if Hong Kong became an economic liability.

ADDENDUM

On 2 May 1975, the Director of Commerce and Industry announced that the preferences granted by Hong Kong to certain Commonwealth imports (see p. 7) would be abolished by 1 January 1976. This was a condition set by the American government before Hong Kong's exports to the United States could be included in its Generalized System of Preferences for developing countries (*South China Morning Post*, 3 May 1975).

1. For example *House of Commons Debates*, 10 July 1967, col. 96; 17 January 1968, Written Answers, col. 615; *House of Lords Debates*, 22 June 1967, col. 1599. See also *House of Common Debates*, 30 January 1973, Written Answers, col. 365; and note 13 below.

2. This point was made by a backbencher and not by a government minister in *House of Common Debates*, 5 April 1973, col. 663. There might be diplomatic difficulties if China objected to such a reinforcement. On 3 Dec 1974 the Minister of Defence told the House of Commons that the Gurkha battalion in Brunei was to be withdrawn, ibid col. 1354.

J. Rear, 'One Brand of Politics', p. 59, in K. Hopkins, *Hong Kong, The Industrial Colony* (O.U.P., Hong Kong, 1971), claims that 'The size of the garrison would seem to be determined much more by London's requirements of a British presence in the Far East than by the needs of Hong Kong', but he gives no arguments in support of this point of view.

3. See *Report on the Riots in Kowloon and Tsuen Wan 1956* (Government Printer 1957), pp. 19–27 and 37–41, *Kowloon Disturbances 1966, Report of Commission of Enquiry* (Government Printer 1967), pp. 72–6; J. Cooper, *Colony in Conflict* (Swindon Book Company, Hong Kong, 1970), pp. 127–43.

4. According to a Joint Services spokesman, in November 1974 the British Forces in Hong Kong consisted of 555 in the Royal Navy, 461 in the Royal Air Force and 9,242 in the Army (4,455 Gurkhas, 3,537 British troops from U.K. and 1,250 locally enlisted Chinese), *Sunday Post-Herald*, 24 Nov 1974. The Defence White Paper of March 1975 announced that the size of the garrison would be cut by fifteen per cent. The armoured squadron and most of the artillery would be withdrawn by 1976 and by 1977 one of the two British infantry battalions is to be replaced by a Gurkha battalion. This will reduce the number of British soldiers in the colony from 3,700 to 2,500. There are also to be cuts in the Royal Navy and Royal Air Force.

5. In the event of a Chinese attack the invaders would also be assisted by a large section of the local population, whereas in 1941 Chinese and British were united in resisting the Japanese.

6. Sir Alexander Grantham, *Via Ports* (Hong Kong University Press, 1965), p. 171.

7. *House of Lords Debates*, 22 June 1967, cols. 1591f, speech by Lord Bourne (formerly Governor and Director of Operations in Malaya 1954–6); also the interview with Lieutenant-General Sir Edwin Bramall, Commander British Forces, *South China Morning Post*, 13 February 1974.

8. For frontier incidents in the early 1950s and one attempt by China to enclose Hong Kong territory see Grantham, op.cit. p. 151.

9. This is stated by Cooper, op.cit. p. 296, who was formerly an army officer in Hong Kong. A spokesman for the army is also quoted as saying this in *Urban Council Proceedings*, 2 November 1971, p. 303.

10. H. Ingrams, *Hong Kong* (H.M.S.O. London 1952), p. 284. This was the first reason given to the troops; the second was British economic interests.

11. By the *Commonwealth Immigrants Act 1968* Parliament removed the automatic right of those holding British passports to enter Britain. However, Britain somewhat redeemed her tarnished reputation in 1972 when she accepted the Asians expelled from Uganda by General Amin, since they had nowhere else to go.

12. Grantham, op.cit. p. 143, quoting a senior British civil servant.

13. *House of Lords Debates*, 12 January 1971, cols. 16 and 83.

14. *H.K. Hansard 1971–72*, p. 22.

15. *Annual Abstract of Statistics* (H.M.S.O., London), Tables 283, 284.

16. *Public Transport Services (Hong Kong Island) Ordinance* (Cap. 317) sec. 22. *Public Transport Services (Kowloon and New Territories)* Ordinance (Cap. 318) sec. 20.

17. *South China Morning Post*, 17 October 1972 (Business News), quoted Mr. Japp,

director of the British Textile Confederation, as saying that the latest quota agreement was less restrictive than the British industry had hoped for: 'On the other hand, the industry could appreciate the government's problem in securing a voluntary agreement with a crown colony without appearing to wave the big stick'.

18. Britain gains similar commercial benefits for her well-established trading links with former colonies, such as Singapore. But in the case of Hong Kong a British withdrawal would be followed, not by independence, but by absorption into China.

19. *House of Lords Debates*, 22 June 1967, col. 1585, Lord Rhodes.

20. Details from *Annual Abstract of Statistics* (H.M.S.O. London).

21. Details of the charges in the sterling reserves from 1967 to 1972 were given by the Financial Secretary, *H. K. Hansard 1972–73*, pp. 217–29. These are summarized in the following table:

	Government Owned. (i.e. accumulated surplus and currency backing)	Bank Reserves	Total
Nov. 1967	?	?	£350m
March 1969	£190m	£200m	£390m
March 1972	£408m	£360m	£768m
May 1972	£418m	£385m	£803m
June 1972	?	?	£900m
Sept. 1973	?	?	£736m

Note. The September 1973 figure is from *The Times*, 24 September 1973. Details of changes in the reserves since September 1973 have not been revealed by anybody.

22. In order to make these bank reserves eligible for protection under the dollar guarantee given by the British government these bank reserves were technically 'borrowed' by the Exchange Fund, from 1968 to 1973. For details of the arrangement see *H.K. Hansard 1968*, pp. 577ff.

23. *The Economist*, 8 June 1968, p. 78 noted that, 'The Crown Colony has been forced by the British authorities to keep all its reserves in sterling: unlike other members of the sterling area it has not been allowed to diversify into gold or foreign currencies.' For example Ghana ran down her sterling balances and built up her own gold reserve after gaining independence in 1957.

24. See *Hong Kong 1974, Report for the Year 1973* (H.K. Government Printer), pp. 34–6.

25. Following the disbandment of the sterling area all restraints on the foreign currency transactions of banks were removed on 1 January 1973. The Hong Kong government was unable to do this with the bulk of its reserves since forward purchases of foreign currency were forbidden by the *Exchange Fund Ordinance* (cap 66, see 3(2)), and the permission of the Secretary of State was needed for any change. The ordinance was amended to permit such transactions in 1975, *H. K. Hansard 1974–75* p. 347. See Chapter 8, note 31, p. 103.

26. For the moves between August 1973 and March 1974 see especially *Far Eastern Economic Review*, 13 August 1973, p. 37, and 24 December 1973, p. 39; *South China Morning Post* and *The Times*, 17 December 1973; *The Economist*, 16 February 1974, p. 84 and 23 March 1974, pp. 85f.

27. *The Economist*, 16 November 1974, p. 115 and *Far Eastern Economic Review*, 29 November 1974, p. 51. Between Nov 1974 and Jan 1975 the proportion of the reserves held in sterling was reduced from 70 per cent to 50 per cent, (*H.K. Hansard*, 8 Jan 1975).

28. A report in the *Daily Telegraph* (London) to this effect on 28 September 1973 led to a drop in sterling of nearly two cents against the U.S. dollar.

29. Of course, Britain's negotiating position would be weakened if the Chinese mounted a swift invasion and were able to capture the Governor and other senior British officials. This is one reason for keeping a large enough military force in the colony to fight a holding action.

30. *South China Morning Post*, 26 May 1971, on the refusal of landing rights to SAS and KLM. KLM has now been granted landing rights, but only after the successful conclusion of Britain's negotiations to enter the Common Market.

31. *H.K. Hansard 1969–70*, p. 359. The Financial Secretary: 'We shall continue to press our moral case in London for a financial contribution towards the expansion of facilities (at Kai Tak), the use of which Her Majesty's Government restricts in the interests of British aviation, and against our interest, which is maximum utilisation.'

2 The Presence of China

THE People's Republic of China has the military power to overrun Hong Kong in a few days. Alternatively it could use its supporters in Hong Kong to instigate a sustained campaign of urban terrorism which would eventually undermine the British government's determination to maintain its authority in the colony. Possibly even such a resort to violence would be unnecessary. If China instituted a total blockade of the colony, it would probably not be too difficult to replace the food and raw materials imported from the People's Republic from other sources (though water rationing would be needed), but business confidence would suffer a fatal blow; all capital investment and building would cease, skilled personnel would leave as soon as they could and the problems posed by economic disruption and rising unemployment would probably be such that the British Administration would have little alternative but to accede to Peking's demands.

Moreover China has strong motives for intervention. There is both the nationalist urge to wipe out the humiliations imposed upon China by the unequal treaties of the nineteenth century, and also the ideological drive of Communism which should direct the followers of Mao Tse-tung to extend the revolution to this citadel of capitalism that lies within their grasp. Yet nothing happens. The colony of Hong Kong is allowed to flourish like a kind of economic nature reserve where primitive untamed capitalists are permitted to roam their market jungle under the watchful eyes of their Chinese keepers, who take a share of the profits but reserve the right to close down the spectacle if ever the beasts become dangerous or threaten the peace of the surrounding region.

Britain's right to remain in Hong Kong is derived from the treaties concluded with the Ching dynasty in 1842, 1860 and 1898. According to international law, as understood in the West, these treaties remain valid in spite of the political upheavals and constitutional changes that China has suffered since then,[1] but this is not the view of the present Chinese Communist leadership. On a number of occasions spokesmen have insisted that all such treaties forced upon China in the days of her weakness are not recognized as binding by the People's Republic and must be renegotiated at an appropriate moment. But China has never formally repudiated the treaties with Britain, since this should logically be followed by action to reincorporate Hong Kong into China. The most recent authoritative statement of the Chinese position is the letter sent by Ambassador Huang Hua, China's permanent representative at the United Nations, to the Special Committee on Colonialism on 10 March 1972:

> The questions of Hongkong and Macau belong to the category of questions resulting from the series of unequal treaties which the imperialists imposed on China. Hongkong and Macau are part of Chinese territory occupied by the British and Portugese authorities. The settlement of the questions of Hong Kong and Macau is entirely within China's sovereign right and do not at all fall under the ordinary category of colonial territories. Consequently they should not be included in the list of colonial territories covered by the declaration on the granting of independence to colonial countries and people. With regard to the questions of Hong Kong and Macau, the Chinese government has consistently held that they should be settled in an appropriate way when conditions are ripe....

This leaves the present position deliberately vague. If China does not recognize the old treaties, then the time might be considered 'ripe' for reincorporation at any time, and the year 1997, when the lease of the New Territories officially expires, has no great significance for China, even though Britain continues to regard this terminal date as valid.[2] In fact, China will probably need to make its intentions towards the colony clear well before 1997 if it wishes to take over Hong Kong as a going concern. Hardly any new investment is likely to be undertaken after about 1990 unless assurances were to be given that the lease of the New Territories would be renewed, since the rump of Hong Kong could hardly survive without them. The realistic options open to China in the late 1980s would seem to be either a swift and unannounced takeover, or an early undertaking to renew the lease, possibly at a high annual rental. Lengthy negotiations would only give the opportunity for capital, movable assets and skilled personnel to flee the colony without any compensating advantages.

But why should China wait till then? The People's Republic has good reasons for taking action, quite apart from the imperative drives of nationalism and anti-capitalism. Firstly, there is the motive of inter-national prestige. China frequently attacks the 'revisionists' of Moscow for deviating from the true tenets of Marxist-Leninism, becoming 'bourgeoisified' and purveying 'goulash communism' to the masses rather than undiluted dialectical materialism. In reply the Soviet Union and her satellites scornfully point the finger at China's tolerance of a profitable imperialist pimple on her border which she could easily scratch out if she had the mind to do so.[3] The occupation of Hong Kong would put a stop to these calumnies and win China increased respect among the nations of the Third World whom she is seeking to draw to her side. In a similar fashion India gained great applause from the poorer countries when she took possession of the tiny Portugese enclave of Goa in 1961.

Secondly, the reincorporation of Hong Kong would eliminate what Lyndon Johnson once called 'a shop window of the free way of life in Asia'. This display must be rather unsettling for the Communist authorities in Canton and South China where travellers from the forbidden city are able to give the subjects of Mao a first-hand description of the capitalist way of life and a basis of comparison to evaluate the merits of communism. Partly as a result of what they have heard, and in hope of a better life than China can offer, thousands of young refugees every year try to swim across Mirs Bay and Deep Bay to reach Hong Kong, in spite of considerable efforts to prevent them by the land and naval patrols of the People's Liberation Army.[4] The existence of these 'freedom swimmers' must be an embarrassment to Peking, and the closing of this escape route would put an end to one outlet for dissatisfaction with the present regime.

Thirdly, Hong Kong offers a base for covert operations against China by agents of Taiwan and the Soviet Union. In deference to China's wishes neither country is allowed to set up a consulate in the colony, but all the efforts of the police Special Branch cannot entirely prevent the activities of spies and saboteurs who try to smuggle guns into China or operate illegal transmitters broadcasting anti-communist propaganda.[5] Whenever such spy rings are discovered (often as a result of information supplied to the police by local communists) the agents are removed from the colony under the Deportation provisions of the *Immigration Ordinance*. But their total elimination could only be achieved by direct communist rule.

THE ECONOMIC BALANCE SHEET

The most common explanation of China's continued forbearance over Hong Kong is the economic advantages which she gains from it. In particular it is said that Hong Kong under British management provides more foreign exchange for China than would be the case if it were reincorporated. Exactly what proportion of Hong Kong's foreign exchange earnings go to Peking is a matter of guesswork. The only firm figures come from the statistics of visible trade between the two countries issued by the Hong Kong government. The mainland provides the colony with an increasing supply of foodstuffs (35 per cent of Hong Kong's total consumption),[6] textile yarn, clothing, raw materials and water every year, but takes only a negligible amount of the colony's domestic exports in return. The figures for the past few years are as follows:[7]

	1969	1970	1971	1972	1973
	(in millions of Hong Kong dollars)				
Merchandise imports from China (excluding re-exports)	1977	2142	2571	2864	4045
—Domestic exports to China	7	30	19	21	49
Visible trade balance	1970	2112	2552	2843	3996
+payment for water supply	17	17	17	21	21
	1987	2129	2569	2864	4017
equals US$m	330	355	428	500	781
approximately £ m	138	147	163	190	325

China also earns foreign exchange by using Hong Kong's facilities as a free port to send exports to third countries. These re-exports through the colony amounted to HK$759m in 1971 (US$125m), HK$983m in 1972 (US$175m), and HK$1,589m in 1973 (US$350m).[8] In addition, the profits of Communist banks, stores, hotels, cinemas and real estate are converted into foreign exchange in Hong Kong's free exchange market and transferred to Peking. Another source of foreign currency for China is the remittances from Chinese in Hong Kong to their families who are still living in the People's Republic, and similar gifts from overseas Chinese channelled through the colony's banking system. Guesses as to the total amount of foreign exchange obtained by China from and through Hong Kong vary widely. The *Far Eastern Economic Review* has given various estimates ranging up to £500m (US$1,200m).[9] The United States consulate in Hong Kong more conservatively estimated a total off-take of over US$700m in 1971 and of over $900m in 1972. The latter figure would mean that in that year Hong Kong provided China with the means to pay for 40 per cent of her hard currency imports from non-Communist countries, or 33 per cent of her total imports. These regular receipts are particularly valuable since China, as a matter of principle, has been unwilling (at least until 1974) to finance her imports by accepting foreign loans or buying on credit.

Quite apart from being a source of foreign exchange, Hong Kong may also be of economic benefit to China by providing a very convenient centre for trade contacts, financial negotiations and the gathering of commercial intelligence about Western technology. The Chinese have always preferred to keep foreigners at arm's length and this colonial enclave which is in, but not of, China has enabled them to do this with the maximum advantage to themselves. Hong Kong's facilities must have been particularly valuable in this respect between 1950 and 1972 when the People's Republic was unable to send ambassadors to most Western capitals. But China is no longer isolated in the world community. Her government is recognized by all the major powers and she is rapidly expanding her diplomatic missions and trading contacts all over the world. Foreigners crowd to the biannual Chinese Trade Fair in Canton and industrial exhibitions are staged by the major Western countries in Peking. Undoubtedly Hong Kong-based firms which have long established trading links with Peking will be in a strong position to take advantage of China's growing trade; but for China itself commercial contacts through Hong Kong and the permanent exhibition of Western goods available here must now be of relatively diminishing importance.

The extent to which China might suffer economically by reoccupying Hong Kong would depend a great deal on the conditions of the takeover and the type of new regime that was established. Obviously, if there was resistance and the People's Liberation Army had to fight its way in, the destruction of the colony's buildings and manufacturing capacity would make Hong Kong a liability rather than an asset. But this eventuality is highly unlikely; if Peking made clear its determination to take over, Britain would hardly choose to fight a hopeless rearguard action but would seek to hand over in as dignified a manner as possible. Any other course would not be in the interests of the local population. After the reoccupation China might choose to leave Hong Kong's trading arrangements much as they are at present without interfering with the status of the free port and free currency market. There is a partial precedent for this in Europe some time ago[10] and at present a number of Asian countries have set up custom-free zones where foreign manufacturers are encouraged to produce goods for export. However such processing zones are measured in acres, not hundreds of square miles; and it would hardly seem rational for China to take possession of Hong Kong and then set up an artificial internal boundary to keep the former colony isolated from the rest of the country under an alien economic system. Public opinion is not of great consequence in the People's Republic, but the mainland Chinese would certainly object if Britain's former colonial subjects were allowed to retain their privileged position after they had been reabsorbed into the motherland.

So it is most realistic to assume that after reincorporation all foreign-owned firms and private businesses would be nationalized (though the Chinese owners might be retained as managers, as happened in Shanghai after 1949); that the renminbi of China would be the official currency and all foreign exchange transactions would be strictly controlled; and that the free port would be abolished and all non-essential imports would be banned. Since Hong Kong has few indigenous resources apart from the skills of her people, foreign exchange would still be needed to import capital goods, fuel and raw materials for industry and some foodstuffs, to the extent that Chinese sources of supply could not be substituted. Nevertheless, Peking might hope to lay its hands on a considerably larger proportion of Hong Kong's overseas earnings than the 25–30 per cent which it now obtains, since precious foreign currency would no longer be diverted to the purchase of California oranges, Japanese cameras, shares on the New York Stock Market, real estate in Australia, university education in Canada or to augment the colony's sterling reserves in London.

However, this would only help China provided that Hong Kong's foreign earnings did not decline under communist rule; and there are a number of reasons for expecting this to occur:

1. All expatriate, and many Chinese, businessmen, managers, engineers and salesmen would emigrate to Taiwan or elsewhere in the developing world, unless the takeover was exceptionally swift and unexpected. The departure of the engineers and managers would probably not be too serious a blow since (unlike in 1949) many could now probably be replaced locally or from the rest of China. But the losses of salesmen and overseas representatives with their commercial contacts and expert knowledge of tastes and changing fashions in Hong Kong's main overseas markets would likely lead to a dearth of future orders.

2. Many factories produce goods to detailed designs specified by foreign contractors or are subsidiaries of international firms making parts for assembly overseas (particularly in such fast growing fields as elec-

tronics). In the event of a takeover most of this work could be expected to disappear: international firms would transfer their production to other subsidaries and overseas contractors would move their custom to agencies elsewhere in Asia.

3. Certain markets, such as Britain, might be closed to Hong Kong products in retaliation for the seizure of Hong Kong, and other countries might refuse to trade with a communist Hong Kong, either for ideological reasons (e.g. Taiwan) or because their non-essential exports to Hong Kong were unwanted by the communists. At the very least Hong Kong would lose the benefits of Commonwealth preference. This is no longer of much advantage to Hong Kong's exports since few Commonwealth countries apart from Britain give a preferential rate of duty to Hong Kong products and these preferences will be eliminated as Britain adjusts to the common external tariff of the European Economic Community. Nevertheless, about 11 per cent of Hong Kong exports enjoyed this advantage over their competitors in 1971, and this was a clear advantage in certain markets such as New Zealand.[11]

4. The ending of the free port would mean the loss of most of Hong Kong's entrepot trade. Re-exports accounted for 25 per cent the colony's total exports in 1973 and only about one-quarter of these originated from China. Loss of this trade would of course be balanced by a corresponding decline in imports, but Hong Kong would lose the profits made on the handling of these goods, the port and airport charges and the money spent here by foreign crews.[12]

5. The tourist trade, which now brings in more than HK$2,000 million a year, would probably be hard hit. The main attraction of Hong Kong is not the scenery or the tropical beaches but the shopping arcades where duty free luxuries from all over the world can be purchased.[13] But under Chinese management visitors would be restricted to Chinese products only. Possibly a new type of tourist might be attracted, interested in seeing the communist transformation of Hong Kong, but most package tour operators would probably omit Hong Kong from their itineraries. In any case many airlines would stop calling at Kai Tak, which would then cease to be the cross-roads of South-East Asia.

6. Multi-national companies which have set up their Asian headquarters in Hong Kong would move elsewhere, probably to Manila or Singapore. According to a survey carried out by the American Chamber of Commerce in 1974, 286 U.S. firms have their regional offices in Hong Kong, spending an estimated HK$440 million a year on housing, office rents and local staff.[14]

7. Capital inflows from overseas would cease. There are no statistics available to measure Hong Kong's balance on capital account, but in some years it has been substantial.[15] The loss of this foreign money would be serious only if equivalent sums for capital investment could not be raised internally by taxation or savings; but there would appear to be no great difficulty in doing this since the rates of tax in the colony are now very low. More than capital, Hong Kong needs foreign expertise to set up new manufacturing industries for the production of more sophisticated

goods. The loss of such potential growth points would be more damaging in the long run than the ending of foreign currency inflows. Most foreign capital which is not used for productive investment goes into stock market and property speculation or is placed in local banks who may reinvest the money overseas. Chinese banks share in the profits to be made from handling foreign deposits and the massive increase in property values over the past few years must have added to China's rising income from Hong Kong. If the free convertibility of the Hong Kong dollar were to be ended all such invisible earnings would be sharply reduced if not eliminated altogether.

However, this is to take the most pessimistic point of view, ignoring the possible counterbalancing advantages for Hong Kong's trade. Under communist management the internal costs of production would be likely to be rigidly controlled, particularly wages and the present soaring rents for industrial premises, while prices charged abroad could be set solely with the aim of maximizing foreign earnings without reference to the profitability of an enterprise by Western accounting methods. The most important benefit from reincorporation would be that trade negotiations on Hong Kong's behalf would be handled by China who would be much more strongly placed to demand equitable treatment for her exports than is now the case; the British government is in a weak position to complain about quota restrictions on Hong Kong's exports when she herself is one of the chief offenders in this matter; and the protests of the Hong Kong administration are easily brushed aside since it cannot threaten retaliations, both because of the small size of the local internal market and because any such action would negate the colony's traditional free trade policy. But China has potentially one of the largest markets in the world and all trading nations are anxious to get their foot in the door.[16] This eagerness could be used by China as a lever to extract concessions for Hong Kong's exports. In a similar fashion China could use her new-found diplomatic weight to insist on fair entry for Hong Kong products from those nations who now seek her friendship. At the very least China could follow the Russian example and propose that those who wish to sell to her should be prepared to take part of the payment in goods that she has not been able to dispose of through normal commercial channels. Such 'switch-trading' is a well-known obstacle for those who want to do business with the Soviet Union; for example an engineering firm may be forced to take part payment in shoes if it wants to conclude a sale.[17] China has not so far indulged in this rather sharp business practice, but if the Russians can succeed in doing so, why not the Chinese? It may not be too fanciful to picture a time when the British Aircraft Corporation may find itself required to take several tons of plastic flowers in part payment for its Concorde airliners.

These are all strategies that China could use to partly counteract the severe drop in Hong Kong's overseas trade which would be likely to follow reabsorption into the motherland. It is impossible to estimate whether China's increased share in Hong Kong's reduced foreign exchange earnings would be more or less than she gets under the present arrangements. Probably the statisticians in Peking do not know either. But if the Chinese decided to take over and found that the calculations they had relied upon proved wrong, it would be impossible to reverse the experiment, and the communists might find themselves with less money but with a sullen and recalcitrant population, whose long experience of the illicit delights of capitalism would make them resistant to Maoist re-education.

How much of a problem the governing of Hong Kong would prove to its new communist masters is hard to say. There would certainly be difficulties, particularly at present when China's own administration is still painfully recovering from the disorganization induced by the Cultural Revolution. But once China has settled down again, the problem would hardly be insuperable. After all, the communists were able to swallow decadent Shanghai so successfully after 1949 that its leadership provided one of the strongholds of left-wing radicalism during the 1960s. A new communist administration in Hong Kong could appeal to Chinese national sentiment. Local party members could provide the nucleus for a reconstituted Special Branch at least as effective as the present police and any troublemakers would be rusticated to Sinkiang or Tibet for re-education in peasant communes. Necessary changes would presumably be introduced gradually and the workers' standard of living would be maintained as an interim measure until control was fully assured. The population would have to adjust to the new regime, since there would be no alternative; resistance movements can only flourish when there is some hope of eventual relief, and the British would never return.

DIPLOMATIC AND STRATEGIC CONSIDERATIONS

If one of the main reasons for China's tolerance of Hong Kong is the economic advantages she derives from it, there are also wider considerations of the diplomatic and military dangers of precipitate action. China's international relationships, of which Hong Kong forms only a small part, have changed radically since 1949 and this in turn has altered the calculation of the potential benefits and dangers of seizing the colony. In the early years of the communist regime the main consideration may well have been a straightforward military one. During 1949 the communist armies swept through China from north to south, but after the fall of Peking in January 1949 the People's Liberation Army had faced little determined resistance. The forces of Chiang Kai-shek were demoralized by the corruption and incompetence of their leaders, who in some cases actually defected to the Communists, taking whole divisions of Nationalist troops with them. These deserters had been incorporated into the P.L.A. together with many hastily raised local volunteer units, but the P.L.A. may have had grave doubts about how they would perform against the newly reinforced British garrison entrenched in well-prepared defensive positions. The Communists were fully extended in mopping up the remaining nationalist guerrillas and organizing a new administration from virtually nothing; the first priority was the reduction of Taiwan; better perhaps to leave Hong Kong aside until more urgent tasks had been dealt with.

There were also considerations of power politics. The Chinese Communists were well aware that they were distrusted by the Russians who had continued to back Chiang Kai-shek in the civil war until he was expelled from the mainland. Mao had no intention of becoming a Russian satellite and his bargaining position with Moscow would be strengthened if he could show that other sources of assistance in restoring the war-ravaged economy of China were open to him. Throughout the 1940s, in spite of considerable discouragement, he had tried to keep his lines of communication with the United States open. Similar considerations applied to Britain, who had been quick to recognize the new Communist regime; surely it would be sensible politics to remain on friendly terms with Britain, at least until the availability of Russian aid was clear.

In 1950 the Korean War broke out and the following year China felt compelled to intervene with 'volunteers' as American forces came near to her border on the Yalu river. In consequence the American Seventh Fleet was ordered to defend Taiwan. All available troops and equipment were now needed to fight the Korean War and to defend the coast opposite Taiwan against any attempt by Nationalist forces to return to the mainland with American backing. There was likely to be little or no spare military capacity for any action to threaten Hong Kong.

By the end of 1952 the Korean fighting was practically over, but the Republicans under President Eisenhower had come to power in the United States, dedicated to 'rolling back communism'. The new Secretary of State for Foreign Affairs, Foster Dulles, threatened 'massive retaliation', if necessary with atomic weapons, against any communist acts of aggression. China's only defence was the threat of counter-retaliation by the Russians; but the Soviet Union showed itself very reluctant to underwrite any Chinese assault on Taiwan. Mao launched verbal attacks on the Americans and their allies as 'paper tigers', but set a careful limit to any provocative action against America's allies, Taiwan or the British in Hong Kong: viewed from Peking, the consequences may have seemed incalculable.[18] Meanwhile the Russians were training and re-equipping the P.L.A. and providing maximum economic assistance to China's five year plans. During the 1950s Hong Kong's contributions of foreign exchange to China were a useful addition, no doubt, but probably not of overriding importance.

During the late 1950s the quarrel between Mao and Khruschev led to the complete withdrawal of all Russian technical and financial assistance. Russian engineers abandoned the plants they were constructing and returned to Russia, in many cases even taking the blueprints away with them. China seemed isolated in a hostile world. The first reaction was the heroic, but ultimately futile attempt at complete self-reliance, the 'Great Leap Forward' of 1958–9 which petered out in the disastrous crop failures of the early 1960s. Foreign currency was now vitally needed to buy raw materials, technical expertise and even food for their own population. The largest market in the world, the United States, was strictly barred to Chinese products. Accordingly the foreign exchange earned by the sale of goods to Hong Kong and the facilities for selling cheap manufactured goods through Hong Kong were now vital. No risks could be taken as to what might happen to these trading links if Hong Kong's status were to be changed. In the latter part of the 1960s there was a further reason for caution: there were troubles on the border with Russia and the dangers of an invasion from the North were well-publicized to the Chinese people. Any adventures against Hong Kong (or Taiwan) would give the Russians an opportunity to strike while the P.L.A. was partially occupied elsewhere.

In the 1970s the picture seems to have changed again. China is now a member of the United Nations, and new embassies are being set up as more Western countries have recognized the People's Republic as the only legitimate government of China; as a result much wider trading opportunities have become available. This may lead to a *relative* decline in Hong Kong's importance, even though China's earnings from and through Hong Kong may still be increasing. But there is also another new factor. China has professed to be strongly in favour of the creation of a united Western Europe; her particular strategic interest is the existence of a credible threat to what is, for China, Russia's rear, and an alternative source of attraction to Russian's uneasy satellites in Eastern Europe. Britain has now joined the European Economic Community and expects to take a leading part in its decision making. If Britain were to be forced into a humiliating withdrawal from Hong Kong it would hardly be helpful for China's efforts to establish good relations with the Common Market countries.

To sum up: Hong Kong is a symbol of China's past humiliations and an embarrassment to her pose as champion of the Third World, it operates an economic system which challenges the fundamental principles of Maoist thought and is a source of disaffection in South China and a possible base for subversive activity; nevertheless, though a takeover would be relatively easy, such an act might have unfortunate repercussions on Peking's diplomatic efforts to secure herself against the Soviet Union, and would very likely involve a reduction in her foreign exchange resources. In these circumstances China seems to be prepared to tolerate the anomaly of Hong Kong's continued separate existence, and in the meantime has taken steps to minimize the inconveniences that the colony might cause her. For example, by insisting on the deletion of Hong Kong and Macau from the list of non-self-governing territories it has put an end to the annual public discussion of Hong Kong in the Decolonization Committee of the United Nations. Britain is happy to cooperate with China in such matters, so long as questions of sovereignty do not arise.

CHINA AND DEMOCRACY IN HONG KONG

However, China's benevolent attitude to Hong Kong would be unlikely to continue if the colony made any move towards internal self-government. There are no effective political parties in Hong Kong at present since there are no worthwhile elective positions to fight for.[19] But, if precedents from elsewhere are any guide, such organizations would quickly spring up as soon as elections to the Legislative Council were instituted. Politicians seek power and in order to be elected they are ready to capitalize on any divisions which exist in the electorate if these can be used to mobilize voters to the polls. Whatever guarantees or safeguards might be incorporated beforehand in the arrangements for the election it would be impossible to prevent the issue of communism and anti-communism being raised either openly or covertly by some of the candidates in any free election, if they thought this was a means of getting votes. At present the colonial administration is usually able to get its views accepted by the Legislative Council because the unofficials are selected from those who have a vested interest in the *status quo* and they have no basis of popular support which would legitimate a posture of unconstructive opposition. The situation would be completely changed by the appearance of elected members in the Council, even if the official majority were still retained. The fact that they were elected would give them the right to voice demands on behalf of their supporters, and the fear of being outbid at the next election would motivate them to go to extremes. The use of the official majority at present to outvote nominated unofficials would arouse little comment;[20] it is the use of an undemocratic device in a situation where in any case normal democratic standards do not apply. But it is quite a different matter to use an official majority to overcome the elected representatives of the people whose expectations have been aroused by the grant of the suffrage and the promises made in an election campaign. In such circumstances government might well feel inhibited against using its constitutional powers, for fear of provoking a confrontation in the streets by seeming to act autocratically in ignoring the popular will. It would make little difference whether the elected members were allies of the K.M.T. proposing restrictions on communist schools, or allies of the C.C.P. attacking foreign business interests. In either case the position of the executive would soon become impossible. The British would not choose to remain nominally responsible for Hong Kong if all decisions were effectively subject to the veto of locally elected communists; nor would the Chinese government be prepared to sit idly by and allow supporters of Chiang Kai-shek to gain a preponderant influence in the councils of the colony. The present delicate equilibrium of British, Chinese and local interests would be upset and the inevitable result would be the reincorporation of Hong Kong into the People's Republic.

It may be objected that this scenario is too gloomy, and that political parties would crystalize and divide upon purely local issues, avoiding ideology and any matters which might provoke China. This is possible; but experience elsewhere suggests that it is exceedingly difficult to insulate certain areas from partisan political controversy when there are free elections and wide popular participation; there are always some politicians who see advantage for themselves in raising issues that more gentlemanly or far-seeing opponents have agreed to sweep out of sight.[21] In any case, as long as there is even the remotest chance of such a train of events being set in motion, it is clear that the British government will never authorize the first step which might lead on to the abyss.

Another objection sometimes made is that there has never been any public pronouncement by Mao Tse-tung or any other leading figure of the People's Republic forbidding the British government to institute democratic elections in Hong Kong. However, it is most unlikely that any Chinese spokesman would go on record as preferring that the Chinese community here should be ruled by an alien British Governor rather than by elected Chinese representatives. Such a statement would be quoted against China for years afterwards by the Soviet Union and her satellites. Nevertheless this is most probably the true situation, as has been asserted obliquely on a number of occasions by British ministers and officials.[22]

Thus it seems that the colony of Hong Kong is allowed to continue its anachronistic existence because of a rational calculation by the Chinese government that the wider interests of China are best served by the present *status quo*. Any change, either in its economic profitability or its constitutional structure, might lead to a reappraisal in Peking followed by a decision to occupy the colony. As long as Britain finds it profitable and convenient to remain in Hong Kong no move will be made which might provoke such a reappraisal.

But can we rely on continuing rationality in Peking? Human beings are not emotionless calculating machines, and top decision-makers, like anyone else acting under stress, may sometimes react irrationally and set in motion policies that prove disastrous for their countries. Some would say that this was what occurred during the Cultural Revolution in 1967. A particular time of danger will occur at the death of Chairman Mao Tse-tung. As is known from what happened in the Soviet Union at the death of Lenin in 1924 or of Stalin in 1953, there is no guarantee that the former ruler's wishes will be respected after his death, and the various contenders for the supreme power may seek to rally support for their personal claims by espousing policies that they hope will win them popularity either among the masses or within the small group (the Central Committee or the Politbureau) in whose hands the decision rests.[23] An insecure successor to Mao might seek to bolster his personal authority by taking over Hong Kong, no matter what damage this might do to China's wider interests. There is nothing that Hong Kong can do to guard against such possibilities.

ADDENDUM

Peking's claim that Hong Kong is an integral part of China was underlined by the presence of delegates from Hong Kong and Macau at the Fourth National People's Congress in January 1975 which adopted a new constitution for China. Two of the Hong Kong deputies were elected to the Praesidium of the Congress (*Ta Kung Pao*, 23–29 Jan. 1975 and *South China Morning Post*, 20 Jan. 1975).

According to calculations made in *Current Scene*, Dec. 1974, p. 5, China may have incurred a trade deficit of up to US$1,000 million in 1974 as a result of the world trade recession and the rising prices for her imports of fertilizers, food and machinery.

The latest figures for China's exports to and through Hong Kong in 1974 suggest that China's total foreign exchange earnings from Hong Kong are now running at an annual rate in excess of US$1,500 million.

1. See for example D. P. O'Connell, *International Law*, 2nd edition (Stevens, London, 1970), Vol. I, p 394: 'Change of government does not affect the personality of the State,

and hence a successor government is required by international law to perform the obligations undertaken on behalf of the State by its predecessor. This is true even when the change is revolutionary.'

Following the deletion of Hong Kong from the list of non-self-governing territories, Britain ceased to transmit information to the Special United Nations Committee on Colonization, but the British delegate stated on behalf of Her Majesty's Government, 'The action of the General Assembly in no way affects the legal status of Hong Kong.... They are unable to accept any differing views.' (22 Dec 1972).

2. Chou En-lai's ambiguous remarks on this point are given in the document in Appendix 1, p. 226.

3. See for example the Czechoslovak newspaper *Rude Pravo*, 6 June 1972: 'Peking's pseudo-revolutionary slogans are an alien element in its relations with rich American, British and Japanese industrialists. The blood and sweat of millions of the Chinese people living in Hong Kong and Macau and working in capitalist factories is being transformed into gold in the banks of Peking.... But Peking is silent and cooperates.'

4. Estimates of the number of illegal immigrants vary. The *Annual Report of the Director of Immigration* gives the number arrested and also his guess at the total number who came ashore:

	Arrested	Total as estimated
1967–8	4,698	10,000
1968–9	1,251	6,000
1969–70	1,624	7,000
1970–1	1,824	10,000
1971–2	3,726	12,000
1972–3	6,338	20,000
1973–4	6,541	25,000–30,000

A higher figure is given in the *Annual Report of the Commissioner of Registration of Persons*, who lists the numbers of those who applied for identity cards without travel documents of any kind, who are assumed to be illegal immigrants:

1967–8	12,825	1971–2	12,141
1968–9	10,584	1972–3	17,815
1969–70	8,018	1973–4	21,258
1970–1	9,610		

5. See *South China Morning Post*, 24 May 1972 for one such arrest. Ten people were deported to Taiwan, and two Hong Kong citizens were charged and sentenced in court.

6. *Hong Kong 1974, Report for the Year 1973* (Government Printer), p. 44. Just under one half of Hong Kong's total food imports by value come from China: in 1973, HK$2,404m out of HK$5,065m.

7. All figures for Hong Kong's trade and balance of payments here and subsequently are taken from the *Hong Kong Trade Statistics* (monthly), the *Hong Kong Review of Overseas Trade* (annually), and the *Estimates of Gross Domestic Product 1966–72*, all published by the Census and Statistics Department. Figures for the trade of China are from *Current Scene* (United States Information Service, Hong Kong), Oct 1970, Aug 1971, Oct 1972, Oct 1973 and Dec 1974. Currency conversions into pounds and U.S. dollars have been calculated at the rate ruling for most of the year.

8. These figures include the costs incurred in Hong Kong for handling, freight, etc.

9. *Far Eastern Economic Review*, 23 April 1973, p. 9. This figure would mean that Hong Kong financed more than half of China's imports from the non-Communist world (US$2,240 million in 1972). In 1974 the *Far Eastern Economic Review* estimated China's foreign exchange earnings from Hong Kong at US$1,300 million (4 Oct 1974, China '74 Focus, p. 39).

10. When the British colony of Heligoland off the German coast was ceded to Germany in 1890 in exchange for Zanzibar, the island retained its status as a free port, outside the German external customs tariff.

11. *H.K. Hansard, 1971–2*, p. 227.

12. Present re-exports from China to third countries would of course continue, except insofar as transhipment via Hong Kong is used as a means of disguising their true origin. Such clandestine exports would probably be transferred to Singapore.

13. A detailed survey of what visitors to Hong Kong do, carried out by the Hong Kong Tourist Association, is reported in the *Far Eastern Economic Review*, 9 April 1973, p. 41.

14. Reported in *South China Morning Post*, 9 April 1974.

15. See *The 1974–75 Budget: Economic Background* (Government Printer, Jan 1974), p. 14.

16. See *The Economist*, 17 March 1973, p. 77, 'The Last Big Market Left'.

17. *The Economist,* 6 January 1973, supplement on East-West trade, p. 17.

18. The Governor of Hong Kong from 1947 to 1957, Sir Alexander Grantham, told American audiences in 1954 that he expected to receive U.S. air support if Hong Kong were attacked (*Via Ports,* p. 171).

19. The Civic Association and the Reform Club will be mentioned in Chapter 14.

20. In fact the official majority has not been so used since 1953.

21. In the Federation of Malaysia the Alliance Party composed of Malays, Chinese and Indians tried to take the racial question out of politics, but some of the smaller parties, such as the Pan-Malayan Islamic Party and the Democratic Action Party sought to gain votes by open or covert appeals to racialism. As a result the May 1969 election led to widespread rioting in Kuala Lumpur, at least 136 deaths and the assumption of emergency powers by the government. Similarly in Ceylon (now Sri Lanka) the communal issue (Singalese/Tamils) was ignored by the parties until Mr. Solomon Bandaranaike deliberately aroused Singalese nationalism to win the 1956 election.

22. Sir David Trench (Governor of Hong Kong 1964–1971) said in his *Dillingham Lecture,* p. 5 in October 1971 at the University of Hawaii East-West Centre; 'China has made it pretty clear that she would not be happy with a Hong Kong moving towards a representative system and internal self-government'. Lord Shepherd (Minister of State responsible for Hong Kong at the Foreign and Commonwealth Office, 1967–1970) said in a House of Lords Debate, 12 January 1971, col. 21: 'Personally, I do not see any real democratic government developments in Hong Kong. The presence of China and the attitude of China will make it necessary for Hong Kong to retain very much the system of government which it has today.'

23. In 1927 Stalin ordered the Chinese Communist Party to stage a revolutionary uprising, mainly in order to prove that his fervour for revolution was as great as that of his rival Trotsky. The result was the disastrous failure of the Nanchang Uprising and the Canton Commune and many leading cadres were massacred. On the other hand, the Communist Party of North Vietnam seems to have managed a smooth transition to a new leadership after the death of Ho Chi Min in 1969.

A somewhat different view of the China-Hong Kong relationship to that given here is to be found in P. B. Harris, 'The International Future of Hong Kong' *International Affairs,* Vol. 48, 1972, pp. 60–71.

3 Chinese Attitudes and British Rule

BOTH Britain and China are apparently now content that the present constitutional arrangements in Hong Kong should continue, but the local population could easily upset this by refusing to accept an accord reached without consulting them. If there were a widespread and persistent demand for reunion with China which manifested itself in frequent demonstrations, riots and strikes and other forms of political protest it would become impossible for Britain to maintain her imperial position. Even if we make the improbable assumption that China would remain indifferent, and the authorities in Hong Kong were able to contain and suppress such violent outbursts by force, public opinion and parliamentary opposition at home would not allow the British government to act in this way for long; and the cost, not only in money but also in military manpower and international embarrassment, would soon persuade Britain to negotiate a handover to China and withdraw. The result would be much the same if local agitation was directed to securing internal changes which went beyond what the administration was prepared to concede or which, though unrelated to reunion with China, would alter the *status quo* beyond what China would tolerate.

All governments to some extent rest on the tacit consent of the governed since no regime can have sufficient coercive power to coerce all the people all the time. But the colonial regime in Hong Kong is far more restricted than other governments in the extent to which it can use force to repress dissent. It operates under the surveillance of China and in an international atmosphere inimical to colonial regimes in general. But in addition it operates subject to two specific restraints: the need for the continued support of British public and parliamentary opinion and the continued confidence of businessmen and bankers (both foreign and Chinese) in its future. Without both these supports it could not survive at all and neither would last long if the administration were seen to be engaged in a perpetual struggle to contain a restless and discontented population.

Thus the present position can only continue so long as the vast majority of the people of Hong Kong are satisfied with their lot. The fact that this has generally been true over the past thirty years tends to obscure how unusual this situation is, for colonial rule is inherently abrasive. The reservation of the most senior posts for foreigners, the fact that English is the main language of government business[1] though it is spoken by only 2 per cent of the population, and the deference given by minor officials to Europeans are a continual source of irritation and annoyance. All Chinese, conscious of their long tradition of cultural and racial superiority over the rest of mankind, must silently resent their present subjection to 'foreign devils', however convenient this arrangement may be as a temporary expedient.[2] This is the pre-eminent reason why Hong Kong must always be inherently unstable, however calm things may appear on the surface. As has been demonstrated in other colonies, there is always the danger that some incident may unintentionally inflame latent nationalist feelings, and once such emotions are aroused they can overwhelm more mundane calculations of present advantage.

Moreover, this is not the only potential source of tension. In order to induce local businessmen to invest here and to attract capital from abroad entrepreneurs are allowed great freedom to run their businesses with the minimum government interference, and rates of taxation are very low. The natural result of such a *laissez-faire* economy is that great disparities of wealth and poverty have appeared which might be expected to arouse the envy and anger of the workers. Furthermore, in a world where the virtues of democracy and participation are widely proclaimed, discontent might also be expected to arise from the lack of any elected assembly with substantial powers to represent the views of the people and to take action to improve their conditions.

Yet in spite of all these potential sources of tension Hong Kong's progress for the last twenty years has been substantially undisturbed by the turmoils and violence to be found elsewhere in Asia. There have been only three outbreaks of rioting, in 1956, 1966 and 1967, and only one of these, the riot of April 1966 against the proposal of the Star Ferry to increase its fares, was the result of local discontent with government policy.[3] The 1956 riot was a faction fight between Kuomintang and Communist supporters which erupted out of a trivial dispute over the flying of Nationalist flags on 10 October, the Republic of China's national day. The 1967 confrontation was largely a spillover from the excesses of the Great Proletarian Cultural Revolution in China; it ended as soon as stable conditions had been restored in Canton and Peking and while it was in progress the communist instigators received little spontaneous support from most of the population.

Not only are violent outbursts rare, but the urban workers show little inclination to protest or organize in legally permitted ways to improve their lot. Out of a working force of 1,582,849 (the 1971 census figure) only 221,619 (14 per cent) are members of trade unions, and this is probably an over-estimate.[4] Strikes are infrequent: only forty took place in 1971-2, a total loss of 21,204 man-days, or about 16.21 man-days for every thousand workers in salaried employment.[5] Many unions are little more than mutual aid societies, more concerned with social and recreational activities than in fighting for improved pay and conditions. Workers generally prefer to change jobs rather than get involved in a direct confrontation with their employers.[6] In the early post-war years the workers showed no interest in the 'Young Plan' to extend the franchise to many of them, and the abandonment of these proposals in 1949 produced no reaction.[7] The occasional peaceful demonstrations mounted by students since 1970 have been ignored. In 1967 the communists had to resort to large-scale bribery and intimidation to persuade workers to take part in political strikes and these all petered out after a few days.[8] The mass of the population seem to believe that they are incapable of influencing the administration and so make no attempt to try. According to a survey of Kwun Tong carried out in 1971, 82 per cent of those interviewed believed that there was nothing they could do about an unjust government regulation.[9]

In any country the number of dedicated political activists is small and most of the population are only intermittently aroused to political activity, but the apathy of the people of Hong Kong and their passive acceptance of the decisions of the administration is more appropriate to a rural backwater than a thriving industrial metropolis. Those who live in cities are notoriously more prone to violence than peasants, yet in Hong Kong there seems to be more active political protest in the rural areas, voiced through the Heung Yee Kuk and the Rural Committees, than is to be found among the urban proletariat. This apathy is the more surprising when it is remembered that as long ago as 1925 workers in the colony staged a general strike which began in June and did not finally end till October 1926, fifteen months later. The strike was called in protest against the shooting of twelve Chinese students by the British-officered police in Shanghai (the 'May 30 incident'). Seamen, port workers and domestic servants all joined the walkout and economic pressure on the foreign merchants was so severe that a special loan had to be arranged to assist them.[10]

There is a similar lack of interest in political activity among the upper strata of the Chinese population. Few of those who have the educational qualifications to make them eligible to vote in Urban Council elections bother to apply for inclusion on the register of electors, and in 1973 less than 25 per cent of those enrolled actually cast their ballots (see Chapter 14 below, p. 159). Though non-Chinese make up less than 2 per cent of the population more than a third of those who have been elected to the Urban Council since 1951 have been non-Chinese.[11] Employers' groups, both Chinese and non-Chinese, are naturally active in lobbying government in their own interests, but expatriates seem to be disproportionately involved in agitation for 'good causes'. For example, Europeans make up two-thirds of the membership of the Conservancy Association, which campaigns against all forms of pollution.[12] The Chinese are more likely to be active in philanthropic associations, such as the Tung Wah Hospital Group and the Po Leung Kuk, or local clan and neighbourhood associations, such as the Kaifongs, rather than groups with a specifically political orientation.

What then is the explanation of the present political apathy? Certain factors are obviously relevant. Between the end of the Japanese war and May 1951 the population of the colony increased from 600,000 to 2,360,000

as a result of the influx of refugees from Kwantung province and many
other parts of China.[13] Since then government has tried by agreement
with the Chinese authorities to limit permanent immigration to fifty a
day, but illegal entrants continue to arrive.[14] Not all these refugees were
political opponents of the communists; many were only seeking safety
and security from the disorders that attended the disintegration of the
Kuomintang regime. But whatever the reason for their original flight,
hardly any have opted to return to China.[15] The traumatic experiences
they have undergone predispose most refugees to political quietism. One
Chinese member of the Legislative Council put the point more colourfully:
'Hong Kong is the lifeboat; China is the sea. Those who have climbed
into the lifeboat naturally don't want to rock it.'[16] This factor must not
be exaggerated. More than half the population is now under twenty-five
and has never felt the terrors of insecurity which shaped the reactions of
their parents and led them to refer to Hong Kong as 'Heaven'.[17] But
the upheavals which have taken place in China since 1949, culminating
in the excesses of the Great Proletarian Cultural Revolution and the
rustication of masses of young people to remote border regions seem
to have convinced the majority that they are best off where they are.

Moreover, everyone in Hong Kong has to live with a continual sense
of uncertainty about the future. At any time China might decide to
reclaim the colony without waiting until 1997, and the wishes of the
inhabitants would not be taken into account. Since they are impotent to
influence a decision that will be taken over their heads by ministers in
Peking and London the people of Hong Kong seem to have adopted a
fatalistic attitude, living for the present and avoiding any thought for
the future.[18] There is little obvious enthusiasm for reabsorption into the
motherland. Anyone who wishes to live under communism can always
cross the border at Lo Wu; there are no difficulties from the British side,
but few choose to do so compared with the thousands each year who
leave the People's Republic legally or clandestinely. More than 80 per
cent of the colony's population have family ties with some part of Kwantung province and many visit their relatives there, especially at the Chinese
New Year, so they are very well placed to appraise the merits of the
communist and capitalist ways of life. What conditions would be like
in Hong Kong under communist rule is uncertain; for the present
apparently most prefer to endure the British devil that they know rather
than run the risk that any attempt at political agitation might unintentionally put an end to the colony's separate existence.

Another factor must be Hong Kong's phenomenal rate of economic
growth, which is third to Japan and Singapore in Asia. Over the six
years to 1973 Gross Domestic Product in real terms grew at an average
compound rate of 8 per cent annually, or 6 per cent per capita. Statistics
have not been computed for previous years, but over the past ten years
the rapid growth of domestic exports—(a fivefold increase at current
prices, that is a compound rate of 16 per cent annually)—suggests that
similar growth in the Gross Domestic Product has been going on for
some time.[19] The benefits of this growth have not been confined to

the owners of capital: between 1964 and 1973 the consumer price index went up by 54 per cent, but nominal wages went up by 138 per cent and so the index of real wages increased by 58 per cent over the period.[20] It seems obvious that such prosperity should tend to siphon off any discontent, so long as the rising standard of living keeps ahead of the aspirations of the workers. This suggestion appears to be confirmed by the antecedents of the 1966 Star Ferry riot, the only one since the war which was entirely domestic in origin. At this time there was a widespread belief that Hong Kong was entering on a period of business depression and price inflation. There was a crisis of confidence in the banking system in 1965: several banks failed, including one with 114,000 depositors' accounts, and there were bank runs in January, April and November. This resulted in tight credit, a recession in the real estate market and a cut-back in the growth rate of imports from 15 to 5 per cent in 1965, which in turn produced a mood of economic uncertainty and frustration. The Commission of Enquiry into the riot considered that this was one of the background factors responsible for the violence.[21]

A further factor is the efficiency of the colonial government machine. Its record in providing housing for 1,800,000 people (42 per cent of the population) in the past twenty years is an exceptional achievement. The necessary infrastructure of roads, communications, port facilities, water supply and other public utilities has been planned and executed to keep in step with the needs of economic development, and the administration has proved equally effective in reacting to sudden emergencies and disasters. Such efficiency does not necessarily result in support for government; but it does mean that the administration is respected and the impression of firmness and consistency that is given to the public is likely to discourage all but the most enthusiastic from attempting to persuade the authorities to modify their announced plans. On the other hand, if government had appeared to be incompetent and vacillating this would certainly have provided a greater incentive for political protest.

Another deterrent to open agitation is the strength of the Police Force. Compared to other countries it is large in relation to Hong Kong's population, and contrary to normal British and Commonwealth practice the police carry revolvers when on duty.[22] The Force claims to have a good record in solving the crimes reported to it,[23] but it is viewed with suspicion and indeed with fear by large sections of the public.[24] The Special Branch (which keeps track of all potentially subversive activities) has a particularly formidable reputation for knowing all that is going on.[25] Its effectiveness may well be exaggerated, but this widespread belief has a deterrent effect on political activity, especially for those—the majority of the adult population—who are liable to deportation.[26]

There are stringent laws regulating Public Order which allow the police to ban or impose strict limits on any meeting. This usually means that any demonstration is confined to a relatively secluded area where it is less likely to attract the attention of casual passers-by. This is not an unreasonable precaution on the part of the police, in view of the density of population in the urban areas, but it does mean that it requires considerable determination and organizing skill to gather a large crowd, and demonstrations have taken place at which the police in attendance practically outnumbered the protesters.

Another factor which makes the organization of protests by the less educated class more difficult is the lack of effective leadership. In most countries dedicated members of the Communist party can be found ready to exploit and exacerbate any dispute in order to build up support for their cause. But in Hong Kong the supporters of Peking generally cause little trouble, since the People's Republic has a strong interest in the continued prosperity of the colony so as to increase its offtake of foreign exchange.[27] The 1967 confrontation showed what could happen when this external curb on communist activity was removed. There also seems to be a shortage of disaffected intellectuals ready to take up the task of organizing mass protests. In the past, government has not been very generous in supporting university expansion and many well-qualified sixth formers seek to enter colleges abroad and so are often lost to Hong Kong. The graduates of Hong Kong University and the Chinese University have little difficulty in finding jobs and apparently soon forget any radical aspirations they may have felt in their student days. In other colonial territories political activity seemed to offer rich prizes: there was the hope that a successful party leader might end up as Prime Minister when the British left. But there is no likelihood of this happening in Hong Kong. The only elections are those for the Urban Council, where the reward for the successful candidates is a load of tedious unpaid committee work. It is small wonder that such voluntary effort holds little appeal for the pragmatic Chinese. Any foreign students studying here are likely to find their applications for visa extensions refused if they have taken part in any agitational activity, presumably out of fear that their example will affect local undergraduates.[28]

The limited time-span of the colony's existence is also relevant, since few expect British rule to continue beyond 1997, if indeed it lasts as long as that. Those who are discontented with life here and apprehensive for the future prefer to emigrate, if they have the requisite qualifications, rather than strive to ameliorate conditions in a 'borrowed place living on borrowed time',[29] since any efforts they may make are unlikely to lead to any permanent changes.

All these arguments help to explain the quiescence or apathy of the Chinese population by reference to specific factors in the Hong Kong situation. It is also possible to look for a more general explanation in the attitudes to government and the beliefs about how men ought to behave towards officials which have long been held in China and which have been inculcated by 2,000 years of schooling in the Confucian classics.[30] According to these writings, the ruler was advised to act towards his people like a father to his children, seeking their welfare, providing for their essential needs and ensuring that they acted morally in their dealings with each other. The benevolent ruler would act justly and provide security for his subjects who in turn would have confidence in him and obey the law willingly. The people could not be expected to understand the business of the state; it was enough for them to be submissive to the government as the grass bends when the wind blows over it. Such a system made no provision for popular participation, either in the choice of rulers of the formulation of policy; at most a limited right of rebellion was recognized, when the rulers reached such a depth of incompetence and moral corruption that they lost the 'mandate of heaven'.[31]

As a result of this instruction, or in consequence of their long historical experience of authoritarian rule, the Chinese people have always been noted for their patience under oppression. In the words of Lin Yu-tang:

There is so much of this virtue that it has almost become a vice. The Chinese people have put up with more tyranny, anarchy and misrule than any Western people ever put up with, and seem to have regarded them as part of the laws of nature. In certain parts of Szechuan the people have been taxed thirty years in advance without showing more energetic protest than a half-audible curse in the privacy of the household. Christian patience would seem like petulance compared to Chinese patience.... We submit to tyranny and extortion as small fish swim into the mouth of a big fish.

So it has been argued that the present political apathy of the Chinese population of Hong Kong can be fully explained as evidence of the survival and continuing strength of traditional attitudes to government.

It is certainly possible to adduce parallels between the paternalistic bureaucratic rule exercised by the mandarins of the Ching dynasty and by the officers of the British Colonial Service.[32] This idea seems most plausible in the relationship between the traditionally-minded villagers in the New Territories and their District Officers, who are colloquially known as *fu-mu-kuan*, literally 'father-mother officers', as were the imperial officials before them. But this and other similarities are superficial. The old regime in China was tenaciously conservative, bound by precedent, suspicious of commerce, and made little impact on the life of the ordinary man. Modern administrators are continually seeking innovations to promote greater efficiency and economic growth, and forever devising new forms, regulations and permits to entangle the individual in the web of government controls. Most important of all, the senior colonial officials are all foreigners, carrying on their business and promulgating laws in an alien tongue. China has known foreign rulers in the past: the Yuan dynasty was Mongol by origin and the Ching dynasty was Manchu; but the Ching emperors made every effort to render their rule acceptable by sinizing themselves and assimilating their administration to the forms of Chinese culture. Not so the British. Submission to authority certainly ranked very high among the Confucian values, but only submission to the authority of morally superior rulers who were Chinese. Confucian traditions cannot be called upon to sanction obedience to foreigners who are widely believed to be corrupt and to be exploiting the people of Hong Kong for the benefit of their masters overseas.[33]

Moreover, concentration upon the official ideology which was fostered by the government and inculcated into the masses to justify the *status quo* overlooks a very different aspect of China's past: the long series of peasant revolts when conditions became intolerable. Confucianism did not prevent the widespread disorders of the Taiping, Nien and Boxer rebellions in the nineteenth century. Political plotting and open protest have a long history in China, going back to the ancient triad societies, Sun Yat-sen's *Tung-meng Hui*, and the 'May Fourth Movement', to say nothing of the progress of the Chinese Communist Party. All these are as much part of the Chinese political tradition as the Confucian ideology preached by the established order.[34]

This is not to deny that there may be some in Hong Kong whose political quietism is the result of devotion to the ideals of China's past.[35] But for most of the population 'Confucian' influence would seem to be confined to the traditional Chinese pattern of teaching children how they should behave: to respect their elders, avoid conflict and keep silent rather than express open disagreement. It seems unlikely that the younger generation, born in Hong Kong and with no memories of the chaos of the Chinese civil war, will be as ready as their parents are to treat government administrators with the same silent respect that they have learnt to show to their elders at home. Young people are exposed to a very different way of life through Western films, television shows, radio programmes and newspapers. They participate in a world-wide teenage pop culture, imitating styles of dress and behaviour created in Europe or America. It will be surprising if they do not go on to repudiate the conformist attitudes of their parents and demand a greater say in the processes of government. Even those who completely reject the Western way of life and look towards the present regime in China can see that even there Chairman Mao emphasizes the rights of the young and the virtue of rebelling against authority.

Moreover the rising generation is far more educated. Already by 1971 nearly a million people, a quarter of the population, had some form of post-primary education and these numbers are certain to increase.[36] Schools in Hong Kong are much more authoritarian than those in the West, but even so those who have passed through them can be expected to be more articulate and self-confident than those who have not. Will they be content to accept the present system of British rule in Hong Kong? So far government appears to have been able to contain the situation by a mixture of firmness and calculated concessions on non-essentials. But none could venture to prophesy how long this will continue.[37]

1. The *Official Languages Ordinance, 1974* declares English and Chinese to be the official languages of Hong Kong, possessing equal status and enjoying equality of use in government communications; however, ordinances will continue to be enacted in English, and proceedings in the more important courts will still be conducted in English.

2. An indication of this is the fact that the anniversary of the surrender of the Japanese in 1945 is officially named as Liberation Day, but is commonly referred to among the Chinese as the 'Reoccupation'.

3. Full accounts of these riots can be found in: *Report on the Riots in Kowloon and Tsuen Wan 1956* (Hong Kong Government, 1957); *Kowloon Disturbances 1966, Report of the Commission of Inquiry* (Hong Kong, March 1967); and John Cooper, *Colony in Conflict, the Hong Kong Disturbances May 1967–January 1968* (Swindon Book Company, Hong Kong, 1970). The first is a despatch to the Secretary of State from the Governor; the second is the report of an independent commission of enquiry; the last is an account by a former

army officer who was stationed in Hong Kong at the time. There has been no official account of the 1967 troubles, apart from the brief details given in the annual report.

Casulty figures were:

1956: 59 killed (15 by rioters, 44 by police fire) (*Report*, p. 44)

1966: 1 killed (*Report*, p. 155)

1967: 51 killed (including 15 by bomb explosions, and 10 policemen (*Hong Kong 1967*, (Government Printer, 1968), p. 19).

4. *Registrar of Trade Unions, Annual Report 1971–72*, p. 5. The figure of 221,619 is that declared by the unions. From an inspection of their accounts the Registrar guesses that the true paid-up membership is about three-quarters of this. The Communist-oriented unions claimed a membership of 126,408 and the Nationalist-oriented ones a membership of 36,005.

5. *Report of the Commissioner of Labour 1971–72*, pp. 10 and 36.

Man-days lost in strikes over the past decade (ibid. p. 193) are as follows:

1962–3	27,153	1968–9	13,902
1963–4	73,371	1969–70	37,682
1964–5	43,344	1970–1	53,737
1965–6	67,156	1971–2	21,204
1966–7	37,535	1972–3	43,350
1967–8	5,231	1973–4	49,311

The low figure for 1967–8, the year of the confrontation, is significant.

6. See Joe England, 'Industrial Relations in Hong Kong', p. 236–46, in K. Hopkins (editor), *Hong Kong, Industrial Colony*.

7. Endacott, *Government and People in Hong Kong*, pp. 189 and 193, citing remarks made by the Governor and a number of unofficial members in 1949. Similarly in 1967–71 the proposed reform of the Urban Council aroused little interest, and the *White Paper on the Urban Council 1971*, could state (para. 3): 'There has not been evidence of much, if any public interest in the introduction of such systems.' (i.e. representative local government).

8. According to Cooper (op.cit. pp. 43, 51, 53 etc.) the communists in 1967 had to resort to bribery and intimidation on a large scale in order to persuade workers to go on strike. Similarly, the Annual Report *Hong Kong 1967*, p. 9, claims that the local communists received $10 million from the China Federation of Trade Unions to support the general strike they tried to call on 24 June.

9. Ambrose Yeo-chi King, *The Political Culture of Kwun Tong* (Social Research Centre, The Chinese University of Hong Kong, 1972), p. 16. Only 14 per cent of those questioned in Kwun Tong thought that they could do something about an unjust regulation. In other countries where similar surveys have been carried out those who believed themselves able to affect government policy were as follows: Britain 78 per cent, United States 77 per cent, Germany 62 per cent, Mexico 52 per cent, Italy 51 per cent. (G. Almond and S. Verba, *The Civic Culture* (Princeton University Press, New Jersey, 1963), p. 185).

In fact, as will be pointed out in later chapters, government frequently gives way to well-organized agitation, see pp. 93, 135, 257ff etc.

10. This strike is briefly referred to in G.B. Endacott, *A History of Hong Kong* (O.U.P., Hong Kong, 1958), pp. 289f. For a full account see Rosemarie Chung Lu-cee, 'A Study of the 1925–6 Canton-Hong Kong Strike and Boycott', unpublished M.A. thesis, Hong Kong University, 1969.

In the *Selected Works of Mao Tse-tung* (Foreign Languages Press, Peking, 1967), Vol. I, p. 21, note 16, the Hong Kong strike is referred to as 'the longest strike in the history of the world labour movement'.

11. Between 1951 and 1973 Chinese elected members sat on the Urban Council for a total of 103 member-years and non-Chinese for 65 member-years, 61.3 per cent and 38.7 per cent respectively.

12. *South China Morning Post*, 12 September 1973.

13. *Report of the Commissioner of Police 1950–51*, p. 1. According to the *Hong Kong Population and Housing Census 1971, Main Report* (Census and Statistics Department, 1972), p. 15, only 185,699 residents gave the place of origin of their family as Hong Kong, less than 5 per cent.

14. The quota of fifty a day from China is first mentioned in the *Report of the Commissioner of Police 1955–56*, p. 87. This has been an unwritten understanding with the Chinese authorities, but it was broken in 1962 when, for reasons unknown, the border was opened and over 120,000 refugees were freely allowed to pass into the colony. Since then the quota was normally adhered to until 1973. See p. 217 below and the *Annual Reports of the Commissioner of Registration of Persons* and of the *Director of Immigration*.

15. *Report of the Commissioner of Police, 1951–52*, p. 40: 'In 1949–50 the Police repatriated voluntarily to China 3,295 people. Last year the figure dropped to 43, but this year there was not a single volunteer. All this intense desire to stay in Hong Kong, despite its adverse economic conditions may be very flattering, but it is far from helpful.'

16. Quoted by J.S. Hoadley, 'Hong Kong is the Lifeboat: Notes on Political Culture and Socialization', *Journal of Oriental Studies*, Hong Kong, Vol. VIII, 1970, p. 211.

17. *Report of the Commissioner of Police, 1952–53*, p. 1: 'To a very large proportion of the Chinese population the colony of Hong Kong is known colloquially as heaven (天堂).'

18. A survey of Kwun Tong in 1971 asked respondents how far into the future they had a clear picture about political matters in the world. 62.2 per cent replied that they could not see clearly at all and less than 6 per cent gave a period of over a year ahead. Surveys elsewhere have given a median reply of over two years. Stan Shiveley, *Political Orientations in Hong Kong, a Socio-Psychological Approach* (Social Research Centre, The Chinese University of Hong Kong, 1972), pp. 24 and 34.

19. *The 1974–75 Budget, Economic Background* (Government Printer, Jan 1974), p. 1. Domestic exports (i.e. excluding re-exports) grew from $3,831m in 1963 to $19,474m in 1973. Government suggests that there is a close correspondence between the growth of exports in quantity terms and the growth of G.D.P. in real terms (ibid. p. 2).

20. *Annual Report of the Commissioner of Labour, 1972–73*, p. 130. However, between March 1973 and March 1974 the index of real wages dropped by 11 per cent, from 159 to 141, as a result of the world-wide rise in the prices of food and raw materials (*Monthly Digest of Statistics*, August 1974, p. 6). Yet in spite of this drop in real wages and rising unemployment the labour scene continued to remain quiet.

21. See *Kowloon Disturbances 1966 Report*, pp. 132–4. In fact real wages rose in every year from 1964 to 1967, but the workers' perceptions of economic trouble ahead seem to have helped precipitate the violence.

A higher standard of living does not by itself guarantee immunity from internal turmoil. Sometimes this may even encourage groups which are enjoying a rising standard of living to challenge the authorities, particularly if growth is not as fast as they expect, or if there is a perceived deterioration after a period of rising prosperity. See J.C. Davies, 'Towards a Theory of Revolution', *American Sociological Review*, Vol. 27 (1962), pp. 5–19. This theory fits the French Revolution of 1789, and also Hong Kong in 1966.

22. Police/population ratios in 1971:

New Zealand	1:890	(3,214; 2,860,475)
Netherlands	1:713	(18,400:13,119,430)
South Africa	1:668	(32,108:21,448,172)
England and Wales	1:520	(93,748:48,815,000)
Hong Kong	1:333	(12,000: 4,045,000)
New York State, U.S.A.	1:290	(62,770:18,237,000)

Sources: *The Statesman's Yearbook 1972/73* (Macmillan, 1972) and *Report of the Commissioner of Police, Hong Kong 1971–72*.

The authorized establishment of the Hong Kong Police in 1973 was 14,963 (1:270), excluding civilian staff.

23. According to the *Report of the Commissioner of Police, 1971–72*, pp. 44f the detection rate for all crimes reported was 77 per cent (including crimes against the person, 76 per cent; crimes against lawful authority, 97 per cent).

24. According to a poll carried out by Survey Research, Hong Kong for *The Star* newspaper, only 27 per cent of the Chinese interviewed thought they were free to criticize the actions of the police without fear of punishment; 40 per cent refused to answer the question, and 33 per cent thought that such action was illegal or that the police would interfere with their business if they spoke out. An earlier survey by the same organization stated, 'Our interviewers reported that they had the impression the "don't know" answer was not always given out of ignorance or indifference, but often because the informant seemed frightened or unwilling to make his political views known.' (*The Star* (Hong Kong), 12 Nov 1966 and 24 July 1966).

25. See for example *Far Eastern Economic Review*, 16 Jan 1971, pp. 5f. Students seem to have inflated ideas that the Special Branch is everywhere.

26. Under the *Immigration Ordinance 1971* (which consolidated previous legislation) the Governor in Council has wide powers to order the deportation of anyone not born or naturalized in the colony if 'he deems it conducive to the public good'. In the case of a Chinese who has lived in Hong Kong for seven years he must first refer the case to a deportation tribunal and consider its report, but he is not obliged to accept its finding, and he can dispense with a tribunal altogether if 'he certifies that the case concerns the security of

Hong Kong or the relationship of Her Majesty's Government in the United Kingdom with another country' (Cap. 115, sec. 20). Social workers told the Commission inquiring into the 1966 riot that the sense of impermanence in Hong Kong was enhanced by unreasonable fears of deportation (*Report*, p. 125). In fact, though several thousand were deported every year in the 1940s this is no longer possible since both the People's Republic of China and Taiwan usually refuse to accept deportees. (*Report of the Commissioner of Police 1952–3*, p. 39.)

27. 'Leftist' elements are sometimes blamed by the press for any agitation or strike (e.g. the teachers' strike of 1973) on what seems to be rather slender evidence.

In September 1974 local communists actively discouraged their members and sympathizers from participating in demonstrations against inflation and unemployment organized by certain student radicals, who were described in the communist press as 'Trotskyists', and 'anti-revolutionaries against communism and China' engaged in 'destroying workers' unity', (*South China Morning Post*, 9 September 1974.)

28. In 1970 three foreigners (one American, one German, one Swede) were required to leave Hong Kong after taking part in a demonstration against the Vietnam War. Very few Chinese joined the protest, but the police were there in strength. (*Far Eastern Economic Review*, 16 January 1971, p. 5).

29. This phrase was coined by Han Suyin. Richard Hughes used it in the title of his book *Hong Kong, Borrowed Place, Borrowed Time* (Andre Deutsch, London, 1968).

In 1967, before the riots, a survey of over 2,000 fifth form students in secondary schools was carried out. When asked, 'If you could live anywhere today, where would you most prefer to live?' only 23 per cent opted to 'stay in Hong Kong'. R.E. Mitchell, *Pupil, Parent and School, A Hong Kong Study* (Asian Folklore and Social Life Monographs, the Orient Cultural Service, Taipei, 1972), p. 338.

30. Political scientists refer to this as the 'political culture' of a people. See for example King and Hoadley, articles cited in notes 9 and 16 above.

31. There is a selection of quotations from the Chinese philosophers in the *Report of the Working Party on Local Administration, 1966*, Appendix A, pp. 89–91. The following passage is from Lin Yu-tang, *My Country and My People* (London, Heinemann, 1938), p. 44.

32. Such a comparison is rather more relevant to the pre-war Colonial Service. See H.J. Lethbridge 'Hong Kong Cadets, 1862–1941' *Journal of the Hong Kong Branch of the Royal Asiatic Society*, Vol. 10, 1970, pp. 36–56, and R. Wilkinson, *The Prefects*, Oxford University Press, 1964, pp. 125–76.

33. A survey of 1,065 ordinary men in Kwun Tong found that 32.6 per cent of them agreed with the statement that: 'The primary reason for being a government official is "to make money" ', while only 25.1 per cent disagreed. (Yeo-chi King, op.cit. p. 13f.) The popular belief that the task of government is to make a profit for Britain and that a substantial proportion of the taxes levied are drained off to Britain is referred to by *Kowloon Disturbances 1966, Report*, p. 126, and the *Report of the Working Party on Local Administration, Nov. 1966*, p. 86.

A survey published in the *Star* newspaper 15 April 1967, p. 16 found that 63 per cent of those interviewed believed that part or all of their taxes were remitted to England as tribute.

34. Thomas Meadows, an early European writer on Chinese history, made the oft-quoted remark: 'Of all nations that have attained a certain degree of civilization, the Chinese are the least revolutionary and the most rebellious'. This was written in 1854. Mao's 1927 *Report on an Investigation of the Peasant Movement in Hunan* (Selected Works, Vol. I) gives little support to ideas of traditional peasant apathy.

35. According to Mitchell (op.cit. note 29 above, pp. 351, 338, 208ff), 62 per cent of all respondents said that they would exercise the right to vote in Urban Council elections if given the chance; but among the small minority of students (9 per cent) who expressed a preference for Chinese music, films and clothes over Western ones, only 39 per cent said they wished to vote.

36. *Hong Kong Population and Housing Census 1971, Main Report* (Census and Statistics Department, Hong Kong, 1972), p. 68.

37. An indicator of increasing politicization are the figures for trade union membership issued by the Registrar of Trade Unions in his *Annual Departmental Reports*:

Declared membership: March 1972—221,619
                        March 1973—251,729
                        March 1974—295,735

4 Economic Constraints and Government's Ideology

'Hong Kong's generally *laissez-faire* economic policies have always been based on considered decisions, not mere paralysis of mind and will.'
Sir David Trench (Governor 1964-71)[1]

HONG KONG must avoid causing diplomatic difficulties for Britain; it must keep China happy with plentiful earnings of foreign exchange; it must respect the susceptibilities of the Chinese population and keep them reasonably contented; but above all it must satisfy its customers overseas. Ninety per cent of its manufacturing output is exported to pay for imports of raw materials and food. Any set-back to the dynamic growth rate of the colony's trade would soon lead to trouble. The workers have become accustomed to a steadily rising standard of living and are eager to enjoy the latest novelties of the affluent societies of the West. If they were to find that their expectations were not fulfilled, or worse, if they suffered a severe cut in their wages and there was substantial unemployment, the present political calm might not long continue. Government would receive the blame even if the causes of such an economic recession were completely out of its control; and Britain would not hesitate long before divesting herself of an unprofitable and unruly colony.

In mid-1973 before the oil crisis the possibility of such an economic calamity seemed remote, since the colony had enjoyed more than twenty years of uninterrupted progress. But this could hardly have been foreseen in 1950 when this tiny territory, which had just begun to recover from the Japanese occupation, found its population virtually doubled by the influx of refugees from China, and then, as a result of the United Nations embargo imposed during the Korean War, almost immediately lost one of its major economic activities—the entrepot trade with China. Viewed objectively, Hong Kong was then one of the most unlikely places to be the scene of an economic miracle. It has few local mineral resources, no indigenous source of fuel except timber, and its inadequate natural water sources have to be supplemented with many expensive reservoirs. Only 12 per cent of the land area is arable, supplying less than 15 per cent of the food needed by the present population. The colony might well have seemed likely to become a vast refugee camp, surviving on international charity.

The success story of Hong Kong since then has often been told. Taking advantage of the established financial institutions in the colony and its world-wide trade contacts local businessmen and industrialists who had fled from Shanghai combined to reorient the economy to manufacturing for export. They began by selling to nearby Asian markets, but now three-quarters of the colony's exports go to Europe and North America. The traditional entrepot trade has revived, but, instead of being mainly the point of entry for China, Hong Kong's free port is increasingly used as a transhipment centre for goods destined for the rest of Asia. Booming invisible exports—the sale of services to foreigners—allow the colony to run a large deficit on visible trade; tourism is the main contributor to this, but shipping firms based on Hong Kong are also growing. In addition it is becoming one of the largest financial centres in Asia, supplying banking, insurance and investment services to trading companies operating in all the neighbouring countries and being used as a regional headquarters for international companies with subsidiaries throughout the Pacific basin.

But this prosperity is highly vulnerable. It is dependent on the belief that China will continue to allow Hong Kong to flourish as a capitalist enclave on its doorstep. At present, so long as Mao Tse-tung is alive and Chou En-lai remains prime minister, the private assurances given by the Chinese government that the colony's status will not be interfered with are credible. But the departure of either of them, particularly if followed by a prolonged power struggle in Peking, would put all this in jeopardy. Industrialists and developers would defer their plans for investment until the situation clarified, and the timid would start to transfer their capital elsewhere. This could easily lead to a panic withdrawal of funds.

Hong Kong is also dependent on continuously rising prosperity in its major markets (now the United States, Britain, West Germany, and Japan), and on freedom from discrimination against its exports. Larger nations can threaten retaliation against such tariff and quota restrictions; but Hong Kong is itself too small a market for reprisals on its part to be effective, and in any case its entrepot trade, and also its tourist industry, depend heavily on its reputation as a free port open to the exports of all nations without tariff barriers or other restrictions. Nor can it look for much political assistance from the metropolitan power. Britain already sets a bad precedent by imposing tariffs and quotas against Hong Kong's textile exports and so is in no position to intervene effectively on her colony's behalf. Britain has her own trading interests to protect and was unable to persuade the European Economic Community to include Hong Kong in the countries to benefit by its generalized system of preferences for developing countries, in spite of the fact that South Korea, one of the colony's competitors, was one of the beneficiaries.[2]

Hong Kong's manufacturers are liable to face such discrimination whenever they develop a new export market successfully, so they must continually seek to diversify their production, making goods of higher quality and expanding into new and more complex fields. The difficulty here is that the majority of Hong Kong's industrial undertakings are small by world standards and do not have the resources that would allow them to undertake the expensive research needed to develop new products. So they generally prefer to undertake part of the production process for foreign companies, using their patents and working to their designs; alternatively government seeks to persuade international firms to set up subsidiary factories here, so that Hong Kong can participate in the latest technological advances. In some fields this policy has been very successful: for example, in 1968 58 per cent of the labour force employed in the fast-growing electronics industry was working in American-owned factories.[3]

In the effort to attract such overseas investment Hong Kong is in competition with its Asian neighbours. A manufacturer proposing to set up a factory in the region is free to shop around and fix his choice on the country which offers him the best bargain. Singapore, Taiwan, South Korea and the Philippines can offer various advantages over Hong Kong such as cheaper land and factory rents, lower wage rates and special tax inducements. As against these, the colony can offer:

1. a labour force accustomed to factory disciplines, with local technicians and supervisory staff available;
2. no discrimination against foreign firms, nor any requirement that a certain proportion of the labour force should be locally recruited;
3. good external and internal communications; efficient services (water, electricity, posts, etc.);
4. low taxes, a free capital market and no restrictions on the repatriation of profits;
5. a stable and efficient administration with prudent budgetary policies;
6. the general use of the English language in government and the British legal system;
7. a minimum of government regulations and detailed interference in business decisions.

So far these inducements have proved sufficient to outweigh both the particular political risks of investing in Hong Kong and the fact that Hong Kong wage rates are high compared to most of its competitors. It was estimated in 1973 that foreign participation in Hong Kong industry amounted to HK$1,000 million.[4] However, the administration must be continually alert to the possibility that the balance of advantage may be changing, and be ready to adjust its policies accordingly. In 1973 the policy of selling the leasehold of all Crown land at open auction was modified to allow privately negotiated land sales to selected industrial ventures which the government wished to attract to Hong Kong.[5] This continuing need for foreign investment makes it highly unlikely that the Financial Secretary will ever feel free to raise the maximum rate of tax on profits and salaries much above the present 15 per cent.[6] This may also be the reason why Hong Kong has never adhered to a number of conventions drawn up by the International Labour Office (for example on workmen's compensation and social security),[7] since legal enforcement of such rights might significantly increase the labour costs of local industry. Some critics of the colony's industrial and social policies fail to recognize the constraints imposed on government by Hong Kong's precarious economic situation and its utter dependence on export earnings to feed its people and provide them with the rising standards of living they have come to expect. It is, of course, possible to argue that the administration is excessively cautious in imposing additional burdens on industry, and that the colony would lose little or no investment if it increased taxes and tightened up its labour laws. But for the last twenty-five years successive Governors and their advisers have been unwilling to take the risk that policy changes of this kind might kill the goose which has laid such golden eggs, particularly when there appeared to be no insistent demands from the local population.

This is the element of truth in the old jibe that Hong Kong is run by the Jockey Club, Jardine and Matheson, the Hong Kong & Shanghai Bank and the Governor—in that order.[8] It is easy to show that on occasion government acts against the views expressed by Jardines or the other great trading firms.[9] However in general government policy must retain the support of the local business interests. Otherwise their unfavourable views will soon filter out to the wider international business community, who are unlikely to be willing to invest in the colony if local industrialists have lost confidence in the administration.

THE IDEOLOGY OF GOVERNMENT

So long as there are no threatening political moves from China, businessmen's confidence in Hong Kong seems likely to continue, since the colonial government is more firmly committed to nineteenth century policies of allowing free play to market forces than is the case anywhere else in the world. The *1973 Yearbook* proclaims:

Hong Kong is probably the only territory still completely faithful to liberal economic policies of free enterprise and free trade.... Economic planning is not a function of the government except in the very broadest sense. Apart from the provision of the infrastructure, either through direct services or by cooperation with public utility companies and autonomous bodies, the government's role remains one of providing a suitable framework within which commerce and industry can function efficiently and effectively with a minimum of interference. The government intervenes in economic processes only in response to over-riding economic and social events. There is also no protection or subsidisation of manufactures.[10]

This description is very close to the truth. The provision of electricity, gas, telephones and public transport is left to private companies. Where services are provided by government, either a handsome profit is made (e.g. the Post Office, the Railway, the Airport, car parks), or an attempt is made to recover the greater part of the cost from the actual users (e.g. the water supply, housing, the Trade Development Council, the Tourist Association).[11]

Such policies would be approved by conservative political leaders all over the world, but in practice democratic governments, including that of the United States, have shown themselves ready to raise taxes for the provision of greater social welfare or to offer subsidies to declining industries in order to prevent workers being dismissed, from fear of losing votes at the next election. The Hong Kong government is under no such temptation to modify its ideology in order to garner a few votes in a marginal constituency. Any such action would be regarded as a distortion of the free market, preventing the movement of the resources of labour and capital to those industrialists who can use these factors of production most profitably and efficiently. Such free scope for entrepreneurs is normally only permitted in very backward countries or military dictatorships where the bureaucracy is too weak or incompetent to impose any restraints. But in Hong Kong, where the administration could easily extend its range of activities, officials deliberately stand aside with self-effacing modesty in the belief that free competition should not be interfered with, and claim that this policy has given local capitalists and foreign investors the opportunity and the incentive to expand and diversify their operations, making their own fortunes and at the same time producing dynamic growth in the economy for the benefit of all.

This policy has always been traditional in Hong Kong, but throughout the 1960s it was pursued with unusual single-mindedness under the direction of the reigning Financial Secretary, Sir John Cowperthwaite. He was always ready to expound the truths of this doctrine with wit and faultless logic to the Legislative Council, particularly when pressed by the unofficial members to stray from the paths of economic rectitude. Most of the unofficials were, and are, businessmen, but their economic views were rather more eclectic than those of Sir John: though they had no doubts about the virtue of low rates of taxation, they sometimes showed a distressing tendency to error by suggesting subsidies for particular industries, or even—the cardinal sin—advocating the collection of statistics and a measure of government planning. All such socialistic deviations were promptly and scornfully rejected.[12]

During his term of office from 1961 to 1971 Sir John's views were rarely overridden. The clearest case was in 1963 when rent controls were imposed on post-war domestic housing, in spite of the fact that he had previously argued that any such interference with the beneficent operations of the law of supply and demand would discourage new investment in building projects. However, government took the view that controls were necessary since this was an 'area of current hardship and potential danger' where economic considerations must take second place.[13] The controls were allowed to lapse after three years but had to be reimposed in 1970.

Apart from this, the main departures from *laissez-faire* economic doctrine before the 1970s were the Fish and Vegetable Marketing Organizations and the Rice Control Scheme. The latter was originally set up in 1954 when wartime rice rationing was finally abolished. Thirty-eight wholesalers were given a monopoly over the import of rice, on condition that they keep at least a three-month supply in reserve in the colony. The purpose of the scheme is to maintain adequate stocks of this stable food and guard against price manipulation. The importers have connections with different sources of supply in South-East Asia and an incidental advantage of the scheme is that in normal years Hong Kong is less dependent on China for its supplies.[14] The Fish and Vegetable Marketing Boards were set up after the war as a means of protecting farmers and fishermen from exploitation by middlemen. Such cooperative schemes were encouraged by the Colonial Office at that time, and these have been successfully operated since then, but they would probably not have been set up in the climate of opinion prevailing in Hong Kong in more recent years.

After Sir John's departure in 1971, and particularly following the arrival of the new Governor, Sir Murray MacLehose, in 1972, the attitudes of the administration appear to have become much less doctrinaire. Long term plans are being prepared in all departments; more statistics are being collected and published; the stock exchanges are to be regulated; and spokesmen prefer to refer to the role of government as being that of 'minimum interference' rather than to expound the benefits of *laissez-faire*. In 1973 the decision was taken to go ahead with an underground railway costing nearly HK$5,000 million. Such a vast expenditure had been virgorously opposed by Sir John, who had insisted that this mass transit scheme would never cover its costs and would require huge and continuing subsidies for its operation. Apparently such arguments no longer carry weight in government, but it is still too early to say how far these new departures in policy will be allowed to go.[15]

1. From a letter to *The Economist*, London, 2 Nov. 1968, p. 4.

2. *South China Morning Post*, 15 Dec. 1973 and *H. K. Hansard, 1973–74*, pp. 155ff. The Director of Commerce and Industry told the Council, 'The British Government intends to press resolutely for the inclusion of Hong Kong's textiles and footwear in the scheme from 1975 onward.... It must be left to Her Majesty's Government to decide the tactics of the operation.' However, in 1974 Britain only succeeded in obtaining some concessions on footwear and discrimination against textiles is to continue. (*Far Eastern Economic Review*, 6 Dec 1974, p. 53.)

3. *U.S. Business Investments in Hong Kong*, 20 Sept. 1968 (quoted in K. Hopkins, *Hong Kong, Industrial Colony*, p. 229). A Survey in the *Sunday Post-Herald* (Hong Kong), 14 Oct. 1973, based on information supplied by the American Chamber of Commerce, claimed that there were more than 400 American-controlled businesses in the colony, employing nearly 50,000 local people and accounting for nearly HK$2,000 million worth of Hong Kong's exports.

4. In a speech by the Governor at the Hong Kong Products exhibition, reported in *South China Morning Post*, 8 Dec. 1973.

5. In December 1973 government sold the lease of a 10 acre site on Tsing Yi island by private treaty to Dow Chemicals Pacific, Ltd. to build a plant for the manufacture of polystyrene for the local plastics industry and for export. The company had considered sites in Taiwan, the Philippines and Thailand, but the offer of the land at below the market price was the decisive factor. *South China Morning Post*, 12 Dec. 1973. See also Appendix 2 Document D, p. 230.

6. In his 1974 budget the Financial Secretary warned that he would have to consider raising the standard rate of tax in 1975–6, ten years after it was last raised from $12\frac{1}{2}$ to 15 per cent; but he added, 'I shall not allow fiscal considerations to override economic realities'. *H. K. Hansard, 1973–74*, p. 606. In 1970 Sir John Cowperthwaite put the upper limit at 20 per cent, *H. K. Hansard 1969–70*, p. 373. Profits tax went up to $16\frac{1}{2}\%$ in 1975.

7. There is a full list of the 30 conventions of the International Labour Office which have been ratified by the British government but which are not fully operative within Hong Kong because 'they are regarded as inapplicable due to local conditions', in *House of Commons Debates*, 23 Nov. 1972, Written Answer, cols. 480–1; 7 others have been applied to Hong Kong with modifications.

In April 1974, 29 conventions had been applied to Hong Kong, and four more were shortly to be made applicable, bringing the total to 33. Compared to other Asian countries, Hong Kong's record is not altogether unfavourable; India has ratified 30, Japan 29, Singapore 21, Philippines 18, Thailand 11, Malaysia 8. (Press conference and letter from the Commissioner of Labour, *South China Morning Post*, 30 March and 2 April 1974).

8. Quoted in R. Hughes, *Hong Kong—Borrowed Place, Borrowed Time*, p. 17.

9. For example, in 1973 the Financial Secretary abolished income tax relief for life insurance payments, in spite of the protests of Jardine's Insurance Department and other insurance companies.

10. *Hong Kong 1973, A Review of 1972* (Hong Kong Government Press), p. 12.

11. Rents in resettlement estates were fixed to cover both recurrent costs and also capital expenditure, notionally amortised at $3\frac{1}{2}$ per cent over 40 years. The Trade Development Council, which engages in overseas promotional activities, is largely financed by an *ad valorem* tax on trade declarations; the Tourist Association is partly financed by a tax on hotel accommodation. *Report of the Commissioner for Resettlement 1971–72* p. 33. *Estimates of Revenue and Expenditure, 1972–73*, p. 531 (Head 79, notes).

12. See the extracts from Sir John's speeches in the documents in Appendix 2, pp. 227–30.

13. For Sir John's views on rent control see *H. K. Hansard 1962*, pp. 5–7. Government's reasons for imposing control are given in *H. K. Hansard 1962*, pp. 279–89, especially p. 287.

14. For details of the history and operation of the Rice Control Scheme, see *H. K. Hansard 1966*, pp. 204f, *H. K. Hansard 1967*, pp. 28–34, and *H. K. Hansard 1973–74*, pp. 710–21. In 1972 Thailand supplied 64 per cent of Hong Kong's total rice imports, but imposed a complete export ban in June 1973. In the same month the previous quantitive restriction on the import of rice from China was lifted, and as a result China supplied 53 per cent of the colony's rice imports in 1973.

15. See *H. K. Hansard 1968*, pp. 208–11 for Sir John's pungent views on the Mass Transit Scheme and the experts' forecasts. Government now claims that the railway will be viable without a subsidy. For a full discussion of the latest trends in government policy see Alvin Rabushka: *The Changing Face of Hong Kong, New Departures in Public Policy* (A.E.I. Hoover policy studies, Washington D.C., 1973).

PART II
The Institutions of Government

5 Hong Kong's Constitution: The Letters Patent and Royal Instructions

CONSTITUTIONS IN GENERAL

MOST countries have found it convenient to set down the main legal rules which determine the composition and powers of the various organs of government in a single document known as the Constitution. Such a document is essential if there has been a break in the continuity of government (e.g. by revolution, foreign conquest or obtaining independence), since it is then necessary to prescribe in detail how the new system of government is to be organized.[1] Thus in the case of Hong Kong its first constitution consisted of the *Charter and Instructions* sent to Sir Henry Pottinger by the Colonial Office, and these came into force immediately upon completion of the formal exchange of ratifications of the Treaty of Nanking and the public proclamation of the Island of Hong Kong as a British Colony on 26 June 1843.[2] A Constitution normally has a higher legal status than ordinary laws, since it defines what is and what is not to count as a law and the procedures by which such laws are to be made. At a minimum, a Constitution should lay down how and by whom the members of the various organs of government are to be appointed, their length of tenure, the powers they may exercise and the limits upon their power. It also needs to include the method of resolving disputes between different institutions, if any system of balance or separation of powers is to be operated, and to state how the Constitution itself is to be amended.[3] Most Constitutions also permit the use of special emergency powers to deal with a crisis, and some also include a list of fundamental rights and liberties of the people. In effect, these are a special limitation on the powers of the Executive or the Legislature. Constitutions vary greatly in length, depending on the complexity of the machinery of government, and the extent to which less important matters are allowed to be regulated by the normal processes of legislation.

But however long the Constitution may be, it is difficult to reduce to writing all the rules which prescribe the way any state is run. Whatever the Constitution may say, some organs of government or the holders of certain offices will in practice refrain from exercising powers which they legally possess and others will act in ways which are not legally sanctioned but which are accepted as right and proper by those who manage the business of government. Such rules, which are recognized as binding by those who obey them, but which are not legally enforceable, are technically referred to as 'conventions'. Some are of such long standing that their breach is almost unthinkable, for example, the convention in Britain that the sovereign never exercises the power to refuse assent to Acts of Parliament, which has been observed by Kings and Queens for 250 years, though it has no legal basis. Others are more recent, and it is always possible to think of possible circumstances in which they might be ignored or altered. The older the constitutional documents, the more conventions will have arisen.

Conventions change and can be changed, just as constitutional documents can be amended. The difference is that the process is usually much simpler in the former case: all that is necessary is that the office-holder or corporate body concerned should decide not to be bound by that particular convention in future; or it may require no more than that the old convention is given a slightly different interpretation or applied in a way hitherto unforeseen. But this flexibility does not mean that governments can ignore at will any convention that stands in their way. Any government which arbitrarily brushes aside a long-standing convention that still continues to enjoy widespread approval risks suffering a damaging loss of authority and public support. Those in power do not lightly disappoint the expectations of their subjects, unless they are convinced that circumstances make this unavoidable and that they can justify their actions to public opinion. Long-established conventions can thus place limits on the freedom of action of governments which are as strong as any restraints in a written constitution.

So a complete description of the constitutional arrangements of any state must include not only the legally enforceable rules, but also the conventions which in practice have sometimes drastically modified what the Constitution says. Anyone who confines his attention entirely to the legal documents would be likely to give a misleading account of how the government of Hong Kong is actually carried on.

THE CONSTITUTION OF HONG KONG[4]

The legal basis for the government of Hong Kong is provided by the *Letters Patent and Royal Instructions*. In form both of these are approved in draft at a meeting of the Privy Council;[5] the *Letters Patent* then become legally binding on the affixing of the Great Seal, and the *Royal Instructions* on the affixing of the Royal Sign Manual and Signet. But these are only the ceremonial details. In fact both these documents, and all subsequent amendments to them, have been drafted by officials in Whitehall and approved by the minister responsible for Hong Kong affairs in the British government. Until 1966 this was the Secretary of State for the Colonies, but with the granting of independence to most of the colonial territories this separate office was amalgamated with the Department of Commonwealth Affairs; and since 1968 Hong Kong has been under the Secretary of State for Foreign and Commonwealth Affairs. The present set of documents was revised and reissued in 1917, and since then minor details have been amended on twelve occasions, but most of the clauses still retain the same wording as appeared in the edition of 1888.

The *Letters Patent** are the earlier and more important document. They create the office of Governor and define his powers in rather vague terms: to make laws for the peace, order and good government of the colony, to make grants of land, to appoint judges and other officers of the government, to suspend or dismiss any officer (except judges of the Supreme Court, for whom a special procedure applies), and to grant pardons. The *Letters Patent* also authorize the creation of the Executive and Legislative Councils; instruct all officers to obey the Governor; and make provision for filling the office of Governor when the holder is temporarily absent. The main emphasis of the *Letters Patent* is on the need to preserve all the rights of Her Majesty's government over the colony. In all the powers given to the Governor he is reminded that they must only be exercised in accordance with any instructions he may be given from London and the power of the Crown (i.e. the British government) to make laws for the colony and to disallow any ordinances passed by the colonial legislature is expressly reserved.

The *Royal Instructions* fill in some of the gaps left by the *Letters Patent*. They are almost wholly concerned with the details of the composition, powers and procedures of the Executive and Legislative Councils, the method of appointment and dismissal of the members, who is to preside, how decisions are to be taken, how ordinances are to be drawn up, and the subjects on which the Governor may not give his assent to bills until he has obtained permission from London. Detailed instructions are also laid down for the action to be taken when the Governor is considering whether to commute or confirm a sentence of death; and a few other minor points are included on such matters as land surveys and oaths.

It is all a very short and simple constitution, because of the concentration of power in the hands of the Governor. This is needed in order to achieve the subordination of the colony to Her Majesty's government in London. In consequence there is no need to go into detail about the Urban Council or the organization of the Colonial Secretariat, since their operations can be completely regulated by ordinances passed by the Legislative Council, or administrative instructions from the Governor. For the same reason there is no need to provide for special emergency powers, since the Governor is already given almost unfettered power to act on his own discretion, provided he reports the facts immediately to London. If legislation is required, an ordinance can be passed through all its stages at one sitting of the Council by the votes of the majority of official members.[6] Alternatively, the Governor could make use of the *Emergency Regulations Ordinance* (cap 241) under which, 'On any occasion which the Governor in Council may consider to be as occasion of emergency or public danger he may make any regulations whatsoever he may consider desirable in the public interest' (sec. 2). Such regulations override any existing law and may impose any penalty, even the death penalty, though this is subject to the agreement of the Legislative Council. The only

*'Patent' means open to the public, not confidential.

special provision included in the *Royal Instructions* to deal with a crisis is that which allows the Governor to give immediate assent to a bill on one of the reserved subjects, so long as he 'shall have satisfied himself that an urgent necessity exists requiring that such a Bill be brought into immediate operation'.[7] This might possibly be needed in the case of a bill concerning the currency issue or the operation of the banking system, both of which are reserved subjects. But such a provision is hardly necessary nowadays when the requisite permission could be quickly obtained by radio-telephone.

As in Britain there are no special safeguards for the fundamental rights of the individual in the colony. The watchfulness of members of Parliament has always been assumed to be sufficient to protect the liberties of the individual from restriction by legislation or arbitrary acts of the Executive, and the Governor and Legislative Council are trusted to be equally zealous in their defence overseas.[8] The only specific precaution is the requirement that any Bill 'whereby persons not of European birth or descent may be subjected or made liable to any disabilities or restrictions to which persons of European birth or descent are not also subjected or made liable' must be reserved for decision by the Secretary of State.[9]

As in Britain there is no provision for the Courts to have the power of Judicial Review. Once an ordinance has been properly passed by the Legislative Council and assented to by the Governor the Courts must enforce it. They are not entitled to invalidate an ordinance, as happens in the U.S.A., on the grounds that it is retrospective or that it conflicts with certain inviolable natural rights. Ordinances can be disallowed by the British government for any reason, but not by the local judges. The most they can do is to rule that a piece of subsidiary legislation is '*ultra vires*' since it goes beyond the powers delegated to the Governor in Council by the ordinance.[10] Since the Courts in Hong Kong have no political function, the details of their organization and the administration of justice will not be further discussed in this book.[11]

There are two other documents which are of constitutional significance: the *Colonial Regulations* and Capt. Elliot's proclamation of 1841. The *Colonial Regulations* are described as 'Directions to Governors for general guidance given by the Crown through the Secretary of State for the Colonies'. It is debatable whether these *Regulations* are legally binding on a Governor, in the sense that he could be prosecuted if he failed to obey them.[12] Probably they are not; but in practice 'guidance' given by a superior is little different from a direct order, and the Hong Kong government adheres to the detail of these rules except where they have been specifically relaxed. For example, a resolution passed by the Legislative Council in 1966 delegating certain financial powers to officials in the Secretariat had to be re-voted in an amended form in 1969 because in certain details it conflicted with *Colonial Regulation 223*; and the Financial Secretary was unable to sign a loan agreement with the Asian Development Bank in 1972 until an authorizing ordinance had been passed by the Legislative Council in accordance with *Colonial Regulation 237*.[13]

Apart from financial matters, the *Regulations* prescribe detailed procedures for the appointment, seniority, conduct and discipline of officials in the Public Service. These rules severely limit the freedom to appoint and dismiss officers given to the Governor by the *Letters Patent,* clauses XIV and XVI. The *Regulations* also include minute detail about dress and ceremonials. Sir Alexander Grantham confesses that he paid little attention to these paragraphs during his Governorship but neglected to get proper permission from the Colonial Office.[14]

When Capt. Elliot first took possession of Hong Kong island he promised that 'the natives of the Island of Hong Kong and all natives of China thereto resorting, shall be governed according to the laws and customs of China, every description of torture excepted'. This declaration was promptly disavowed by the British Foreign Secretary, Lord Palmerston, on the ground that Hong Kong had not yet been formally ceded to Britain.[15] Nevertheless it has been regarded since then by the Chinese population as a solemn declaration of policy by the Colonial government. When a Public Health Bill was proposed in 1886 which imposed minimum standards of housing with adequate space for ventilation to deal with an outbreak of plague, the Chinese organized a petition against the bill which called in evidence the Elliot proclamation as a reason why their traditional methods of house building should not be disturbed.[16] And when a bill for the reform of Chinese marriage customs was finally brought to the Legislative Council in 1970 after seventeen years of discussion one unofficial member, Mrs. Ellen Li, blamed the administration for its pedantic adherence to the words of Captain Elliot.[17] It would seem that the proclamation makes a good debating point whenever Chinese rights appear to be infringed, whatever its lack of legal validity. The nearest constitutional parallel is perhaps the Directive Principles of the Indian Constitution, which have no legally binding force, but which indicate the sort of society which the authors hoped would be achieved.

CONSTITUTIONAL CONVENTIONS

So much for the formal documents. It is more difficult to describe the conventions of government, since it is necessary to rely on the way officials behave and the remarks they make about what they consider is right and proper to do. The most important difference between the constitutional position as set out in the *Letters Patent* and *Royal Instructions* and what actually happens is that the British government very rarely exercises its legal right to give detailed instructions about the way the internal affairs of the colony are to be conducted. Parliament has the right to pass laws which are binding upon Hong Kong, but by convention this is only done when uniformity of law is desirable throughout Britain and all the remaining territories of the Colonial Empire for which Britain remains internationally responsible (see Chapter 19, p. 203). The Secretary of State can advise the Queen to disallow any ordinance passed by the Legislative Council; but this right has not been exercised since 1913, and it would be very surprising if it were to be revived now. In practice, if the British government is unhappy about any ordinance, detailed negotiations take place between Hong Kong and London until a mutually acceptable compromise is reached and then an amending bill is introduced into the Hong Kong Legislative Council. The British government has the legal power to overrule the local legislature, but by convention it proceeds by persuasion and argument rather than by open use of the prerogative powers of the Crown. (See below, Chapter 8, p. 99–100.)

British interference is now very largely confined to matters which have a bearing on Hong Kong's international position. The powers still actively exercised by London and the circumstances under which British views may become important are best described in Part III of this book. They rarely intrude on the day-to-day business of administration, and it is possible to describe the way Hong Kong is run with hardly a reference to Britain's nominal sovereignty.

Other conventions will be referred to in subsequent chapters but a few more examples may be given here. Clause XVIII of the *Letters Patent* orders all officers to be obedient to the Governor, but following U.K. practice, the Attorney General is entitled to determine whether or not to initiate a prosecution in a criminal case, and the Governor will never interfere with his discretion.[18] The Governor is only 'advised' by the Public Service Commission how he should exercise his powers of appointment to the Public Service, but it would be most unusual if he ignored their recommendation and chose someone else. Though there is a majority of 'official' votes on the full Legislative Council, this is never used to overrule a decision taken in the Finance Committee, where the unofficials are in the majority.

It is not only officials who consider themselves bound by conventions. When Sir Yuet-keung Kan was the senior unofficial member of the Legislative Council he stated that it would be improper for the unofficial members to attempt to influence the appointments made by the Governor by voting to reduce or abolish the financial provision for the salary of the person so appointed; he also stated that it would be wrong to breach the convention of the independence of the universities by using the power to vote or withhold funds from the University Grants Commission, as a means of influencing the internal allocations made by the universities.[19]

Until 1972 the oldest convention in Hong Kong government was the tradition that the unofficial Justices of the Peace[20] and the General Chamber of Commerce were each entitled to select one of their number to sit on the Legislative Council. The J.P.s had enjoyed this customary privilege since 1849 and the Chamber since 1883, though it was nowhere mentioned in the *Royal Instructions* or in any other legal document.[21] Successive governors had followed their predecessors' example and nominated the representatives so 'elected' to seats on the Council, and it had come to be assumed that this would always continue. At the time this system was instituted it seemed a reasonable means of finding representatives of a substantial body of opinion in the colony without putting government to the trouble of organizing a ballot. However, the electorates were fairly small: the unofficial J.P.s numbered about 200, and though about 2,000 firms are members of the Chamber the nomination was in fact made by the General Committee.[22] Moreover, the persons so chosen were in fact very little different from the other unofficial members of the Council. So there was no public objection when in 1972 the Governor took advantage of the impending retirement from the Council of the J.P.s' representative, Mr. J.C. Browne, to announce that the custom would be discontinued, and that Mr. Hilton Cheong-Leen, an elected member of the Urban Council, would be nominated to the vacant seat.[23] The J.P.s were somewhat mollified by the reference to the fact that Mr. Cheong-Leen was himself a J.P., and any dissatisfaction they may have felt was lost in the general approval of this enhancement of the status of the elected members of the Urban Council. Appointed members of the Urban Council had frequently been elevated to the Legislative Council in the past, but never before had this honour come to a sitting elected member.

At the same time the Governor informed the General Chamber of Commerce that its traditional privilege would also be discontinued, though the term of office of its existing member on the Council, Mr. P.G. Williams, was extended, in a personal capacity, for a further two years.[24] Most of the leading businessmen in Hong Kong are members of the Chamber of Commerce, and it continues to be well represented on the colony's policy-making bodies, even after losing this right of nomination: in 1973 three of the Chamber's General Committee were unofficial members of the Legislative Council, and three others sat on the Executive Council.[25] Before 1941 there was continuing friction between the officers of the Colonial Service and the local business community, so the provision for the Chamber to 'elect' its own nominee to the Legislative Council served a useful purpose in ensuring that the views of the commercial interest were vigorously expressed to government at the highest level by a representative who enjoyed their confidence.[26] But since the Japanese occupation business and government have collaborated together in an intimate partnership, so such a constitutional arrangement, though valued by the Chamber, was by 1972 unnecessary if not anachronistic. Accordingly the Governor was able to abrogate this convention without any loss of public support.

1. China did not have such a Constitution until after the revolution of 1911. Japan's first written constitution was drawn up in 1889. Of course, both countries had a constitutional structure before these dates, but it was regulated entirely by conventions (see next paragraph) and not by a legally binding document.

2. See G.B. Endacott, *Government and People in Hong Kong*, p. 19ff for details.

3. This last point applies only to the Constitution of an independent state, and not to a colony.

4. The texts of the *Letters Patent* and *Royal Instructions*, can be found in Volume 19 of the *Laws of Hong Kong*. They are reproduced in Appendix 3, pp. 232–44. Copies of *Colonial Regulations* are not readily available in Hong Kong. Texts of Capt. Elliot's Proclamation and the treaties of 1842, 1860 and 1898 can be found in *Laws of Hong Kong*, Volume 20, Appendix IV.

5. The Privy Council no longer has any effective functions in the government of Britain; it meets formally to issue such Orders, which are the normal means for altering colonial constitutions. The Judicial Committee of the Privy Council is also the final Court of Appeal from a Colonial Judiciary and certain Commonwealth governments.

6. This procedure was followed, with the unanimous approval of the unofficial members,

on 28 January 1970, to pass all stages of the *Security of Tenure (Domestic Premises) Bill 1970*. (*H. K. Hansard 1969/70*, pp. 269–78, 299 & 304). This was necessary to prevent landlords imposing rent increases or evicting tenants before a permanent system of rent control was devised. Of course, if the unofficials were to be given an overall majority, special constitutional provision for overriding this in an emergency would have to be made, in order to preserve the final authority of the British government so long as Hong Kong remained a colony.

7. *Royal Instructions XXVI*, last paragraph.

8. During the 1967 disturbances regulations were made under the *Emergency Regulations Ordinance* to permit detention without trial. Twenty-six questions were asked in the House of Commons about the conditions of these detainees and related matters in the 1967–8 session, and this pressure was probably one reason why this regulation was revoked in 1969. Not one question was asked on this subject in the Legislative Council, though Mr. Woo Pak-chuen has complained about the excessive zeal shown by the police on a number of other occasions (see for example *H. K. Hansard 1966*, pp. 303–5, 318–19 and 426–7). He also questioned the wide investigative powers given to the police under the *Prevention of Bribery Ordinance* (*H. K. Hansard 1970–71*, pp. 192–4) and requested certain safeguards to be added to the bill instituting preventive detention (*H. K. Hansard 1972–73*, p. 897).

9. *Royal Instructions XXVI*, see 9. Similar provisions were and are included in the constitutional documents of all colonies with a non-European population; see M. Wight, *The Development of the Legislative Council* (Faber, London, 1946), p. 153.

10. A case of this kind occurred in 1971 where in an appeal against a magistrate's order for the detention of a minibus, the Full Court ruled that part of the regulations which authorize the impounding of this kind of vehicle was *ultra vires*. One of the grounds of this judgment was that the word 'used' in the original Ordinance could not be legally construed to include 'driven'.

Legislation was subsequently passed, first to revalidate the regulations, and finally, to include them as part of the ordinance itself. See *H. K. Hansard 1969/1970*, pp. 719–23, & 777–83, and the *Hong Kong Law Journal*, Vol. I, 1971, pp. 74–80.

11. The magistrates and judges are, of course, a politically very important group within the administration when giving their views on new legislation.

Full details of the organization of the Courts are given by Rear in K. Hopkins (ed.), *Hong Kong, The Industrial Colony* (O.U.P., Hong Kong, 1971), pp. 390–406.

12. Sir Kenneth Roberts-Wray, *Commonwealth and Colonial Law* (Stevens, London, 1966), pp. 239–40.

13. *H. K. Hansard 1969*, pp. 491–6, & *H. K. Hansard 1971-72*, pp. 858ff.

14. Grantham, *Via ports*, pp. 145–6.

15. See Endacott, *Government and People in Hong Kong*, p. 28.

16. Ibid. p. 152.

17. *Hong Kong Hansard 1969/70*, p. 732. The Elliot Proclamation was also cited by one writer to the newspapers in 1973, who was complaining about the Crown's decision to reprieve a convicted murderer. (*South China Morning Post*, 19 May 1973.)

18. See *South China Morning Post*, 24 May 1972. The Attorney-General, Mr. D.T.E. Roberts, announced that none of the young people who took part in the Tiao Yu Tai demonstration would be prosecuted, and said 'As Attorney-General, I am in sole control of all prosecutions and the decision whether or not to pursue a particular case is entirely mine, not that of the Commissioner of Police nor of the Government'. He added that he had consulted other government departments and officials 'whom I think may be able to tender useful advice to me'.

19. See letters by Mr. J. Rear, Sir Charles Hartwell and Sir Yuet-keung Kan, *South China Morning Post*, 2, 4, 5, 11 & 14 January 1971.

20. Certain government officials, such as District Officers in the New Territories and City District Officers, are made Justices of the Peace; but they did not vote on these occasions.

21. For the origins of these practices see Endacott, *Government and People in Hong Kong*, pp. 45–55 and 98–103. Election by the J.P.s lapsed between 1857 and 1883.

22. Endacott, *Government and People in Hong Kong*, p. 215. Since the war the Chamber had always nominated its chairman.

23. An official announcement at the time stated that after a careful consideration of the historical and legal background the Secretary of State had approved that a nomination from the Justices of the Peace should not be called for. 'It is emphasized that this departure does not reflect any change in the Government's view of the high status of Justices of the Peace in the community, or of their fitness to serve on the Legislative and Executive Councils.' *South China Morning Post*, 26 April 1973. All unofficial members of the Executive and Legislative Councils are in fact Justices of the Peace.

24. See the speech made by the outgoing chairman of the Chamber, Mr. P.G. Williams, on 2 April 1974: 'Since 1883 the Chamber has enjoyed the tradition of being asked to nominate for the Governor's consideration a member for appointment to the Legislative Council. It was disappointing therefore that this practice has been discontinued in parallel with a similar tradition relating to the J.P.s. However, I know of the importance the Governor attaches to the Chamber and I have every confidence that there will continue to be Unofficial Members of the Legislative Council who can speak with a knowledge of Chamber affairs and points of view. It is perhaps significant that my own appointment was extended in a personal capacity for two years.'

25. On the Executive Council: Sir Douglas Clague, Sir Yuet-keung Kan, and Mr. G.R. Ross. On the Legislative Council, Mr. Ann Tse-kai, Mr. G.M. Sayer and Mr. P.G. Williams. Two other members of the Council of the Chamber also sit on the Executive Council: Dr. Chung Sze-yuen and Sir Sidney Gordon.

26. See the article by H.J. Lethbridge, 'Hong Kong under Japanese Occupation: Changes in Social Structure', in I.C. Jarvie and J. Agassi (eds.), *Hong Kong: A Society in Transition* (Routledge and Kegan Paul, London, 1969), pp. 77–127.

6 The Governor and the Executive Council

THE Governor is the symbolic representative of the Queen's sovereignty over Hong Kong and exercises by delegation the powers of the royal prerogative. This delegated authority is circumscribed by the general limits set out in the *Letters Patent*, the *Royal Instructions* and *Colonial Regulations*, by the specific directions that he may receive from the Secretary of State for Foreign and Commonwealth Affairs, and by the constitutional conventions which have been observed by former governors. He is also subject to British Law as far as it is applicable in the colony and to all the Ordinances passed by the Hong Kong Legislative Council. Concurrently with his office as Governor he is the Commander-in-Chief of the Armed Forces, entitled to receive the 'obedience, aid, and assistance of all military and air force officers in the colony', but not to exercise direct operational control over them.[1] In normal times this appointment is a nominal one; the organization of the British Forces is almost entirely separate from the civil government and the Commander British Forces deals directly with the Ministry of Defence in London. But in an emergency the Governor, as Commander-in-Chief, can personally order that troops should be called out to assist in the maintenance of internal security without any prior need to refer to Whitehall.[2]

In his public role the Governor is seen as the representative of the imperial power, relaying the decisions of the British government and endeavouring to explain them and make them as acceptable as possible to the local population. But in private he is usually much more active as the spokesman of the colony to Britain, putting the point of view of Hong Kong and attempting to safeguard its interests. The Colonial Service has always had a good reputation for the vigorous defence of the dependent territories against unreasonable demands from London. For example, Sir Alexander Grantham (Governor 1947–1957) fought for many years with the Treasury to prevent the closure of the Naval Base in Hong Kong and the transfer of all repair work to Singapore.[3] Similarly every five years when the amount of the Defence Contribution to be paid towards the maintenance of the British Forces is reviewed the vigorous representations of the Hong Kong government have achieved substantial reductions from Britain's original demands.[4] Such arguments are conducted in secret, but the views of the administration will often be publicly supported in protests voiced by the unofficial members of the Executive

and Legislative Councils. Though the Governor is formally the representative of the British government he may on occasion covertly encourage
such activity when he hopes it will persuade the ministers in London to
change their policy.[5]

The Governor's legal powers are such that if he chose to exercise his
full authority he could turn himself into a petty dictator. In theory he is
constitutionally entitled to ignore the advice of the Executive Council
and the Public Service Commission; he could override any opposition in
the Legislative Council by directing the official majority to repeal or pass
any ordinances he wished; he could completely reverse past policies and
set the whole colony in turmoil. At least one nineteenth-century Governor
showed signs of acting in such a high-handed way;[6] but such colourful
characters are no longer to be found, or at least, not in the higher ranks
of the Public Service. If any modern Governor were tempted to follow
such a buccaneering course, the Crown's dormant powers of disallowance
would certainly be revived, detailed directives would be sent from London,
and in the last resort a Governor, who like all the Public Service only
holds office during the Queen's pleasure, could be summarily dismissed.

In fact, of course, there are built-in obstacles against any such behaviour
without the need to call in the aid of the British government. Chief of
these is the Public Service itself. Any long-established organization tends
to get settled into a routine and produces a standard repertoire of responses to any demands made upon it. A large part of the business of
government is concerned with the detailed implementation of decisions
taken long ago, and these basic policies cannot be re-examined and
reversed overnight without considerable cost and administrative dislocation. This is also true of plans which have reached an advanced stage
before a new Governor's arrival. Naturally civil servants, like anyone else,
prefer to keep to their accustomed ways and passively resist any inconvenient innovations. If any changes are to be made they can only be
effected successfully with the active cooperation of the officers concerned.
Any attempt to suppress opposition, to flout established conventions or
by-pass standard procedures often achieves very little except to destroy
goodwill. Any Governor who hopes to achieve anything worthwhile
during his term of office can only do so with the full cooperation and
whole-hearted support of the Public Service. Though he has the final
authority to give orders he will normally work more by questioning and
persuasion than by issuing peremptory instructions. Of course, a Govern-
or is not without weapons for achieving his ends. The decisions he takes on
routine matters will influence the shape of proposals being put forward in
the Colonial Secretariat and the departments. His views will influence
promotions, particularly at the top of the service. He can, within limits,
transfer officers to different duties when vacancies occur.[7] He can push
forward action by showing continued interest in a project and discourage
other lines of policy by neglect. Where a department is unwilling to put
forward sufficiently bold plans, he can set up a committee to examine
proposals and set new targets, and then point to the popular enthusiasm
aroused by the publication of the report as an argument for accelerated

implementation. But whatever his ambitions, he cannot hope to achieve an overnight transformation in the face of the inevitable inertia of an entrenched bureaucracy.[8] For example, Sir David Trench became Governor in 1964, and in 1966 he put forward tentative proposals for setting up a new system of local authorities, particularly in the New Territories. When he retired in 1971 the system of local government, or lack of one, was exactly the same as when he arrived. This was in part a consequence of the 1967 riots, but it was chiefly because of the opposition of senior administrators and heads of departments to any significant devolution of power from the centre.*

A Governor also has to take account of the likely reactions to new policy initiatives, particularly the attitudes of those well-organized groups whose goodwill and cooperation are essential for the efficient administration of the colony. For instance, most of the schools are not directly run by the government but by voluntary agencies who receive subventions from public funds. So any policy changes in education must first be agreed with these bodies who will largely have the responsibility for putting them into practice. Similar considerations apply to aspects of Social Welfare. Labour legislation and measures to reduce industrial accidents will have to be worked out in consultation with the representatives of employers and trade unions if they are to be effective and easy to administer. Many other such examples could be given.

Public opinion must also be considered. The administration in Hong Kong does not need to worry about the possible effects of its policies on the results of the next general election, as does a British government, but as far as possible it must ensure that its policies are generally acceptable to the Chinese population and that they have reasonable confidence that the government is taking their interests into account. If this basic confidence disappears then even a minor administrative muddle may trigger off a riot such as occurred in 1966 when the decision to authorize an increase in fares on the cross harbour ferry sparked off demonstrations which escalated into two nights of stone-throwing and arson.[9] Such riots have been extremely rare in post-war Hong Kong. But any such troubles on the streets tend to lead to unfavourable publicity for the colony. This may provoke enquiries from Whitehall and the minor irritation of questions in the House of Commons. More seriously, they might cause foreigners to hesitate before making investments or setting up factories in the colony.

Any serious rioting would also be liable to attract the attention of Peking. The government of China could hardly be expected not to make any protest if Chinese rioters were hurt by those 'running dogs of imperialism', the Hong Kong police. There are a number of ways in which Peking can cause difficulties: for example, supplies of food and water from across the border could be temporarily interrupted; Hong Kong fishermen could be interfered with; visitors to China could be harassed. Any or all of these pressures might be used in the event of a riot,

*See below, Chapter 15. There may have been good reasons for making no changes; the point is that the Governor, in spite of his nominal power, felt constrained to accept this.

or on any occasion when China felt that the government of the colony was failing to pay proper regard to her interests. Almost every policy decision has implications for China or her communist supporters in the colony, and the calculations of possible reactions are a further factor that limits the Governor's freedom of action, even though in any particular case the possibility of such a reaction from China is not decisive in determining what decision is taken.

But most of all there is the problem of shortage of time. The most important decisions of government are preceded by extensive technical studies of the factors involved, which sometimes, as in the case of the Cross-Harbour Tunnel or the proposed Mass Transit Underground Railway Scheme, take years to complete. These cases are exceptional. But similar questions of costs and alternative strategies must be thoroughly examined in the lower echelons of government before any changes are made, for example, in education or housing policy. The conclusions reached after prolonged consultations at departmental level are then processed by the Colonial Secretariat and passed up to the Executive Council for decision. If the Governor then wishes to challenge these recommendations and persuade the other members of the Council to support him, he needs to master the detail on which the original conclusion was based, and the time for this study must be subtracted from the other demands upon his time.

These demands are very numerous. In Britain the 'dignified' aspects of government—the laying of foundation stones, the presiding at degree congregations, the opening of hospitals, the receptions and presentations, the entertainment of distinguished visitors—are largely filled by the Queen and other members of the royal family who preside at such ceremonial occasions, leaving the Prime Minister and his ministers to concentrate on the 'efficient' processes of government.[10] But the Governor of Hong Kong has to fill both roles; he not only rules but he also reigns, and he would give justifiable grounds for offence if he failed to appear at the numerous public and private functions which Governors have attended in the past.

Much of this ceremonial may be boring and time-consuming, but it is not entirely a waste of his time. Being at the top of the social pyramid gives the Governor and his Lady the greatest influence in setting the tone of society. In the past it was important to set a standard of inter-racial social contact between the Chinese and the Europeans.[11] This is now hardly necessary, but by showing interest in all kinds of social welfare activities the Governor can encourage others to do the same. One potent inducement to this end is the fact that twice a year the Governor makes his recommendations to London of those who should be included in the Honours List. These awards enable a decent and proper recognition to be given to humble and unassuming service to the community; but they also provide an incentive to reasonable ambition and a spur to generosity for some who would not otherwise be inclined to make such efforts for the common good. Appointments to the unofficial seats on the Urban Council and the Legislative and Executive Council are also made on the

Governor's recommendation and can be used to harness varied talents for the service of the community. A Governor who immersed himself entirely in the details of administration would hardly be in a position to fill these posts wisely; and he also needs as wide a range of social contacts as possible so as to keep in touch with all levels of public opinion.

How a Governor apportions his time and sets his priorities will depend on his personal inclinations and his past experience. Colonial Governors have normally come from the Administrative Service. The usual pattern in the past has been to promote a senior officer from another colony, who has preferably served in Hong Kong earlier in his career, or perhaps elsewhere in Asia, but not so recently that he might be embarrassed by personal friendships and contacts made when he was at a lower level. Occasionally, though never yet in Hong Kong, an active politician is made a Governor at the end of his ministerial career. This is not often done since such an outside appointment naturally causes resentment among serving officers. But the talents for negotiation, compromise and concilia-tion developed in a lifetime in politics may enable a way to be found out of an explosive situation, particularly when a colony is on the verge of independence and the main need is to conclude a workable agreement with newly emerged political leaders rather than a talent for administra-tion.[12] Politicians are also likely to be more adept at public relations than the average administrator, and there are times when this is a great asset.

A third kind of appointment is a transfer from the diplomatic service, as in the case of the present Governor, Sir Murray MacLehose. Diplomats have to cultivate much the same talents as politicians, and they have been used in a trouble-shooting role elsewhere in the final stages of the colonial empire.[13] Sir Murray is the first ex-ambassador to govern Hong Kong, but he is unlikely to be the last, since Britain's other few remaining colonies are too small and rural to provide the necessary experience for dealing with Hong Kong's problems. As a former diplomat Sir Murray may be somewhat hampered by his lack of experience of administration at the grass-roots; but his advantage over a career colonial officer is that his views will carry greater weight among the officials of the Foreign and Commonwealth Office in Whitehall where he previously held a very senior post. Diplomats are usually transferred fairly frequently so that they do not become too attached to the country where they are serving, to the detriment of British interests. Presumably Sir Murray has quickly acquired the rather different attitudes of the Colonial Service officer. He had already served in Hong Kong as Political Adviser to the then Governor from 1959 to 1962.

According to *Colonial Regulations* Governors are usually appointed for a term of five years, but this may be extended if they are very popular or if there is difficulty in finding a suitable successor. Since the war, Sir Alexander Grantham served for 10 years (1947–1957), Sir Robert Black for 6 years (1958–1964) and Sir David Trench for 7 years (1964–1971).

THE EXECUTIVE COUNCIL

The *Letters Patent* authorize the creation of the Executive Council and direct that appointments to it are to be made by the Crown (i.e. by the Secretary of State), though the Governor is empowered to suspend any member pending a final decision from London. The *Royal Instructions* go into more detail: the Commander British Forces, the Colonial Secretary, the Attorney-General, the Secretary for Home Affairs and the Financial Secretary are all made permanent members of the Council *ex officio* (as long as they hold that particular appointment), and it is provided that further official and unofficial members may be appointed on the instructions of the Crown, though the Governor is allowed to make a provisional appointment when a vacancy occurs. Since 1966 the Council has consisted of the five *ex officio* members, one other official member and eight unofficials. According to the *Royal Instructions* unofficial members may be appointed for a maximum period of five years and are eligible for reappointment. In practice all the nominated members, official and unofficial, are appointed for periods of one or two years. There is no requirement, either by law or convention, that the single nominated official member should be the most senior government official below the permanent members. Since 1972 the seat has been filled by Dr. Choa, the Director of Medical and Health Services, who was appointed to head his department only in 1970. At the time he was made a member of the Council he was the senior Chinese departmental head. His predecessor, Dr. Teng, was also on the Council; he served for four years from 1966 to 1970.

In recent years the Governor has invariably recommended the appointment of one of the senior unofficial members of the Legislative Council, though not necessarily the most senior, when a vacancy occurs among the unofficials on the Executive Council.[14] Between the end of the war and 1974 half the unofficial members were always Chinese and half were British or Portuguese. In 1974 the balance was altered to give the Chinese six seats and the British two. Unofficial members are normally reappointed for as long as they are willing to serve: Sir Albert Rodrigues was a member from 1959 to 1974 and Sir Douglas Clague from 1961 to 1974. Some unofficials appointed to the Legislative Council resign from the Legislative Council at the end of their current term (e.g. Mr. S. S. Gordon in 1966 and Mr. Tang Ping-yuan in 1968); others feel able to combine both roles, though this involves a heavy burden of part-time service. At the beginning of 1975 Dr. Chung Sze-yuen and Mr. Oswald Cheung were members of both councils. This overlap in membership is valuable since it helps the Executive Council to anticipate the reactions of the unofficials on the Legislative Council and its Finance Committee, and so avoids the possibility of friction between them. But it can also cause embarrassment if the unofficials on the Executive Council agree to a bill which they then find is unacceptable to their colleagues on the Legislative Council (see below, p. 66).

Since 1966 the unofficial members have been a majority in the Council, but this has no great constitutional significance. The Governor is required by the *Royal Instructions* to consult the Council in all cases except where the matter is urgent, trivial or highly confidential ('cases which may be of such a nature that Our service would sustain material prejudice by consulting the Council thereupon'); but he is within his rights to act in opposition to its views provided that he informs the Secretary of State at the first opportunity.[15] However, it is a very long established convention that the Governor respects the majority view of the Council—(he would be a very self-opinionated man if he did not do so)—and he would probably be very reluctant to act over the determined opposition of a minority composed of unofficial members.[16] The main importance of this clause is to preserve the authority of the British government over the colony and to enable the Governor to carry into effect any instructions that he may receive from London, however much opposition there might be to them in the Council. Since the Council's proceedings are secret and the minutes of its meetings are not available to the public until after thirty years have elapsed, discussion can be quite free with official and unofficial members disagreeing among themselves. The Governor normally sums up the sense of the meeting and a formal counting of votes for and against a proposal is usually unnecessary. Clause XII of the *Royal Instructions* allows any member who disagrees with the final decision to insist that his objection should be recorded in the minutes. Such notes of dissent are rare and are not likely to have much practical effect. Copies of the minutes are despatched to London only every six months and such an opinion would be outweighed by the views of the majority.[17]

The position of the Executive Council in the government of Hong Kong corresponds to that of the Cabinet in Britain. Both are the authoritative final decision-makers for the whole of the government machine, and though many of their conclusions are legally subject to ratification elsewhere, by the Legislative Council and its Finance Committee or by Parliament, in practice this is normally achieved without much difficulty. But there are significant differences between the Governor in Council and the Prime Minister meeting with his Cabinet. The Governor seems to be in a stronger position than the Prime Minister since his power rests upon explicit legal foundations and binding instructions. He is constitutionally entitled to ignore the advice offered by the Council, and he is secure in his office for at least five years (subject only to the remote possibility of premature dismissal by the Crown). The Prime Minister's power, on the other hand, rests mainly upon long-standing conventions. His views in Cabinet will carry very great weight, but he can on occasion find himself outvoted if his colleagues combine to reassert the old principle that he is only 'first among equals'. More seriously he is continuously dependent on the support of his ministers and his party in the House of Commons, and if they should decide at any time that he is no longer fitted to remain at the head he can be forced to resign.[18] However, he is stronger than the Governor in a most important respect, that he is free to pick his own Cabinet, to allocate ministries as he chooses, and to demand a minister's resignation at any time. A Governor of Hong Kong is in a much weaker position. The five *ex officio* official members may have been in office under his predecessor and retain their seats as long as they hold their official positions. For example, Sir John Cowperthwaite was appointed Financial

Secretary under Sir Robert Black, and remained there for ten years, until the final year of Sir David Trench's governorship. Furthermore, though a Governor could in theory change the unofficial membership of the Council as the members' one or two year terms expire, in practice this would give great offence and he must normally wait until they die or choose to retire. Since a Governor's power to 'hire and fire' is very limited, particularly at the beginning of his term, the members of the Council can be expected to speak their minds with far more freedom than if they were dependent on him for future preferment, particularly as most of them have been in Hong Kong far longer than he has. Moreover, a new Governor lacks the 'legitimacy' which a British Prime Minister acquires from winning a general election. This success at the polls gives him great moral authority in pushing ahead with the changes he wants, however inconvenient they may be to the bureaucracy, whereas a Governor can make no such claim to represent the will of the people. Consequently, though he is legally entitled to demand that the officials in the Executive Council should vote as he directs, in practice he is more likely to feel obliged to defer to their greater experience of Hong Kong conditions.[19]

The Executive Council usually meets once a week. There is always a large amount of routine business to be attended to since many ordinances allow appeals to the Governor in Council from an administrative decision, for example against a draft town plan or the de-registration of a private medical clinic. The number of these relatively minor matters has grown so great recently that a number of ordinances have been amended to allow the Governor to decide some of these appeals personally (e.g. those from Tenancy Tribunals) without reference to the Executive Council.[20] For similar reasons the *Royal Instructions* and *Colonial Regulations* were amended in 1969 to allow the Governor to confirm the recommendations given him by the Public Service Commission on appointments, promotions and disciplinary matters without the need to refer them first to the Executive Council.[21]

Another frequent item on the agenda is new legislation. Most proposals for changes in the law originate from departments; the decision to begin drafting a bill and on the degree of priority to be accorded to it is normally taken within the Colonial Secretariat, though occasionally a directive may come from the Executive Council. When the draft is complete it is submitted to the Council together with a memorandum setting out the reasons for the bill written by the Secretary responsible. The Council may then approve the bill as drafted for introduction into the Legislative Council, or alternatively refer it back for further amendments to be made.[22] The views of those unofficial members who are also members of the Legislative Council are particularly important at this stage. They can normally predict the likely reactions of their colleagues on the Legislative Council, and if they consider that any proposal will be unacceptable to them the suggested change in the law will probably be abandoned before it ever has a chance to reach the First Reading. This previous vetting of bills by the Executive Council explains why so few ordinances are ever rejected by the Legislative Council. For example, in 1969 the Attorney-General revealed that a proposal he had made to introduce a bill to legalize abortion on the lines of recent British legislation had been rejected by the unofficials on the Executive Council and so had not gone any further.[23]

Very occasionally this system breaks down. One such instance occurred in 1960 when the Executive Council allowed a bill to legalize gambling on football pools to go forward. Opposition to the bill unexpectedly arose among the Chinese community, and the proposal was voted down on the Second Reading. The only unofficial to speak in favour of it was Mr. Ngan Shing-kwan, the senior unofficial and a member of the Executive Council, but he abstained in the final vote in deference to the opinions of the other unofficials, who all voted against the bill. All the official members also abstained.[24]

While a bill is going through the Legislative Council the Executive Council will be called upon to consider what concessions, if any, should be made to meet criticisms raised during the second reading debate, or by outside interests. When such points of detail are being discussed the Council may ask the Head of Department concerned to attend the meeting in order to elucidate any technical points. After an ordinance is finally passed into law detailed regulations to implement it are often required. Most of these items of subsidiary legislation must be laid before the Executive Council and be approved by it before they become legally valid.

Questions of finance rarely appear on the Council's agenda. It is left to the Financial Secretary to decide how much the colony can afford to spend each year and how the burden of taxation is to be distributed. He discusses the general shape of his budget proposals with the Governor some months previously, but the Executive Council is only told the details the day before the Appropriation Bill is introduced in the Legislative Council.[25] In theory the Council could then ask for changes to be made, even at this late stage, but in practice they do not do so. Bills to effect the taxation changes announced in the budget come before the Council later in the same way as other pieces of legislation. Otherwise financial matters only come before it if the question is highly political. This applies for example to changes in the rate of exchange of the Hong Kong dollar. In the past, tenders for the largest public works contracts were decided by the Governor in Council,[26] but the only one to come up in recent years was the contract for the Mass Transit Underground Railway; quite apart from the colossal sum of money involved, the decision whether to divide the contract into several parts or to negotiate a complete package deal with one of the consortiums who were ready to bid for the contract had important international political implications. But except in the case of such major issues detailed examination of expenditure proposals is left to the Finance Committee of the Legislative Council (see Chapter 9).

Finally, all sentences of death passed by the Courts are considered by the Executive Council with the aid of a report submitted by the judge who presided at the trial. Clause XXXIV of the *Royal Instructions* requires the Governor

...not to pardon or reprieve any such offender unless it shall appear to him expedient so to do, upon receiving the advice of the Executive Council thereon; but in all such cases he is to decide either to extend or withhold a pardon or reprieve, according to his own deliberate judgment, whether the Members of the Executive Council concur therein or otherwise, entering nevertheless on the Minutes of the Executive Council a Minute of his reasons at length, in case he should decide any such question in opposition to the judgment of the majority of the Members thereof.

In form this is very close to the general authority given to the Governor by Clause XII to go against the advice of the Council, except that he is not required to make an immediate report to London, and that particular stress is laid upon his personal responsibility for deciding whether the offender shall live or die. But this does not mean that he can settle the matter simply by considering the facts of the case and his own personal moral principles and beliefs about the efficacy of capital punishment as a deterrent. Since he bears the final responsibility for the colony's welfare he must also take into account the effect of his decision on the morale of the forces of law and order, the police and prison service, and also the state of public opinion. The people will lose confidence in the government if they believe that it does not pay sufficient attention to their reasonable anxieties about their personal safety. This is why the Governor is required to take his decision in the light of the views expressed by the Council, since these must normally be his main guide to the state of public feeling. In practice, Governors are very loath to act against the advice of the Council in such cases: the Minutes of the Council from 1936 to 1939 show that there was not a single case where this was done.[27]

However, it appears that this clause is now effectively obsolete and that the death penalty will never again be carried out in Hong Kong so long as it remains under British rule. The last execution took place in November 1966. In 1967, in spite of the riots, Lord Shepherd, the Minister of State responsible for Hong Kong, made it clear that the Labour government would disapprove of any return to hangings.[28] In April 1973 the Governor refused a reprieve to a murderer for the first time in six-and-a-half years but the Conservative Secretary of State, in an almost unprecedented intervention, overruled the Governor and recommended the Queen to exercise the royal prerogative of mercy. It seems extremely unlikely that any Governor will risk such an open rebuff again, now that both the major political parties in Britain have made their position on executions clear.

1. *Colonial Regulation 105.*

2. This point was confirmed by Lord Shepherd, Minister of State at the Commonwealth Affairs Office, in a debate in the House of Lords, 9 November 1967, column 574.

This does not apply to the use of troops in an international incident. On 8 July 1967 permission had to be obtained from London before the army could be used to rescue a police unit who were pinned down by automatic fire from across the border at Sha Tau Kok. See J. Cooper, *Colony in Conflict. The Hong Kong Disturbances May 1967–January 1968.* (Swindon Book Company, Hong Kong, 1970), pp. 105ff.

3. See Appendix 4. Documents B(i) & (ii), p. 246.

4. See *H. K. Hansard, 1967,* p. 266, and *H. K. Hansard 1971–72,* pp. 19–23, speech by the Colonial Secretary. Britain originally asked for about £12 million a year, but finally agreed to accept the equivalent of £8 million. Note particularly p. 19: 'Our view, as was made very clear by you, Sir, to London....'

For similar expostulations by the Financial Secretary on the question of safeguards for Hong Kong's sterling reserves see *H. K. Hansard 1971–72,* pp. 949–50.

5. See Appendix 4, Document B(i), p. 246; also see Chapter 19, p. 208.

6. Sir John Pope Henessey, Governor 1877–1882. His obituary, quoted by Norton-Kyshe, *History of the Laws and Courts of Hong Kong,* Vol. II, p. 355, states that 'he quarrelled with most of the officials, many of the leading inhabitants, and, hot as the place is owing to climatic influences and geographical position, he made it much hotter than nature ever intended it to be. Mr. W.H. Marsh, the Colonial Secretary was one of the most placable and good-tempered persons living, and a businesslike and efficient officer. Even he was compelled to run away and told the Governor to his face that he would never return so long as he (Sir John) remained on the island.' See also Endacott, *Government and People in Hong Kong,* pp. 95f.

7. A Governor is limited in his dealings with the Public Service not only by the advice of the Public Service Commission and the requirement to clear all the most senior appointments with London, but also by the need to safeguard the morale of the Service by not ignoring the claims of seniority. This may be contrasted with the position of a new American President who brings with him to the White House a completely new staff of personal advisers, who enable him to bypass the established channels of the bureaucracy. The most notable of Mr. Nixon's appointees was Henry Kissinger, who was orginally engaged in 1968 as a person-al assistant to the President in the White House, but who in fact had far more influence on foreign affairs than the State Department. (In Mr. Nixon's second term in 1973 he was actually appointed to the post of Secretary of State.)

There is no financial provision for a Governor to act in this way; at most he might bring in a few officials on secondment from the U.K. Civil Service, provided the Public Service Commission agrees.

8. This point may be illustrated by the comments on the United States federal bureaucracy by two of the most successful presidents of this century.

Franklin Roosevelt (1933–1945): 'The Treasury is so large and far-flung and ingrained in its practices that I find it almost impossible to get the action and results I want.... But the Treasury is not to be compared to the State Department. You should go through the experience of trying to get any changes in thinking, policy and action of the career diplomats and then you'd know what a real problem was. But the Treasury and State Department put together are nothing compared with the Navy.... To change anything in the Navy is like punching a feather bed. You punch it with your right and you punch it with your left until you are finally exhausted and then you find the damn bed just as it was before you started punching.' (M. Eccles, *Beckoning Frontiers* (New York, 1951), p. 336.)

Harry Truman (President 1945–1952): 'I sit here all day trying to persuade people to do the things they ought to have enough sense to do without my persuading them.... That's all the powers of the President amount to.' (Neustadt, *Presidential Power,* Wiley, New York, 1960, p. 9).

No similar forthright comments by past governors of Hong Kong can be traced, though Sir Alexander Grantham does refer to 'government organizations, which tend to suffer from the ponderous slowness of the bureaucratic machine'. (*Via Ports,* p. 102).

While paying tribute to the Hong Kong Public Service in the Legislative Council, Sir Murray MacLehose remarked, 'A new Governor can be a demanding and somewhat unruly colleague'. (*H. K. Hansard, 1972–73,* p. 3).

9. See *Kowloon Disturbances 1966—Report of Commission of Enquiry* (Government Printer, 1967).

10. For this distinction between the 'dignified' and the 'efficient' aspects of government, see W. Bagehot, *The English Constitution* (Collins, Fontana Library, 1963), pp. 61ff.

11. See M. Perham, *Lugard: the Years of Authority* (Collins, 1960), pp. 290–1 & 372–3. Lugard was Governor of Hong Kong 1907–1912.

To give a modern example, it would appear that Sir Murray and Lady MacLehose have shown a much more active interest in the work of the Family Planning Association than previous Governors.

12. An example is the appointment of Sir Richard Sharples, formerly Parliamentary Secretary to the Ministry of Works, as Governor of Bermuda in 1971. (He was subsequently assassinated.)

13. An example is Sir Humphrey Trevelyan, formerly ambassador to Egypt, who was the last colonial governor of Aden.

14. Mr. Dhun Ruttonjee, the senior unofficial member of the Legislative Council, was not appointed in 1968, since the vacancy was for a Chinese member.

15. *Royal Instructions,* Clauses X and XII.

16. 'It would have been perfectly correct, constitutionally, for me to have directed the government members to vote in favour of the Bill, which would then have been passed. Moreover some of the unofficials would have voted with them. But when the public is strongly opposed to a certain course of action, one does not pursue it unless a matter of fundamental importance is involved. None was in this case, and government bowed to the public will.' Sir Alexander Grantham, *Via Ports,* p. 109. This refers to an incident in the Legislative Council, but similar considerations apply in the Executive Council. I have checked through the Minutes of the Council from 1936 to 1939 (the latest peacetime years for which these records are open) and there was apparently no instance where the Governors at that time decided to act against the Council's advice; nor was there any despatch to London in the correspondence notifying such a disagreement.

17. This is extremely rare. The sole instance in the years 1936–1939 is given in Appendix 4, Document C, p. 248.

According to Clause XI, a member is also entitled to have his views recorded in the Minutes if the Governor refuses his request to have an item put on the agenda. It is difficult to imagine any circumstances in which a Governor would rebuff a member of the Council in this way, and no such instance could be found in these years.

18. Cases of such enforced resignations this century are Asquith (1916), Lloyd George (1922), Chamberlain (1940) and possibly Eden (1957). The precise limits of a Prime Minister's power is a much disputed point. A reasonable summary of the argument can be found in R.M. Punnett, *British Government and Politics* (Heinemann, London, 1968). pp. 199–207.

19. *Letters Patent,* Clause XVIII: 'We do hereby require and command all Our officers and ministers, civil and military, to be obedient, aiding and assisting unto the Governor....'

Grantham, op.cit. p. 108: 'The official members must vote as directed by the Governor who presides at both Councils'.

20. In taking such decisions the Governor would be guided by advice from the relevant head of department.

21. *Town Planning Ordinance,* (Cap. 131) sec. 8. *Medical Clinics Ordinance* (cap. 343), sec. 12. *Landlord and Tenant Ordinance,* (cap. 7), secs. 4, 5. *Report of the Public Service Commission for 1969. Hong Kong Additional Instructions 1969* (L. N. 21 of 1969). This process has now been carried further by the *Miscellaneous Amendments (Powers of the Governor in Council) Ordinance 1973.*

22. An example of this occurred in 1970. The Commissioner of Labour explained the origin of certain clauses in the Employment Bill to the Legislative Council: 'The draft bill was considered by the Executive Council and, on its advice, you, Sir, directed that it should be redrafted chiefly for the purpose of bringing the procedure for applying for a warrant for the arrest of an absconding employer as closely as possible into line with The Rules of the Supreme Court. The revised bill was subsequently reconsidered by the Executive Council, and on its advice, you, Sir, ordered that the bill, with some further minor changes, should be introduced into this Council.' (*H.K.Hansard 1969–70,* p. 688.)

23. *Hong Kong Hansard 1969,* p. 515. 'As will be known to some honourable members, Government did give consideration in 1968 to the introduction of this English legislation which had been enacted in 1967 and Unofficial Members of the Executive Council were consulted at that time. The consensus of opinion was that such a change in the law was not required in Hong Kong and indeed it might be in conflict with traditional views on this subject in the community.'

24. *Hong Kong Hansard 1960,* pp. 180–2, and pp. 222–31. A somewhat similar case seems to have occurred in 1973. The unofficials on the Legislative Council unanimously opposed the *Crown Leases Bill,* even though three of them were on the Executive Council when the draft was approved. Either they were outvoted in the Executive Council, (which seems unlikely), or they changed their minds as a result of discussions with their Legislative Council colleagues and their assessment of public reaction. See Appendix 6, Document E, pp. 258–60.

25. This is exactly the same procedure as in Britain: the Chancellor of the Exchequer consults with the Prime Minister, but the full cabinet is informed only the day before the Budget is presented to Parliament.

26. This was the position in 1960. Details of tendering procedure then are given in *H.K. Hansard 1960*, p. 124.

27. See note 16 and item for 26 May 1937 in Appendix 4, Document C, p. 247.

28. See *House of Lords Debates*, 9 November 1967, col. 573. Lord Moynihan said, 'I would congratulate Lord Shepherd, if I may, on his remarks in Hong Kong regarding the death penalty. I am extremely happy to hear that there is no consideration of a return to the death penalty in the present crisis.' The 1973 reprieve is further discussed in Chapter 19, note 1, p. 212.

7 The Public Service

'The claims of officers for promotion will be considered on the basis of official qualifications, experience and merit.'

Colonial Regulation 25

HOWEVER wise and far-seeing the Governor and his Executive Council may be, this is of little use if the conclusions of their discussions are not properly carried into effect. In the eyes of the average citizen the quality of decision-making at the top matters less than what is actually implemented by the servants of the government in his own street, tenement or place of work. He will decide whether the administration is benevolent or not according to the treatment he receives at the hands of its officials, and not by an analysis of the pronouncements made in the Legislative Council. Without a sufficient number of able and honest officials to implement their decisions, the deliberations of government bodies are a pointless waste of effort.

THE COLONIAL SECRETARIAT AND THE DEPARTMENTS

At the end of 1973 the Hong Kong civil service was in a process of reorganization following the report of a firm of management consultants, and it is not yet clear how the new changes will work out in practice. This chapter will therefore describe how the machinery of government functioned up to 1972, the faults that were found in it, and how it is hoped that the new arrangements will improve matters.

The day-to-day business of government is carried out by forty departments which either supply goods and services directly to the public (e.g. Education, Police, Housing), or provide support services to government as a whole (e.g. Treasury, Printing, Audit). The number of these departments has steadily increased over the years as administration has become more complex and specialized, and government has become more involved in social welfare. Thus immigration control was originally a responsibility of the Police, but became a separate department in 1961. The Transport Department similarly emerged in 1968, taking over functions from the Police and Public Works Departments. The Social Welfare Office began as a section in the Secretariat for Chinese Affairs in 1947 with a staff or two officers; it became a department in its own right in 1958 and in 1973 employed over 1,500 people.

The activities of all these departments are supervised and coordinated by the Colonial Secretariat, which was originally the office of the Colonial Secretary, who is deputy to the Governor and the official head of the civil service. All the operations of government are tightly controlled from the centre. Departments carry out the duties laid upon them by various ordinances and the decisions of the Executive Council, but all suggestions for changing policy (e.g. to create new services, to extend existing services, or to change standards), and all requests to recruit more staff, buy new equipment, or spend money in a different way from that authorized in the annual department estimates had to be referred (at least until 1974) to the appropriate branch of the Secretariat. There these proposals were passed for comment to the other branches and departments likely to be concerned, and assessed in the light of the general policies and priorities of government and the resources of men and money available. Secretariat officials would then take a decision themselves, if the matter was minor, or draft a paper for consideration by the Executive Council or the Finance Committee of the Legislative Council.

This highly centralized system was designed to ensure that the Governor and his immediate staff were fully informed about all that was going on, and in a position to carry out directives sent from the Secretary of State in London, who is responsible to Parliament for the good government of the colonies. It worked reasonably well twenty years ago when the Secretariat was small and the task of coordinating departmental activities and dealing with any matter which did not fall within the purview of any particular department could be managed by a few senior officers working closely together. But as departments grew bigger and more departments were set up, the Secretariat also had to expand to deal with the increasing volume of business. Separate branches were set up within the Secretariat to deal with the papers generated by a group of departments; responsibilities became increasingly fragmented; and more and more *ad hoc* committees had to be set up to reconcile the differing views of officials dealing with particular aspects of a single proposal. All this made for delays, and from the point of view of department heads at the bottom of the pyramid the Secretariat too often appeared to be a bottleneck where their requests and proposals were lost in endless committees by procrastinating officials who spent their time demanding unnecessary scraps of information in order to complete their processing of the case. In return, officers serving in the Secretariat complained that 'departmental submissions are not always entirely comprehensible or the argumentation immediately self-evident'.[1]

Such mutual grievances might be expected however good the system was, but departmental heads did have reasonable grounds for complaint.[2] Administrative officers serving in the Secretariat were frequently moved about to fill the gaps created as other officers disappeared on leave.[3] Each new occupant of a post needed time to familiarize himself with the policy area for which he was responsible, before he was likely to be able to make useful comments on the problems raised. Moreover, the heads of most branches in the Secretariat were junior in rank to the heads of departments with whom they had to work. So when disagreements arose, heads of departments would insist that issues be passed upwards for decision by the Colonial Secretary or the Financial Secretary or their deputies, who consequently became overloaded, often with relatively unimportant matters. In practice, the detailed scrutiny of proposals and the consideration of possible alternatives usually took place in Finance Branch, in default of adequate examination in the policy branches, since the Financial Secretary and his assistants had to assess the immediate and long-term budgetary implications of any decision.

Another fault in the system was the low priority given to long range planning.[4] In theory branch heads were expected to assist departments in the formulation of policy and instigate proposals, and this aspect of their duties had been increasingly stressed in recent years. But in practice, for the reasons already given, they did very little, and what planning there was tended to take place on a departmental basis; for example programmes were drawn up for the provision of water resources to meet expected demand, and for the expansion of the fire service, and an outline development plan for the whole colony was prepared. But such exercises did not cover all government operations, and departments tended to develop their plans in isolation, with the result that programmes requiring coordinated action by several departments were seldom attempted. For instance, a comprehensive long-term crime prevention programme would involve not only the Police, but also the Social Welfare, Prisons, Home Affairs, Education and Legal Departments, quite apart from the Finance and Establishment Branches and other organizations outside government.

These and other failings were fully investigated in 1972 by McKinsey and Company, the management consultants engaged by government, and a summary of their report was tabled in the Legislative Council in May 1973. They made a large number of suggestions for improving government effectiveness and obtaining better value for money, which are too detailed to be considered here. Their main proposals for increasing the efficiency of the Secretariat and reducing the overload at the top may be summarized under three headings: that many decisions should be entirely delegated to department heads, particularly minor financial changes and matters involving technical expertise without any policy implications; that programmes covering all policy areas should be drawn up and should thereafter be regularly revised and updated; and that a number of high level posts should be created in the Secretariat directly below the Colonial Secretary and the Financial Secretary whose holders would have the authority to plan and control programmes within particular policy areas and could be held responsible for monitoring progress and ensuring that targets were met.* In theory these changes should cut down the number of staff working in the Secretariat, and enable senior administrators to undertake a more dynamic and positive role, dealing

*Under the pre-McKinsey system each branch head in the Secretariat was responsible for the affairs of a particular *group of departments*; the new secretaries are responsible for *programmes* which may involve a number of different departments, depending on the policy area concerned.

with major questions of policy without becoming involved in detailed operational and executive decisions.

These proposals were accepted by government and by the end of 1973 the Secretariat was reorganized into two resource branches dealing with money and manpower under the Financial Secretary and the Secretary for the Civil Service respectively, and six new policy branches, each under a newly appointed Secretary, covering the following areas:

Economic: responsible for policy and programmes covering the commercial and industrial field, monetary and foreign exchange, banking, securities and stock exchanges, primary products, public utilities such as electricity, gas and telephones, mass transit (overall control of finance and establishment of the Authority) shipping, transport franchises and external aspects of civil aviation.

Environment: responsible for policy and programmes covering land matters, colony planning, the design, timing and construction of new towns, pollution, urban services, roads, road transport, traffic, railway, car parking, mass transit (construction, engineering aspects and land) and operational and works aspects of the airport and harbour.

Home Affairs:* responsible for policy and programmes covering information services, public relations, broadcasting, television, information on public attitudes, cultural activities, tourism, City District Officers, and residual New Territories affairs.

Housing:* responsible for policy and programmes covering housing, resettlement, flatted factories, rent control, and coordination of departmental services—e.g. education, health, law and order—in new towns.

Security: responsible for policy and programmes covering external security (liaison with British Army) emergencies, internal law and order, immigration, prisons, narcotics, and fire services.

Social Services: responsible for policy and programmes covering education, medical and health services, social welfare, charities, labour and recreation.

These six new secretaryships were all filled between May and November 1973. Five of those appointed are administrative officers, but one, Mr. J.J. Robson, the new Secretary for the Environment, was formerly Director of the Public Works Department. This is in line with the recommendation of the report that in future top posts should be open to all officers and not be reserved for those in the administrative grade. The report also argued that more emphasis should be placed on merit than length of service and seniority when promotions were made; as can be seen from the staff list, this principle has been followed in making these appointments.

These tidy arrangements were upset in March 1974 as a result of protests from the leaders of the Heung Yee Kuk, who claimed that the new system

*This new Home Affairs portfolio should not be confused with the former Secretariat for Home Affairs, which continues to exist under a new Director, but is now only one of the departments coordinated by the new Secretary for Home Affairs. Similarly the Secretary for Housing must not be confused with the Director of the Housing Department, which was created in April 1973 by the amalgamation of the former Resettlement Department and the former Housing Authority staff.

ignored the special needs and status of the New Territories. They objected to the division of responsibility for their affairs between the Secretaries for the Environment, Home Affairs and Housing, and represented that their District Commissioner should be elevated to a position of equality with the secretaries. The Governor in Council decided that it would be politic to heed their views; and so the post of New Territories Commissioner was upgraded to an equal rank with the secretaries. His responsibilities for the co-ordination of all departmental activities in his area are much the same as they were before the McKinsey consultants arrived, though he now has increased authority. The position most affected under the revised arrangements would seem to be the Housing Secretary who has been deprived of his recently acquired responsibilities for the co-ordination of the provision of departmental services in the new towns, all of which are in the New Territories.

The consultants envisaged that one result of their proposals would be a reduction of the role of Finance Branch. For some years it has taken the main responsibility for assessing projects and determining priorities, largely by default of any effective mechanism for doing this elsewhere in government; also some matters concerning personnel had been determined in the Finance Branch rather than by the Establishment Branch. According to the McKinsey blueprint much of this scrutiny could be taken over by the new secretaries, and the Finance Branch should be confined to raising the resources needed, setting expenditure limits and ensuring that value is obtained for the money spent.[5] The difficulty here is that any increased delegation of financial powers carries with it the danger that department heads might exercise less care in keeping strictly within the limits set down in the Estimates, and commit government to future expenditure for which the money may not be available. It is a tiresome discipline to have to make out a case to Finance Branch for every additional man or new piece of equipment required, but it is no doubt a very salutary one. Some increased latitude has been allowed: in the Estimates for 1974–5 sub-heads within the permitted expenditure of each department have as far as possible been assimilated to a common pattern and their number reduced, allowing heads of departments a greater degree of flexibility than before.[6] But all requests for supplementary provisions, to engage additional staff or to transfer funds from one sub-head to another (the technical term for which is 'virement') still require the agreement of Finance Branch. So from the point of view of department heads, the net result of McKinsey so far would seem to be that, though some operational decisions have been delegated to them, they will be subject to more high-powered direction from the new policy secretaries, without being compensated by any very significant loosening of the Financial Secretary's reins.

If the new system works out successfully one consequence might be some lessening of the work load of the Executive Council and the Finance Committee of the Legislative Council. The consultants were told that they must not make any proposals that would require any changes in the roles and responsibilities of the Executive and Legislative Councils.

But if programmes are to be agreed on for a long period ahead there may be less opportunity for changes than if each project is considered individually. At most, the Finance Committee could suggest that a programme should be stretched out over a longer period if there was need to save money in a particular year. The Governor and the Colonial Secretary hold meetings on a regular basis with the new secretaries and with department heads to discuss broad problems and policy proposals and agree on priorities, but this in no way diminishes the need for the Executive Council to take the final decisions.

Similar proposals to those of the McKinsey consultants had been put forward in earlier years. In 1965 the senior unofficial member of the Legislative Council, Mr. Dhun Ruttonjee, suggested the decentralization of the administration into seven or eight mini-secretariats, each under a single official, with the Colonial Secretary as first among equals, like the Prime Minister in his cabinet. In 1971 another unofficial member, Mr. G.M.B. Salmon, advocated the creation of 'Overlords' much on the lines of the present scheme. Mr. Ruttonjee's proposal was rejected by the then Colonial Secretary on the ground that a new super-secretariat would then be needed to co-ordinate the work of the eight sub-secretariats. Mr. Salmon's proposal of 1971 was turned down by the Financial Secretary, Mr. Haddon-Cave, on the ground that such devolution would relax financial control and allow the growth of expenditure to get out of hand.[7] It will be interesting to see if either of these prophecies comes true. A similar experiment in appointing non-departmental ministers as 'over-lords' to coordinate groups of departments was tried out in Britain by the Conservative government of 1951, but was abandoned within two years.[8]

Apart from the two resource branches and the seven policy branches the Colonial Secretariat also contains a number of minor units. These include the Councils Branch, which looks after the arrangements for meetings of the Executive and Legislative Councils, a small Management Unit responsible to the Deputy Colonial Secretary, and the office of the Political Adviser, a Foreign Office official seconded to the Hong Kong government from London.

ADMINISTRATORS AND SPECIALISTS

The civil service is divided into the general classes, whose members may be posted to serve in any department, and the occupational classes whose members will normally spend all their careers exercising their special skills in one department only. The latter include both the uniformed and disciplined services such as the police, prisons, preventive and fire services, and also such occupations as teachers, nurses, architects and lawyers. The general classes comprise the administrative and executive officers, personal secretaries, interpreter/translators and supply officers.[9]

In practice most executive officers remain for long periods in the same department, but this is not true of administrative officers, who are generally considered to be the elite of the public service. Their first posting is often in a district office in the New Territories, or as a City District Officer. They then go on to learn and practise administrative skills in the

Secretariat or perhaps in one of the other departments where staff work in the office of the department head needs strengthening.[10] Normally they can expect to move to a different department or back to the Secretariat at two to three year intervals, punctuated by leave or training courses.

The wider opportunities open to an administrative officer mean that he must be ready to turn his hand to anything. For example, Mr. J. Cater was successively Director of Agriculture and Fisheries (1963), Defence Secretary (1967), Head of the Trade Development Council (1968), Director of Commerce and Industry (1970) and Secretary for Information (1972). He became Commissioner in charge of the Independent Commission Against Corruption in 1973. Similarly Mr. Li Fook-kow, the Secretary for Social Services in 1973, had previously served as Director of Social Welfare, Acting Secretary for Home Affairs, Deputy Director of Commerce and Industry and Deputy Financial Secretary, as well as filling various other posts in the Resettlement Department, the Labour Department and the Colonial Secretariat.

Until 1973 civil servants in the professional and technical classes could not normally expect to rise higher than the headship of their own specialist department, and even this eminence was not open to them in all cases. Quite apart from monopolizing the highest posts in the Secretariat, the New Territories Administration and Home Affairs, administrative officers have also customarily headed the Census and Statistics, Commerce and Industry, Labour, Resettlement, Social Welfare, Transport, and Urban Services Departments; and occasionally other departments have also had an administrative officer put in charge. There is no rule reserving these posts solely for administrative officers: from 1953 to 1962 the Director of Commerce and Industry was a former executive officer, Mr. H.A. Angus, who had originally entered the department in 1924 as a clerk and then worked his way up to the top. It might be thought that a technical department would function more efficiently under a professional head who had first-hand experience of the work and in whom the staff had confidence, rather than under a generalist administrator. However, government may be in real difficulty if a department is small or recently formed and there are doubts about the competence of the senior professional officer to manage the whole of its business, particularly if it deals with a sensitive political area, such as, for example the Social Welfare Department. In such cases the appointment of an administrator as head may on occasion be the safer course, particularly if, as is usually but not always the case, he has served in the department at some time previously.

When a new department is set up an administrative officer is normally put in charge. But once it is well established and specialist officers have acquired the necessary standing and experience they can normally expect to take over the senior position. Thus the police and fire brigade were directed by an administrative officer until 1935, the Education Department until 1938, and the Post Office until 1950. In similar fashion the first professional head of the Labour Department, Mr. I.R. Price, was appointed in 1973, and in the same year the Housing Authority and the

Resettlement Department were merged under Mr. Liao Poon-huai, a former architect, as Director of Housing. In 1974 Mr. Lee Chun-yon became Director of Social Welfare having joined the department twenty-two years before as a probation officer.

However, this does not mean that administrative officers will never again be appointed to head these departments. In August 1974 the post of Director of Education was given to an administrative officer, Mr. K.W.J. Topley, in spite of the fact that this position had been held by professional educationalists for the previous thirty five years. The Education Department has been a frequent target for public criticism in recent years, so presumably the Governor and the Public Service Commission considered that an administrator from outside would be better able to supervise the new programme of educational expansion than any of the senior professional officers in the department.

The frequent postings of Hong Kong administrative officers have no real parallel in Britain. Civil servants of the administrative grade there also form a single class and are liable to serve in any ministry; but in practice the vast majority spend all their time in one ministry and so become specialists in its particular problems as they work alongside their professional colleagues. It is only at the very top of the service, at the permanent secretary and deputy permanent secretary level, that movement normally occurs. The moves of Hong Kong administrators most closely resemble the shifts of ministers between different departments of state. The varied career of Mr. Cater given above suggests that in some cases this is a very apt parallel. However, the crucial difference is that British ministers are only expected to give political direction to their departments and do not take over the management themselves; whereas in Hong Kong the top administrators are expected to fulfil both roles.

RECRUITMENT AND THE PUBLIC SERVICE COMMISSION

According to article XIV of the *Letters Patent* the Governor has the right to determine all appointments and promotions in the colony's Public Service. As with all the Governor's powers this is subject to the overriding authority of the Crown, and the *Establishment Regulations* of the Hong Kong government lay down that all appointments to posts with a salary of more than HK$11,950* a month require the approval of the Secretary of State, together with a few other senior posts in the Administrative class, the Police, the Audit and Legal Departments and the Judiciary. In practice London is most unlikely to go against the Governor's recommendation, but it does have to consider whether a 'transfer from another territory would be preferable.

Applications for posts carrying a maximum salary of less than HK$ 3,380* a month are entirely decided by department heads. Above this level all new appointments or promotions must be referred for consideration by the Public Service Commission. This body was set up by ordinance in 1950 to advise the Governor on appointments to all senior posts, with

*These figures are periodically adjusted to take account of rises in salary scales.

the exception of the *ex officio* members of the Executive and Legislative Councils (the Colonial Secretary, the Financial Secretary, the Attorney-General and the Secretary for Home Affairs), the Deputy Colonial Secretary, judges and magistrates, military, naval, air force and police officers, and the Director of Audit. At the end of 1972, 11,149 posts fell within the scope of the Commission. Until 1967 all members of the Commission were local business and professional people giving voluntary service to the government on a part-time basis. Since 1967 there has been a full-time salaried chairman, assisted by two (or sometimes three) part-time local members. The Commission's staff is small and does not organize recruitment and interviews, but confines itself to a broad regulatory role over what is done by the departments and the office of the Secretary for the Civil Service. However, members of the Commission occasionally sit as observers on promotion and selection boards. All advertisements and conditions of service are referred to the Commission, as well as all requests to recruit staff overseas. The Commission is also consulted when an officer is not considered suitable for confirmation of appointment after a period of probation, and when an officer is not recommended to pass an efficiency bar. Files from departmental boards are circulated among the members of the Commission and are then forwarded to the Governor with their recommendations. In law the Commission only advises the Governor, but by convention he is most unlikely to go against their recommendation. The Commission's annual reports for the last few years have noted that there was no case where its advice was rejected.

In 1971 *Colonial Regulations* were amended to allow the Commission to advise the Governor on all matters relating to the disciplining and dismissal of government officers. Previously the Governor had been required to consult with the Executive Council on all cases where the officer concerned was above a certain rank, but he now decides such cases himself on the basis of the advice of the Commission. After the last war Public Service Commissions were set up in all the larger British colonies on instructions from London. The main objectives were to encourage the recruitment of local candidates, and, as far as possible, to insulate the civil service from political interference and patronage as colonies moved towards independence. The latter object is not relevant to Hong Kong, but the fact that promotion proposals have to be examined by an external body gives civil servants some protection and confidence that their abilities will receive impartial consideration and be less likely to be subject to the whims or prejudices of their departmental head.

The policy of giving preference in recruitment to local candidates—in practice this means Chinese candidates—has been frequently reiterated by government and in the Commission's reports. Since 1961 it has been government policy that where external recruitment is necessary expatriates shall normally only be engaged on contract terms and shall not be appointed to the permanent establishment unless there appears to be no possibility of Chinese with the appropriate qualifications being available in the next few years. The only general exceptions to this policy are that a proportion of the vacancies for Administrative and Police Officers will regularly be filled by expatriates on permanent terms.[11] Such an exception would be unacceptable if the colony were destined for early independence; but since it now appears that Britain is likely to retain control for many years ahead, there is an obvious need to retain a number of experienced British officials who can fill some of the senior posts in the administration and the police for as long as Britain remains ultimately responsible for the order and good government of the colony. Peking tolerates Hong Kong's existence only so long as it remains firmly under British control, and would be unlikely to accept a situation in which Britain exercised only nominal sovereignty while all policy-making posts were in fact held by Chinese.

This political need to recruit expatriates may be irksome to the local Chinese, but after the original appointments have been made promotions are based solely on merit without regard to race, and must be referred to the Public Service Commission. Since Hong Kong is a cosmopolitan city which lives by international trade it is an advantage that a number of its senior officials who deal with foreign businessmen have had experience outside the rather narrow confines of the colony.

THE PROGRESS OF LOCALIZATION

In January 1973 there were about 90,000 employees in the public service, of whom only 1,905—just over 2 per cent—were overseas officers. Over the past twenty years the actual number of expatriates has almost doubled, but since the whole of the service has expanded four times, the proportion of expatriates in it has been halved, as can be seen below.

	Local	Overseas	% Local	% Overseas
April 1952	22,900	1,063	95.56	4.44
Jan. 1962	48,277	1,625	96.74	3.26
Jan. 1968	71,057	1,879	97.42	2.58
Jan. 1973	88,121	1,905	97.88	2.12

Source: Staff Lists and the Annual Reports on the Public Service.

However, these global statistics are misleading, since approximately 40 per cent of the service consist of lower levels of staff (labourers, artisans etc.) and expatriates are proportionately heavily concentrated at the top, as can be seen from the table opposite.

Progress in localization over the past few years has been steady, but slower in some classes than others. The slowest growth in the proportion of Chinese is in the superscale posts (heads of departments and those of equivalent status). This is the result of the relatively low intake of Chinese in the 1950s, especially into the administrative grade from which many of the top posts are filled. Between 1947 and 1960 only seven Chinese were appointed as administrative officers, compared with 41 expatriates.

Except in the case of certain highly specialized skills the continued need to recruit overseas for the professional classes is not caused by lack of educational facilities in Hong Kong. It is possible to qualify for most professional posts at the two universities or at other institutions in the

PROPORTIONS OF LOCAL AND EXPATRIATE OFFICERS
IN UPPER LEVELS OF GOVERNMENT SERVICE,
1967, 1970 and 1973

	Jan. 1967			Jan. 1970			Jan. 1973		
	Local	Expat.	% Local	Local	Expat.	% Local	Local	Expat.	% Local
Superscale	47	206	18.6	62	264	19	92	270	25.4
Administrative Grade	23	74	23.7	40	71	36	52	74	41.3
Medical Officers	396	46	89.6	416	49	89.5	597	69	89.6
Dentists	41	1	97.6	56	–	100	51	–	100
Police Inspectors	484	405	54.4	554	434	56.1	611	412	59.7
Engineers	63	63	50	88	55	61.5	140	90	60.9
Executive Grade	154	109	58.6	262	95	73.4	505	93	84.4

Source: The Annual Reports on the Public Service.

colony; and even where the necessary training is not available locally, as for example in dentistry, it can be seen from the table that some local Chinese are prepared to qualify overseas and then return to practise their skills. Since 1971 there has been no differential in favour of expatriates in salaries, and there had been equal pay in the senior grades for many years before this. Local officers earning above HK$4,970 a month are housed in government quarters or receive a housing allowance in lieu at the same rate as expatriates; and both are eligible for overseas education allowances for their children. The only additional perquisites enjoyed by expatriates are that they have somewhat longer vacation leave with passages paid to their homes overseas for themselves and their families, and that they all qualify for housing or housing allowances, whatever their salary. In most of the professions where overseas officers are still being recruited, qualified Chinese such as doctors, engineers or architects find that they can earn more when employed by local firms or in private practice than in government service.[12] As long as government can fill its needs by recruiting overseas when sufficient local applicants are not available it is not prepared to bid up its salary offers to the inflated levels that would be needed if it wished to have an entirely Chinese civil service. Another reason why qualified Chinese prefer private employment is that many of them are considering eventual emigration, and if they find a post with an international company they may hope to transfer to one of its branches overseas in due course.[13]

There should not be the same difficulty in recruitment to the administrative grade. The academic qualification required is unspecialized—a first or second class honours degree in any subject from a Commonwealth or American university[14]—and the salary level is comparable to that obtainable in the private sector. Up to 200 applications are received each year when vacancies are advertised, and in 1974 there were over 500 applications. Yet until recent years very few Chinese graduates from outside the civil service have been chosen. The first appointment was Mr. Paul Tsui Ka-cheung in 1948, and the next was not appointed until ten years later. Up to 1968 a total of only fourteen had been accepted. Since then the position has improved: 1969–six; 1970–two; 1971–two; 1972–none; 1973–ten. A few others were offered appointments but declined to take them up.

This low intake has not been due to any lack of vacant posts. The authorized establishment of the administrative grade has grown rapidly in recent years:

1960	80	1972	145
1965	99	1973	168
1971	132	1974	209

Source: Staff Lists and the Annual Reports on the Public Service.

These new positions have been filled from three main sources in addition to local graduate recruitment: recent British graduates, colonial service officers who retired from other colonies on independence, and promotions from the executive class and elsewhere in the civil service. This last group has provided more Chinese administrative officers than external recruitment: up to the end of 1973, 37 had come up in this way compared to 34 by direct entry.[15] In 1971, 4 Chinese were promoted to the administrative grade from within the service, 1 in 1972 and 9 in 1973.

Why have only 34 Chinese candidates from outside government service been appointed to the administrative grade in the past twenty-five years? There are three possible explanations: either selection boards discriminate against Chinese candidates; or the most able Chinese graduates do not apply, possibly because they are intent upon emigration or private employment, or because they are unwilling to serve under an alien regime; or the Hong Kong educational system, operating in a restricted urban environment, fails to develop the required qualities.

The first explanation, that alleging racial prejudice, is commonly believed in Hong Kong, but there is no evidence for it apart from the figures already quoted. Although a proportion of the administrative grade must remain British as long as Hong Kong remains a colony, government would certainly prefer to have more Chinese officers in contact with the public and in policy-making positions, in order to have the advantage of their local knowledge and to help to win public acceptance for government decisions. The second explanation is similarly speculative. But the number of candidates who apply suggest that unwillingness to serve under the British government is not a great deterrent. The third explanation is the one favoured by the administration. According to government spokesmen, applicants have the necessary academic qualifications, but seem rather limited in their outlook, show little knowledge or interest in public affairs and do not display the qualities of character and intelligence needed in an administrative officer (see Appendix 5, Document B, p. 250).

This emphasis on 'character' as assessed by interviews is a peculiarly British phenomenon. In France, entrance to the administrative class is entirely determined by written and oral examinations in academic subjects only;[16] and this was also true of appointments to the colonial administration in Hong Kong up to 1933 when the competitive examinations for 'Eastern cadetships' were abolished in favour of lengthy interviews and enquiries into a candidate's background and leadership potential.[17] Such a method is also quite foreign to Chinese bureaucratic traditions; the old imperial examinations for the Ching civil service were completely anonymous in order to be scrupulously fair to all candidates.

However, if this system of selection works to the disadvantage of newly graduated Chinese, it seems to have proved less of a barrier to those graduates who were prepared to enter the civil service in a lower grade and then applied again when they had acquired maturity and self-confidence after a few years working experience. A few Chinese executive officers who had no degrees have also been promoted to the administrative grade because of the personal qualities which they had shown in the performance of their duties.

These factors suggest that Hong Kong might do well to follow the lead of the British civil service where the administrative and executive grades were merged in 1971 to form a continuous structure with promising entrants being marked out for faster promotion.[18] This would make it possible to give greater weight to an officer's performance on the job and thus reduce the need to rely so much on the assessment made at the time of recruitment. Though the first three years after entry are supposed to be on probation it appears that very few administrative officers now fail to pass this barrier.[19] A change on these lines was proposed by the 1971 Salaries Commission, who noted the difficulty of attracting enough suitable local recruits to the administrative grade. They recommended the establishment of a special three-year training grade, mainly for potential administrative officers, but also for trade and labour officers; executive officers who showed administrative ability could also be transferred to this group after two years. According to the Commission, this would allow government to make conditions easier for initial entry, but institute a tougher weeding out process during the first three years.[20] However, government has decided against this.

BOARDS AND COMMITTEES

As government operations become larger and more complex an increasing number of committees are set up, some to harmonize the views of different departments within the administration, and others which include the representatives of outside interests with whom government finds it necessary to cooperate in order to make its own work easier and to provide a more efficient service for the public. The *Civil and Miscellaneous Lists* issued by the Colonial Secretariat give details of 134 committees in existence at the beginning of 1973, of which 75 have been set up under various ordinances. But there are far more than 134, since a number of important ones such as the Rural Committees and the Heung Yee Kuk in the New Territories are omitted, as well as the numerous *ad hoc* committees set up to deal with a particular problem and dissolved when the task has been completed.

Many of these committees are of minor importance and have little to do with influencing government policy. The *1973 List* includes 18 boards concerned with the investment and distribution of Trust Funds, 9 management committees and councils of hospitals, temples and universities, 13 administrative tribunals and boards for the assessment of compensation, 4 licensing and censorship boards, and other similar bodies. Besides these committees, and the 17 standing committees consisting entirely of civil servants, there are (at a conservative estimate) between 60 and 70 other committees which are partly composed of members of the public and which are consulted before government policy is finally decided.

Looking at these committees and their terms of reference it is possible to suggest the reasons why they were originally set up. The following categories are not exclusive since any one committee may serve a number of different purposes.

1. To tap expert advice in an area where government must exercise control; e.g. the Pharmacy and Poisons Board, the Radiation Board, the Dangerous Goods Standing Committee, the Exchange Fund Advisory Committee.

2. To stimulate action by businesses and other outside interests in directions which government considers desirable; e.g. the Hong Kong Productivity Council, the Metrication Committee.

3. To take politically embarrassing decisions for which government prefers to avoid responsibility; e.g. the Standing Committee on Superscale Salaries,[21] the Advisory Committee on Corruption, the Public Service Commission. The Social Welfare Advisory Committee recommends how the global sum approved by the Finance Committee for subventions should be divided up among the various voluntary agencies.[22]

A classic example of government's use of this expedient occurred in 1966. The Star Ferry Company had applied to government for permission to raise its fares. The application was justified according to the terms of its franchise, but there was strong public agitation against any increase. Government set up a committee to consider the application on which the official members were in a minority of 6–9. The committee advised government to approve the increases by 14–1 (Mrs. Elsie Elliott dissenting), but despite this three nights of rioting followed.

4. To keep its clients happy, where a government department provides a service for businessmen or the general public and the committee provides a forum where the 'consumers' can raise their complaints and suggest improvements; e.g. the Airport Facilitation Committee, the Airport Operations Committee and the Aviation Advisory Board, where the Director of Civil Aviation and his staff meet with representatives of the airlines and travel services. The Port Committee, the Port Executive Committee, the Trade and Industry Advisory Board etc. have similar functions. Most of these committees are composed of experts in the particular field. Until 1974 the Transport Advisory Committee was an exception since the non-official members had little specialized knowledge of the subject when first appointed, though they presumably learnt a great deal over the years.[23] This Committee was reorganized in March 1974 to bring in more expert advisers, such as a director of one of the ferry companies and the manager of the cross-harbour tunnel.

5. To ensure the cooperation of voluntary agencies which provide services on government's behalf; e.g. the Social Welfare Advisory Committee, the Medical Advisory Board, the Board of Education. The departments which administer the social services are heavily dependent on the schools, hospitals and welfare services run by missionary societies and charitable institutions such as the Tung Wah Hospital Group. Since their help is essential, government must allow them a major voice in the determination of policy.

6. Finally, a cynic might suggest that some committees are set up solely to satisfy the public that government is concerned about a particular problem and is doing something about it. The appointment of a committee gives an excuse for postponing any action, and there is always the possibility that by the time the committee reports public interest will have shifted elsewhere and nothing need be done.[24] It would be invidious to suggest that any recent committees had been set up for this purpose, but an example might be the committee set up in 1968 after the riots to consider

the wider use of Chinese in government business which led to no action whatsoever until the issue was resurrected by student agitation in 1971.[25]

Committees such as those in categories 4 and 5 have most impact upon policy-making, since the non-official members are likely to be experts with a substantial business or professional interest in ensuring that the government does what is right—or at least what is most convenient for themselves. If dissatisfied, they are in a position to embarrass the administration by public criticism. So a head of department will normally take great care to keep his committee happy and secure their agreement to all changes which he may put forward. Such support can be of great importance in getting the proposal accepted by the Secretariat and the Executive Council.

Government takes pride in the fine crop of committees it has raised. A recent White Paper boasted, 'Public participation in the management of public affairs is already achieved, and to a very considerable extent, by a highly developed network of advisory bodies which are an important and very characteristic feature of the Hong Kong scene.'[26] This claim is exaggerated. Most committees consist of experts and interested parties, and the few laymen involved are almost invariably either members of the Legislative and Urban Councils or business and professional men[27] from the upper strata of society who have the spare time to take on these commitments. Moreover, these committees have important limitations which impair their role as a surrogate for democracy. They meet rarely, usually at intervals of several months. They do not have the time to go into any proposal in depth and so are dependent on the selected information supplied to the committee by the department.[28] Most important committees are chaired by the departmental head who determines the agenda;[29] it is possible for a persistent unofficial member to raise a matter, but the committee may never have a chance to air its views on projects which have been considered and rejected by the department. Other proposals which are known to be unacceptable to the committee may never be referred to it at all. A committee's decision is not necessarily final, and may be reversed later at a higher level in government.[30] Few committees issue annual reports and all proceedings are secret and unpublicized. An ordinary member of the public with a complaint or suggestion would require some tenacity to discover which was the relevant committee and find a member of it willing to pursue his problem. A number of departments still have no advisory committees attached to them, such as the Fire Service, the Immigration Department, the Post Office,[31] the Prisons Department and the Railways.

The proliferation of committees has recently been criticized from the point of view of government efficiency. In 1972 McKinsey & Company, commissioned to conduct a survey of the administration, recognized the 'valuable and essential' function that these bodies perform, but pointed out that senior staff typically spend 25–50 per cent of their time attending *ad hoc* and standing committees, whose 'effectiveness is uneven and frequently the benefits hardly seem to merit the increasing demands they make on the time of top level staff and busy private citizens'. They recommended that, after other reforms to the government machine had been completed, there should be a comprehensive review of their roles and responsibilities which could lead to a reduction in their number and improvements in their effectiveness.[32] Such a rationalization may appear eminently desirable, but it leaves political considerations out of account. Most redundant committees were originally set up to fulfil a government need or to pacify particular groups, who would now object strongly to their demise. Similar considerations can be expected to operate in future and it may be confidently predicted that new committees and sub-committees will continue to burgeon and flourish.

1. Comment by the Financial Secretary, Mr. Haddon-Cave, *H. K. Hansard 1971–72*, p. 88.

2. This account of difficulties in the Secretariat is largely taken from the summary of the recommendations of McKinsey and Company tabled in the Legislative Council 23 May 1973: *The Machinery of Government: A new Framework for Expanding Services*, esp. paras. 36, 37, 72 and 73.

3. Ibid. para. 67: 'In the last seven years the average tenure in the four posts most concerned with planning future education expansion—three in the Secretariat and one in the Department—was only nine months.'

4. Ibid. para. 45: 'At present there is little in the way of either carrot or stick to induce staff to think ahead in this way. Without pressure, long-term planning tends to get a low priority from a department head who will have retired, or from Secretariat staff who may have been posted, long before the deficiencies of the plan, or the sheer lack of one, come home to roost.'

5. Ibid. paras. 73 and 79.

6. See the memorandum at the beginning of the *Estimates for 1974–75*, p. 30. para. 13, and the Financial Secretary's comment, *H. K. Hansard 1973–74*, p. 566.

7. See *H. K. Hansard 1965*, pp. 100f and pp. 233f, and *H. K. Hansard 1971–72*, pp. 51f and pp. 87f.

8. See H. Morrison (Lord Morrison of Lambeth) *Government and Parliament*, 3rd edition, (O.U.P., London, 1964), pp. 58–67, for a critical account of this experiment. The British 'overlords' were politicians (not officials as in Hong Kong) and were all in the House of Lords. The main criticisms of the system were the unclear division of responsibility between ministers in the Commons and the Lords, and the inability of the Commons to question the overlords and call them to account.

There was a previous experiment with overlords in Neville Chamberlain's first wartime government in 1939. Churchill at the time thought little of the idea:

'I naturally preferred a definite task to that exalted brooding over the work done by others which may well be the lot of a Minister however influential, who has no department. It is easier to give directions than advice, and more agreeable to have the right to act, even in a limited sphere, than the privilege to talk at large....'

'A group of detached statesmen, however high their nominal authority, are at a serious disadvantage in dealing with Ministers at the head of the great Departments vitally concerned.... They tend to become more and more theoretical supervisors and commentators, reading an immense amount of material every day, but doubtful how to use their knowledge without doing more harm than good. Often they can do little more than arbitrate or find a compromise in interdepartmental disputes.' (W.S. Churchill, *The Second World War, Vol. 1. The Gathering Storm* (Cassell), 1948, pp. 320 and 327.)

9. Details in this and the following sections are taken from the government *Staff List*, the *Report on the Public Service* and the *Report of the Chairman of the Public Service Commission*, all issued annually.

10. Treasury Accountants are also seconded to most departments to supervise accounting and accounting systems.

11. *A Report on the Public Service 1971 & 1972*, p. 26. Eight new British graduates were recruited as administrative officers in 1972 and six in 1973. For the three years 1974–77 the target is that five local officers should be recruited for every three overseas officers and that about one-third of the entrants should have had some previous administrative experience, *H. K. Hansard 1973–74*, p. 866.

12. *A Report on the Public Service 1971 & 1972*, p. 26, and the *Report on the Committee Appointed to Review the Doctor Problem in the Hong Kong Government Service*, May 1969, p. 18: 'Competitive salary scales which could match the remuneration obtainable in a well-established private practice are not a realistic objective.'

13. A survey of 253 Chinese civil servants found that just under 60 per cent would like to emigrate if possible, A.K. Wong, *The Study of Higher Non-Expatriate Civil Servants in Hong Kong* (Chinese University of Hong Kong, Social Research Centre, June 1972), p. 43.

14. American university degrees were first accepted in 1971, *H. K. Hansard 1970–71*, p. 501. Degrees from non-Commonwealth universities are accepted if they are of equivalent standard, *H. K. Hansard 1973–74* p. 866.

15. This has also been a route by which expatriates have entered the administrative grade. Between 1947 and 1973, 115 new expatriate administrative officers were appointed, of which 58 were by direct entry from Britain, 38 came from other colonies and 19 were promoted from within the civil service.

16. See F. Ridly & J. Blondel, *Public Administration in France* (Routledge and Kegan Paul, London, 1969) p. 35. Some attention is now paid to character in the examinations for entry to the *École Nationale d'Administration*, but this is a recent development (p. 39).

17. 'Eastern cadets' for service in Ceylon, Hong Kong and Malaya were chosen on the results of the same competitive examination used to select members of the Home and Indian Civil Services. (Sir Alexander Grantham began his colonial career as an Eastern cadet in 1922.) As a result of the Warren Fisher Committee's report in 1930 administrators for these colonies were thereafter selected on the same basis of interview as had been used in the African and Carribean colonies. See Sir Ralph Furse, *Aucuparius, Recollections of a Recruiting Officer* (O.U.P., London, 1962), esp. pp. 206 and 239.

18. This followed the recommendations of the Fulton Committee, *Report of the Committee on the Civil Service 1966–68*, Cmnd 3638 H.M.S.O. 1968, Vol. I, paras. 16, & 192–243.

At that time about 40 per cent of the administrative class in Britain had previously served in other grades (ibid. Vol. 3(1) p. 40). For further details and a summary of the changes see R.G.S. Brown, *The Administrative Process in Britain* (Methuen, London, 1971), pp. 46 and 309. In the case of Hong Kong, 59 out of 191 entrants to the administrative grade between 1947 and 1973—30 per cent—were promoted from within the service: 37 Chinese, 19 expatriates, and 3 local Asians.

19. It appears from the *Staff Lists* that since the war four administrative officers left the service before they were confirmed, but it is not shown whether this was because they failed their probation, or for other reasons. Two were Europeans and two Chinese. The last case was in 1967.

20. *Hong Kong Salaries Commission Report 1971* (The Mallaby Report), p. 17, para. 96.

21. This committee is entirely composed of unofficial members.

22. See *H. K. Hansard 1973–74*, p. 159. The Director of Social Welfare makes the final allocations, but he is unlikely to reject the Committee's views.

23. The unofficial members of this committee in 1973 were an architect, a barrister, a chartered accountant, a solicitor, an economic journalist and a teacher. Of these only the teacher (Mrs. Elliott) remained on the reconstituted committee. This mixed membership may have been one reason for the lack of harmony on the committee. See Appendix 5, Document D, pp. 251–3.

24. cf. Mr. Dhun Ruttonjee (then senior unofficial member of the Legislative Council): 'This government is by no means unique in stepping from expediency to palliative. When in doubt appoint a Commission or a Working Party would seem to be the motto. This I trust is the last time that an already involved subject is made even more so by the inch by inch attitude of Government. I get the impression that, just occasionally, we in Hong Kong spend too much of our time putting off decisions because they are uncomfortable.' (*H. K. Hansard 1965*, p. 399.)

25. *H. K. Hansard 1968*, p. 50.

26. *The Urban Council* (1971, Government Printer), para. 3.

27. The Consumer Council set up in April 1974 to take action against rising prices and complaints of profiteering was a notable departure from this pattern: it included several housewives from the lower-income groups and a factory worker. (*South China Morning Post*, 8 April 1974).

28. *The Machinery of Government—a New Framework for Expanding Services*, McKinsey & Company, Inc. (Government Printer, May 1973) para. 18 (published in all Hong Kong newspapers, 24 May 1973). 'The volume of decisions has now reached such proportions that the various committees can afford to examine in depth only the really major items. Thus, in practice, substantial decision-making powers are delegated to the staff serving the commit-

tees; what is more these staff have extensive negative decision powers, since it is they who decide which items are to be put forward for debate and decision by the committees.'

29. In 1973 the Board of Education was reconstituted with an unofficial member of the Legislative Council, Mr. Woo Pak-chuen, as chairman, replacing the Director of Education who held the post previously.

30. For examples of all these points see Appendix 5, Document D, pp. 251–3.

31. Oddly, the telephone service, which is a private monopoly, does have an advisory committee attached to it, which issues an annual report. This committee was set up in 1964 after a proposal by the company to raise its charges had been criticized in the Legislative Council.

32. McKinsey & Company, op.cit. paras. 37, 90 and 91.

8 The Legislative Council: Composition and the Passing of Ordinances

MEMBERSHIP

THE composition of the Legislative Council is laid down in Clause XIII of the *Royal Instructions*. Since the end of 1972 it has consisted of five *ex officio* members (the Governor, the Colonial Secretary, the Attorney General, the Secretary for Home Affairs and the Financial Secretary), ten nominated officials and fifteen nominated unofficial members. With the exception of the Commander British Forces the *ex officio* members are the same as those on the Executive Council. The Commander British Forces had always been a member of the Legislative Council from its inception in 1843 until 1966, when the *Royal Instructions* were amended; but holders of that post had normally spoken only twice during their membership, once on taking the oath, and again in replying to the customary valedictory on their departure. The conduct of the British Army in Hong Kong is not politically controversial and has not been discussed in the Council for many years.

Formally, all the nominated members are appointed by the Secretary of State in London, though the Governor is entitled to make a provisional appointment when a vacancy occurs (subject to the possibility of future disallowance). In practice, the choice is made by the Governor and ratified by the Secretary of State, though there might be consultations beforehand if the Governor proposed a controversial nomination.[1]

The nominated official members are chosen to speak for their offices or departments, and not on the basis of seniority or personal qualifications. When an official member goes on leave his seat is taken by the official acting in his place. The size of the Council has been steadily increased since the war, as shown in the following table.

	Ex officio (including the President)	Nominated officials	Nominated unofficials	Total
1947	6	3	7	16
1951	6	4	8	18
1964	6	7	13	26
1966	5	8	13	26
1973	5	10	15	30

When there were only three nominated officials in addition to the *ex officio* members, the departments represented were Urban Services, Public Works, and Medical and Health Services. More heads of departments were added as the Council was subsequently enlarged, but this process was reversed after the creation of the new posts of secretary in the McKinsey reorganization. In 1974 the ten nominated officials were the Secretaries for the Environment, Housing, Social Services, Security and the New Territories, and the Directors of Urban Services, Education, Medical and Health Services, Public Works, and Commerce and Industry.

The *Royal Instructions* do not impose any fixed racial quotas among the unofficial members. The usual pattern since the war has been to appoint three Europeans, one member of Portuguese or Indian origin, and the rest Chinese. As the Council has been steadily enlarged this has meant an increasing proportion of Chinese members, as can be seen in the table below.

	Chinese	Indian	Portuguese	European
1950	3	–	1	3
1952	4	–	1	3
1954	4	1	1	2
1959	4	–	1	3
1960	4	1	–	3
1966	9	1	–	3
1969	10	–	–	3
1971	11	–	–	2
1973	11	–	1	3

The nominees of the General Chamber of Commerce and the 'unofficial' Justices of the Peace were all Europeans, with the exception of Mr. Dhun Ruttonjee who was nominated by the J.P.s from 1953 to 1958.[2]

Now that these two bodies are no longer entitled to 'elect' members to the Council (see Chapter 5, p. 55) the Governor has gained greater freedom in chosing European members, since the nominees of the Chamber of Commerce and Justices of the Peace normally pre-empted two of the three seats customarily held by European unofficials. It will be interesting to see whether the appointment of Mr. Hilton Cheong-Leen will serve as a precedent for future elevations of elected Urban Councillors to the Legislative Council. At any rate, the Governor has avoided giving the impression that he will allow any future appointment to be decided for him by the Urban Council electors; Mr. Cheong-Leen is not the most senior elected member, nor the one who gained most votes at his last election.[3]

Membership of the Legislative Council is not representative of the Hong Kong ethnic communities in any statistical sense. The Europeans (about 30,000 residents) have three members, but the Indian community of 40,000 has not been represented in the Council since the retirement of Mr. Ruttonjee in 1968. The Indians are very active commercially and in the export trade and the appointment of one of their number would give great psychological satisfaction.[4] However, their views are adequately conveyed to government through the Indian Chamber of Commerce and there can be few occasions when a distinctively Indian viewpoint needs to be heard in the Council.[5] The section of the population which is most under-represented is the women. The first lady member, Mrs. Ellen Li Shu-pui, was appointed in 1965, and two further ladies, Mrs. Joyce Symons and Mrs. Mary Wong Wing-cheung, joined her in 1972. However, Mrs. Wong died suddenly a few months later and Mrs. Li retired in 1973, leaving only one woman on the Council. The number was brought up to two again by the appointment of Mrs. Kwan Ko Siu-wah in 1974.

Service on the Council is unpaid, and (unlike the Urban Council) there is no provision for the payment of expenses. Instead, unofficial members can now obtain clerical assistance and some help with research from the UMELCO office staff. Contrary to what has been asserted,[6] members do not need to be wealthy to serve on the Council, but they do need to have sufficient time and energy to spare not only for the fortnightly sittings of the Council and its Finance Committee, but also for the numerous committees and advisory boards on which members serve, to say nothing of the study groups set up by the unofficials themselves to look at particular bills in detail.[7] Those appointed to the Council have already shown their willingness to engage in this kind of work at other levels of the community, often as appointed members of the Urban Council. Obviously, the rich are more likely to be free to take up this activity than the poor; but service on the Council can be, and in fact has been, combined with the practice of a number of professions such as teaching, architecture, medicine, and the law.

Since 1972 speeches at the Council may be made in either Chinese or English, and a simultaneous translation system has been installed. But in practice most of the Chinese members make their speeches in English and any unofficial not fluent in English would have difficulty in dealing with the mass of documents he will have to consider in the course of his duties.

VOTING

The administration can always command an overall majority in the Council since the official members are bound to vote as directed by the Governor unless specifically released by him,[8] and the Governor himself, as President of the Council, has both an original and also a casting vote if there is a tie. So even if the unofficials are unanimous they can always be outvoted 16–15. But it is over twenty years since the official majority was last mobilized to outvote the unanimous opposition of the unofficials. Nowadays government takes great pains to avoid having any contested votes in the Council at all. There are a number of mechanisms to avoid this. Some ideas for new legislation are dropped while still being investigated at the departmental stage if it is found that they would be unacceptable to an influential pressure group or an advisory committee. For example in 1966 the Director of Medical and Health Services proposed that motor cyclists should be compelled by law to wear crash helmets, but the Transport Advisory Committee turned this down and recommended that there should instead be a campaign of publicity and persuasion.

Consequently this change in the law was not enacted until 1973 after the Committee had changed its mind as a result of a threefold increase in fatalities due to head injuries over the intervening years.[9] Other bills are killed at the Executive Council stage by the opposition of the unofficial members there; for example, the bill to legalize abortion on social grounds put forward by the Attorney General in 1968.[10] If any bill which has survived this filtering process nevertheless arouses opposition in the Legislative Council, government's normal reaction is to seek a compromise in private negotiations outside the Council so that amendments can be put forward at the committee stage which will command unanimous support. For example in 1950 the Financial Secretary proposed to raise the standard rate of income tax from 10 to 15 per cent. This was bitterly attacked by the unofficials as certain to bring about the ruin of Hong Kong's business; but later a compromise of $12\frac{1}{2}$ per cent was endorsed by the Council without a division.[11] At other times a proposal may be dropped completely rather than face open opposition. In 1956 government reversed its stand and decided to permit the operation of a privately-owned commercial radio station in competition with the government-owned Radio Hong Kong, when its White Paper on broadcasting policy was criticized by the unofficials;[12] and in 1969 the proposal to appoint an 'Ombudsman' to conduct independent investigations into complaints against government departments was dropped after all except one of the unofficials had indicated their opposition.[13]

This compliant readiness to compromise would not be possible if the administration were anxious to push through a far-reaching programme of change either because of its ideological commitments or in order to satisfy those who voted for it at a free democratic election. But this is not the case. Government is secure so long as China's tolerance of the colony continues; and officialdom is firmly wedded to the philosophy that it should intervene as little as possible. So when any controversy arises it normally prefers to drop a proposal. The *status quo* is almost always preferred to facing an open clash.

This appearance of unanimity between the unofficials and the government which is so earnestly sought has been helped by the new *Standing Orders* of the Council adopted in 1968. Previously any member could claim a division and members' individual votes for and against were recorded in the official report. This procedure enabled a determined member to divide the Council even if he were the sole dissentient. Thus Mr. Dhun Ruttonjee was outvoted by 16 votes to 1 when he protested against the terms granted to the company building the cross harbour tunnel; and Mr. Kan Yuet-keung was defeated by 24 votes to 1 when he objected to the proposed increase in the Defence Contribution.[14] But under the new Standing Order 36(5) the President may refuse a division if, in his opinion, the division is unnecessarily claimed after a voice vote. If the member persists in his request, the President may ask those who voted 'aye' or 'no' to stand up in their places in turn and declare the result on this basis, without asking the clerk to take a note of the votes of individuals.[15] As a result of this change there have been no divisions since the new *Standing Orders* were introduced in 1968, though certain government policies have been severely criticized.

The full potential official majority has been used twice since the war to overcome the unanimous opposition of the unofficials. The first occasion was in 1947, to defeat a motion of censure demanding that the government should 'modify its present unfair and repressive policy in regard to the renewal of seventy-five year Crown Leases'.[16] The other occasion was in 1953 on a resolution to amend the royalty to be paid by the Yaumati Ferry Company so as to bring it into line with that levied on the Star Ferry Company.[17] The former company had been promised that if more favourable terms were granted to the Star Ferry, then the terms of its own franchise would also be revised. The unofficials wanted to make this revision conditional upon the Yaumati Ferry altering its articles of association so as to make its shares freely transferable and not subject to the discretion of the directors. Government refused to accept this amendment, on the grounds that its original promise to the Yaumati Ferry had been unconditional, and that other monopoly franchise holders had similar restrictions in their articles.

Since 1953 there have been a few occasions when government has pressed ahead with its policy over the objections of a majority of the unofficials, but never when they were unanimously in opposition. In 1973 the unofficials threatened that they would all vote together against the proposals for the renewal of Crown Leases, and government immediately gave way in spite of the very considerable loss of revenue involved (see Appendix 6, Doc. E, pp. 258–60). It thus appears that it has now become an established convention that government will always concede to the views of the unofficials when they can agree on a united stand. As with any convention it is possible to imagine circumstances in which this one might be broken. If some vital imperial interest were at stake orders could conceivably be sent from London that the full official majority should be mobilized; but in such a case the European unofficials might perhaps support the officials. However, for practical purposes this convention sets a political limit in domestic affairs beyond which the administration will not go.

The other occasions when government declined to modify its policy in spite of the opposition of most, but not all, of the unofficials are listed at the end of Appendix 6. They seem to fall into three categories:

1. When an agreement reached by government with an outside body has to be ratified, in order to preserve its credibility in future negotiations. This covers the 1969 undertaking to compensate the China Motor Bus Company and the Kowloon Motor Bus Company for the legalization of minibuses. The question of the good faith of government was involved here. (This also explains the 1953 vote.)

2. When a question of principle is at stake. This covers the 1970 debate on the financing of the Motor Bus Companies. As Mr. Haddon-Cave made clear, government was utterly opposed on ideological and practical grounds to any subsidies for commercial firms.[18]

3. When government believes that it is safeguarding the interests of

the majority of the Hong Kong population against a demand for unreasonable concessions to the rich. This covers the refusal of the Financial Secretary in the 1973 budget to abandon his proposed income tax changes.

But such confrontations, as can be seen from the list, are very rare. Government is normally able to achieve a satisfactory compromise through private talks with the unofficials so as to avoid any open clash in the Legislative Council.

* * * * *

Traditionally, legislatures and assemblies have been regarded as having three main activities: the passing of laws, the voting of money (in British parliamentary terminology, the 'granting of supply'), and the scrutiny and control of the acts of the executive. These three functions will be considered in the remainder of this chapter and in the two which follow.

THE PROCESS OF LEGISLATION

Almost all bills are introduced by official members. Standing Orders allow the presentation of bills by unofficial members, but in practice this facility is only used for bills to incorporate a charity or educational establishment in order to enable it to hold property. Such bills follow a standard pattern and are usually introduced by an unofficial who has some connection with the institution concerned. In Britain private members' bills are frequently used to propose measures of social reform for which the government in power does not wish to take responsibility, out of fear of losing votes at the next election, and members are allowed a free vote. This fear does not exist in Hong Kong, and so all such measures (e.g. divorce, abortion, cruelty to animals) are proposed by government. However, it is very reluctant to introduce any such legislation unless assured beforehand of the support of the unofficials.

The majority of government bills are concerned with matters of minor administrative detail, a part of the continuous process of keeping the law up-to-date with changing social circumstances and the latest decisions of the courts. Of the seventy-eight bills presented to the Council in the 1970–1 session about forty-five were of this nature. These included such matters as:

1. Clearing up minor ambiguities in drafting.
2. Closing possible loopholes discovered by a decision of the courts or when a prosecution was contemplated.
3. Simplifying court procedures; allowing certain powers to be exercised by delegation to a deputy.
4. Bringing Hong Kong procedures into line with international agreements (e.g. the new signalling code to be flown by a ship in quarantine).
5. Repealing obsolete ordinances.
6. Altering and increasing penalties for certain offences.
7. Altering the composition of legally constituted bodies (e.g. the Medical Council, the Council of Hong Kong University).

None of these measures are likely to cause any controversy. They are normally initiated by the head of the department concerned or by the Attorney-General's department. Occasionally the first move may come from an outside body, as in item 7.

About twenty-five bills a year make more substantial changes in the law. These may be classified as follows:

A. *Finance Bills.* The Appropriation Bill in February authorizes the money needed for government services in the next financial year. There are also the Supplementary Appropriation Bill, usually in October, and the bills to implement any taxation changes announced in the budget speech.

B. *Law Revision.* British legal reforms are routinely examined by the Legal Department to consider whether they could usefully be adopted in Hong Kong. For example, in 1970–1 the laws relating to Intestacy, the Administration of Probate, Magistrates, and Criminal Procedure were revised on the model of British legislation.

C. *Legislation on completely new subjects.* In Hong Kong this is not normally a new departure in government activity, but rather the filling in of gaps in the law. In 1970–1 there were bills dealing with Legitimacy, Affiliation Proceedings and a bill giving the courts power to order that certain dependants of a deceased person should receive benefits from his estate. All these were modelled on British laws. The only purely local innovation was a bill setting up the Hong Kong Polytechnic.

D. *Incremental additions to the powers of government departments.* In 1970–1 the Director of Fire Services was given authority to make regulations for the licensing and control of fire service installation contractors, and the Director of Urban Services was authorized to regulate slaughterhouses in the New Territories; there were five similar bills that year.

E. *Substantial amendment or the complete recasting of old ordinances.* In 1970–1 four of these bills aroused controversy: a bill to amend the *Inland Revenue Ordinance* on the lines of a report submitted by a joint committee of civil servants and outside experts; a bill amending the *Trade Union Registration Ordinance* to increase the controlling powers of the Registrar; a bill to consolidate and tighten up the law relating to immigration; and a bill completely recasting and strengthening the law against bribery and corruption by government officials.

When a bill seems likely to arouse some controversy the administration will consult not only the advisory body attached to·the department but also other interested parties before the bill is finally published. This enables officials to discover beforehand the practical difficulties likely to be met in implementing the bill in order to make provision to overcome them, to avoid ambiguities and to make the bill as watertight as possible. It also allows the government to make concessions beforehand to important pressure groups without publicity, if it judges that any clause is likely to provoke strong opposition. Sometimes important provisions of the bill may be leaked to the press so that some idea of public reaction may be obtained. Very occasionally the whole of the tentative draft may be released for public comment.[19] It is only after all these consultations have been completed and the resulting changes embodied that the bill is finalized, approved by the Executive Council and published in *Legal Supplement No. 3* of the *Government Gazette* for presentation at the next session of the Legislative Council.

This pre-legislative stage is much the most important in the bill's formation. It is rare for further substantial changes to be made during the passage of the bill through the Legislative Council since all likely criticisms have been foreseen and, it is hoped, forestalled. The formal stages of the bill in the Council serve mainly to publicize its provisions and give a last opportunity for objections to be raised. Unlike the United States Congress the Hong Kong Legislative Council does not 'make' laws; it endorses and formally ratifies, (and only rarely challenges), decisions that have already been taken elsewhere in the Secretariat after very full argument and consultation with all those interests thought likely to be concerned.

The stages of a bill follow the model of those in the House of Commons, though their actual significance is rather different. In Britain a bill is not made publicly available until it has been formally introduced at the First Reading. In Hong Kong a bill is published in the *Government Gazette* immediately it is received by the Clerk of the Council. This publication is accompanied by an explanatory memorandum setting out the contents and objects of the bill in non-technical language. Only the latter is published in a Chinese translation.[20] The bill must then be introduced at the next session of the Council, usually a week later and never more than a fortnight.[21] The first reading is nothing more than the formal recitation of the title of the bill and the Council proceeds immediately to the Second Reading. The official member introducing the bill (usually the Attorney-General) then makes a brief speech covering the main points of the bill and the debate is immediately adjourned.[22]

In the interval before the second reading debate is resumed the unofficials have a further opportunity to look at the bill and if necessary they may set up a sub-committee to consider it in detail together with any representations that may be made by members of the public to the unofficial members' office (UMELCO). Except for the very infrequent cases where a draft bill is published for public comment several months beforehand the second reading debate will normally be the first time that any groups or individuals who might be affected by the bill hear of its existence, unless they are on the select list of organizations granted prior consultation by government. Thus in 1972 a bill was introduced to regulate the accounting profession and establish a Hong Kong Society of Accountants, after extended negotiation with local accountants who had qualified in Britain or Australia. The effect of the provisions of the bill as originally presented to the Council would have been to forbid certain Chinese 'tax agents' to practise their profession at all. These gentlemen lodged a protest with UMELCO and after their case had been taken up by the unofficials government agreed to move certain amendments at the committee stage making a distinction between *professional* accountants and others, who were now to be allowed to continue their businesses as before.[23] The second reading debate is also the first time that the public at large may hear of the bill (unless there have been any prior leaks to the press). What has been comfortably agreed between officialdom and the privileged groups and individuals it consults may not be equally acceptable to the general public. For example, in 1971 government found itself obliged to make a large number of amendments to its omnibus *Immigration Bill* as a result of a public outcry.[24]

The second reading debate is resumed in the next or the next but one session of the Council unless substantial difficulties have emerged in the interim. If there are none, or none which the unofficials are prepared to take up,[25] there will be no further speeches and the bill will be immediately considered in committee. If the unofficials have any objections (which may be either newly discovered, or matters which have been previously raised with officials and rejected at the drafting stage), these will be voiced at the resumed debate. Though a few general remarks on the subject of the bill may be made, this debate does not, as it does in Britain, function as a wide-ranging discussion of the principles of the bill—these are taken to be agreed between government and the unofficials—but is rather a minute consideration of the case for and against certain possible amendments in an attempt to persuade the administration to accept them at the committee stage. The Attorney-General (or the official member in charge of the bill) has been informed of the substance of what is to be said beforehand, and he will have already decided what concessions, if any, are to be made. He replies to the debate either to rebut the criticisms or to indicate what amendments he proposes to move later. On a very controversial bill the second reading debate may be adjourned a second time to allow an opportunity for the decisions to be taken by the Governor in Council.

The Committee Stage is normally taken immediately after the close of the second reading debate, in committee of the whole Council. There is provision in Standing Orders for a bill to be sent to a select committee but this only occurs in the case of the annual Appropriation Bill.[26] Since detailed arguments on the amendments have already taken place there are usually no long speeches at this juncture. The Attorney General moves various amendments 'as set out in the paper before you' and these are quickly passed. Amendments may be either to remove ambiguities in the draft which have been noticed since the publication of the bill, or new concessions by government. Though they may have originated in representations made by the unofficials they are normally for convenience drafted and introduced by the official side, though occasionally they may be moved by one of the lawyers among the unofficials.

Thereafter the Attorney General reports to the Council that the committee stage has been completed and moves the Third Reading of the bill. This is invariably passed without any speeches or division.[27] All that now remains to be done is the signification of the Governor's assent which is announced in the next edition of the *Government Gazette*. Since no bill is ever introduced into the Legislative Council without the consent of the Governor in Council, and since the official majority could be used at any stage to reject unacceptable amendments, the Governor's assent is almost, but not quite, a formality. In the whole 130 year history of the colony it has been refused only once, in 1946. In that year Sir Mark Young, acting on instructions from London, refused assent to the *British Cinematograph Films Bill*. Representations against this bill (which laid down a compulsory quota of British films in local cinemas) had been received by the Secretary of State, and the Governor only received notification of this after the third reading.[28] The bill was reintroduced the following year in substantially the same form after correspondence with the Colonial Office and was then passed into law.

Apart from the need for the Governor's assent there are two other limitations on the legislative competence of the Council. By Clause XXVI of the *Royal Instructions* the Governor is forbidden to assent to any bill on the following subjects unless he has previously obtained the consent of the Secretary of State or unless the bill contains a clause suspending its operation until such consent has been notified:

1. Divorce
2. The grant of land or money to himself
3. Currency and the issue of banknotes
4. Banks and banking practices
5. The imposition of differential duties
6. Anything inconsistent with treaties binding upon Britain
7. The discipline and control of the armed services
8. Anything prejudicing the rights, property, trade or shipping of British subjects not living in Hong Kong
9. Discriminatory legislation against non-Europeans
10. Any provision previously disallowed or not assented to.

In practice the agreement of the Secretary of State is always obtained beforehand, not only on these classes of bills, but also on any others which might cause him embarrassment in the House of Commons; for example, bills affecting public order.[29]

The only matters on the reserve list on which Hong Kong is normally likely to wish to legislate are items 1, 3 and 4, that is bills affecting divorce, currency and banking. Divorce law causes no difficulty. The local law on the dissolution of marriage generally follows that in Britain and modifications of British law are subsequently enacted by the Legislative Council after a short delay. Currency and banking are much more important. All currency notes issued by the three authorized note-issuing banks are backed by the assets held by the Exchange Fund, which owns nearly half of the colony's external reserves.[30] The activities of this Fund are controlled by the *Exchange Fund Ordinance*, which lays it down that the consent of the Secretary of State is necessary for certain operations; his consent would also be required for any amending legislation. This power of veto held by the Secretary of State might potentially be an important bargaining factor if Hong Kong wished to diversify all her external assets out of sterling.[31]

Any bill on any subject passed by the Legislative Council and assented to by the Governor may be disallowed by the British government; that is to say, the bill is in effect repealed as from the date of notification of the disallowance. In the first year of the Council's existence, 1844, four bills were disallowed, including the first one ever passed. This power was occasionally exercised throughout the nineteenth century; the last time was the *Sugar Convention Ordinance* of 1913. However, disallowance is not yet completely dead. It has been used since then against legislation in other colonies, and the remote possibility that it might be revived in the case of Hong Kong encourages the administration here to consult Britain during the drafting stage on any bill where there is a possibility of a clash of interests, so that an agreed formula can be settled beforehand. If any points of difference are noted in London only after the ordinance has been passed into law negotiations are set in motion to find an acceptable compromise for subsequent amending legislation. For example the Council was told in 1960 that the *Mining (Amendment) Bill* then being introduced had been drafted as a result of detailed comments by the Secretary of State on the 1954 *Mining Ordinance,* followed by lengthy consideration and correspondence to reach agreement.[32]

DELEGATED LEGISLATION

Many ordinances contain enabling clauses permitting the Governor in Council or some other body such as the Chief Justice or the Urban Council to issue detailed regulations to facilitate the implementation of the law. This device is commonly used now in almost every country; it prevents the overloading of the legislature with technical details; and it is a flexible means for quickly incorporating minor changes without the need to go through the whole process of amending the original law. For example, during 1971 regulations were made by the Commissioner of Labour on safety requirements for the operation of woodworking machinery under the *Factories and Industrial Undertakings Ordinance*; rules to authorize three new legal forms needed for proceedings under the *Fixed Penalty (Traffic Contraventions) Ordinance* were made by the Chief Justice; and an order altering the charges for radiotelegrams was made by the Governor in Council under the *Telecommunications Ordinance.*

If the original ordinance authorizes such subsidiary legislation to be made by the Governor in Council, the new order, notice or regulations are drafted in the department concerned. Relevant interest groups are normally consulted and the draft may be seen and agreed by the appropriate advisory board. The order is then submitted to the Executive Council for its approval. After this the order is formally laid on the table at the next meeting of the Legislative Council. There is a provision in the *Interpretation and General Clauses Ordinance* (Sec. 34(2)) which allows the Legislative Council to pass a motion amending any such order or regulations within a fortnight of their being laid, in which case the amendment takes effect from the date of its publication in the *Government Gazette.* Though this power has been available to the unofficial members for many years, the first time that it was ever used was in June 1974 when Mr. O.V. Cheung moved a resolution to amend three provisions of the *Road Traffic (Construction and Use) (Amendment) Regulations 1974.*

These regulations extended the powers of the police to remove and dispose of vehicles apparently left abandoned on the roads and laid down the procedures to be used, and the amendments were designed to protect the interests of the owner. These changes were accepted by government without a division.[33]

Where the power to make rules is delegated to some body other than the Governor in Council (such as the Commissioner of Labour, the Pharmacy and Poisons Board, the Chief Justice etc.), the authorizing ordinance normally requires the passage of a motion to approve them by the Legislative Council before they become legally valid. Such motions are normally the first business at a session of the Council and are invariably approved after a brief speech by the official proposer. Before its reorganization in 1973 by-laws made by the Urban Council to regulate beaches, libraries etc. needed the validating approval of a motion by the Legislative Council, but since then this requirement has been repealed.

The Legislative Council normally meets for only about two hours once a fortnight so it can hardly be claimed that delegated legislation is necessary to relieve its members from overwork. The main justification in Hong Kong must be the abstruse technicality of most subsidiary legislation, which is best worked out in discussions between government officials and experts from the main interest groups concerned. If these technicians are satisfied, there is little that the members of the Council can usefully add, whether they are official or unofficial members.

1. For example, the decision to abolish the convention that the unofficial J.P.s should 'elect' one of their member to the Legislative Council was taken only after consultation with London. See the official statement quoted in Chapter 5, note 23, p. 56.

2. Mr. Ruttonjee was subsequently reappointed by the Governor from 1960 to 1968 and became the senior unofficial member.

3. The senior elected member in 1972 was Mr. Bernacchi, first elected in 1952. Mr. Cheong-Leen came second in the poll in 1971 to Mrs. Elsie Elliott who gained 7,578 votes to his 5,790.

4. See the letter by Mr. Vaid to the South China Morning Post, 18 July 1972.

5. No occasion can be found when Mr. Ruttonjee thought it necessary to speak out on behalf of the Indian community in the Council, but he did speak very eloquently against the inadequacies of administrators who had no roots in or commitment to Hong Kong's future:

'I am aware that what I have said is not going to be pleasing to many influential people in Hong Kong. But I say this to them: and I speak as a man who was born and bred here, who has his home here and who is vitally interested—like the majority of people in Hong Kong—in what the future holds for Hong Kong. I am not, Sir, one who is looking forward to a comfortable retirement in those green and pleasant lands across the sea....' (H. K. Hansard, 1968, pp. 82f.)

6. See for example, Rear's attack in K. Hopkins, Hong Kong, Industrial Colony, pp. 72ff: 'Since the councillors are unpaid, wealth has become in practice the first criterion of selection'.

7. According to the Second Annual Report of the UMELCO Office, Hong Kong 1971–72, p. 7, the 19 unofficial members of the Executive and Legislative Councils then held a total of 187 seats on various committees.

8. H. K. Hansard 1952, p. 31 (Debate on the architecture of the new City Hall): The President: 'On this resolution official members may speak and vote as they wish'.

9. H.K. Hansard, 1972–73, p. 355.

10. See Chapter 6, note 23, p. 69.

11. H. K. Hansard 1950, pp. 159 and 184, and Grantham, Via Ports, p. 109.

12. H. K. Hansard 1956, pp. 46–57.

13. H. K. Hansard, 1969–70, p. 31. Only one unofficial spoke in favour of an Ombuds-

man, Mr. Wong Sien-bing, p. 39. According to the *Far Eastern Economic Review*, 27 November 1971, p. 17, a bill to introduce a New Zealand-type Ombudsman had already been drafted but was pigeon-holed after the unofficials had expressed their opposition. The British government had been pressing for action along these lines. (See for example *House of Commons Debates*, 16 December 1968, written answer col. 239 and 21 July 1969, oral answer col. 1225.) But the views of the unofficials were decisively against it.

14. *H. K. Hansard 1965*, p. 520; *H. K. Hansard 1967*, p. 273.

15. *Standing Orders 1929–1968*, Sec. 24 (2). 'At the conclusion of a debate the question shall be put by the President and in any committee by the Chairman and the votes may be taken by voices aye and no and the result shall be declared by the President or Chairman, but any member may claim a division when the votes shall be taken by the Clerk asking each member separately how he desires to vote and recording the votes accordingly.'

Standing Orders Revised 1968, Sec. 36 (5). 'The President or Chairman may, if in his opinion the division is unnecessarily called, take the vote of the Council or the committee, as the case may be, by calling upon the Members who support or who challenge his decision successively to rise in their places; and he shall thereupon, as he sees fit, either declare the determination of the Council or the committee or order a division.'

16. *H. K. Hansard 1947*, pp. 191–247.

17. *H. K. Hansard 1953*, pp. 339–45.

18. *H. K. Hansard 1969–70*, p. 530. 'The Government simply cannot accept that there should be hidden subsidies when royalty has been eliminated.... I am afraid that philosophy is neither acceptable, nor, in our view, practicable.

19. Such releases are usually published in *Special Supplement No. 5* of the *Government Gazette*. As a result of public comment four changes were made in the *Trade Union Registration (Amendment) Bill (H. K. Hansard 1970–71*, pp. 459ff). For the very full consultations on the *Prevention of Bribery Bill*, see Appendix 6, Document A ii, pp. 254–5.

20. Since the full text of the bill is not available in Chinese, misapprehensions are very likely to occur if the Chinese press does not summarize its provisions adequately. The Commissioner for Labour, when introducing the *Labour Tribunal Bill*, deplored the fact that some criticisms showed a misunderstanding of the scope and purpose of the bill. This is hardly surprising since he was not proposing to publish a booklet setting out the full details of the bill in Chinese until *after* the bill was passed, so that any amendments made during the Committee Stage could be incorporated. (*H. K. Hansard 1971–72*, p. 627.)

21. *Legislative Council Standing Orders*, Sec. 40 and 41.

22. Until 1973 non-controversial bills passed immediately to the Committee Stage without adjournment, if none of the unofficials wished to speak on them. The second reading debate is now always adjourned (except for emergency bills), following a request made by the Senior Unofficial Member, Mr. Woo Pak-chuen (*H. K. Hansard 1972–73*, p. 53).

23. *H. K. Hansard 1971–72*, pp. 995–8 & 1051, and *H. K. Hansard 1972–73*, pp. 167–76. Similarly in 1969 government neglected to consult the Association of Pawnbrokers on a bill to make it more difficult to dispose of stolen property to pawnbrokers until after it received representations from them on the day of the second reading debate. As a result of these consultations a further amending bill was introduced later in the year. *H. K. Hansard 1969–70*, pp. 134f, 215f, & 579. See also Appendix 6, Document C, p. 256.

24. *H.K. Hansard 1971–72*, pp. 101–145, parts of which are included in Appendix 6, Document D, p. 257.

25. There were considerable complaints by trade unionists about the *Trade Union Registration (Amendment) Bill 1971*, but there were no speeches on the second reading except that by the Commissioner of Labour introducing the bill, and no amendments moved in committee (*H. K. Hansard 1970–71*, pp. 455ff & 578).

26. For the special procedure with this bill, see Chapter 9, pp. 112f.

27. In the House of Commons the Report stage is the last stage at which amendments to a bill may be proposed, when the full House receives the report of the standing committee which has made a detailed study of the bill.

28. These details are taken from the Governor's address to the Council on the presentation of the 1947 bill, *H. K. Hansard 1947*, p. 105. Presumably the protests were made by American film interests who would expect to be more influential in London than in Hong Kong. The bill had passed through all its stages in the Hong Kong legislature in a fortnight without any objections being raised (*H. K. Hansard 1946*, pp. 151 and 165). The Secretary of State has power to instruct the Governor to refuse his assent under the *Letters Patent*, clause X.

The 1947 ordinance was repealed in 1971 (*H. K. Hansard 1971–72*, p. 248). It had not been enforced for some years and the Secretary of State indicated that he had no objection to the repeal.

29. The prior approval of the Secretary of State was sought for the *Public Order Bill* (*H. K. Hansard 1967*, p. 475). *The Prevention of Bribery Bill* was submitted to the Secretary of State for his comments in view of its importance and the nature of some of its clauses. He put forward a number of suggestions which were embodied in the bill and gave his approval to it (*H.K. Hansard 1970–71*, p. 133). See Appendix 6, Document B(ii), pp. 255f.

30. The details of the holdings of the Exchange Fund are kept secret (*H. K. Hansard 1969*, p. 206). It appears that the Exchange Fund owns about half Hong Kong's sterling assets from the disclosures made by the Financial Secretary in his reply to a Question on 19 December 1972 (*H. K. Hansard 1972–73*, pp. 221 and 225).

31. According to section 3 (2) of the *Exchange Fund Ordinance* (cap. 66) the Fund may hold its assets in Hong Kong currency, foreign currency, gold, silver or securities approved by the Secretary of State. Thus the Fund, which is managed by the Financial Secretary, has the power to move all its assets into foreign currency or bank deposits abroad, but not to make long-term investments without London's permission. The Secretary of State's approval is also required for variations in the borrowing limits of the Fund and for the transfer of any profits made by the Fund to general revenue (sec. 3 (5) and sec. (8)). Refusal of permission on such matters could be inconvenient. There were some complications with the Secretary of State over amending the ordinance in 1968 (*H.K. Hansard 1969–70*, p. 682). The limits imposed by this ordinance were important in 1974; see Chapter 1, note 25, p. 14.

32. *H.K. Hansard 1960*, p. 260.

33. *H.K. Hansard 1973–74*, pp. 900–1 and *Fourth Annual Report of the UMELCO Office, 1973–74*, p. 29.

9 The Legislative Council: Financial Control

FINANCIAL CONTROL IN BRITAIN AND HONG KONG

LONG ago members of parliament sought to control the executive—the king and his ministers—by refusing to grant financial supplies for royal projects until their grievances were satisfied. The attempt of Charles I to levy taxes without the authority of parliament so as to avoid the scrutiny of his policies by the House of Commons was one of the causes of the English Civil War and his own execution. However, the executive in Britain is no longer the monarch but the leaders of the party which commands a majority of the seats in the Commons. Members of the government party on the back-benches no longer regard it as their duty to keep a close check on the extravagant tendencies of the Cabinet; on the contrary, they loyally support their party in power, voting in favour of all requests for money put before them. In this, they are motivated partly by the desire for promotion to ministerial office and partly out of fear of offending those who voted for them. It is more than fifty years since the House of Commons insisted on a reduction in any item of the annual budget laid before it. Financial control is now little more than the efforts of various parliamentary committees to study the details of public spending, in the hope that their reports may have some influence on future ministerial decisions.

Party discipline is not the only reason for the impotence of the Commons to control government expenditure. The sheer size of the sums involved—£54,000 million in 1975–6—and the bulk of the documentation giving the details of how the money is to be spent make it seem trivial and pointless to quibble about items involving thousands, or even millions of pounds. Moreover the average M.P. is far more conscious of the demands of the electorate for an ever-increasing level of expenditure on social and environmental services, and less worried about the complaints of the tax-payers who have to foot the bill. M.P.s seeking re-election may talk about the need for economy in general terms, but they are well aware that any specific proposals for cuts in expenditure will lose more votes than they will gain. Consequently the total of public expenditure has gone soaring upward under both Conservative and Labour governments until nearly 60 per cent of the British gross national product is now disposed of by central government, local authorities and the nationalized sector of the economy.[1]

The situation of Hong Kong is very different. As in Britain the total amount spent by government has been rising steeply over the past few years, from just over HK$1,113m in 1962–3 to an estimated HK$6,615m in 1975–6. But this is still a relatively manageable figure compared to the British total (approximately £600m as against £54,000m spent by the British government). More surprisingly, Hong Kong government expenditure in 1973 represented approximately 14.2 per cent of the estimated gross domestic product, and over the previous seven years this percentage remained relatively stable around 13–15 per cent. (See the table below.)

Year	G.D.P.	Govt. expenditure	%
1966	$11,196m	$1,796m	16.0
1967	$12,111m	$1,776m	14.7
1968	$12,961m	$1,846m	14.2
1969	$15,136m	$1,992m	13.2
1970	$18,407m	$2,347m	12.8
1971	$20,587m	$2,789m	13.5
1972	$23,738m	$3,394m	14.3

Note: All figures at current market prices. The 1971 budget was the last one of Sir John Cowperthwaite.

Source: Statistical Appendix to a speech by Mr. Haddon-Cave 'The Economic Future of Hong Kong' to a business conference in Singapore, 2–4 Oct. 1973, copy from Financial Secretary's Office.

In his budget speech on 26 February 1975 Mr. Haddon-Cave estimated that government expenditure reached nearly 20 per cent of G.D.P. in 1974–5 and would be a little over 20 per cent in 1975–6, as a result of increasing government expenditure and stagnant economic growth.

Why this difference between 20 and 60 per cent? One reason is that the figures are not entirely comparable. The small size of Hong Kong means that it is unnecessary to delegate power to a network of local authorities. Certain services which are provided by the public sector in Britain are run by private enterprise in Hong Kong, such as electricity supply and the telephone service. Most important is the fact that Hong Kong spends only 2 per cent of its budget on Defence compared to over 10 per cent in Britain.[2] But even when all these and similar qualifications have been made, the difference in scale of government expenditure in the two countries is very impressive.

There would appear to be three main reasons for this divergence: the constraints imposed by the colony's economy, the absence of elections, and certain structural mechanisms in the system of government which make it easy to inhibit expenditure.

The need to keep taxes low in order to attract foreign investment and persuade local entrepreneurs to build up their businesses here has already been explained in Chapter 4. This sets an upper limit on the amount of resources which government can raise, and so enforces economy on all branches of the administration. In addition, government's commitment to almost undiluted free enterprise means that Finance Branch does not have to find the money for any open or disguised subsidies to commercial firms. During the 1960s these policies were vigilantly defended by Sir

John Cowperthwaite, the Financial Secretary, who was convinced of the virtue of leaving money to 'fructify in the pockets of the taxpayer'.[3] Though he always modestly claimed that his influence was exaggerated, his pre-eminent position in the government and his intellectual gifts enabled him to set the imprint of his passion for economy on all government policy documents throughout the 1960s.[4]

Government has been able to keep to such principles because it is never required to submit itself for re-election and campaign for votes. Politicians soon forget the need for financial discipline when they are in danger of losing their seats; free primary education would certainly have come many years sooner if this demand had been raised by opponents in an electoral contest. Even without elections government might have been stirred to spend more if it had been faced by prolonged riots and demonstrations. But the passivity of the vast majority of the Chinese population never put it under any real pressure to make concessions. Even in the 1968 budget debate, when the experiences of the previous year aroused several unofficial members to press the Financial Secretary for more generous expenditure on social welfare, he was able to shrug off these pleas with a remark repudiating 'the implication that the people of Hong Kong have to be given a reward, like children, for being good last year, and bribed, like children, into being good next year'.[5]

These are the two main reasons for the comparatively low level of government expenditure. But their effectiveness is enhanced by certain institutionalized checks in the government machine, which are situated at three levels: the Secretariat, the Legislative Council and the Finance Committee. All proposals involving new expenditure originating from the departments are processed in the Secretariat, where their success or rejection will depend on how vigorously these plans are advocated by the policy secretaries against the criticisms of Finance Branch, which has the unpopular task of trying to accommodate all these requests for more money within the limited resources available. When agreement cannot be reached within the Secretariat and the policy secretary concerned has the support of the Colonial Secretary against the Financial Secretary, the dispute between them will ultimately be resolved by a decision of the Governor.

This system is very like that which operates in Britain, where ministers whose departmental requests are turned down by the Treasury have the right to appeal to the Cabinet. But there is an important difference: ministers in charge of spending departments have seats in the Cabinet, they argue the point in person against the Chancellor of the Exchequer, and they can sometimes win if they secure the support of the Prime Minister.[6] Whereas in Hong Kong heads of departments have to rely upon the secretaries and the Colonial Secretary to speak on their behalf against the Financial Secretary, who is thus in a stronger position than the Chancellor of the Exchequer.*

*A head of department has the right to approach the Governor directly if he considers that he has reasonable grounds for complaint; but this right is seldom exercised, and such an appeal is even more rarely successful on financial matters.

Secondly, paragraph 24 of the *Royal Instructions* (which is incorporated in *Standing Order* 23 of the Legislative Council) forbids any unofficial member to move any motion or amendment which would have the effect of imposing a charge upon the revenues of the colony, except upon the recommendation of the Governor. In practice, such permission is never asked or granted.[7] Unofficials may propose cuts in expenditure, but not increases. This rule is derived from a similar one in the House of Commons which dates from 1706, a time when party discipline was very weak and the government of the day might find itself unable to carry its budget through the Commons unless various proposals for increased expenditure to benefit special interests were accepted. This rule ensures that the responsibility for proposing expenditure and the task of raising the revenue to pay for it rests in the same hands. It is easy to gain applause by advocating new expenditure but less popular to propose the new measures of taxation to pay for it.[8] It might be argued that such a precaution is unnecessary in Hong Kong since any proposals for increased public spending could be defeated by the built-in government majority. However, it would cause the administration considerable embarrassment to mobilize its majority to defeat the unofficials on a motion, for example, to increase social welfare disability allowances. This standing order prevents unofficials from doing any more than raising such points in their speeches, and so puts the government under less pressure to increase its outlays than if it needed to defeat such a proposal in a division.

The final structural mechanism to inhibit expenditure is the Finance Committee of the Legislative Council. This has no equivalent in the House of Commons. The committee is composed of all the unofficials and sits in judgment on all new items of government expenditure, to either approve or reject them. It is rather as if the spending proposals of the British Cabinet had to be passed, not by its own compliant party majority, but by a committee composed entirely of opposition members. Of course this is not a fair comparison, since the unofficials are not, and do not act as if they were, an Opposition in the British parliamentary sense and they do not behave in a deliberately obstructive way. Nevertheless, this imaginary parallel does suggest the important role that the Finance Committee can play in the Hong Kong system of government and its operations must now be considered in more detail.

THE FINANCE COMMITTEE

The Finance Committee is not mentioned in the two major constitutional documents of the colony, the *Letters Patent* and *Royal Instructions* to the Governor, though it has been in existence since 1872. Its composition and powers are given in one paragraph, no. 60, at the end of the *Standing Orders* of the Legislative Council, but it is rarely mentioned in the sessions of the Council, except when its report on the Estimates is tabled in the annual debate on the Appropriation Bill. Nevertheless, it can be argued

However, in a dispute between the Colonial and Financial Secretaries, the Governor does on occasion overrule Finance.

that the meetings of this committee are of far more importance than the formal open sessions of the Legislative Council itself and second only to the meetings of the Executive Council in their significance for the working of the Hong Kong governmental system.

It consists of all the unofficial members of the Legislative Council plus the Colonial Secretary, the Financial Secretary and one other official member nominated by the Governor (usually the Director of Public Works). The Colonial Secretary is the chairman of the committee but neither he nor the two other official members have a vote. Thus it is hardly correct to say that the unofficials have a majority on the committee; effectively they *are* the committee and the official members are only in attendance. Two sub-committees have been set up: the Establishment Sub-Committee consisting of four unofficial members plus the Secretary for the Civil Service and the Deputy Financial Secretary, which considers all requests for additional staff; and the Public Works Sub-Committee consisting of five unofficials plus the Financial Secretary (who is *ex officio* chairman) and the Director of Public Works, which keeps a check on the government building programme and decides the degree of priority to be given to individual projects.

Legislative Council *Standing Order* No. 60, sec. 6, lays down that all proposals for additional financial provision arising during the current financial year after the Appropriation Bill has been passed must first be referred to the Finance Committee for its approval. Sec. 8 of the same standing order states that the Estimates presented with the Appropriation Bill *may* be referred to the Finance Committee who may call before them to give evidence the public officer responsible for the service provided under any head of the Estimates. In practice this always happens. Since the examination of the Estimates has to be completed within a few weeks to enable the Appropriation Bill to be passed at the beginning of the new financial year, new items of expenditure to be included in the coming budget are in practice considered by the Finance Committee and its sub-committees at any time during the previous financial year, as soon as the documents setting out the reasons for the proposed changes have been finalized in the Secretariat; but most of its work is concerned with requests for additional expenditures in the current year. The Committee normally meets once a fortnight after the open sessions of the full Council, and its agenda is very heavy: for one meeting in 1972 the papers to be considered were over one-and-a-half inches thick and weighed more than four pounds.[9]

The power of the Committee stems from the well-established convention that government will not use its majority in the full Council to reverse an adverse decision by the Committee. Sec. 7 of *Standing Order* no. 60 allows an official member to move a motion in the full Council to authorize expenditure which has not been previously approved by the Committee, but this procedure has been used against the Committee only once since the war. In 1956 the Finance Committee disagreed over a request to authorize an additional grant of $1 million to the University of Hong Kong in order to allow it to offer more competitive salaries. This sum had been recommended by an independent committee of enquiry after the University had been unable to attract applicants of sufficient academic merit to fill certain professorships and other vacant posts. Apparently the Finance Committee was divided, with four members supporting the request and four wishing to reduce the sum by $300,000. Since there were only eight unofficial members at this time and the chairman of the Committee, the Colonial Secretary, had no vote to break the deadlock, government had no choice but to bring the matter before the full Council where the official majority was used to pass the full additional provision for the University. The unofficials again divided four to four.[10]

Nowadays the only occasions when a resolution authorizing a specific item of expenditure is put before the full Council are motions proposed under section 95 (1) of the *Interpretation and General Clauses Ordinance*. This provides that the Legislative Council may by resolution award compensation to any person who is injured in the execution of a moral or legal duty to assist in the prevention of, or resistance to, a crime, and to the dependants of a person who dies after being so injured. In order to give the fullest publicity to these *ex gratia* awards for gallantry the resolution is moved at a full meeting by the Attorney General who gives an account of the action which led to the award.[11] But this procedure does not derogate from the powers of the Finance Committee; it is always consulted beforehand and the amount of compensation agreed.

The convention that the Committee has the final say on all spending proposals is fully recognized by both officials and unofficials. Mr. Oswald Cheung, an unofficial since 1968, stated flatly in a radio discussion, 'We have an absolute veto on expenditure'.[12] But does the Finance Committee make full use of this power? It is widely believed that the Committee is nothing more than a rubber stamp which tamely accepts every proposal which is put before it by the Secretariat.

Unfortunately for its public reputation the Committee always deliberates in secret. This system is defended on the ground that it allows the unofficials to speak with complete freedom, uninhibited by any fear that what they say may be recorded and quoted later in the press.[13] Those who have attended such meetings say that argument can become fierce and the atmosphere is far removed from the formality of the public sessions of the Legislative Council; and that government proposals are indeed sometimes rejected or sent back for reconsideration and amendment.

Such reports from participants are suspect, since they cannot be checked. But there is some open evidence available. The attitude of the main Committee can perhaps be inferred from that of the Establishment Sub-Committee, which does publish an annual report. This sub-committee works in conjunction with the Establishment branch of the Secretariat, which processes the applications for increases in staff from the departments and forwards those which it is prepared to support for final decision by the sub-committee.[14] The figures for the original departmental requests and the number of additional posts finally approved by the sub-committee are as follows:[15]

Year	Departmental requests	Accepted
1969–70	4,700	1,700
1970–1	4,155	2,565
1971–2	7,190	3,450
1972–3	5,358	3,430
1973–4	4,788	2,816
1974–5	2,127	272

This sub-committee was first appointed in 1961. In the three previous years the Public Service had increased by 12.1, 12.65 and 10.72 per cent respectively. In the three years following the setting up of the sub-committee the rate of increase dropped to 5.62, 6.83 and 5.95 per cent, and has remained close to this level ever since.

But the power of the committee cannot be gauged merely by adding up the number of times they turn down or reduce a government proposal. The fact that every estimate has to be approved by the committee means that the government officers responsible for proposing expenditure must always take account of the views of the committee and their likely response when framing their requests. The influence of the committee is felt when officials *anticipate the reactions* of the committee and modify their proposals accordingly.[16] Thus the committee can have a preponderant influence over the whole field of government policy, even though it might never have turned down a single estimate.

This point may be illustrated by the controversy which erupted in May 1971 over the decision of the Director of Education to make a drastic reduction in the subsidy paid to European schools, forcing them to impose a steep increase in fees. The Legislative Council had approved a White Paper on educational policy six years previously in 1965 which proposed that the rate of subsidy for schools attended by Chinese and European children should be equalized, even though it was recognized that this would necessitate a rise in the European school fees. However, the Education Department had procrastinated over the implementation of this decision, for fear of the outcry that would certainly be raised by the expatriate parents concerned; so for the following five years the excessive subsidy for European schools was continued on a 'transitional' basis. In 1971 the Department finally took action to end this anomaly and the expected storm of protest from European parents quickly followed. Soon afterwards there was a debate on the subject in the Legislative Council in which the Senior Unofficial Member, Mr. Kan Yeut-keung, revealed the background to the decision and the crucial role played by the Finance Committee in forcing the Education Department to take action. In Mr. Kan's words:

In July last year Finance Committee was asked to accept the financial commitment of a higher recurrent subsidy for the two schools, the Beacon Hill Junior School and the Island Secondary School for a further transitional year, the academic year 1970–71.... Later in November a proposal was put to Finance Committee to vote $1,866,000 by way of recurrent subsidy to these schools. This amounted to a subsidy of approximately $1,134 per place for Beacon Hill Junior

School and $1,241 per place for Island Secondary School, both of which are far in excess of the amounts allowed for other subsidized schools. Notwithstanding this, the Finance Committee voted the amount asked for.... However, it was made clear to the schools that the higher subsidy would only be granted as an interim measure and that the level of subsidy would be brought into line with that granted to equivalent Chinese schools with effect from September 1971.[17]

Thus, though the proposal to equalize the subsidies paid to European and Chinese schools, and so force the European schools to impose a steep rise in fees, was technically brought forward by the Director of Education —(and the unofficial members made considerable play with this fact in the debate)—the reason why the proposal was brought forward at that time was because the Education Department knew that further requests for 'transitional' subsidies for the European schools would not be countenanced by the Finance Committee.

A similar case occurred in 1972. It is fairly clear that the decision to grant very generous educational allowances to civil servants for the education of their children at schools abroad was mainly devised as an inducement to attract and retain European staff. But this allowance has also been made available to Chinese civil servants, largely because it is well known that the Finance Committee is most unwilling to tolerate different terms of service for Chinese and expatriate officials.

There are two main limitations on the work of the Committee: it cannot vote to increase the sum requested by government, but can only either approve, reject or reduce it; and it only discusses government expenditure and not the ways in which revenue is raised and possible changes in taxation. With regard to the first point, the Committee is bound by *Standing Order* 23 just like the full Council, and the reasons for this limitation have already been given (see p. 107 above). However, this formal ban on moving a motion to increase expenditure need not, and does not, inhibit members from making speeches in the Council pointing to specific areas where government expenditure should be increased; and similarly in the Committee members can indicate that they would be happy to approve an even higher sum next year. Thus the attempt of officials to anticipate the reactions of the Committee may not always serve to depress the level of expenditure; sometimes it may encourage departments to ask for more.[18]

With regard to taxation changes, unofficials certainly show no hesitation in suggesting desirable modifications, both in the debates on the Appropriation Bill and at other times. Occasionally the Financial Secretary alters his proposals immediately in the light of what is said in the debate; for example, in 1970 Sir John Cowperthwaite amended his proposals on estate duty to raise the exemption limit from $100,000 to $200,000, as suggested by Mr. Woo Pak-chuen.[19] Other advice given by the unofficials may be implemented after a lapse of time. Mr. Cheung's suggestion in January 1973 that child relief should be granted to the parents of an incapacitated and unemployable dependent child of whatever age was taken up in the budget a month later,[20] but Mr. Li Fook-shu's 1963 plea for tax exemption for gifts made to charities had to wait until the budget of 1970.[21] As with other financial matters the Financial Secretary's taxation proposals have to be framed to take account of the anticipated reactions of unofficials; Sir John Cowperthwaite told the Legislative Council in 1966, 'It was made plain to me some years ago, on grounds I have difficulty in wholly accepting, that an orthodox full income tax would not command the support of a substantial part of this Council'.[22]

The real limitation on the Finance Committee lies not so much in these formal prohibitions as in the fact that the members are busy men, who have their own businesses to run or professional duties to perform in addition to their part-time service on the Council; consequently they find it difficult to spare the time to go into the estimates in detail; nor are they provided with highly qualified staff to assist them.[23] When faced with a complex proposal that has been worked out in detail over many months by the Secretariat in consultation with outside interests and approved by the Executive Council it is difficult for the Committee to send the whole project back for reappraisal.[24] Similarly when asked to approve the recommendations of a Salary Review Commission there is little the Committee can do but accept the report, since the only alternative is in effect to do the job of the Commission all over again themselves.[25] So members are more likely to make their views prevail over relatively simple and straightforward issues such as the building of a new police station, the upgrading of certain posts, or the purchase of a particular item of capital equipment rather than on the more far-reaching strategic decisions on the balance of government expenditure between different departments and services. However, these lower level decisions with which the Committee is chiefly concerned have their cumulative effect in enforcing a proper regard for economy throughout the Public Service, and members can make their influence felt on the wider issues not only by the attitudes shown to particular requests in the Committee, but also by their speeches in the Legislative Council and in the various advisory bodies on which they also serve.

THE ANNUAL FINANCIAL CYCLE

Throughout the previous financial year proposals for the next budget are being put forward by the departments, processed in the Secretariat and passed on to the Finance Committee and its sub-committees for their approval. At the end of January the draft estimates for the coming year incorporating these changes and others which the Committee has not yet seen are finalized and sent for printing so that they are ready to be published and laid before the Legislative Council on the same day as the Financial Secretary presents his Budget. This is normally the last session of the Council in February.

The Appropriation Bill is very short, merely listing the main heads of expenditure and the total sum to be authorized for the coming year. It is accompanied by the Draft Estimates of Revenue and Expenditure, a bulky volume which subdivides and itemizes each head in detail. Unlike other bills, the Appropriation Bill is not published in the *Government Gazette* until the day of the First Reading. This is to avoid prior speculative comment in the press on the likely budget proposals.[26] The Second Reading Debate begins immediately after the formal announcement of the First Reading, and the Financial Secretary then sets out his forecasts for the coming year and explains his proposals for changes in taxation. If there are to be any increases in taxes or government fees the Governor is authorized by the *Public Revenue Protection Ordinance* to sign an order which brings these changes into force immediately without waiting for them to be approved by the Legislative Council. So, for example, if the Financial Secretary proposes an increase in driving licence fees, as he did in 1973, the increased fee becomes payable at the licensing offices the very next morning after the budget. If this were not done, everyone needing a driving licence in the next six months would immediately queue up at the offices to buy it at the old rate before the law was passed, thus depriving Government of the additional revenue it hoped to obtain. The signing of this Order by the Governor does not prevent the Legislative Council from rejecting the proposed increase in taxation, nor does it prevent the Financial Secretary from withdrawing his proposal during the debate if he is convinced by the arguments brought against it. If this happens, the Order imposing the temporary increase ceases to have effect as soon as a notification is published in the *Government Gazette*, and any excess payments made while the order was in force are refunded by the Treasury. This actually occurred in 1974, when the Financial Secretary modified the stiff increases in vehicle licence fees which he had originally proposed, in order to reduce the cost for owners of smaller cars.

As soon as the Financial Secretary has finished his opening speech on the Second Reading the debate is adjourned and the Draft Estimates are referred to the Finance Committee for further study. During the next few weeks the Finance Committee meets three or four times. A number of heads of department and other officials, as requested by the Committee, appear before it to answer questions and the unofficials use the detail provided in the Estimates as a basis for a close examination of the policy and programmes of the department in question.

Meanwhile, two weeks after the Financial Secretary's speech, the open debate is resumed in the full Council and the unofficials make their public comments on his proposals. In the following sessions, at the end of March, the report of the Finance Committee is tabled and the Second Reading Debate is again resumed to allow the official members to reply to the criticisms that have been made of their departmental policies and expenditures; the debate is closed by the Financial Secretary. The Appropriation Bill is then immediately considered in Committee of the whole Council. Each head of expenditure is called in turn and members may make further detailed comments on the head as a whole or any of the sub-heads detailed in the Estimates. Amendments to increase or decrease any head or sub-head may be moved at this time, though only an official member may move for an increase.[27] Finally the total sum as modified by any successful amendments is voted upon. The Third Reading is moved at the conclusion of the day's session and the Bill then becomes law with the Governor's assent. During the next few sessions the bills to impose new taxation or to modify existing tax ordinances are passed through the Council in the normal way.

As soon as the new financial year begins on 1 April the Accountant General's Department begins to release money to the various government departments up to the limit authorized by the various heads and sub-heads of the estimates. But almost immediately unforeseen contingencies arise, such as a typhoon, a landslide or an unexpected rise in prices, which necessitate additional financial provision. These requests are all considered and approved or rejected by the Finance Committee as they arise. Every three months a paper is laid before the Legislative Council listing the supplementary provisions already approved by the Committee and the Financial Secretary moves a motion asking for the covering approval of the full Council. This is a formality since by this time the sums involved have in most cases already been paid out. At the end of the financial year on 31 March departments close their books and see that all their receipts and documentation are in order. These are then checked by the Accountant General's Department and made ready for auditing. When the final total of expenditure during the financial year has been arrived at, a Supplementary Appropriation Bill is presented to the Legislative Council, usually in October, which seeks retrospective approval for all the changes which have been made since the original Appropriation Bill was passed eighteen months before. This is again a purely formal requirement and the Bill is passed without debate.

THE AUDIT DEPARTMENT

The function of the Director of Audit and his staff is to see that all expenditure by departments is made within the limits laid down by, and for the purposes set out in, the Appropriation Bill, and that all receipts and payments are properly controlled and documented. Formerly the Audit Department was directly responsible to the Director-General of Overseas Audit at the Colonial Office in London, who certified the colony's accounts on the basis of assurances and reports sent to him by the Director of Audit in Hong Kong. There was a unified audit service and auditors could be transferred and promoted between different colonies. With the run-down of the Colonial Empire such an elaborate organization was no longer appropriate and it was wound up in 1971. The Director of Audit is now a member of the Hong Kong Public Service responsible to the Governor and the Legislative Council, but his independence is safeguarded by the *Audit Ordinance 1971* which lays down that he can only be appointed, or dismissed before retiring age, with the prior approval of the Secretary of State.[28] This is to give him complete freedom to comment criticially on the government accounts and to ensure that adequate systems of control exist for the collection of revenue and the avoidance of unauthorized or wasteful expenditure. During the course of the year his staff make spot checks on different departments but their main activity is the audit of the government accounts submitted by the Accountant General within five months of the close of the financial year.

When this audit is complete, usually by the following February, the

Director of Audit's Report is tabled in the Legislative Council together
with a despatch from the Governor giving the replies of departments to
the criticisms that have been made against them.[29] By tradition the
Director speaks out strongly on all cases of waste and inefficiency discovered in the course of the audit, and these criticisms are widely reported
in the press. This is the main sanction to ensure that effective action is
taken to correct these failings, since no departmental head likes to be
publicly pilloried year after year. The Report and the Governor's despatch
are also sent to the Secretary of State. There is no public debate on them
in the Legislative Council, but members can make use of the criticisms
to provide material for Questions; presumably they also refer to the report
when examining requests for additional staff and funds in the Finance
Committee, and when interviewing heads of departments on the Estimates.

FINANCIAL CONTROL FROM LONDON

Before 1948 Hong Kong's finances were closely supervised by the
Colonial Office. The draft estimates had to be submitted for the Secretary
of State's approval before the beginning of the financial year and all
supplementary provisions also required his sanction. All this was in
addition to the passage of the appropriation bills in the Legislative
Council. Control was slightly relaxed in 1948 when supplementary
provisions of less than $1 million for capital expenditure or $250,000 for
recurrent expenditure no longer required Colonial Office approval, unless
some important point of principle was involved.[30]

Such fussy supervision may have been needed when Hong Kong was
still recovering from the aftermath of the war, but it was hardly appropriate to the colony's financial strength ten years later. This was recognized
in 1958 when the Secretary of State decided that the estimates and
supplementary votes should no longer require his authorization, provided
that the Financial Secretary kept London informed of the colony's
financial affairs and took account of the views of the financial advisers of
the Secretary of State when formulating his policy. At the same time
Colonial Regulation 279 was relaxed, to allow the colony to raise a loan
without first seeking the permission of London. This was of little immediate consequence since throughout the 1960s Sir John Cowperthwaite
showed very little desire, on grounds of principle, to borrow any money.[31]

It is clear that Sir John did not allow the need for consultation with
London to cramp his style. When it was suggested in 1966 that his decision
to raise the standard rate of Earnings and Profits Tax to 15 per cent had
been taken under pressure from London, he informed the Legislative
Council that there was no truth in this whatsoever;[32] on the contrary, the
Colonial Office had not even been informed beforehand and he understood
that there had been substantial betting in the corridors of Whitehall as
to whether he would do it or not.[33]

In practice the convention that government will never override the
views of the Finance Committee on questions of expenditure had made
the submission of the Estimates to London a futile exercise long before
1958. The Colonial Office might offer comments and suggestions, but

such policy changes could not be put into effect unless the unofficials endorsed them. This fact was fully recognized by the ministers concerned, though it was not so clear to Members of Parliament who then and now still continue to talk as if binding instructions could be issued from Whitehall which officials in Hong Kong would jump to obey. For example, there was a short debate in the House of Lords in 1968 in which the Minister of State responsible for Hong Kong, Lord Shepherd, was pressed on all sides to ask the colony's administration to provide grants for poor school children to pay for textbooks. Lord Shepherd admitted the force of the points made in the debate but then went on to point out the constitutional difficulties:

The noble lord is aware that there is a Governor in Hong Kong with an Executive Council and a Legislature, and I do not think it would be right to use influence, if by 'influence' we mean pressure, on decisions that they must make, taking into account the needs of these school children and the moneys that are available.[34]

Britain's formal acknowledgement in 1958 of Hong Kong's financial autonomy in managing its own internal affairs was no more than a recognition of the actual situation. In legal theory the British government could still reassert full financial control at any time, but in practice this would be politically out of the question after such a lapse of years. Any such action would raise a huge outcry and senior officials (and unofficials) might well resign rather than carry out any such instructions from London. This possibility is not worth discussing. The financial controls still exercised over Hong Kong by the Secretary of State now relate entirely to the management of its external reserves; but even in this area Britain relies more upon contractual agreements made with the Hong Kong government rather than on the constitutional powers which are theoretically available. (See Chapter 19, p. 209.)

1. The figures for the last 25 years are conveniently collected in Sir Richard Clarke. 'Parliament and Public Expenditure', *Political Quarterly*. 1973, Vol. 44, No. 2. The post-war low point was 41 per cent in 1957 and it then increased. See also *The Economist*, 30 June 1973, p. 88, 23 Nov. 1974, p. 78, 1 Feb. 1975, p. 63, and 19 April 1975, p. 80.

2. According to the *Estimates of Revenue and Expenditure 1975–76*, the Hong Kong Government expected to spend 1.8 per cent of the budget on defence in 1975–76. The high point was 4.8 per cent in 1967–8. It is difficult to believe that Hong Kong will be allowed to get off so lightly in the next review of the Defence Contribution. This would be less than $\frac{1}{2}$ per cent of G.D.P. Britain spends $5\frac{3}{4}$ per cent of G.D.P. on Defence.

3. *H. K. Hansard 1963*, p. 41.

4. See his disclaimer in Appendix 7, Document A. Someone less impressed with the sinfulness of government expenditure described one white paper on Social Welfare as 'marred by the tramplings of a stray hyena from the Treasury zoo'. (*H. K. Hansard 1965*, p. 308.)

5. Mr. Dhun Ruttonjee had previously told him, 'There can be few times or few places where an increase in taxation would have been so acceptable and would have raised so little protest.' Mr. K.A. Watson had similarly warned, 'Capital investment may be discouraged by things other than higher taxation. Dissatisfaction with labour and living conditions, frustrations and grievances, feelings of neglect and injustice...could have been highly dangerous to our economic well-being, but for the steadfast loyalty of our people.' *H. K. Hansard 1968*, pp. 83, 105, & 215.

Since 1971 spending on Social Welfare has greatly accelerated: 1970–1, $39.9m; 1971–2, $60.4m; 1972–3, $87.7m; 1973–4, $153.2m; 1974–5 (Estimate), $270.1m; 1975–6 (Estimate), $326.7m.

6. For example in January 1958 Prime Minister Macmillan supported the spending ministers against his Chancellor of the Exchequer, who resigned from the government in protest.

7. The sole exceptions since the war are the ceremonial resolution moved by the Senior Unofficial Member in 1947 to vote a wedding gift of $50,000 to Princess Elizabeth, and the similar resolution and gift to Princess Margaret in 1960.

8. Of course, from 1966 to 1974 revenue always exceeded expenditure, so it would be possible to propose increased expenditure without the need for any rise in taxation.

9. The amount of detail put before the committee enables it to probe the reasons behind any spending proposal, if it wishes to do so. Sometimes the committee asks for more information before giving its approval; for an example of this, see note 24 below.

To reduce the load on the committee, power to approve certain items of expenditure within existing policies has been delegated to the Financial Secretary and other officers in the Secretariat by resolution of the Legislative Council. The limits of this delegated authority are periodically revised to take account of inflation. The last occasion was in 1973: see *H. K. Hansard 1972–73*, pp. 964–70. In certain cases the Financial Secretary may now sanction supplementary expenditure in an existing subhead of up to $600,000.

10. *H.K. Hansard 1956*, pp. 3–29. The vote in the Finance Committee was not revealed in the debate; but the assumption that the unofficials voted then as they did later in the full meeting of the Council is the only way of explaining the necessity for this public debate.

11. Examples are *H.K. Hansard 1969*, pp. 117–19 and *H.K. Hansard 1969–70*, pp. 18f.

12. *Radio Hong Kong*, 18 February 1971.

13. See Appendix 7, Document B(iv), p. 265.

14. For the full procedure for appointing more staff, see Appendix 7, Document B(iii), p. 264.

15. *Annual Reports of the Establishment Sub-Committee of Finance Committee* (Government Printer). For the setting up of the sub-committee, see *H. K. Hansard 1961*, pp. 125f.

The reports of the Public Works Sub-Committee are also published, but do not reveal very much. They consist mainly of the details of various projects and the recommendations of the P.W.D. as to which category they should be placed (e.g. investigation only, detailed planning, to be put out to tender, to be deleted from the current programme etc.). With the exception of one project in 1970 and one project in 1971, the recommendations of the Director are almost always accepted by the sub-committee. In 1970 the unofficials deferred the inclusion of an item for small arms ranges in police stations, pending a reappraisal by the police of their requirements (*Second Review*, 25 August 1970, p. 6); in 1971 the unofficials objected to the deletion of the project to build a market at Chang Sha Wan (*Third Review*, 28 December 1971, p. 75). However, the Director was presumably influenced as to what projects he brought before the sub-committee by the general discussions on priorities which is recorded in the minutes at the beginning of each meeting.

Another case of the Finance Committee rejecting a government request is given in note 24 below.

16. The concept of 'anticipated reaction' in the assessment of influence is further expounded in C.J. Friedrich, *Man and His Government* (McGraw-Hill, New York, 1963), pp. 199–215.

17. *H. K. Hansard 1970–71*, p. 698f.

18. Of course, such proposals still run the risk of being reduced in the Secretariat before they can reach the Committee, if they exceed the resources that can currently be made available.

19. *H. K. Hansard 1969–70*, pp. 417 and 492f.

20. *H. K. Hansard 1972–73*, pp. 321 and 485.

21. *H. K. Hansard 1963*, p. 106.

22. *H. K. Hansard 1966*, p. 79.

23. Possibly the UMELCO office may in time be expanded to provide such assistance. It already does some research on legislative proposals, looking into the past history of a controversy (as over Crown Leases) or finding out what the law is in other countries. In 1974 the equivalent of one-and-a-half senior staff at UMELCO were engaged on this.

24. The Finance Committee does do this occasionally when it feels that it is being rushed into a decision. In 1971 government had agreed to postpone the fee increases at European schools pending a review of the fee remission system. The new fees were due to be introduced in January 1972 but the new remission proposals only reached the Finance Committee on 19th November. The Committee were not prepared to take an immediate decision on what they considered to be important points of principle, as government was requesting them to do. So they decided instead to defer consideration of the proposals pending the report of a select committee of the Legislative Council on the costs of running the European schools. The motion for a select committee was moved on 1st December 1971 (*H. K. Hansard 1971–72*, pp. 262–4). The committee appointed by the Governor consisted of four unofficials plus the

Director of Education. Its report is summarized at *H. K. Hansard 1971–72*, pp. 683–6.

25. Recent salary commissions have always included one unofficial member who would be on the Finance Committee when the report was referred to it; e.g. Mr Lo Kwee-seong in 1971.

26. *H. K. Hansard 1970–71*, p. 410. In the previous year the Bill was published a week previously leading to what Sir John Cowperthwaite called 'premature uninformed comment'.

27. Normally any such changes are more conveniently made by the procedure for supplementary estimates described in the next paragraph.

Speeches made by unofficials at this point are mainly to call public attention to the need for minor increases in particular items. Mr. Wang Tse-sam once threatened to move a reduction of $1 in the Education Head, in protest at the inadequate provision of primary school places, but did not in fact do so (*H. K. Hansard 1969*, p. 138).

28. See the Attorney General's speech on the *Audit Ordinance, H. K. Hansard 1971–72*, pp. 210–12.

29. See Appendix 7, Documents C(i) and C(ii), pp. 266–7.

30. See *H. K. Hansard 1958*, p. 46, for this and the following paragraph.

31. Sir John's views on borrowing can be found most fully set out at *H. K. Hansard 1966*, p. 74–6. He did not rule it out under all circumstances but was deeply concerned about its inflationary consequences. He also considered it morally disreputable (p. 74).

32. *H. K. Hansard 1966*, pp. 154 and 207.

33. This was a momentous change for Hong Kong, since Earnings and Profits Tax had stood at $12\frac{1}{2}$ per cent for the previous fifteen years.

34. *House of Lords Debates*, 3 April 1968, col. 1221ff. Similarly in November 1974 the Foreign Secretary, Mr. James Callaghan, rejected a suggestion that he should instruct the Hong Kong Government to introduce a wealth tax: 'Introduction of any new tax in Hong Kong would be a matter for the Hong Kong Government . . . and not for me'. In response to further questions he added, 'I should think there is a good case for increasing taxation in considerable measure in Hong Kong, but that is a matter for them. The fact that I am not able to issue a directive should not lead the hon Gentleman to assume that there are not many aspects of the taxation system which could be improved.' *House of Commons Debates*, 6 Nov 1974, cols. 1066–8.

10 The Legislative Council:
Controlling the Administration

THE power of the Finance Committee is the power of veto. It can say 'No' to propositions put before it by government, but it cannot formulate counterproposals. At most it can ask questions and suggest alternatives; but if government stands firm then the Committee has to accept or reject the proposal before it. In theory it might perhaps be argued that the Committee should use its control over expenditure as a bargaining counter to achieve policy changes. For example, it might refuse any increase in salaries for the Administrative Class until it was agreed that all future appointees should be Chinese. But such behaviour, if acquiesced in by government, would have the effect of making the Finance Committee, and not the Governor in Council, the supreme decision maker in the system. Inevitably, rather than submit to such blackmail, the official majority in the full Council would be used to override the Finance Committee. The convention that the Committee is allowed the final say on expenditure is balanced by a complementary convention that the unofficials will not be deliberately obstructive or seek to usurp the functions of the executive. Any such attempt to exercise power without responsibility would serve to weaken, not strengthen, the influence which the unofficials at present exercise over the policies of government.[1]

It is out of the question for the unofficials to seek to 'control' government in the sense of dictating the lines of policy and the content of legislation. There are very few legislatures in the world which wield such power. Proceedings in the Legislative Council are more in the nature of a dialogue, a conversation between the rulers and the representatives of the ruled, in which government puts forward its policies and explains the reasons why they have been adopted, and the unofficials point out where they find these policies ineffective, inappropriate or objectionable, suggest alternatives and indicate areas of neglect where government ought to take action. This feed-back of criticism and scrutiny should serve to keep officials responsive to the needs and anxieties which are uppermost in the minds of the people, and so make it less likely that feelings of dissatisfaction may erupt into violent confrontations in the streets. The unofficials do not control the executive by issuing orders, but rather by thrusting upon the attention of government the problems which it must tackle successfully if it is to retain the respect and confidence of the governed, and by forcing officials to reassess projects and methods when these are failing to achieve their objects and alienating the population. The un-officials are listened to and their criticisms are taken seriously because they are able to indicate where government is failing and so enable officials to take early action to avoid worse troubles in future.

DEBATES

All the activities of the unofficials are aimed at influencing government policy in the broadest sense, but this is particularly so in the case of general debates and questions. There are two occasions in the year when the whole range of government activities comes up for debate: the debate on the Governor's speech at the beginning of the new session in October, and the debate on the budget in March. The first debate is technically on a motion thanking the Governor for his address, but after a few flattering remarks by the first speaker all the unofficials in turn comment on the whole field of government activities, both those matters mentioned in the speech and those that should have been but which were unaccountably omitted. The unofficials usually agree among themselves which areas each shall cover to avoid unnecessary repetition; but even so fifteen speeches take up two afternoons before the official side replies a fortnight later. The speeches in the budget debate are similarly wide-ranging, since it is impossible to discuss the appropriation for any department without also scrutinizing the policies which make such expenditures necessary.

These are normally the only two long debates of the year. Standing Orders allow an official or unofficial to propose a motion for debate, but this happens very rarely.[2] In 1965 there were two such debates on motions moved by official members to discuss the White Papers setting out new policies on Education and Social Welfare.[3] But the next one did not take place till 1969, when Mr. Woo Pak-chuen moved a motion asking government to revise the law relating to intestate succession. This was the first motion to initiate a debate moved by an unofficial since 1949 when Sir Man Kam Lo moved the rejection of the Young Plan for constitutional reform.[4] Since then there have been two further debates introduced by unofficials: in 1972, on a motion moved by Mr. Oswald Cheung, asking government to review its policy on Crown Leases; and in 1973, on a motion by Mr. Wong Sien-bing, advocating a change in the retirement age for civil servants from fifty-five years to sixty.[5] Apart from these occasions short debates also sometimes take place on government motions to approve pieces of subsidiary legislation.

Much more frequent are debates on the adjournment. This was an innovation introduced in 1966 whereby at the end of the day's business an unofficial may raise any matter for which government is responsible with a view to eliciting a reply from an official.[6] The member must normally give three clear days' notice of his intention and may speak for a maximum of twenty minutes. The President then calls on an official member to reply for not more than ten minutes. This procedure enables a topical matter of public interest to be aired at greater length and under less restrictive conditions than is possible at question time. The first such debate was a model of its kind. A police inspector had been reported in the press as having told a magistrate that he was required by his superiors to issue a certain 'quota' of summonses each month. Mr. Woo Pak-cheun pointed out that the belief that the police acted in this way was widespread; he spoke about the bad effect this had on police-public relations and asked for an assurance that this was not the case. The Attorney General replied, going into considerable detail on the background to the reported incident and the general policy of the police in order to refute the allegation. Since then these debates have covered a wide range of topics, from fears of pollution from a proposed oil refinery on Lamma Island to the moral dangers of permitting 'topless' exhibitions in nightclubs. When adjournment debates were first introduced they proved popular with the unofficials and as many as ten were held in 1968. Since then the number has dropped to only two in 1973.

QUESTIONS

The rules about asking questions generally follow the restrictions imposed in the House of Commons, which are designed to ensure that questions are short, precise and factual.[7] The questioner must be prepared to substantiate any statement included in the question and must not seek an expression of opinion, or ask what government would do in some hypothetical future situation; nor may he ask if a statement in the press is accurate. Thus the subject of the adjournment debate described above would be inadmissable as a question. Either the original questioner or any other member may ask supplementaries after hearing the official answer but must not use this as a pretext for a general debate. At present about 40 per cent of questions are followed by one or more supplementaries.

Until recent years unofficials did not make much use of the opportunities afforded by question time for pressing government. Less than two questions a year were asked in the 1950s. Since then the numbers have been as follows:

1960	9	1967	7
1961	14	1968	64
1962	12	1969	84
1963	3	1970	95
1964	35	1971	140
1965	15	1972	155
1966	30	1973	167

The record for the highest number of questions asked at one meeting is held by Mr. K.A. Watson who in 1966 directed ten questions (and three supplementaries) at the Financial Secretary in an attempt to prove that an excessive profit was being made out of government car parks.[8] Possibly to avoid this in future the 1968 Standing Orders limit each member to three questions at any one sitting. The most persistent questioner in recent years has been Dr. Chung Sze-yuen who asked twenty-six in the 1970–1 session, twenty-seven in 1971–2 and twenty-three in 1972–3. No more than fifteen questions may be asked at any one sitting. This limit was reached four times in 1973.

Questions may be roughly grouped into four broad categories according to what appears to be the main object of the questioner, as the following examples indicate:

1. *Asking for information, either about facts or government policy*
   Would government provide details of the multi-storey car park projects which are now under consideration (a) to be constructed with public funds, (b) to be constructed by private developers?   (29 Nov. 1972)

   Will the government inform this Council what is the policy of the police in regard to the towing away of cars?   (6 Jan. 1971)

   Will government explain why the recruitment of auxiliary police, unlike that of regular police, is confined to constables only and does not include inspectors?   (29 Nov. 1972)

2. *Making suggestions*
   Would government introduce legislation to make it a requirement for refuse chambers to be provided in all new multi-storey buildings? (29 Nov. 1972)

   Would government consider the construction of a bridge across Lei Yue Mun to further improve road transport between Kowloon and the Island?   (13 Dec. 1972)

3. *Pressing for action*
   Has any conclusion been reached on the setting up of a cadre of traffic wardens to perform some of the duties now undertaken by traffic policemen? If not, when can a decision be expected?   (29 Nov. 1972)

   Will government say what progress has been made on Stage IV of the Kai Tak Airport terminal development?   (13 Dec. 1972)

   Has government any plan to stabilize the price of rice which has risen sharply during recent weeks?   (14 March 1973)

4. *Criticizing government decisions*
   In view of the large backlog of driving tests, will government reverse the decision requiring the holders of overseas driving licences to take a Hong Kong road test?   (25 April 1973)

   The honourable Financial Secretary in reply to a question put by me in this Council on 5th November 1969 said that he found it difficult to gauge the urgency of making laws to deal with mutual funds and that he had no evidence at that time of any fraud having taken place in connection with mutual funds. Does he recall that I had then suggested that prevention was better than cure? In the light of recent developments is he in a position now of gauging the urgency of making such laws?   (10 Feb. 1971)

   Is government aware that its departments usually insist on members of the public with whom they correspond, quoting the departments' references but fail to quote the reference used by members of the public? Is this government's policy?   (10 Feb. 1971)

As can be seen, any such classification as this is very arbitrary. Some of the above questions might equally well have been placed in a different category, and a question which apparently only asks for information may be followed up by a supplementary blaming the government for the state of affairs revealed and pressing for action.

Very occasionally, questions are asked at the suggestion of an official member who wishes to correct a false report or to gain publicity for an announcement. Officials are permitted by *Standing Order* 20 to make a statement to the Council after question time, but this method is normally used only when a report or a piece of subsidiary legislation is laid on the table. The following questions seem likely to have been 'inspired' in this way:

In view of the fact that varying interpretations appear to have been placed on the words 'radical or major change in the present constitutional position in Hong Kong' used by Lord Perth in his statement at the airport on Saturday, 29th October, can the government say whether the inclusion of elected members in this Council would be regarded as a 'radical or major change' in the context of Lord Perth's statement?

Colonial Secretary: Yes, Sir, it would. The Governor has been authorized by the Secretary of State to make it clear that the inclusion of elected members in this Council is not contemplated. (9 Nov. 1960)

In view of the prevalence of Asian flu, will the Director of Medical and Health Services give some advice to the public on increasing resistance to infection other than the avoidance of crowds?

Dr. G.H. Choa:—Sir, I am grateful to my honourable Friend for giving me the opportunity to clarify the situation concerning influenza and influenza-like diseases in Hong Kong, which has been the subject of some editorial comments in the local press recently.... (23 June 1971)

THE UMELCO SYSTEM

There are very few questions in the Legislative Council concerned with the specific grievances of individuals against the administration.[9] Allegations of unfair treatment, incompetence, unreasonable delays, failure to take all relevant factors into account and discrimination on the part of officials in their dealings with the public arc frequently the subject of questions in the House of Commons. M.P.s are active in taking up such cases on behalf of their constituents and questions are asked in Parliament when private letters to the Minister concerned have failed to produce satisfaction. M.P.s have every incentive to do this since they hope to gain votes from their grateful clients at the next election. But in Hong Kong the unofficial members, being only part-time legislators, have no time to spare for such detailed enquiries, and though the unofficials have had an office open to the public during normal government hours since 1963 comparatively little use of it was made by complainants before 1970.

In view of this there was an agitation between 1965 and 1969 for the setting up of the office of 'Ombudsman' in Hong Kong, an independent commissioner to investigate the abuse and misuse of power by officials, which had long been established in Sweden. During the 1960s a number of countries copied this institution, including New Zealand in 1962 and Britain in 1967. The features of such a Commissioner in Commonwealth countries have been his complete independence from the Executive, his full power to see any relevant file or hear any witness, and the limitation of his power to recommendations addressed to competent legislative and administrative organs. Because of his independent position and the publicity given to his findings these recommendations are usually accepted and acted on by the Executive. Although the idea of such an Ombudsman in Hong Kong was advocated by leading members of the legal profession, government showed little enthusiasm for the idea.[10] Members of the Public Service were hardly likely to welcome a commissioner whose main function was to uncover their mistakes; and the unofficial members felt that the establishment of such an office would detract from their own position.

Finally, as a compromise, in 1970, the Office of the Unofficial Members of the Executive and Legislative Councils (UMELCO) was strengthened by the appointment of a senior administrative officer seconded from the Public Service, Mr. R.W. Primrose. His duties were to institute a more effective system for dealing with public complaints and representations, and to organize administrative and secretarial assistance for the unofficial members of both councils.[11] Mr. Primrose is not an independent commissioner. He is responsible to the unofficial members for the discharge of his duties and takes his instructions from them. However, by an administrative instruction from the Governor, UMELCO has access to all relevant files and policy documents that may be required for the purpose of investigations, with the exception of those that are top secret.[12]

In 1974 UMELCO had a staff of twenty-six, including six officers who are immediately available to deal with all callers without delay. First of all a client is interviewed to establish the facts of his complaint, and this may be supplemented by a visit to the site if necessary. The Administrative Secretary (Mr. Primrose) then gets in touch with the relevant government department to call for any necessary files or documents and asks the departmental head or a senior officer for his comments on the case. At this stage it may be possible to ask for the decision complained of to be reconsidered if facts have been discovered that were not previously available, or where the client has not been competent to put his case adequately. Sometimes, where the main grievance is delay, the intervention of UMELCO may dramatically speed up the processes of government. In other cases where there is no suggestion of maladministration and the decision is fully in accordance with government policy, the client may be satisfied, after the matter has been explained to him, that everything possible has been done. However, it is always open to the unofficials, if they consider that a particular policy decision is causing injustice, to press government either in private discussions or at meetings of the Councils to modify this policy. In all routine matters the Administrative Secretary takes action himself under the general directions of the unofficials, though all cases are reported to them. A client may ask to have an interview with one of the two unofficials who are on duty each week, and the unofficials may intervene in any case where they consider that a grievance needs to be pursued or where there is a need to press for a change of policy at the highest level.

The increase of staff and the improved procedures instituted in 1970 have encouraged the public to make more use of UMELCO. About a quarter of these callers need no more than general advice on their personal problems and are referred for help to the appropriate authority such as the Social Welfare Department or the Legal Aid Department. Of the remaining cases with real grievances about 30 per cent had their complaint rectified either because the department's rules were not properly applied in the first place, or because the decision was reconsidered in the light of the particular circumstances of the client (Type A cases). Another 40 per cent received some satisfaction, though less than they hoped for (Type B cases); and the remainder had to be told that their complaint was unjustified or that the rules could not be altered in their case (Type C) Statistics given in the first three UMELCO reports are as follows:

	1970/71	1971/72	1972/73
New cases	834	1,208	1,689
No further action required	158	347	382
Completed cases			
Type A	120 (25%)	255 (31%)	359 (29%)
Type B	228 (46%)	326 (39%)	524 (42%)
Type C	144 (29%)	244 (30%)	366 (29%)
	429	825	1,249

Examples of all three types of case are given in Appendix 8, pp. 270–2. These statistics can be compared with those of the Urban Council Ward Offices (see below p. 165).

These reported results were achieved entirely by private persuasion and not by invoking the provisions of an ordinance—(there is none)—nor by an appeal to public opinion. Selected case studies, two a week, are released to the press when a file is closed, in order to tell the public what UMELCO is doing; but this is never done while a case is in progress. This makes it easier for a senior officer to rescind a decision when there is no question of his past conduct being dissected in the newspapers. It has been claimed that the lack of a legal basis for UMELCO's work is a positive advantage since an ordinance would have set precise limits to UMELCO's activities, (as it does in Britain), whereas under the present system the office can take up any case where it feels there is a justifiable grievance.[13] The effectiveness of UMELCO rests on its right to be furnished with information, its right to put the case for its clients at the highest level, and the willingness of government to concede policy changes when the unofficials put the weight of their influence into the scales. Above all, it depends on the conscientiousness with which the UMELCO staff put together their client's case and the zeal shown by the unofficial members and the Administrative Secretary in pressing this case on a possibly reluctant department. The present administrative arrangements cause the minimum of inconvenience to government and the maximum benefit in public relations.

Critics would say that the informal intimacy of these arrangements lays them open to suspicion. But it is hardly realistic to expect the colonial government—or any other government, for that matter—to provide a scourge for its own back by appointing a crusading outsider as Ombudsman, armed with legal powers to turn every complaint into an open public confrontation under the banner of The People versus Bureaucracy. This would no doubt provide a highly enjoyable spectacle; but UMELCO's clients are probably more likely to get their grievances rectified by the present method of confidential discussions. Abrasive methods do not necessarily get the best results, particularly when the administration has no need to fight elections.

Nevertheless, it might be helpful if UMELCO made some effort to disengage itself more obviously from government. One well-publicized controversy between the unofficials and government over a poor widow's eviction would do more for UMELCO's reputation than the hundred anodyne case studies put out every year. As one unofficial member pointed out, 'For the purpose of redress, the people have the impression, however wrongly, that the UMELCO office is too much with the government'.[14] Compared to the ward offices of the Urban Councillors, who have to rely on part-time clerks and voluntary helpers, UMELCO is lavishly staffed; yet many more people prefer to take their problems to the ward offices, particularly to those Councillors who have gained a reputation for reckless pugnacity. Ward Offices also have the advantage that they are situated near where people live, whereas UMELCO has to be near the Central Government Offices in order to be able to serve the unofficial members.

UMELCO does what it can to overcome these difficulties.[15] The office stays open during lunch time and till six in the evening, though in fact almost all clients now arrive during government office hours. The case studies which it publishes are featured in a regular weekly programme on the Chinese service of Radio Hong Kong. Publicity is also obtained from stories in the newspapers and interviews on television. There is also the word-of-mouth recommendation from clients who have been helped. About half of those who come to the office have heard of it in this way.

When UMELCO was reorganized on its present basis in 1970 the post of Administrative Secretary was publicly advertised, and there was some criticism of the fact that the appointment was given to a serving government officer who would return to his former duties in the administration after his tour of duty with UMELCO was completed.[16] In other countries such a potential conflict of interest is avoided by appointing retired officers, who have nothing to look forward to except their pensions, to similar sensitive posts, such as the British Parliamentary Commissioner for Administration and the judges of the French Administrative Court (the *Conseil d'Etat*). However, these cases are not strictly comparable; these officials have an independent, legally defined status, whereas the UMELCO Administrative Secretary is in theory nothing more than the servant of the unofficials, even though in practice he has considerable discretion in pursuing his enquiries. The advantage of having a government officer in this post is that he has an intimate knowledge of how the bureaucratic machine actually works; but this is offset by the suspicion of the administration and its officials which is prevalent among the Chinese population.[17] It will take a long time to overcome this.*

*It must be emphatically stressed that this paragraph is not in any way intended as a criticism of the UMELCO staff or Mr. Primrose, but is a comment on public attitudes in Hong Kong.

1. See above, Chapter 5, p. 54 and note 19, p. 56.

2. *Standing Orders of the Legislative Council* 21 and 22.

3. *H.K. Hansard 1965*, pp. 270ff and 295ff. These debates took place in the year after Sir David Trench became Governor, a natural time for a reassessment of policy.

4. There were a few formal and ceremonial motions moved by unofficials in these twenty years, but none intended to give rise to a debate.

5. *H.K. Hansard 1971–72*, pp. 725–64. *H.K. Hansard 1972–73*, pp. 360–9.

6. *Standing Order* 9. The first such debate at which the procedure was explained was *H.K. Hansard 1966*, 425ff.

7. *Standing Orders* 15–19.

8. *H.K. Hansard 1966*, pp. 295–303.

9. One such question was asked by Mrs. Ellen Li Shu-pui on 30 July 1969: What assistance has been rendered by government to the family of the man who was recently convicted and sentenced for illegally selling his three daughters? *H. K. Hansard 1969*, pp. 442–3.

But such questions come up all the time in the House of Commons, e.g. Mr. Symonds asked the Minister of Pensions and National Insurance why Mr. J.R. Thompson of 43, George Street, Whitehaven is not entitled to draw his pension from 15th to 17th December 1960, having ceased to draw his unemployment benefit on 14th December 1960 and having been informed that pension was not payable until 19th December 1960. (*House of Commons Debates*, 20 February 1961.)

10. See Report by Justice (Hong Kong Branch) *On the feasibility of instituting the office of Ombudsman in Hong Kong*, July 1969. The details in this paragraph are taken from this Report.

References in Legislative Council Debates are *H.K. Hansard 1966*, pp. 120f; *1967*, pp. 169f; *1969*, 63f; *1969–70*, pp. 11, 20, 28–31, 39, 95.

11. This is the order in which his duties were given in the *Second Annual Report of the UMELCO Office, 1971–72*, p. 1.

The detail in the next two paragraphs is taken from these reports.

12. This is similar to the restriction imposed on the Parliamentary Commissioner for Administration in Britain by the law which set up his office. Mr. Primrose says that in practice he has never been refused any document he asked for.

13. *Annual Report 1970–71*, p. 8.

14. *H.K. Hansard 1969–70*, p. 39. Mr. Wong Sien-bing.

15. The following details are from an interview with Mr. Primrose.

16. For example, *Far Eastern Economic Review*, 4 June 1970, p. 8. The report by Justice (see note 10 above) stressed that any future Ombudsman must not be a past or present member of the Hong Kong Government Service (p. 16).

17. On this see the restrained statements of Sir Alastair Blair-Kerr, *Second Report of the Commission of Inquiry*, Hong Kong, September 1973, pp. 20f. A more vivid account of public feeling is by Mrs Elsie Elliott, *The Avarice, Bureaucracy and Corruption of Hong Kong* (Friends Commercial Printing Factory, Hong Kong, January 1971), *passim*.

The same conflict between the demands of efficiency and public trust arose over the question whether to separate the Anti-Corruption Branch from the Police. (Sir Alastair Blair-Kerr, op. cit. pp. 42–52.)

11 The Role of the Unofficial Members

THERE are two views current in Hong Kong about the impact made on government policy by the unofficial members. One view, which is most commonly expressed by student groups, lays stress on the powerlessness of the unofficials, claiming that they are mere stooges and puppets chosen for their willingness to give supine assent to all the demands of their imperialist masters and rewarded for their docility with knighthoods and O.B.E.s. If any of them should ever show any sign of indiscipline the official majority is immediately used to crush all dissent. The opposite view, held by certain liberal-minded expatriates, depicts the unofficials as exercising a predominant and malign influence over the whole machinery of government in the interests of the owners of industry and commerce, and thwarting any attempt by officials to ameliorate the conditions of the workers or diminish the privileges of the rich.[1]

Obviously such views are caricatures of reality, and they also contradict each other. The unofficials cannot be both ineffective ciphers and at the same time the evil genius of the government, though one recent author comes close to asserting both propositions in the space of a single article.[2] Probably the truth, as usual, lies somewhere between the two extremes, depending on the particular issue at stake. But before trying to assess the power of the unofficials let us consider some of the more detailed criticisms thrown at them: that they are unrepresentative; that they are part-time and so do not take their legislative responsibilities seriously; that they do not offer vigorous open opposition to government policy; and that they are illiberal.

THE 'UNREPRESENTATIVENESS' OF THE UNOFFICIALS

It is claimed that they are 'drawn from a narrow class', 'directly representative of the interests of big business and banking, the industrialists and the employers' and are 'without exception the representatives of wealth'.[3]

No legislature or assembly in the world is an exactly representative statistical sample of the whole population, a microcosm in which every significant group is given a part exactly equivalent to its proportion of the whole total. This is true both of nominated assemblies and also those elected by universal suffrage. Voters tend to chose as their representatives men who are more educated, more wealthy and of a higher social class than themselves, in the expectation that they will be able to advance their interests more effectively than a member who is poor and inarticulate. For example, 66 per cent of British M.P.s have been to university, but less than 2 per cent of the population as a whole; so it could be said that graduates are grossly 'over-represented' in the House of Commons. This tendency applies to both political parties. At least two Labour members in the 1966–70 parliament were self-made millionaires, and one of them was in the Labour cabinet, but they were elected by working class constituencies because the voters trusted them to use their talents in the interests of the poor.[4] Similarly in Hong Kong Urban Council voters have elected Mrs. Elsie Elliott in spite of the fact that, being an expatriate, she is not 'representative' (in this sense of the word, i.e. 'typical') of the Chinese population.

The real criticism of the present unofficial members is not that they are mostly very rich.[5] There is no discredit in being rich (provided the money was honestly gained); wealth can give a man independence from government pressure, while a poor man might be very anxious to please the powers that be in order to get reappointed. What is objectionable is that past Governors have used their power of nomination to appoint to the Council only those, whether rich or not so rich, who were prepared to support the fundamental assumptions of the administration about the proper limits of official activity, the desirable level of public spending, the incidence of the burden of taxation, and the present distribution of privilege and power between employers and employees. All troublemakers who might rock the boat were passed over in favour of those who favoured the official ideology of free enterprise and the maintenance of the *status quo*. Membership of the Council was treated as a reward for meritorious service to the government and the community, which is not unreasonable; but others who had been equally active in community welfare were excluded if their views did not generally coincide with government policy. Such people were available, and some have been appointed to the Council by the present Governor.

If there were more diversity of viewpoints on the Council, it would acquire greater prestige, and hence greater legitimacy, among the population, and this would make its endorsement of official policies that much more valuable to government in helping to build support. Such a Council would be more cantankerous, but in the long term it would probably bring greater stability to the regime.

THE UNOFFICIALS AS PART-TIME LEGISLATORS

It is claimed that the unofficial members are only part-time amateur legislators who must inevitably devote the majority of their time to their professions and private businesses; consequently they do not criticize government policies effectively, they do not carry out a detailed scrutiny of legislation and they do not present worked-out alternative policies for public discussion.[6]

There is clearly a good deal of truth in this argument. Persuasive criticism of a complex bill must be informed by detailed knowledge of the subject matter; otherwise a critic can expect to be overwhelmed by the mass of detail accumulated by the official side when preparing the legislation. Unless he has specialist knowledge, an unofficial needs to be properly briefed if he is to put forward a convincing case. Until the reorganization of the UMELCO office in 1970 there was no proper provision for research assistance of this sort for the unofficials and even now it is only available on a limited scale.[7] In the past government has assumed that members are able to provide such back-up services from their own office staffs. It should not be necessary for members to draw on their private resources in this way. If the membership of the Council is to be broadened in future to comprise a wider spectrum of opinion, an allowance for such expenses similar to that paid to Urban Councillors and greater facilities in the UMELCO office would be highly desirable.

On the other hand, it could be argued that the perfunctory despatch of legislation by the Council is not such a serious defect. Detailed considera-tion of legislation takes place not in the Council, but during the long process of a bill's gestation in the Secretariat. The interest groups which government considers relevant are normally given full opportunity to comment while a bill is being put together and use is made of their technical expertise during the drafting stage. Before it goes to the Executive Council the final draft is considered by the appropriate advisory committee which contains representatives of the main interests involved. Most unofficials sit on several of these committees. When proposing a bill at the opening of the second reading debate the official member in charge is frequently able to assure members that the bill has been unanimously endorsed by the appropriate advisory committee, and as a result unofficials usually see no reason to go over the ground again to no purpose.[8]

The suggestion that unofficials ought to propose worked-out alternative policies for discussion seems impractical. In Britain the Opposition consists of members who have joined the party by deliberate choice because they are in sympathy with its principles, and their loyalty is cemented by the hope of ministerial office when their party comes to power. If their opinions change they can resign from the party, or in the last resort they can be expelled and this will almost certainly end their parliamentary career. The Opposition party has a corporate existence and in order to make a convincing appeal to the electorate it must adhere to a reasonably consistent line of policy. It is on the foundation of this policy consensus that a detailed programme for the future can be drawn up.

None of this applies to the unofficials on the Legislative Council. They are chosen as individuals without any prior policy commitments, and they remain members of the Council as long as the Governor reappoints them. They may have roughly the same upper class background and a general contentment with the *status quo*; but when it comes to detailed questions of policy they do not find it easy to reach an identity of views. They have in the past disagreed among themselves on gambling, on rent control, on marriage reform, on abortion, on the appointment of an Ombudsman, and many other matters.[9] There is similar dissension in British political parties, but there party unity can be imposed by various sanctions and rewards. But in Hong Kong, even if the unofficials did attempt to draw up a detailed programme by majority vote among themselves they would have no means of enforcing it on the minority. Such an exercise would in any case be futile, since, unlike the British Opposition, they can never hope to take office to implement their plans, and such schemes, drawn up without the help of the bureaucracy (and consequently without detailed knowledge of what is and what is not administratively practicable), would be unlikely to appear very impressive either to government or public opinion. A more useful function of the unofficials would seem to be to point out their objections to the policies proposed by government, and then leave it to government to find some alternative scheme, since it alone has the resources for such a task.[10]

It is this activity of the unofficials—telling government what the public will tolerate and what it will not—which seems to me their most valuable contribution to the colonial system of government.[11] In Britain it is the minister in a department with his political knowledge of what the people will stand for who tells his civil servants how far they can go. He has a great incentive to predict popular reactions accurately since if he is wrong his party will risk losing the next general election. But the senior administrators in Hong Kong suffer from a double handicap: they are expatriate and so find it very difficult to understand what the Chinese really feel, however long they may have served here; and secondly there are very few Chinese in positions of real authority in the Secretariat to enlighten them. (Chinese subordinates would find it embarrassing to correct their superiors, and also might fear it would be damaging to their careers.) This gap in understanding is—or should be—filled by the unofficial members of the Executive and Legislative Councils. For example, in 1971 government, following the best modern penological theories, proposed to allow magistrates to pass suspended sentences on first offenders; but the unofficial members voiced the growing concern of ordinary people about crimes of violence and insisted that, in accordance with traditional Chinese views about punishment, all serious crimes must be excluded from this provision.[12] Faced with this unanimous opposition government swiftly gave way. This function of expressing the mind of the people to government is one which only the unofficials can perform with authority, and they do not need to be full-time professional legislators to do it.

Indeed, part-time legislators have positive merits. In Britain the top bankers, businessmen, trade unionists and professional men do not sit in parliament; they consider, rightly, that they have more important matters to attend to than fighting elections and sitting around the chamber of the House of Commons waiting for a division to be called. But because of the limited commitment involved such people do serve as unofficial members in the Executive and Legislative Councils. This offers a number of advantages. It gives prestige to the Council and so gives its endorsement of official policy an added value for government. It also brings to the Council rare expertise in certain fields. For example, Dr. Chung Sze-yuen, a leading industrialist, was described by the Commissioner of Labour as knowing more about the *Factories and Industrial Undertakings Ordinance* than any other person outside the Labour Department;[13] and Mr. J. Saunders was Chairman and Chief Manager of the largest bank in the colony. British M.P.s can only acquire such knowledge at second hand or from past outdated experience and not from present involvement at the highest level. But unofficials in Hong Kong, when dealing with matters relevant to their business or profession—this qualification is important— can speak with unrivalled authority and independence and feel no need to defer to the superior competence of officials, who might be able to mislead a less qualified questioner.

The high status of the unofficials within their own professions and communities gives a further advantage. When government's proposals are judged to be unacceptable by the unofficials, government can then negotiate with them to find a mutually acceptable compromise, knowing that such an agreement will stick. Because of their acknowledged pre-eminence in their own fields, any agreement concluded by the unofficials will normally be accepted as binding by the interests concerned. Once government has satisfied the unofficials it usually feels, with some justification, that other outside critics can be ignored. The unofficials are the intermediaries between government and the governed. Officials can negotiate with them in the confidence that they are dealing with men whose leadership is acknowledged and who can therefore commit the Chinese community to support the terms of any agreement concluded between them.

This situation may be contrasted with that in Britain, where the real bargaining over policy no longer takes place in parliament because M.P.s are professional legislators, second rank figures who do not have the authority to take such decisions. The central issues of economic policy in Britain are hammered out at meetings between Cabinet ministers, and the leaders of the Confederation of British Industries and the Trade Union Congress, by-passing the House of Commons which will subsequently be called upon to ratify willy-nilly the commitments which have been thrashed out elsewhere. One reason why the Legislative Council in Hong Kong has not yet been devalued in this way is because its members are still 'part-time amateurs'.

THE LACK OF A VIGOROUS, OPEN OPPOSITION

It is claimed that officials are never seriously challenged for their actions and called to account for their policies; that proceedings in the Council are ritualistic and unaggressive, more an exchange of bland assurances than the lively cut and thrust of debate; and that members prefer secret negotiations to open argument and so fail in their duty to educate and inform the public.[14]

This description of proceedings in the Council is not an unfair account of the position in the 1950s and early 1960s, but there has been a striking change in the tone of debates in recent years. One indication of the un-officials' increasing activity is the growth in size of the yearly volumes of Hansard. In the early 1960s these filled 300 pages or less, while the latest volumes are over a thousand pages long. Questions asked have increased fivefold since 1966 and about 40 per cent are now followed up with supplementaries.[15] In part this is the result of the increasing complexity of administration and the need to pass about twice the number of ordinances in each session. There is also the fact that the number of unofficials has almost doubled since 1964. But even so it is clear that unofficials are now willing to play a much more active role, and some recent questions, and supplementaries, notably from Sir Yuet-keung Kan, have been biting (see Appendix 8, Document A(i) p. 268).

However, Legislative Council proceedings never approach the fierceness and uproar which are not infrequent in the House of Commons. It would be surprising if they did. In Britain, as soon as one election is over the Opposition is already thinking of the next. Meetings of the House are treated by the minority party of a five-year electoral campaign, designed to impress the voters and gain publicity for their criticisms of the government. There is little expectation that any arguments produced by them will impress the government or modify cabinet decisions to any appreciable extent, much less that they will be able to overthrow the government.[16] The scoring of points in debate or skilfully catching a minister out is a means of raising party morale and strengthening party solidarity, not an attempt to persuade the government to change its mind; divisions are called more to impress the party's supporters outside parliament with the dedication of their representatives than to have any effect on government policy.

Such theatrical displays are quite out of place in an assembly where the unofficials have no electorate to worry about and where there is no clear dividing line between 'Government' and 'Opposition'. Several unofficials are concurrently members of the Executive Council where they have participated in taking many of the policy decisions which later come before the Legislative Council for ratification. In this respect they almost form part of the 'Government', and they may sometimes feel obliged to keep silent in a debate because they have seen confidential background papers which are not available to the rest of the unofficials. Quite apart from this inhibiting factor, the unofficials generally prefer to proceed by quiet reasoned argument than by hectoring denunciations because their tactics are designed to win specific concessions on the immediate matter under discussion. Often the best way to achieve this may be to say nothing in public at all and allow the official side to make its withdrawal from an exposed position with the minimum of fuss, avoiding any open exposition of where the bureaucracy has erred. No parliamentary opposition would willingly pass over a chance to expose ministerial ineptitude. But the unofficials may hope that their reticence on one occasion may be reciprocated by official concessions at a later date.

Moreover, such a method of procedure is more congruent with Oriental traditions of politeness. The Chinese would normally consider it the grossest bad manners to humiliate a dignitary in public, to make him 'lose face'. In the Western, and particularly the American, tradition political conflict and open confrontations are considered a legitimate and wholly admirable way of elucidating and resolving a conflict situation.

But there is no reason to regard this standard as a universal norm, to which every assembly the world over must conform. A traditionally minded Chinese might, with equal justification, regard the usual slanging matches in the legislatures of the Occident as most uncivilized and unbecoming behaviour.[17] It is noteworthy that in almost all the disagreements in the Council between officials and unofficials which have been pressed to a division since the war, the leading role was taken by a non-Chinese unofficial.[18]

It may be objected that though this style of legislative opposition is perhaps explicable in terms of Chinese culture, it is nevertheless undesirable in the modern world, since such private negotiations and compromises fail to educate the people. Many Western political theorists would hold that one of the main functions that a legislature should fulfil is to inform the public about the great issues of public policy, so that they can understand and, if they wish, participate in the great debate.[19] A long Western democratic tradition stresses that popular participation in government is of value in itself for the enrichment of the lives of individuals, quite apart from the hope for beneficial effect on policy decisions.[20] However, the proceedings of both officials and unofficials in the Hong Kong Legislative Council are hardly calculated to stir up intense popular debate. Probably both sides of the Council would regard any such outcome as positively undesirable, if not abhorrent, on grounds of both tradition and expediency. This is not democratic, but it is realistic. Since the colony's international position and the attitudes of China and Britain rule out the possibility of an indigenous elected government in the foreseeable future, what is the point of disturbing the traditional passivity of the population and whetting an appetite for popular participation in government which can never be satisfied and can only lead to frustration?

THE ILLIBERALITY OF THE UNOFFICIALS

Those in the colony who take a stand on such traditional liberal concerns as individual freedom, strict limits on police activity and full legal protection for the rights of the accused do not find much sympathy for their views among the unofficial members.[21] While it is unfair to say that questions of civil liberties are never raised in the Council—Mr. Woo Pak-chuen in particular has spoken on these matters—there is certainly far less interest than is shown by members of the House of Commons.[22] Much of the agitation on such matters arises outside the Council and is largely voiced by expatriates and academic lawyers.

This appears to be a matter on which the unofficial members, in spite of their propertied background, are highly representative of the opinions of the mass of the Chinese population. The rights of the citizen against the state and the inherent value of the individual have never excited much interest among Chinese thinkers, and the Hong Kong public in its present anxieties about violence in the streets would probably support much tougher measures against criminals and more stringent curbs on liberty than government has proposed. Those critics who wish the Council to become more democratic in its composition must accept that this would be likely to make it even less liberal in its attitudes to crime and criminals than it is at present. This is indicated by the fact that Mr. Hilton Cheong-Leen, the only member of the Council who has won an election, welcomed the government's proposal to introduce preventive detention for habitual criminals, a method of dealing with them that had already been tried and then abandoned in Britain.[23]

THE POWER OF THE UNOFFICIALS

Power is notoriously difficult to measure.[24] On many matters the attitudes of the unofficials and government generally coincide and any disagreement is not over ends, but over methods and the detailed application of agreed principles. No question of the power of one party to outvote the other arises and the questions at issue are settled on the basis of administrative convenience and the various pressures involved. For example, it is agreed on both sides that a certain amount of regulation of private enterprise is necessary to protect consumers, but the unofficials are more eager to suggest areas for government intervention than officials are willing to take up. For some time the unofficials have been pressing for the proper control of hire-purchase agreements, on which there is no legislation in the colony, but without success.[25] On the other hand, government at first refused and then gave way to demands that it should set up an organization to test the purity of hall-marked gold articles on sale.[26] In the latter case the demand for action was supported by the Hong Kong Tourist Association which was concerned about the colony's reputation as a 'shoppers' paradise'; in the case of hire-purchase it is only the local population which is liable to suffer.

On matters of Chinese custom and social traditions the views of the unofficials are paramount. In general, government has no desire to institute changes or to stir up trouble for itself by interfering, so it always defers to their superior knowledge.[27] However, in recent years at least one area has emerged where the interests of government and Chinese traditional morality appear to be in conflict. Various forms of gambling are forbidden by law, and this accords with ancient Chinese views. But this vice, or pastime, is apparently extremely popular among Chinese of all classes. Consequently the efforts of the police to enforce the law are ineffective and only expose them to the danger of corruption. It seems clear from various leaks in the press that government would be very glad to legalize certain forms of gambling favoured by the poorer classes and thereby free the police to deal with more serious crimes. However, the opposition of certain unofficial members inhibited the government from taking action until 1973.[28] Having appointed them as the representatives of Chinese opinion the governor feels that he has to accept their views even though in this case they did not appear to correspond with the way the mass of the Chinese actually behave.

At the other extreme there are certain matters where the unofficials recognize that the British administration must have its way and where any attempt to intervene will be brushed aside. These include such matters as the need for a substantial expatriate element in the police force and the administrative class, the retention of certain key posts by expatriates, the payment of the annual Defence Contribution and the question of which foreign airlines shall be granted landing rights at Kai Tak. Normally the unofficials do not challenge government on these matters because all they would achieve would be to cause embarrassment to officials to no purpose; for no concessions can be made on these points so long as Britain remains responsible for Hong Kong.

Finally there is an uncertain area involving such matters as taxation policy, rent control, Crown leases and labour legislation where the outcome of any trial of strength will depend on such matters as the degree of cohesion and persistence of the unofficials, the view of the Governor and his chief advisers (who may be in conflict, when much will depend on the strengths of the personalities involved), the state of public opinion and even possibly the interest shown by London. In such matters one might say that there is a predisposition on government's part to do all they can to accommodate the unofficials in order to boost their prestige, since their general support for government policy is a vital factor in legitimizing an alien regime. But sometimes government may decide that the cost of concessions to the unofficials (either in revenue forgone, or administrative dislocation, or loss of support elsewhere) is too great to be tolerable.

1. This latter point of view is to be found in the *Far Eastern Economic Review*, e.g. 16 July 1970, p. 42. 'The Commissioner of Labour had to eat his words over a controversial move to safeguard workers from unscrupulous employers.... He made the basic mistake of annoying the powerful clique of wealthy, ultra conservative industrialists who have an armlock on the colony's lawmakers.'

2. John Rear, 'One Brand of Politics', in Hopkins, *Hong Kong, the Industrial Colony*. 'When Government has made up its mind about the terms of a particular piece of legislation after the usual process of consultation it usually feels able to ignore most of the small suggestions for amendment occasionally thrown out by unofficial members.' (p. 76).

'Because the interests of employees are not directly represented in these corridors of power, such protective labour legislation as exists has to be fought for tooth and nail by the Labour Department. All too often its proposals, not initially far-reaching are further watered down in the process.' (p. 88)

3. Rear, op.cit. pp. 72 and 73. Strictly speaking, only one unofficial who spoke for the Hong Kong General Chamber of Commerce in the Legislative Council was a 'direct representative' of the business interest, in the sense of being an elected delegate. The rest of the unofficials were chosen by the Governor for their personal qualities and achievements to speak (it is to be hoped) on behalf of Hong Kong as a whole.

4. Robert Maxwell, a publisher, and Harold Lever, a lawyer. The latter was Chief Secretary to the Treasury.

5. This and the following remarks apply mainly to those nominated before 1972. Sir Murray MacLehose has made some appointments outside the normal pattern. For example, Mrs. Joyce Symons, the headmistress of an aided school who has had many years experience in education in Hong Kong, is unlikely to be counted as wealthy by Hong Kong standards; and Mrs. Mary Wong Wing-cheung had been deeply involved in social welfare work for many years.

6. Rear, op.cit. pp. 80, 81 and 116.

7. *Annual Report of the UMELCO Office 1971–72*, p. 9, para. 31; *H. K. Hansard 1971–72*, p. 29.

8. The Legislative Council is very like the House of Commons in this respect. Detailed consultations on bills take place between the civil service and pressure group representatives before a bill is published. The proceedings in the standing committees of the House are not

a painstaking independent scrutiny of the contents of the bill, but the tiresome repetition by opposition members, briefed by pressure groups, of a case that has already been rejected by the minister at the pre-legislative stage. Government members are expected to keep silent and vote as directed, and a bill rarely emerges from committee with any significant changes.

For a full description of what happens in Britain, see G.A. Walkland, *The Legislative Process in Great Britain* (Allen & Unwin, 1968), and J.A.G. Griffin, *The Parliamentary Scrutiny of Government Bills* (Allen & Unwin, 1974).

9. *H.K. Hansard 1960*, pp. 222–31; *1962*, pp. 80ff; *1969–70*, pp. 735ff; *1969*, p. 515. *1969–70*, p. 39. The extent of dissent among the unofficials is difficult to measure, since there are now no divisions, and wherever possible members prefer to keep silent rather than disagree openly with their colleagues. Mr. Ngan Shing-kwan was obviously embarrassed to find himself the only dissentient among the unofficials on the question of legalizing football pools in 1960; so, in spite of his approval of the measure, he abstained: 'You will have gathered, Sir, that I do not believe that the Pools are as bad as they have been made out.... In view, however, of the public opposition to this bill, and the fact that I have no wish to go against the unanimous opinion of my unofficial colleagues on a matter of this nature, I shall abstain from voting.' (*H.K. Hansard 1960*, p. 224.)

10. In fact opposition parties in Britain do not normally draw up detailed programmes for the future. They concentrate on destructive criticism of the government and leave their future plans very vague, for fear of alienating some group of voters if they spelled out what they propose to do in detail.

11. More accurately, the unofficials can best tell government the reactions of that *section of the public* they themselves know most intimately.

12. *H. K. Hansard 1970–71*, pp. 348–56.

13. *H. K. Hansard 1969*, p. 38.

14. Rear, op.cit. pp. 82, 83, 85 and 89.

15. See table and details on p. 121.

16. The Cabinet does sometimes make notable retreats, but this is normally in deference to the opinions of its own backbenchers, or because it is afraid of losing votes, and not because of the demands of the Opposition. In fact the tactics of the unofficials are much more like the activities of the government backbenchers in the Commons rather than those of the Opposition.

17. This is of course no longer true of modern China. Dialectical materialism emphasizes the value of conflict, as was particularly seen in the excesses of the Cultural Revolution.

18. The most notable exception was the division forced by Mr. Kan Yuet-keung in 1967 over the Defence Contribution—see p. 93 above, and Appendix 6 pp. 260–2. In 1966 Mr. Wong Sien-bing vigorously attacked the bill which raised the salaries and profits tax to 15 per cent and said that he would vote against the second reading; but he did not press his opposition to a division, *H.K. Hansard 1966*, pp. 306–15.

19. See for example, A. Kornberg and L.D. Musolf (eds.), *Legislatures in Developmental Perspective* (Duke University Press, Durham, N.C., 1970), esp. pp. 39–51.

20. Also in modern China intense political participation is required of every citizen, and compulsorily enforced.

21. Rear, op.cit. pp. 87 and 92.

22. See Chapter 5, note 8, p. 56. The predominant view among the unofficials was voiced by Mr. Wong Sien-bing, 'In modern jurisprudence, too much emphasis is laid on individual justice and too little on social justice. Fairness to the individual must be weighed against fairness to society.' *H.K. Hansard 1972–73*, p. 898.

23. *H.K. Hansard 1972–73*, p. 898.

24. For a discussion, see R.A. Dahl, *Modern Political Analysis* (Prentice-Hall, 1963), Chapter 5.

25. *H. K. Hansard 1965*, p. 165; *1967*, p. 163; *1969–70*, pp. 831–3; and *1973–74*, p. 866; all these are remarks and questions on hire-purchase control by Mr. Woo Pak-chuen.

26. See *South China Morning Post*, 23 October 1971 and 4 November 1971, and *H.K. Hansard 1971–72*, p. 155.

27. In 1971 the Attorney General proposed to abolish the legal actions for damages for adultery, seduction and enticement, following the pattern of recent law reforms in Britain. However, the unofficials felt this protection for marriage was still needed in Chinese society, and government immediately dropped the proposed change, *H.K. Hansard 1970–71*, pp. 725–7.

28. For examples of 'leaks', see *South China Morning Post*, 5 June 1972 and 19 October 1972, 'We are aware that consideration is being given by the government to introduce some form of legalized gambling....'.

The opposition to any such relaxation was led by Sir Cho-yiu Kwan, the senior Chinese member of the Executive Council and chairman of the Gambling Policy Committee (who died in December 1971). The main opponent on the Legislative Council was Mrs. Li Shu-pui (see for example, *H.K. Hansard 1972–73*, p. 66). After her retirement from the Council in August 1973 government felt able to introduce a bill to permit the Jockey Club to organize off-course betting on horse racing, under strict controls. This bill was welcomed by the senior unofficial member, Mr. Woo Pak-chuen, and passed without opposition, *H.K. Hansard 1973–74*, pp. 47, 146, and 197. Mr. Szeto Wai said on the second reading. 'I agree— and my unofficial colleagues go along with me—that the provisions of this bill represent a sensible approach to the problem.'

12 Local Government: The New Territories

THEIR ACQUISITION: PROBLEM OF THE WALLED CITY OF KOWLOON

In 1895 China was defeated by Japan, and the Western powers promptly took advantage of her weakness to enforce further concessions. Britain demanded and obtained the lease of the New Territories for ninety-nine years from 1 July 1898; but as a sop to Chinese dignity the imperial officials then stationed in the old walled city of Kowloon were allowed to continue to exercise jurisdiction there 'except so far as may be inconsistent with the military requirements for the defence of Hong Kong'. British forces took over effective control of the New Territories in April 1899 against light resistance from the local inhabitants. Using this opposition and the alleged complicity of the imperial officials as an excuse the British expelled them and their bodyguard in May; and in December the recently signed Convention with China was unilaterally amended by a British Order in Council which declared that the city of Kowloon should be 'part and parcel of Her Majesty's Colony of Hong Kong...as if it had originally formed part of the said Colony'. The pretext given was that the presence of the officials had been found to be inconsistent with the military requirements for the defence of Hong Kong. The Chinese government protested but was impotent to take any action; the walled city soon became deserted and the British, who had never intended to make more than a token concession to Chinese feelings, assumed that the matter was now closed.[1]

But subsequent Chinese governments, both the Nationalists and their Communist successors, have never abandoned their claim to jurisdiction over the area of the old walled city, even though its boundaries are now somewhat indeterminate, since the ruins of the original walls were quarried by the Japanese during 1943–4 to provide materials for the enlargement of Kai Tak airport. The first reassertion of China's rights took place in 1933 when the Hong Kong government proposed to resettle a few squatters who had taken up residence in the ruins. When China protested, the British government at that time was unwilling to exacerbate relations with the Nationalist government by arguing the point, and most of the squatters were persuaded to move out by an offer of generous compensation. The threat of similar evictions in 1948 and 1962 likewise provoked Chinese protests at such a 'gross violation' of her sovereignty and on both occasions the Hong Kong government preferred to defer action indefinitely to avoid diplomatic complications. Legally the British Order in Council is recognized as binding upon the Courts of Hong Kong and the police patrol the area. Any offenders arrested there are put on trial under Hong Kong law. But by longstanding convention no attempt is made to enforce the provisions of the *Buildings Ordinance* or the law of Landlord and Tenant. The inhabitants pay no rates on their property and no piped water supply is officially provided though the inhabitants have made their own arrangements from wells and illegal connections to water-pipes outside. For the moment this expedient compromise suits both Britain and China, so long as the government in Peking is anxious to foster friendly relations with the colony. But if China ever wished to cause trouble or put pressure on the Hong Kong government, the status of the 'Walled City' would be a very convenient issue to raise.

THE ADMINISTRATION OF THE NEW TERRITORIES

From the beginning no legal distinction was made between the leased territory and the original area of the colony which had been ceded to Britain in perpetuity by the treaties of 1842 and 1860. All laws and ordinances in force in Hong Kong were made applicable to the New Territories after a declared date, and the area of the Kowloon peninsula north of Boundary Street and south of the hills was attached for administrative purposes to the urban area under the general supervision of the existing Secretariat for Chinese Affairs. The rest of the leased area was administered by newly appointed District Officers whose first duties were to enforce law and order and carry out a land survey. All the original inhabitants at the time of the British take-over were confirmed in the possession of their existing farms ('the Old Schedule Lots') and the remaining land was deemed to be unallocated Crown Land, the leases of which could be sold by public auction (the 'New Grant Lots'). At the time of the occupation the Governor, Sir Henry Blake, issued a proclamation promising, 'Your commercial and landed interests will be safeguarded and your usages and good customs will not in any way be interfered with'.[2] This declaration has much the same status in the New Territories as Captain Elliot's 1841 proclamation has for the rest of the colony.

Between the wars the administration of this isolated and scattered population presented few problems, apart from chronic unemployment. There were two District Officers, North and South, who also served as magistrates for criminal and civil matters. They were mainly concerned with the collection of Crown rents and the control and allocation of land, but they also worked in cooperation with the Police and officials of the Agriculture, Fisheries and Forestry departments and did any other jobs which government wanted done, sometimes with help from other government departments, but usually on their own.

This situation was much changed after the war with the influx of refugees and the growing prosperity of the colony. This made more money available for rural development and also made it necessary for the New Territories to provide space for housing and industrial use. These developments greatly increased the work load of the District Officers, both in their traditional field of land administration, and also in public health, licensing, squatter control and labour disputes. This burden was partly offset by the deployment of specialized staff from other departments to the New Territories. For example, a full-time magistrate was appointed in 1954 who took over all the police court work, and all civil jurisdiction was taken over by the District Court in 1961. In 1958 the District Officers ceased to act as local agents for the Registrar of Births; in 1959 the Social Welfare Department set up its first office in the New Territories; and in 1960 the Urban Service Department took over responsibility for refuse removal, sanitation and public health. Government decided in principle in 1959 that the District Commissioner's organization ought to retain only such executive powers as were inseparable from his primary political functions, on the understanding that he would be constantly consulted on the development of all departmental, professional and technical services.[3] However, control of land still remains in the hands of the District Officers because of its crucial importance to a rural community.

Until 1974 the New Territories were divided into five districts, each under a District Officer with a staff of a hundred or more. Their work was coordinated by the District Commissioner, whose office is in Kowloon. The area and population of these five districts, based on the 1971 census with an estimate of the marine population added, was as follows:[4]

	Square Miles	Population
Tai Po	123	167,500
Yuen Long	86	181,000
Tsuen Wan	26	278,000
Sai Kung	67	22,200
Islands	63	45,500

In April 1974 two new districts were created, making seven in all. The Tai Po district was divided to create the new district of Sha Tin, and the Yuen Long district was similarly split to create the district of Tuen Mun (Castle Peak). These new districts were formed to deal more effectively with the development of the new towns being built there.

At the same time the post of District Commissioner was upgraded to 'Secretary for the New Territories', becoming the equal of the new policy secretaries set up in the McKinsey reorganization (see Chapter 7, p. 75).

In spite of the loss of most of their executive powers the District Officers and their staff still have plenty to do. Their remaining functions may be roughly listed as follows, though the order of importance may alter at different times.[5]

1. *Gathering political intelligence*, in the broadest sense. District Officers need to know what is going on in their area and where trouble is likely to occur so that preventive measures can be taken. This may involve anticipating communist subversion, as in 1967, or keeping an eye on an ancient feud between neighbouring villages which might erupt into violence.[6]

2. *Representing the interests of the New Territories to higher authority.*

The Secretary for the New Territories sits on the Legislative Council and on various boards and committees such as the Town Planning Board, the Housing Authority, the Advisory Committee on Environmental Pollution, and the Transport Advisory Committee. He is able to use these and similar opportunities to see that the needs of the rural areas for their proper share of amenities are not neglected.

3. *Coordinating the activities of government departments at the local level.* All departments operating in the New Territories need to work closely with the District Officer who knows the peculiar problems of his area. It is his interest to see that the possibly conflicting plans of different agencies fit in with each other and go forward harmoniously with proper consideration for the wishes and anxieties of the local residents. The complexity of this task is particularly seen when a new reservoir is planned or a new development is being prepared for housing or industry. This involves roads, water supply, drainage, bus services, fire stations, clinics, police stations, telephone services, schools and much else besides.

4. *Explaining and supporting government programmes.* This may mean, for example, persuading villagers to adopt improved methods of sanitation recommended by the Medical and Health Department; or to have their livestock inoculated by the Department of Agriculture, or to plant more trees. This activity by District Officers is supplemented by the work of an Army Information Team and a civilian Information Team which visit all parts to show films and give tape-recorded programmes.

5. *Land administration.* The New Territories Administration is responsible for approving land exchanges, for varying the terms of leases and granting new ones, and for approving plans for new buildings within villages. When land is required for government purposes District Officers attempt to negotiate an agreed sum in compensation for the termination of the lease or arrange for the grant of a lease on other land in exchange. Where a new development threatens the *fung shui* (geomantic propitiousness) of a village they arrange compensation or pay for the appropriate rituals to be performed.

6. *Controlling squatters.* Refugees have been allowed to put up temporary huts in certain areas, but constant checking is necessary to see that they keep within the permitted locations.

7. *Encouraging local development.* If a group of villagers agree to supply voluntary labour to improve their locality, for instance, by building a new pathway, bridge or breakwater, or by piping water from a local spring, the New Territories Administration will help them by supplying the materials needed (cement, bars, piping etc.) and specialist advice from a small engineering unit attached from the Public Works Department. Normally the initiative for such schemes should come from the local people but District Officers can make suggestions and draw attention to the assistance that is available.[7]

8. *Arbitrating disputes.* Although the District Officers have now been relieved of all their judicial powers there is a tradition that any individual who lives in the New Territories has the right to approach his District Officer with a personal problem at any time. The courts are often distrusted

and many prefer to settle a dispute over land, debts or marital problems by asking the District Officer to act as a mediator, perhaps with the help of the official village representative or the chairman of the rural committee.[8] District Officers are colloquially known as *fu-mu-kuan* (father-mother officer) as were the Ching imperial officials before them.

9. *Assisting in educational administration.* District Officers help the Director of Education to evaluate applications from villagers and groups of sponsors for land and subsidies to build or extend schools. District Office staff then supervise the construction of the building and pay out the government subsidy on behalf of the Education Department.

10. *Organizing relief work in emergencies.* When a typhoon strikes, or when there is a landslide, a fire or a flood, the District Officer is the man on the spot to take charge until specialist emergency services arrive and to organize immediate relief for the victims, providing meals and temporary accommodation.

11. *Social Welfare activities.* In the remoter areas the District Office acts as an agent for the Social Welfare Department in administering the Public Assistance Scheme and also in distributing various aid funds. After a disaster, teams from each District Office assess the damage and pay out grants for rehabilitation from the Community Relief Trust. Villagers may also get informal help when they are having difficulties with a government department. On occasion the District Officer may act as a substitute Ombudsman since the services of the UMELCO office are far too distant to be of use.[9]

12. *Liaison with the British Army.* This particularly involves sorting out problems over land use and arranging compensation payments when crops are damaged by stray shells from a nearby range or by military manoeuvres.

13. *Organizing Recreational Activities and Youth Camps.* Money is provided by the Social Welfare Department to finance such activities, particularly in the summer holidays, and various local coordinating committees are set up. Plans are also being drawn up by the New Territories Advisory Committee on Recreational Development and Nature Conservation under the Chairmanship of the Secretary for the New Territories to set up four or more country parks.

VILLAGE REPRESENTATIVES, RURAL COMMITTEES AND THE HEUNG YEE KUK

In their manifold activities District Officers are often advised and assisted by an elaborate system of locally elected elders and councils who maintain a channel of communication between government and their communities. Though the New Territories are, in parts, the most underdeveloped area of the colony they have a formalized representative system which is in some respects more advanced than that of the urban areas.

The lowest tier is formed by more than 900 village representatives who are elected or appointed according to local custom by the heads of households in the 651 villages throughout the New Territories. A village may

have up to a maximum of three representatives, each nominally representing about fifty families; in practice this means that the largest villages
and towns are under-represented. The person selected by the villagers
must be approved by the Secretary for the New Territories, and if this
approval is not granted or recognition is later withdrawn he is not entitled
to participate in the elections for the Rural Committee. During the 1967
disturbances the recognition of forty-one representatives was withdrawn
because they had engaged in subversive activities.[10] This power has not
been used since then, except in the case of one rural committee chairman
who was convicted of bribery.

The 900 village representatives are grouped into twenty-seven Rural
Committees. The constitutions of these Committees vary slightly, but all
except one elect an Executive Committee with a Chairman and Vice-
Chairman every two years by a secret ballot of the village representatives
in their area. These Executive Committees keep in close touch with the
District Officer, acting as spokesmen for local public opinion and
arbitrating in clan and family disputes. They are paid a small sum by the
government to cover their running costs. The Secretary for the New
Territories is empowered to withhold or withdraw his approval from any
Rural Committee and if this were to happen the Committee would then
become an unlawful society under the *Societies Ordinance* and its Chairman and Vice-Chairman would be disqualified from membership of the
Heung Yee Kuk.[11] This power has never yet been exercised.

The apex of this pyramid of representation is the Heung Yee Kuk,
(normally translated as 'Rural Consultative Committee'). This was
originally set up in 1926 as an assembly of appointed village elders to
advise government, but over time it developed into a self-perpetuating
body, making its own choice of members to fill any vacancies that arose.[12]
In 1957 this system broke down in dissension when a number of elders
resigned and the majority faction claimed that the Kuk was the only body
entitled to speak authoritatively on behalf of the people of the New
Territories and that government had no right to interfere with its own
constitution.[13] Such an assertion was obviously unacceptable to government; recognition of the Kuk was withdrawn, making it an unlawful
society; and a new ordinance was passed reconstituting the Kuk as a
statutory advisory body with a completely new organization.

Under this new constitution the Full Council of the Kuk consists of
the Chairmen and Vice-Chairmen of the 27 Rural Committees, the
unofficial Justices of the Peace in the New Territories (14 in 1973),[14] and
also 21 Special Councillors who are elected every two years by the Chairmen, Vice-Chairmen and unofficial J.P.s sitting together as an electoral
college. These Special Councillors are elected either from among the other
village representatives or from other residents of the New Territories.
The latter are, like the village representatives, subject to the veto of the
Secretary for the New Territories, though there is the possibility of appeal
to the Governor in Council.[15] For the purposes of this election the New
Territories are divided into three electoral districts—Yuen Long, Tai Po
and Southern. Seven Special Councillors are elected from each district by

the Chairmen, Vice-Chairmen and unofficial J.P.s who reside there.

The Full Council of the Kuk normally meets only once every six months. Its most important function is to elect its own Executive Committee, which consists of a Chairman and two Vice-Chairmen, each of which must come from a different electoral district, and fifteen ordinary members from among the members of the Full Council. These then sit with the Chairman of all the twenty-seven Rural Committees and the unofficial J.P.s to form the Executive Committee. This Committee meets monthly with the Secretary for the New Territories to discuss matters of interest to the New Territories and give its views on bills which are to be presented to the Legislative Council. Since 1972 it has also set up fourteen specialized sub-committees on Public Works, Education, Transport, etc., whose chairmen meet with the heads of departments responsible for their areas of concern.

According to the *Heung Yee Kuk Ordinance*, its functions are to promote mutual cooperation within the New Territories, and between the New Territories and government, to advise government on social and economic developments, and to encourage traditional customs and functions. Unlike the Urban Council, it has no executive powers, and its only activity is to offer advice. Since this advice is largely given to the New Territories Administration, which itself now has only limited executive authority, this pyramidal structure of indirect elections—(the villagers elect their representatives, who in turn elect the rural committee chairmen, who in turn elect the Full Council of the Kuk, who in turn elect the Kuk's Executive Committee)—might seem unnecessarily elaborate.

However the influence of the Kuk is much greater than its constitutional functions might suggest. All governments need the consent of the governed to function efficiently, but this is particularly true in the rural areas of the New Territories where the District Officers must largely work by persuasion and need the willing cooperation of the villagers to achieve their ends. In 1958, when the then Heung Yee Kuk was at loggerheads with the government, this dispute created distrust and soured relationships between the administration and sections of the rural population. In one incident serious local opposition temporarily halted work on the construction of catchwater channels for the new Tai Lam Chung reservoir since the farmers in the area refused to believe the assurances of officials that the construction work would not interfere with their own essential supply of water for irrigation. The colony was at that time suffering from a severe water shortage and completion of the reservoir project was a high priority task. Coercive force could no doubt have been used and the work completed under police protection, but there would then have been the danger that the channels might be destroyed as soon as the police guard was withdrawn. The administration had no choice but to defer operations until it had succeeded in persuading the farmers that their livelihood would not be endangered.[16]

Since government needs the public endorsement of its policies by the Heung Yee Kuk in order to administer the New Territories effectively and economically, the Kuk is in a strong bargaining position to put pressure on government for modifications of policy. For example, in 1970 government put forward an amendment to the *Prevention of Bribery Bill* which allowed officials to accept entertainment from members of the public without being deemed to be guilty of corruption. The Attorney General told the Legislative Council that one of the parties pressing for this amendment had been the Heung Yee Kuk, and according to newspaper reports the councillors had threatened to stage a mass resignation if their traditional custom of lavishing hospitality on members of the administration became a criminal offence.[17] In 1972 the Kuk achieved a similar success when it threatened to organize a protest march to Government House to demand changes in land policy and the relaxation of building regulations about village houses. Within three weeks the Commissioner for the New Territories was able to announce that agreement had been reached with representatives of the Kuk on all their demands.[18]

THE FUTURE PATTERN OF ADMINISTRATION

The organizational pattern described above was devised to suit a scattered rural population, and it is still largely run in the interests of the indigenous inhabitants whose ancestral roots in the New Territories go back for generations. In practice only heads of families who have lived in a village since before the war are usually allowed to take part in the choice of the village representative; new settlers are thus effectively disenfranchized unless they are prominent enough to be elected as Special Councillors or appointed as Justices of the Peace. But the original inhabitants are now a decreasing minority as a result of squatting on waste land by refugees and the building of new housing estates to decant the growing population of the urban areas. The 1971 census found that out of a total New Territories land population of 665,700 only 82,706 people—less than 13 per cent—claimed that Hong Kong was their family's place of origin.[19] Further massive housing developments are projected in the next ten years. The town of Tsuen Wan grew from 61,000 in 1961 to over 300,000 in 1973, and is planned to reach 850,000 by 1983. By the same date Sha Tin and Tuen Mun are each expected to house 500,000 people.

At present District Officers keep in touch with urban opinion by their contacts with local Chambers of Commerce and various clan, welfare, trade and guild associations. In Tsuen Wan and Yuen Long these groups have formed federations with official encouragement to make it easier for them to express their views to the administration. Similarly, the New Territories General Chamber of Commerce has been formed as a federation of the Chambers in the eleven largest towns.[20] But such improvised channels of communications are not entirely satisfactory and as long ago as 1966 the Dickinson Working Party on Local Administration recommended that a proper Urban Council should be set up for Tsuen Wan and subsequently also in other towns when their size justified it. To date no action has been taken on this proposal, but clearly some such development will be needed in future, since it is difficult to see how the rural committee/Heung Yee Kuk system can be adapted to take account of the needs of the new urban areas. However, the Kuk will certainly object to any innovation which would derogate from its present role as the leading spokesman to government on behalf of the New Territories.[21]

1. The details in this and the following paragraph are taken from Endacott, *Government and People in Hong Kong*, pp. 126–34; P. Wesley-Smith, 'The Kowloon Walled City', *Hong Kong Law Journal*, Vol. 3, pt. 1, 1973, pp. 67–96; *Far Eastern Economic Review*, 20 February 1969, pp. 332–4. *House of Lords Debates*, 11 June 1974, cols 463–76; and *China Mail*, 16 May 1974.

2. *Supplement to the Hong Kong Government Gazette 1900* (after p. 635) p. xxx, Appendix IX.

3. District Commissioner, New Territories *Annual Departmental Report 1958/59* para. 23.

4. *H.K. Hansard 1972–73*, pp. 702f. *Annual Report 1972–73*, p. 13. The land population was 665,700 and the marine population 28,215 (p. 6).

5. The list of functions has been compiled from reading all the N.T. Annual Reports since 1946.

6. For an example of this, see Appendix 10, Document ii, p. 276.

7. *The Annual Report 1960–61*, pp. 62–6 gives a detailed account of these local public works. In that year projects completed included 192,903 feet of pathways, 19,286 feet of drainage channelling, 71 dams, 50 footbridges, 37 village playgrounds, 28 wells and 14 small piers.

8. *Annual Report 1954–55*, para. 72 and *1958–59*, para. 20.

9. In the past District Offices acted as a kind of employment agency, finding work with the Army or government departments, and organizing the recruitment of labour for phosphate mining on Ocean and Nauru islands and for the Brunei oilfields. This activity of the N.T. administration is last mentioned in the 1955–56 report. In recent years there has been considerable emigration to Britain to set up Chinese restaurants.

10. *Annual Report 1967–68*, p. 3.

11. *Heung Yee Kuk Ordinance* (Cap. 1097) clause 3 (3) and *Societies Ordinance* (Cap. 151) clause 7 (1) and (2).

12. Endacott, *Government and People in Hong Kong*, p. 134.

13. This is the account of the dispute given by the Attorney General, in *H. K. Hansard 1959*, p. 253. The full details are very complex; complaints over land resumption and compensation were also a factor.

14. This excludes the District Officers who are all Justices of the Peace.

15. When the *Heung Yee Kuk Ordinance* was passed in 1959 the Attorney General gave an assurance that such power of veto would be used in the most exceptional circumstances, 'perhaps in the case of a candidate who either had a serious criminal record or who, on the basis of his past activities, was known to be likely to introduce into the conduct of rural affairs irrelevant matters related to international political issues'. *H. K. Hansard 1959*, p. 268.

16. This paragraph is largely taken from the *Annual Report* for 1958–59, pp. lf. The first words of the report are, 'This was not an easy year'.

17. *H.K. Hansard 1970–71*, p. 278. *Far Eastern Economic Review*, 12 December 1970, p. 51.

18. Reports in the *South China Morning Post*, 26 February, 3, 9, and 18 March 1972.

19. *Hong Kong Population and Housing Census 1971, Main Report*, p. 15. The indigenous population has declined absolutely as well as relative to newcomers: between 1961 and 1971 those living on land in the New Territories who claimed Hong Kong origin declined from 99,868 to 82,706.

20. *Annual Report 1972–73*, p. 3.

21. *H.K. Hansard 1968*, pp. 18f. *Annual Report 1971–72*, p. 20.

13 Local Government: The City District Offices

HONG KONG was taken over in 1841 primarily to further British trade, and until comparatively recent times most of the activities of government were directed to provide the services needed by the port and the business community. So long as the Chinese population kept within the law and paid their taxes they were largely left to administer their own affairs under their traditional system of elders. The main channel of communication between government and the Chinese community was the Secretary for Chinese Affairs* and his staff who were required to maintain and improve their contacts with all lawful Chinese societies and advise government departments on Chinese attitudes and traditions. Over the years this department has also acquired a number of other miscellaneous functions which include the control of narcotics, the administration of the Landlord and Tenant Ordinances and land matters in Kowloon and Hong Kong Island; it also assists in the management of various trusts and charitable foundations.

In the discharge of its primary duty of liaison with the Chinese population the department up to 1967 adopted a rather passive role.[1] It kept in touch through its officers with the large colony-wide social service organizations such as the Tung Wah Group of Hospitals and the Po Leung Kuk, and also with a multiplicity of religious, district and clansmen's associations. In 1949–50 encouragement was given to the formation or revival of Kaifong Welfare Associations on a traditional pattern to attend to the social needs of a local area, providing clinics, libraries and recreational facilities and rendering assistance to the victims of typhoons and other natural disasters; but generally the initiative in founding such societies was left to local residents. Such traditional associations tend to be officered by a very small minority of the population, active middle-class citizens with some ambitions in public life, and their reports upon popular opinion are likely to be coloured by their perceptions of what government officials would prefer to hear. Moreover, such contacts can give little insight into the views of the poorer sections of the community, who would be unlikely to join such associations.[2] The only

*From 1845 to 1913 this official was entitled the Registrar General; from 1913 to 1969, the Secretary for Chinese Affairs; from 1969 to 1973, the Secretary for Home Affairs. Finally since 1973, following the McKinsey reorganization, he has become the Director of Home Affairs.

attempt to make wider contacts with the general public was the provision in the early 1960s of two tenancy enquiry bureaux and four public enquiry centres manned by junior staff and providing simple information about government rules and procedures.

These deficiencies in organization did not appear in the ten-year period of calm which followed the Kowloon Riot of 1956. But in 1966 government was caught unprepared by disorderly hooliganism occasioned by a proposal by the Star Ferry Company to increase the fares on its cross harbour services. The Commission of Enquiry set up to investigate these disturbances blamed the administration for failing to communicate its views effectively and for the existence of a gap between government and people which was aggravated by the excessive centralization of the government machinery. It advocated as a partial remedy the setting up of more intermediary bodies at the local level (see Appendix 11, Document A, p. 278). This conclusion, reached by a commission the majority of whose members were not government officers, was reinforced by the report of an internal working party set up to look into the question of local administration. A minority reservation to the main report signed by the senior ranking Chinese officer in the administrative service, Mr. Paul Tsui, and two others, emphasized the frustrations of the people in the urban areas who felt that they lacked sufficient means of access to put their point of view to those in authority and proposed the early introduction of a system of regional administration in the urban areas to improve understanding, which should be modelled on that prevailing in the New Territories (see Appendix 11, Document B, p. 279).

The confrontation of 1967 further underlined the relevance of these suggested measures. Though the inspiration for the riots came from outside the colony the administration was certainly surprised at the extent of anti-government feeling which was revealed. New initiatives were clearly needed to convince the population of government's essential benevolence and to improve the efficiency of services at the local level. One expedient was the City District Officer Scheme.

The central idea of the scheme was to set up a 'regionalized, approachable local manifestation of the central government' to carry out the same 'political and coordinating functions' which are the responsibility of the District Officers in the New Territories.[3] In the original area of the colony specialized government departments had been set up to run particular government services. Since any part of the city can be reached in less than an hour there had appeared to be no advantage in setting up local offices, and the coordination of the work of different departments was managed by committees in the central government offices or on a personal, *ad hoc* basis. Such a system could work effectively in pre-war Hong Kong with an urban population of 700,000 when the public service was relatively small. But it was not so well adapted in the 1960s to a population of 3,250,000 and a vastly expanded bureaucracy which was trying to do far more than its predecessors of the 1930s. As new government departments were created (e.g. the Social Welfare Department in 1958, the Transport Department in 1966) better coordination of the increasingly fragmented work of these agencies became more necessary, but also more difficult to arrange in the absence of a territorially based organization at the local level. The aim of the C.D.O. scheme, in the words of the original report, was to 'superimpose on the functionally oriented executive departments a geographically based advisory and coordinating organization in order to strengthen the ability of the Government to give everyone a fair hearing and a fair share of the services which the community can afford'.[4]

As soon as the worst of the confrontation was over at the end of 1967 detailed planning for the scheme began and there was great pressure to get it into operation as quickly as possible. A preliminary outline of the proposal and the first request for money was put to the Legislative Council in January 1968, the first offices were opened in May and the last C.D.O. was appointed in January 1969. The urban area was divided into ten city districts, corresponding to the police divisional areas, four on Hong Kong Island and six in Kowloon (which has the larger population). Each district was originally staffed by a general grade administrative officer, eight executive officers and a number of junior staff, and additional sub-offices have now been set up in seven districts. The Executive Officers were volunteers taken from all departments of government who were expected to benefit from three years of dealing directly with the public before they returned to their specialized duties. The offices have been set up in central shopping areas with attractive window displays to encourage people to come in. The old public enquiry centres have been incorporated in the scheme and enquiries dealt with rose from 300,000 to more than a million in three years.

The functions of the C.D.O.s can be roughly listed as follows:[5]

1. *Explaining and defending government policy.* This is partly achieved by making information available at the C.D.O. offices, but senior staff are expected to go out and actively seize any opportunity to speak to groups or individuals so as to put across the official point of view.

2. *Reporting back to government on the opinions and attitudes of the public.* This is partly achieved by noting comments made by those who come to ask questions at the enquiry counters and partly by cultivating contacts with as many local associations as possible. Surveys are also carried out with the help of student volunteers, sometimes in response to a specific request from government (e.g. to ascertain public reactions to the clock changes in summer time).[6] Each week a digest of local opinion, 'Town Talk', is made up and sent to headquarters.

3. *Liaison with and coordination of the work of departments in the district.* For example, organizing a campaign to improve conditions at the Aldrich Bay squatter area involved the Resettlement Department, the Urban Services Department, the Public Works Department and the Police. At the request of the Urban Services Department district Hawker Consultative Committees have been set up, and the C.D.O.s are always consulted before a hawker clearance operation is undertaken. At headquarters there is an interdepartmental committee concerned with the environment and amenities of housing estates; local sub-committees of this body at district level are chaired by the C.D.O. and include representa-

tives of the Public Works, Urban Services, Social Welfare, Education, Housing, Transport and Police Departments.

4. *Drawing attention to neglected local needs.* These may be matters which are not the specific responsibility of any department, or minor improvements which are too insignificiant to be noticed at the centre but make a great deal of difference to local residents. For example, getting a standpipe for a squatter area or a supply of low-voltage electricity (which does not constitute so much of a fire hazard), arranging for a bus service to a neglected area, levelling waste land for a football pitch with help from the Army, or asking the P.W.D. to repair broken pavements.

5. *Stimulating local activity and community involvement.* This has been a major focus of activity since the encouragement of local associations to take on new responsibilities, and the formation of new groups not only provides help and opportunities for individuals, but also enables the C.D.O. staff to enlarge their range of contacts and build up a favourable image of government's concern. Examples include the organization of swimming competitions and football matches, entertainments and variety programmes, outings for the handicapped and aged, picnics, youth camps, seminars on career prospects and tutorial classes for the underprivileged (with student help). Various Youth and Recreational Committees have been set up, help has been given in the formation of management committees in multi-storey buildings (in accordance with an ordinance passed in 1970) and district federations of these committees have been encouraged. Seventy-four area committees were set up by the C.D.O.s in 1972 for the 'Clean Hong Kong' campaign.

6. *Providing services for individuals.* All C.D.O.s are Justices of the Peace and can witness sworn declarations. Advice is given to those in difficulties with government departments and help may be provided in putting a case, though C.D.O.s are not in general expected to act as amateur Ombudsmen. Matrimonial problems may be brought to the office and some districts have set up a Family Disputes Mediation Panel with the help of the local kaifongs. In other cases those in trouble may be referred to the local offices of the Social Welfare Department or Legal Aid Department.[7]

7. *Rendering relief in emergencies.* Unlike their counterparts in the New Territories, C.D.O.s are unlikely to be required to take charge in a fire or other disaster since the fire brigade or other civil aid services can quickly reach the scene. But they often coordinate relief work and find accommodation for the victims with the aid of the Social Welfare Department and the kaifongs or district disaster committee.

All these functions can be paralleled in the similar list of the activities of District Officers in the New Territories. The main difference is that C.D.O.s have no executive powers whatsoever and so do not spend a large amount of their time on problems of land administration and the control of building. Similar problems of land resumption, lease exchanges and compensation arise in the rural areas of Hong Kong Island which are included in the Western and Eastern City Districts, but such matters are dealt with by the specialized staff in the Lands Division of the department headquarters and the local C.D.O. is only involved in an advisory capacity. This explains the relatively small size of the C.D.O. staffs. The normal city district has a staff of about twenty in all, dealing with a compact population of more than 300,000. No district in the New Territories except Tsuen Wan approaches this figure, yet even the smallest district there, Sai Kung with 22,500 people, has a normal staff of over 80 because of the distances involved and the land administration for which it is responsible.[8]

In general, the C.D.O. scheme has been well received and it has had a very good press. However a number of criticisms of details have been made: that C.D.O.s are transferred too frequently; that some of those appointed have been too junior for their suggestions and complaints to carry weight with departments; and that they lack sufficiently wide experience to make useful recommendations for changes. The first charge is an unwarranted generalization from a few instances where temporary appointments have had to be made to fill an unexpected hiatus. In fact the average length of posting for the first ten C.D.O.s was twenty-two months, and three of them remained in the same district for more than three years.[9]

There is more substance in the other criticisms. Up to March 1973 twenty-three officers had been put in charge of districts. The average length of service as an Administrative Officer or at an equivalent rank (i.e. an Assistant Secretary for Chinese Affairs), previous to their appoint- ment was just under four years, the longest being ten years and the shortest a few months. Three were made C.D.O.s within a year of entering the Administrative Class but two of these had already served for a number of years as Executive Officers. District Officers in the New Territories are usually more senior than this. Over the same five year period D.O.s on first appointment averaged over six years previous service in the Admin- istrative Class. It is certainly desirable that more senior officers should be made C.D.O.s (provided such men are available) so that they can speak with greater authority when dealing with departments. But in recent years the strength of the Administrative Class has always been less than the permitted establishment and so it is probably unavoidable that C.D.O. posts, which have no specific executive responsibilities, should take a lower priority at a time of staff shortage. In order to broaden their outlook and provide points for comparison three C.D.O.s and seven other staff went on a fourteen-day study tour of Singapore in 1971. This tour was repeated for other officers in 1973.[10]

A more general criticism is that so far there has been no attempt to use the C.D.O. organization as a basis for some kind of elected local government bodies on the lines suggested in the Dickinson Report.[11] One district appears to have set up a formal District Consultative Committee,[12] but in general it seems that C.D.O.s consult informally with various groups on different subjects as need arises. There is no equivalent of the elected Rural Committees in the New Territories and no intention at present to initiate any such development.

Nor has there been any attempt to link the C.D.O.s with the ward system of the Urban Council (see Chapter 14, pp. 163–5). This has been in operation since 1965 to attend to complaints brought by members of the public, and in 1969 the areas served by the ward offices were revised to make them coincide with the city district boundaries. But government has resisted all suggestions from Urban Councillors that there should be any formal connexion between the two organizations or that Councillors should be able to make use of the C.D.O. office facilities or the help of their staff. The ground for this refusal is that C.D.O.s are already fully occupied by their present duties for central government and are not intended to investigate private grievances—the main function of ward offices—though they may give help where they can.[13] Unfriendly critics have even suggested that the C.D.O.s were deliberately set up as a counter to the influence the Urban Councillors have under the ward system, but this has been emphatically denied by government.[14] In some wards C.D.O.s cooperate easily on a personal basis with Councillors, but their main contact is with the Urban Services Department, the executive arm of the Urban Council.[15]

The government claims that no scheme similar to the C.D.O.s has been attempted in any other modern city.[16] This may well be true; but the reason is that elsewhere their job is done either by elected local government bodies or by local agents of the dominant political party. The closest parallel to the City District Officer is a Chinese Communist cadre working full time on party business at district level. However the C.D.O. is not required to participate periodically in manual labour to 'learn from the masses', as a communist party cadre is supposed to do; nor does he have the full coercive power of the state behind him to reinforce his suggestions.

1. This point is made by way of self-criticism in *The City District Officer Scheme, A Report by the Secretary for Chinese Affairs*, 24 January 1969, p. 6.

2. Ibid. p. 12. On the setting up of the kaifongs, see *Departmental Report by the Social Welfare Officer 1948–54*, pp. 31–5. On Kaifongs generally see Aline K. Wong, *The Kaifong Associations and the Society of Hong Kong*. Orient Cultural Service, Taipei, 1972.

3. *The City District Officer Scheme, A Report*, p. 2, p. 34.

4. Ibid. p. 3.

5. This account of the activities of the C.D.O.s is taken from the 1969 special report and the *Annual Departmental Reports of the Secretariat for Home Affairs, 1969 to 1972*.

6. *H.K. Hansard 1970–71*, p. 819.

7. There is also a mediation office at the headquarters of the Department of Home Affairs which can deal with matrimonial problems and helps to negotiate compensation for traffic accident victims.

8. In 1974 Sai Kung had additional staff concerned with the building of the new High Island reservoir.

9. These figures and those in the following paragraph have been calculated from the appointments listed in the *Annual Reports* and the biographical details in the *Government Staff Lists*.

10. *Annual Report 1971–72*, p. 45. *Annual Report, 1972–73*, p. 37.

11. John Rear comments in *Hong Kong, The Industrial Colony*, p. 119, 'The scheme is basically paternalistic, an extension of better government for the people rather than an attempt to build mechanisms for government by the people. It seems apparent that initially at least the main object was to make Government more palatable to the mass of the people, to send information down rather than to convey information from the bottom to the top.'

12. This was mentioned in the notes from Shamshuipo district in the *Annual Report, 1970–71*, p. 11. In response to a proposal on these lines by Mr. Hilton Cheong-Leen, the

Secretary for Home Affairs claimed that formal District Committees had been set up in all districts in 1973 (*H.K. Hansard 1973–74*, pp. 126 and 227).

13. *Proceedings of the Urban Council*, 23 December 1969, p. 369; 3 November 1970, p. 277; 1 December 1970, p. 350.

14. *Proceedings of the Urban Council*, 5 March 1968, p. 485; 27 November 1968, p. 258.

15. Particularly on matters of hawker control, but also with the Amenities and Recreation Department of U.S.D., e.g. *Proceedings of the Urban Council*, 4 February 1969, p. 384.

16. *The City District Officer Scheme, A Report*, p. 3.

14 Local Government: The Urban Council

THE Urban Council is the only government body which both includes elected members and exercises executive powers in directing the work of a government department. As a consequence it has become the focus of what little popular agitation there is in the colony for constitutional changes. It also figured prominently in the proposals put forward by Sir Mark Young in 1946, which were not finally abandoned until 1952 (see Chapter 15 below).

The presence of elected members came about almost by accident in 1887. Lack of proper sanitation in Hong Kong had been severely criticized by an inspector sent out from Britain and under pressure from the Colonial Office a Sanitary Board was set up to organize the scavenging of the streets and houses and to draft new public health regulations. These measures aroused bitter local opposition; so in order to strengthen their authority members of the Board took the initiative by suggesting that two of its members should be elected. In the event the Executive Council decided to remove all the contentious clauses from the draft bill, but at the same time agreed that two of the unofficials on the board should be elected by those ratepayers whose names appeared on the jurors roll. Both these concessions were intended to mollify public opinion. They may have succeeded in this, but they did little or nothing to safeguard public health in the colony which continued to suffer from outbreaks of cholera every spring and periodic visitations of the plague.[1]

The Sanitary Board continued in much the same form for the next fifty years. In 1908, after a Commission of Enquiry had uncovered widespread corruption, its powers were substantially reduced so that it became little more than a consultative committee to the Sanitary Department, which was run by an administrative officer.[2] In 1936 it was renamed the Urban Council and its supervision was extended to cover a wider range of public health and other miscellaneous matters, though hardly enough to justify its new and more grandiose title. After the Japanese occupation the Council was revived in its pre-war form, but without any elected members. The first post-war election to fill two seats was not held until 1952, after government was prompted to take action by a question in the Legislative Council.

In the twenty years since then the Urban Council has gradually increased in size and acquired a mixed collection of additional functions, though this growth has not been the result of any preconceived plan. Two extra elected members were added in 1953 to compensate for the final abandonment of the Young Plan for more extensive constitutional reforms. In 1956 six more unofficial seats were created, two for appointed members and four for elected members. This was in reply to a request from the Council which claimed that the amount of work to be done justified the increase. In 1964 it was announced that a further four unofficials were to be added, two elected and two appointed, though no initiative had come from the Council. This was to coincide with an increase in the size of the Legislative Council. The increase in the size of the Urban Council can be seen in the following table.

	Ex officio members	Appointed unofficials	Elected unofficials	Total
1946	5	6	–	11
1952	5	6	2	13
1953	5	6	4	15
1956	6	8	8	22
1965	6	10	10	26
1973	–	12	12	24

The accumulation of functions proceeded in a similar haphazard manner. In 1951 the Council took over the administration of resettlement areas for squatters and as a result became responsible for the housing estates built there later. In 1953 parks and playgrounds were added, followed by street-naming in 1954, multi-storey car parks in 1957, the new city hall in 1959, libraries in 1965 and the Hong Kong stadium in 1970.[3]

In 1966 various committees and working parties were set up to consider a wide-ranging reform of local government but progress was interrupted by the 1967 confrontation and then by the need to defer final decisions until the arrival of the new Governor. Finally in 1973 a modest measure of reform was implemented. All functions relating to housing were removed from the Council and centralized in a new separate Housing Authority.[4] The Council was given more financial autonomy and a small increase in its licensing powers. The latest arrangements as set out in the 1973 ordinances are given below. As yet it is too early to say how they will work out in practice.

COMPOSITION AND ELECTIONS

The Council now consists of twelve elected and twelve appointed members. All members must be qualified to be registered as an elector (see below). Formerly candidates were also required to be proficient in English, but this was abolished in August 1974.[5] Certain persons are disqualified from membership including bankrupts, those found guilty of treason or corruption, those serving a sentence of more than a year's imprisonment, office holders under the Crown, members of foreign parliaments or assemblies and officials of foreign governments.[6] This provision would exclude any functionary of the Peoples' Republic of China or the government of Taiwan. Until the 1973 reorganization six

Hong Kong government officers sat on the Council *ex officio*, to reply to questions and to the complaints against government made in the annual conventional debate. Otherwise they did not take an active part in the Council's public proceedings and always abstained from voting when motions relating to the constitution of the Council were discussed.

Elected members hold their seats for four years, six seats being subject to re-election every two years.[7] Appointed members may be nominated by the Governor for any period up to a maximum of four years. The normal period is four years, but they may resign earlier. They are usually reappointed for as long as they wish to serve. In practice appointed members rarely remain on the Council more than eight years. The exception is Mr. Arnaldo de Oliveira Sales who has sat as an appointed member continuously since 1957. Elected members tend to remain longer, provided they are not compulsorily retired by the voters. Mr. Brook Bernacchi has been on the Council for twenty-three years since elections were reinstituted in 1952, apart from a three-month gap in 1957 when he resigned and was immediately re-elected. Mr. Hilton Cheong-Leen has been a member since 1957 and Mrs. Elsie Elliott since 1963. Five other elected members who are no longer on the Council served for eleven years or more.[8]

Members of the Council may claim up to the maximum of $2,000 a month to recover the costs actually incurred by them in the services of the Council, for such matters as secretarial assistance, transport and stationery. According to one elected member he may spend up to ten hours a week on Council business—attending committee meetings, reading papers and seeing complainants at the ward office for which he is responsible.[9]

The qualifications for inclusion on the electoral register are highly complex. A potential voter must be over the age of twenty-one, have lived in Hong Kong for at least three years and must satisfy the registration officer that he is qualified in at least one of twenty-three categories. Broadly speaking these include all those who have passed the School Certificate Examination or a similar or higher certificate or diploma, who are jurors, salaried taxpayers, ratepayers or businessmen, or who are members of some listed professional organization, ranging from airline pilots and barristers to midwives, nuns and newspaper reporters. Anyone who comes into one of these categories and who is not in prison, in a lunatic asylum or in the British Army may apply to be entered on the electoral roll. In 1973 the staff of the Commissioner of the Registration of Persons calculated that the sum total of those qualified in each category came to 803,744; but since many people are eligible in two or more groupings (e.g. a graduate solicitor who pays salaries tax) the true maximum possible number of voters is probably less than 600,000.[10]

This list of those eligible for the franchise was last revised in 1965 by a working party of civil servants together with two elected members of the Council, Mr. Brook Bernacchi of the Reform Club and Mr. Hilton Cheong-Leen of the Civic Association. The report of the Committee was unanimous. Since it opened the franchise to many groups who had not previously been eligible because they did not understand English, it was expected to lead to a large increase in the number of voters on the register.[11] The committee regarded the vote as a privilege to be bestowed on those 'who make a valuable contribution to Hong Kong through service to the community, or professional knowledge and skill, or educational stand- ard'.[12]

Such a limited franchise, which excludes at least three-quarters of the adult population, cannot be considered 'democratic' by any 'Western' standard (or by any Communist standard, for that matter). Yet it was endorsed by the representatives of the two main political clubs in the colony and it has since been reaffirmed as acceptable in documents issued by the Council in 1966 and 1969.[13] In 1971 when the government's White Paper on the reorganization of the Council was discussed in the annual conventional debate only one member, an elected independent, Mrs. Elsie Elliott, advocated universal adult suffrage.[14] The limited representative- ness of the Council should be remembered when members make demands for increased powers in order to 'arouse in young people an interest for political participation' and to 'allow the people of Hong Kong to take a more active part in their own affairs'.[15]

New voters can apply to be registered in alternate years from February to June. A full-scale publicity campaign is then mounted by the govern- ment information services and forms are freely available from professional associations and from post offices, C.D.O. information counters, etc. The provisional register is published in September and finally comes into force the following January, two months before the biennial elections. The names of voters on the old register are automatically carried forward to the new one unless they are known to have died or left the colony. Once every six years everyone on the register is sent a pre-paid reply form asking if they wish to continue to be registered. If no reply or a refusal is received they are then excluded from the new register. This sextennial check explains the drop in the number of electors in 1967 and 1973.

	New enrolments by personal application	Removed, dead or left H.K.	Removed, no reply	Electors on register
1965	3,417*	2,288	–	29,529
1967	10,897	–	14,151	26,275
1969	8,412	295	–	34,392
1971	3,987	591	–	37,788
1973	5,438	–	11,942	31,284
1975	3,270	476	–	34,078

Source: the Annual Reports of the Commissioner of Registration of Persons.
*Excluding 2,468 jurors automatically enrolled.

A candidate for election, in addition to fulfilling the qualifications already mentioned, must have his nomination form signed by ten electors and pay a deposit of $1,000, which is forfeited if he fails to obtain at least one-eighth of the votes cast.[16] Two political associations, the Reform Club and the Civic Association, put up lists of candidates and a few independents also stand. To an outsider there does not seem to be much difference between the programmes of these two organizations; both want more powers and more money for the Council and a majority of elected members on it. The Civic Association appears to be slightly more conservative. Since it is difficult to make fighting campaign speeches on policies dealing with the real workaday responsibilities of the Council, for example the treatment of nightsoil, or the cleanliness of hawkers' stalls, candidates prefer to orate about the dangers of violence on the streets or the need for more schools, though neither subject has any relevance to what the Council actually does. In fact it is pointless for either association to put forward detailed programmes of action (except as a means of ventilating grievances), since even if one of them were to win all the elected seats (that is to say, was completely successful in two successive elections) it would still only be equal in numbers to the appointed members and so would be unable to carry its policy through.

On election day in March there are ten polling stations. Each elector is allocated to the one nearest his home. This may not be the one which is most convenient for him if he is away at work all day. Although the Urban Council does not operate in the New Territories anyone who is resident there and who satisfies the requirements may be enrolled as an elector or even stand as a candidate. The 1973 register included 2,401 electors with addresses in the New Territories. However, until 1975, no polling stations were set up there and electors had to go to Kowloon to vote.

Few of the registered electors bother to exercise the privilege or duty of casting their ballots. The highest turnout was in June 1967 (38.8 per cent) when voting perhaps served as an affirmation of loyalty to the government in the face of Communist rioters.

	Electors on register	Votes cast	%
1965	29,529	6,492	22.0
1967	26,275	10,189	38.8
1969	34,392	8,175	23.8
1971	37,788	10,047	26.6
1973	31,284	8,675	24.4
1975	34,078	10,903	32.0

Source: the Annual Reports of the Commissioner of Registration of Persons.

The lower turnout in 1969 was blamed on the bad weather but no such excuses were available in 1971 and 1973. The 1967 percentage turnout is roughly comparable with that in local government elections in Britain where all adults are automatically included on the register.[17] A higher poll might perhaps have been expected in Hong Kong, since the electors are mostly middle class and many of them have made a particular effort to get themselves included on the roll. Surveys in many countries have shown that educated middle-class voters are much more likely to go to the polls than manual workers. However, the remarkable fact is not that so few people vote but rather that there are several thousand people in the colony who are prepared to take the trouble to apply for inclusion on the roll and then go to the polls in an election where there are no issues except the personalities of the candidates and no guarantee that those who are elected will be able to carry out their promises.

FUNCTIONS AND POWERS

The Urban Council has certain duties which it must perform and it is also permitted to exercise certain other powers if it wishes to do so. The mandatory functions include the following:[18]

Environmental Public Health

Construction and management of markets and abattoirs, licensing and control of hawkers and offensive trades.

Street cleansing, refuse disposal, conservancy; public conveniences and bath-houses; sewers, drains and wells.

Licensing and inspection of food premises, sampling and testing food and drugs, food poisoning.

District public health; house inspections, investigation and abatement of nuisances, pest control, malarial control, infectious diseases.

Licensing and control of laundries, commercial bath-houses, funeral parlours and undertakers; management of cemeteries and crematoria.

Recreation and Amenities

Management and maintenance of bathing beaches, swimming pools, tennis courts, parks, playgrounds and stadia.

Licensing of billiard saloons, bowling alleys, skating rinks, table tennis saloons and places of public entertainment.

Licensing of places where liquor is sold.

Cultural Services

Management of the City Hall, public libraries, museum and art gallery.

In addition, the Council is given general powers to provide facilities for recreation, culture and sport; to sponsor and promote theatrical and musical performances; and to conduct literary, artistic and sporting competitions and displays.

In all these matters the Urban Council is restricted to Hong Kong Island, Kowloon and New Kowloon. In the New Territories the same functions are performed by the New Territories Division of the Urban Services Department, but there the Director of Urban Services is acting on his own authority and not as the chief executive of the Urban Council. A few of these functions (such as licensing) are there vested in the Secretary for the New Territories and not in the Director of the Urban Services Department.

Policy decisions on all these matters are mostly made in the thirteen select committees of the Council, of which the most important is the Finance Committee which prepares the annual budget.[19] Every Councillor is a member of at least four of these committees and their chairmen may be either elected or appointed members. Committees may include persons who are not members of the Council, provided they do not exceed one-third of the membership of any committee, and the Director of Urban Services or senior members of his staff may also be co-opted as members.

The Director may attend any committee meeting to give his advice, even if he is not a member of that committee.

The full Council meets once a month in public, usually for an hour or less, since there is little business to transact. First, various papers are formally laid before the Council, including the monthly report on its activities, and committee chairmen may make statements. This is followed by questions, which are answered by the committee chairmen and often give rise to miniature debates, since the strict limits imposed on question time in the Legislative Council do not apply. Then by-laws and regulations drafted by a committee are put before the Council for ratification. The proposed rules are sometimes debated and criticized, but more usually they are passed after a brief introductory speech. Until 1973 these by-laws had also to be approved by the Legislative Council before they became legally valid, but this requirement has now been dropped.

Finally there may be a debate on a motion proposed by a member. Before 1972 motions proposed by elected members were often very tenuously connected with the responsibilities of the Council and gave an opportunity to ventilate matters of current public interest. For example in 1967 Mr. Cheong-Leen moved a motion that 'This Council is concerned about the number of primary age children in resettlement estates who are not attending school.'[20] At that time the Council was responsible for the management of resettlement estates, but the real purpose of the motion, as the proposer made clear, was to call for universal compulsory primary education—a matter which had nothing to do with the Urban Council. This facility was apparently embarrassing to government and under pressure the Council voted to amend its standing orders in March 1972 so as to confine all motions to matters within the jurisdiction of the Council.[21] It had been made clear that government proposed to take power to exercise control if the Council itself did not amend its standing orders.[22]

The Urban Council now has the power to elect its own chairman; before 1973 the Director of Urban Services held this post *ex officio*. He may be either an elected or an appointed member, or even an outsider who has agreed to serve. At all meetings of the Council or its committees the chairman has an original vote and if necessary also a casting vote to break a tie. At the meeting to elect the first chairman the elected members split their votes between Mr. Bernacchi of the Reform Club and Mr. Cheong-Leen of the Civic Association, while the appointed members all voted for the senior appointed member Mr. de Sales, who consequently won the election. He was re-elected as Chairman in 1975.

The decisions of the Council are carried out by the Urban Services Department which, according to the *Urban Council Ordinance* (see 27), 'shall, under the direction of the Director of Urban Services, do all acts and things necessary for implementing the decisions of the Council or of any committee thereof to which the Council may have delegated the exercise of any of its powers under this or any other ordinance'. However, the staff of the U.S.D. are not directly employed by the Council, but are members of the colony's public service, subject to the *Regulations* of the Hong Kong government and, as far as the senior officers are concerned, liable to be disciplined or dismissed only on the advice of the Public Service Commission. The Urban Council pays over to the central government the full cost of their salaries, pensions, housing and other allowances, but is otherwise precluded from interfering in staff matters. Obviously this system of divided control may lead to friction since the Council lays down policy but is unable to supervise its detailed execution and cannot discipline or transfer any member of its staff who is thought to be negligent in carrying out its intentions.[23] The Chairman of the Council will in future be consulted about senior appointments in the U.S.D. and the choice of Director, but this is a matter of courtesy set out in a letter sent by the Governor to the Chairman and not a statutory obligation.[24]

FINANCE

The most important change made in 1973 was the grant of increased financial autonomy to the Council. Previously the Council's annual spending proposals had been sent to the Colonial Secretariat in the same way as those of other government departments, and were liable to be pruned and altered by the Finance Branch before they were submitted with the other estimates to the Finance Committee of the Legislative Council. Under the new arrangements the Council's main source of income is a proportion of the revenue from rates in the urban areas.[25] This is automatically paid over to the Council as it is collected. The Council also receives a much smaller sum from fees collected at its swimming pools, sports grounds, libraries, etc. The Council can spend this money as it pleases, provided it keeps within its statutory powers and obligations, and it has the right to make its own by-laws to control its financial procedures.[26] Its detailed estimates must be submitted to the Governor four months before the beginning of the financial year and these are then laid before the Legislative Council. This is for information only, since the Legislative Council's approval is not now required. As with all public expenditure the Urban Council's accounts are checked by the Director of Audit at the end of the financial year. The Council is also now empowered to raise a loan to finance any large item of capital expenditure, though the terms of such a loan must be approved by the Financial Secretary, who must also approve all investments made with surplus funds.[27] The Council's estimated expenditure for 1975–6 is $335 million, an increase of $38 million over the previous year's estimate. Just under 80 per cent of its revenue is expected to come from rates.

The proportion of rates allocated to the Council was calculated on the basis of its expenditure in previous years. The total yield from rates has been rising rapidly in recent years from $128 million in 1962–3 to $383 million in 1972–3 as a result of new building and the periodic revaluations of older property. Assuming this rise is maintained, the Council's future share of the revenue from rates should be sufficient to cover expected increases in costs caused by inflation and also a continuing expansion of its services. If this does not happen the Council is permitted to apply to the Legislative Council to authorize an increase in its percentage share. As a transitional measure government agreed to complete all outstanding projects being undertaken in 1973 by the Public Works Department for the Council without making any charge, in order to avoid a hiatus in construction work while the Council is setting up its own organization. In addition, government will continue to take responsibility for all the larger and more technical projects such as abattoirs, stadia and civic centres, and has made an initial once-for-all grant of money to the Council to provide it with a reserve fund.[28] With this help it seems unlikely that the Council will need to raise any loans in the near future.

Government has retained three reserve powers to control the Council if it should seem to be acting irresponsibly in financial matters. First is the need to get the permission of the Financial Secretary before it can raise a loan. Secondly, the approval of the Legislative Council is required if it wants a larger share of the rates. Thirdly, the Governor is empowered to give general or specific directives to the Council if it is failing to discharge its functions.[29] This power would only be used as a last resort. But within these broad limits the Council can draw up its own budget and spend its money according to its own priorities.[30] As far as the elected members are concerned, they are liable to be turned out by the voters if they fail to take account of the wishes of the public. But since they are not in a majority on the Council, they will always be able to put the blame for any unpopular decision on the appointed members and so may attempt to escape responsibility.

NON-STATUTORY FUNCTIONS

Not all the activities of the Council are specifically mentioned in the Ordinances which lay down its responsibilities and powers. For instance it is engaged in an extensive programme of health education, advising the public of preventive measures against diseases. This is an offshoot of the Council's public health activities and is carried on in close liaison with the Government Information Service and the Medical and Health Department. Another example is the naming of streets which has been done by a committee of the Council since 1954.

The most important of these non-statutory activities is the system of Ward Councillors. This was instituted in 1965 as the result of a motion introduced in the Council by Dr. Raymond Lee which proposed that the urban area should be divided into wards each with a ward office where a Councillor would be available at fixed times to hear complaints, give advice and gain detailed local information about the effectiveness of the Urban Services Department.[31] The motion was unanimously adopted by the elected and appointed members (the *ex officio* members abstaining) and was soon put into practice. Ten wards were delimited with one elected and one appointed member assigned to each. The Director of Urban Services arranged office accommodation, stationery and secretarial assistance as required. At first government only accepted the scheme on condition that the Councillors confined themselves to complaints and grievances falling within the scope of the Council's statutory powers. This limitation soon proved to be unrealistic. All sorts of difficulties were brought to the ward offices and Councillors were unwilling to do nothing when faced with a case concerning another department. So all heads of departments were instructed that Councillors might approach them on any matter and that they should take appropriate action, keeping the Ward Councillor informed of what had been done.[32] However, there was, and is, no question of Councillors being given access to the departmental file concerning any case.[33] These are only available to officials and to the Administrative Secretary of the UMELCO office.[34]

Ward offices are close to where people live—a number are situated in resettlement estates—and Councillors try to be available in the evenings, at times convenient to those who have to work all day. Elected members of the Council should have every incentive to follow up cases of apparent injustice since they may hope to gain goodwill and further their own chances of re-election. However, though the number of people making use of the ward offices has grown steadily over the past few years, it is clear from the table opposite that the load of work has been disproportionately borne by a few Councillors. In the last few years more than five times as many people have taken their troubles to the Ward Offices as go to the UMELCO office for help, but there is no way of gauging the relative difficulty of the cases dealt with by each agency.[35]

Another useful activity of the Council is the annual conventional debate. Since 1974 this takes place in February on a motion that the Council endorses the Statement of Aims for the coming year. This Statement is an unexceptional list of the Council's activities containing generous promises of improvements to come. But by long-standing convention the debate ranges widely over all topics of current public concern without regard to the Council's limited statutory responsibilities. In this respect it is like the annual debate in the Legislative Council at the beginning of the session nominally on the subject of the Governor's speech. In spite of the tightening up of the Council's standing orders in 1972 the Chairman allowed this tradition of a free debate to continue. All members speak on this occasion and so debate continues for two days. In the past, when the *ex officio* members still sat on the Council, they replied at the following meeting to the points raised, though they confined their speeches to matters within the Council's competence. These replies can now no longer be made, but the annual debate still serves to provide a channel of communication between the people and government and it is to be hoped that members' complaints are noted by government as giving an important indication of informed public opinion.

Finally, in the case of the appointed members, the Urban Council has in the past provided a period of probation and training for many of the appointed members before being nominated to the unofficial seats in the Legislative Council. All the Chinese members who were so nominated between the end of the war and 1964 had previously sat on the Urban Council, and every one of the fourteen Chinese members of the Urban Council between 1951 and 1964 went on to the Legislative Council, as also did five out of the nine non-Chinese. Others have followed the same upward path since then, but promotion is now more uncertain, and several

Ward/District H.K. Island	Cases attended to				Ward Councillors in 72/3 (Elected member first)
	1969/70	1970/71	1971/72	1972/73	
Western	527	826	822	849	Mr. Hu Hung-lick, Mr. Ng Ping-kin
Central	34	88	82	68	Mr. Kan Yat-kum, Mr. R.H. Lobo
Wanchai	3	8	176	279	Mr. H. Cheong-Leen, Mr. Wu Man-hon
Eastern	569	778	911	1305	Mr. B.A. Bernacchi, Mr. Lo Tak-cheung
Kowloon Yau Ma Tei	358	396	258	245	Mr. Sin Cho-chiu, Mr. A. de O. Sales
Mong Kok	238	157	172	121	Miss Yeung Lai-yin, Mr. Chan Po-fun
Sham Shui Po	106	76	102	101	Mr. H. Wong, Mrs. C.J. Symons
Kowloon City	27	19	30	14	Dr. Huang Mong-hwa, Mr. J. MacKenzie
Wong Tai Sin	1457	4145	5814	5524	Mrs. E. Elliott, Mr. Lo Tak-shing
Kwun Tong	230	273	640	277	Mr. Chan Chi-kwan, Mr. H.M.G. Forsgate
	3549	6766	9007	8783	

Source: Monthly Reports of the Work of the Urban Council.

of the present members seem to have been passed over. Not all the un-officials on the Legislative Council have served previously on the Urban Council, but seven out of the fifteen on the Legislative Council at the beginning of 1973 had done so. In 1973 Mr. Hilton Cheong-Leen became the first elected member to be promoted to the Legislative Council while still sitting on the Urban Council. Previously Mr. Woo Pak-chuen had been an elected member from 1953 to 1957 before he was nominated to the Legislative Council in 1964.

1. For further details on this and the following paragraphs, see Endacott, *Government and People in Hong Kong*, pp. 148–62, 201–4.

2. At this time administrative officers were called 'cadets'.

3. See *Annual Reports of the Urban Council and Urban Services Department*, 1951 onwards.

4. According to the *Housing Ordinance* passed in 1973 eight of the thirteen members of the new Authority are to be members of the Urban Council, (cap 283, sec 3).

5. One attempted nomination was refused on these grounds by the returning officer in 1973 (*South China Morning Post*, 9 & 16 February 1973). For the repeal of the language requirement see *H.K. Hansard 1973–74*, pp. 1081–2 and 1162–3.

6. *Urban Council Ordinance*, cap. 101, clauses 6–12.

7. One member was elected for two years in 1973 as a transitional measure when the number of elected members was increased by two, allowing the election of seven members.

8. Raymond Lee, 14 years, 1953–67; Chan Shu-woon, 11 years, 1956–67; Dr. Mary Bell, 11 years, 1956–63 and 1965–69; Li Yiu-bor, 13 years, 1956–69; Dr. Woo Pak-foo, 13 years, 1956–69.

9. Mr. Bernacchi makes this estimate in *Far Eastern Economic Review*, Vol. 54, 6 October 1966, p. 39.

10. See the *First Schedule of the Urban Council Ordinance* (cap. 101) for full details of the qualifications for electors, and *Annual Report of the Commissioner of Registration of Persons*, 1973–74, p. 15.

11. *The Report of the Working Party on the Urban Council Franchise and Electoral Registration Procedure* (Government Printer, August 1965). Previously the right to vote had been confined to jurors ('good and sufficient persons resident within the Colony between the ages of 21 and 60, of sound mind and not deaf, blind or similarly infirm and who have good enough English to understand proceedings in Court'), those qualified for jury service but exempted, teachers, taxpayers and members of the Defence Force and the Auxilliary Forces. Those on the jury list were automatically enrolled as electors; those in the other categories had to apply. As a result jurors made up 56 per cent of the electors in 1965:

Jurors and Special Jurors	16,581
Exempted jurors	2,841
Teachers	7,525
Taxpayers	83
Auxiliary Services	2,499
	29,529

The 1965 working party recommended the ending of automatic registration but allowed those at present on the register to remain, subject to the new sextennial check. Unfortunately, the operation of this check reduced the number of voters by 14,151 who did not send back their prepaid reply forms. 10,897 applied to be enrolled under the new categories, so the unexpected result of this exercise was a *decrease* of 3,254 in the number of electors and not a vast increase, which the working party had expected to achieve. The 1973 register still contains the names of 10,929 who were on the 1965 register.

12. Ibid. p. 3.

13. *Report of the Ad Hoc Committee on the Future Scope and Operation of the Urban Council*, August 1966, p. 17; *Report on the Reform of Local Government*, March 1969, p. 3.

14. Two members of the Reform Club referred in passing to the need for an extension of the franchise, Mr. Bernacchi and Mr. Hu Hung-lick. *Proceedings of the Urban Council*, 2 Nov. 1971, pp. 287, 302 & 310.

15. *Report of the Ad Hoc Committee*, August 1966, p. 3.

16. No attempt is made here to summarize all the detailed provisions to be found in the subsidiary legislation to the *Urban Council Ordinance*, in the First Schedule part III.

17. At the elections for the Greater London Council in 1967, 1970 and 1973 the voter turnout was 37 per cent, 35 per cent and 38 per cent respectively.

18. This list is not exhaustive. For full details see the *Annual Reports of the Urban Council and Urban Services Department* and the *Public Health and Urban Services Ordinance* (cap. 132).

19. The number of committees is frequently changed. Over the last 15 years it has varied between 35 and 8. See the latest *Annual Report*. The details which follow are taken from the *Urban Council Ordinance* (cap. 101).

20. *Proceedings of the Urban Council* 4 April 1967, pp. 41ff.

21. It is almost incredible that government should have been bothered about this occasional exhibition of free speech, or what harm it thought could come of it.

22. The 1971 *White Paper* proposed that the Council's Standing Orders should be subject to the approval of the Legislative Council. The Unofficial members of the Legislative Council

objected to being put in this invidious position (*H.K. Hansard 1971–72*, p. 416). Government then agreed to withdraw its proposal to control the Council's Standing Orders, provided that Order 10 (1) relating to Motions was tightened up. According to Mr. Cheong-Leen (who voted for the restriction) it was indicated to members that if this were done there would be no interference with the annual conventional debate. See the speeches by Mr. Bernacchi, Mr. Cheong-Leen and Mr. Sales in the debate on this, *Proceedings of the Urban Council*, 4 April 1972, pp. 17, 18 and 22.

23. Mr. Lo Tak-shing, Chairman of the City Hall Select Committee of the Council, gave a good example of the difficulties caused by this in *Proceedings of the Urban Council*, 19 June 1973. There had been a brawl at the City Hall involving a newspaper reporter and a member of the staff, but the committee of the Council was precluded from investigating the matter. As Mr. Lo said, 'The position of paying the piper, but not being able to call the tune, engenders not just theoretical but very substantial practical difficulties' (p. 55). The incident was investigated by three senior officers of the Urban Services Department, who reported their findings to the Director of the U.S.D. and the Colonial Secretariat. The report was shown to Mr. Lo on a confidential basis, but other councillors were not permitted to see it (*Proceedings*, 10 July 1973, pp. 80–4).

Similarly Mr. J. MacKenzie complained that certain other U.S.D. files and reports were not made available to Councillors (14 Feb 1974, p. 299). In such a situation, where the Urban Council's decisions are executed by an agency over whose internal procedures it has no control, friction is bound to arise.

24. *White Paper, The Urban Council 1971*, para. 20. *H.K. Hansard 1972–73*, p. 383.

25. From 1973 to 1975 rates were levied at 15 per cent of the rateable value of property. The product of a 6 per cent rate is paid over to the Council. *H.K. Hansard 1972–73*, pp. 434–9. In the 1975 budget rates were increased to 17 per cent.

26. *H.K. Hansard 1972–73*, p. 382. *Urban Council Ordinance* (cap. 101) clause 37.

27. *Urban Council Ordinance*, clauses 42 and 43.

28. *H.K. Hansard 1972–73*, p. 434–9.

29. *Urban Council Ordinance*, clause 45. It is highly unlikely that this would ever be necessary; the appointed members could be expected to vote together in order to block any irresponsible or extravagant proposals put forward by the elected members. (It is hard to imagine the present elected members doing any such thing.)

Normally the appointed members disagree among themselves and criticize government as much as the unofficials do on the Legislative Council. See Sir Yuet-keung Kan's remarks on this, *H.K. Hansard 1971–72*, pp. 363f.

30. The Council can only authorize the expenditure of money on matters which are within its statutory responsibilities, or on matters specifically permitted by the *Urban Council Ordinance*. For example, clause 39(3)(a) permits the Council to pay for the cost of official ceremonies. This was sufficient authority for the Council to vote for the purchase of a prestigious official car for the use of its Chairman.

31. *Proceedings*, 4 May 1965, pp. 81–90.

32. *Proceedings*, 5 January 1971, pp. 378f.

33. *Proceedings*, 4 November 1969, pp. 248–52.

34. According to the Administrative Secretary of UMELCO, a few Urban Councillors refer difficult cases to the UMELCO office for further investigation.

35. Compare the UMELCO figures given at p. 125 above.

15 The Reform of Local Government: 1946–1973

THE YOUNG PLAN

DURING the course of the last war the British government made various declarations to the effect that, when the fighting was over, the colonies would be given a fuller and more responsible share in managing their own affairs, leading to eventual self-determination. The first moves in Hong Kong were initiated in May 1946 when Sir Mark Young returned to resume his governorship after the interim military administration had completed the first stage of reconstruction. He announced the intention of the British government, subject to local consultation, to hand over certain functions of internal administration to a new Municipal Council, constituted on a fully representative basis. Details took some time to work out, and the draft ordinances were not finally published until 1949. The new Council was to have an elected majority with the franchise open to all who were permanent residents and were literate in either Chinese or English; it was to be financially autonomous out of the revenue from rates and licences, employ its own staff and would eventually take over all urban services, education, social welfare, town planning and other functions. At the same time there were to be minor changes in the Legislative Council, including the indirect election of two of the unofficial members by the new Council.[1]

The decision to set up what was virtually a new municipal authority rather than begin with the democratization of the Legislative Council was presumably an attempt by Britain to keep her imperial interests in Hong Kong—the port facilities and the naval dockyard—insulated from the area of activities of any newly emergent Chinese politicians for as long as possible. But the effect of constituting such a body elected on a broad franchise would inevitably have been to make its leaders more authoritative spokesmen for the local population than the nominated members of the Legislative Council. Whatever the legal or constitutional position might have been, government would have been bound to pay greater attention to the views of these elected representatives and would have eventually had to concede effective power into their hands, as in fact happened in other colonies where similar expedients were tried.

This prospect of being superseded by a newly created body was unwelcome to the unofficial members of the Legislative Council, and when the draft bills setting up the new Council were presented to them they tabled a motion asking that the whole scheme should be shelved until after the Legislative Council had been reformed to give the unofficials a clear majority. This motion was passed unanimously by the unofficials with the official members abstaining on the Governor's instructions.[2] The bills could have been forced through by the official majority but it was decided to defer a decision and recommence consultation. The unofficials claimed during the debate that there was little public demand for constitutional changes and this seemed to be confirmed by the lack of significant protest at the postponement of any reform. In June 1949 this was hardly surprising. Communist armies had captured Peking in January, and Shanghai in May; refugees were beginning to flood into the colony and the first reinforcements for the British Army were on their way. Discussions about a municipal council must have seemed irrelevant at a time when the colony's very survival was in doubt. Talks on constitutional revision continued in a desultory fashion for three years, but a possible modification of the 'Young Plan' was killed by the private opposition of the unofficial members in July 1952, just before the Governor left to confer with the Colonial Office, and the final burial of the project was announced in the House of Commons in October 1952.

The 'Young Plan' is now an historical curiosity. It only made sense as a step on the road to Hong Kong's eventual self-determination—a goal which may have seemed plausible in 1946, but which is now clearly out of the question. Its main significance is that it continues to excite the imagination and ambitions of Urban Councillors who see their future role as constituting the elected government of Hong Kong. But any such scheme is ruled out for exactly the same reasons which preclude an elected majority on the Legislative Council (see pp. 24–6). At present the Urban Council's limited functions, and the parity of elected and appointed members on it, make it an unattractive target for Communist or Nationalist sympathizers. But such reticence might well disappear if the Council were to be given an elected majority and increased powers. The Council could then be used as a platform for ideological demands which might call the whole colonial regime into question; its staff could be packed with partisans and the vital urban services it provides could be abused to serve the political ends of the party controlling it. No prudent Governor would dare to risk the consequences for the stability of Hong Kong if control of the Urban Council became a political prize worth fighting for.

1966–1973

For the next fourteen years the colony was too preoccupied with the problems posed by the refugees and the need to reorient its economy after the loss of its traditional entrepot trade with China to spare any thought for constitutional reform. But by the mid-1960s the future seemed reasonably assured and a new Governor, Sir David Trench, decided to reopen the question of local government in his budget address of February 1966. After giving his opinion that 'An effective method of providing controlled channels for the exercise of local initiative in the management of purely local affairs is a valuable—indeed an almost essential—adjunct to the government of any country', he went on to give a careful definition of a local authority as a body to which the Legislature allots certain prescribed powers and duties to be exercised within a specified geographical area. He then referred to the developing urban areas of Tsuen Wan, Castle Peak and Sha Tin where it seemed desirable to provide the people with a method of influencing purely local affairs, and added that certain features of the Urban Council might also be amended with advantage. Accordingly he proposed to solicit the views of members of the public and set up a study group of officials to consider the practical problems involved.[3]

The unofficial members gave a guarded welcome to these suggestions. Mr. Kan Yuet-keung seemed to sum up their view when he said that he supported the provision of a further opportunity for wider participation by members of the community in the administration of public affairs, but stressed that such local authorities must not become 'debating societies or public platforms for political gambits'.[4]

The Urban Council promptly set up an *ad hoc* Committee to formulate proposals. Its report, completed in August, was, broadly speaking, a resurrection of the 'Young Plan' and in some respects went far beyond it.[5] The Urban Council was to be expanded into a greater Hong Kong Council with an elected majority which would take over the responsibility for Education, Fire Services, Housing, Medical Services, Town Planning, Public Works, Social Welfare, Transport and many other functions, not only in the urban area but throughout the entire colony. Below this Council three or more District Councils would be set up for Hong Kong island, Kowloon and the New Territories to carry out sanitary and public health functions. Apart from these new Councils at the bottom, this scheme bore little resemblance to the local authority concept as carefully formulated by the Governor. It was more like a takeover bid by the Urban Council for half the Colonial Secretariat and its departments, with the New Territories and the Heung Yee Kuk thrown in for good measure.

The report drawn up by the working party of officials under the chairmanship of Mr. W.V. Dickinson not surprisingly took a different line.[6] It carefully analysed possible boundaries for local authority areas and concluded that a mixture of major and minor authorities (Municipal Councils, District Councils and Urban District Councils) would be required to take account of the peculiar needs of the concentrated urban areas of Kowloon and Hong Kong Island, the rural areas of the New Territories and the new townships such as Tsuen Wan. The maximum possible number of Councils proposed was nine, and the minimum, four. The functions to be devolved to these authorities from the Departments were much the same as those now performed by the Urban Council with the addition of the management of housing estates, the provision and management of schools, and certain social welfare services. The effect of these recommendations would have been to abolish the Urban Council as such and divide the area served by it between three or more new local councils, each exercising within its own territory the same or greater powers which the Urban Council had formerly exercised over the whole. A similar partition of the New Territories was also tentatively proposed.

The difference between the two schemes can be summarized as follows: the Urban Council proposed a three-tier structure for the government of Hong Kong, with a debilitated central government at the top, a powerful new municipal council in the middle and new district authorities at the bottom; the Dickinson Report more parsimoniously proposed a two-tier structure, with the central government at the top left much as before and a number of new local authorities at the bottom which were to be called into existence by the dismemberment of the Urban Council and the Heung Yee Kuk.

The confrontation of 1967 put a stop to all theorizing for the next few years, though the Urban Council produced a further report in 1969 which did little more than elaborate on its earlier grandiose plans. The final result of Sir David Trench's initiative was the *White Paper* on the Urban Council published by government in October 1971.[7] This disparaged the whole idea of devolution of power to local authorities and implicitly condemned the intellectual effort of the past five years as a waste of time. According to the White Paper the grant of executive powers to local representative bodies was quite unnecessary and would probably lead to a decline of efficiency in the provision of services to the public; if people wished to participate in government there was a highly developed network of advisory bodies available to serve this need. A few changes in the Urban Council were proposed and substantially carried into effect in 1973, as already described.[8] Up to the time of writing no new provision whatsoever has been made for the local administration of the new townships in the New Territories, in spite of the fact that this problem had been the original inspiration for the whole exercise.

THE CASE FOR ELECTED LOCAL AUTHORITIES

There is little argument that the most efficient way to coordinate the local operations of specialized departments is to have a territorially based agency in each area which can help to adjust the policies laid down by the central authority to fit the peculiar needs of each locality and see that the development projects of different departments are sensibly meshed in with one another. Similarly, government policies do not merely need to be appropriate to the requirements of a particular area as they might be objectively evaluated; if such schemes are to win popular support they must also be accommodated to the expressed desires of local opinion, which may subjectively rate the importance of various projects in a different order of priorities to that determined by an official from outside. So there is also the need for some kind of spokesman to put the local point of view to decision-makers at the centre, to reconcile conflicts within the local community and to conduct negotiations on its behalf.

But is it necessary that these two functions—the co-ordination of centrally administered services and the articulation of local pressures to the central authorities—should be done by elected local authorities? In Hong Kong both these functions are primarily the responsibility of the

District Officers in the New Territories and the City District Officers in urban areas, with the assistance of local advisory bodies. These officials work largely by persuasion and the influence that comes from an intimate knowledge of their own locality.[9] It is difficult to assess how well they do their job, but their performance would seem to be at least adequate (to put the case at its lowest), since government has every incentive to see that these functions are carried out efficiently. Ineffective coordination of local services causes delays and wastes money, and any failure to assess and take proper account of local opinion loses support for the government and so makes its task more difficult. It is not at all obvious that the subordination of District and City District Officers to elected local authorities would lead to any improvement.

To some people such a suggestion is outrageous. The 1966 Urban Council Report did not see any necessity to argue in favour of popular participation in government: 'To ask, in this day and age, for a case to be made for the people to be given more responsibility in public affairs is to fly in the face of progress and may even be said to negate the rights of man'.[10] Nevertheless, this allegedly outmoded point of view is predominant in Hong Kong government circles and it is moreover in accord with traditional Chinese ideas of the proper relationship between rulers and ruled. The case that local government should not only be *responsive* to local people (which it is now, to a large extent) but also *responsible* to them (which it is not), might be made on the following lines. The arguments are given in the order in which they appear most plausible to the author, beginning with the strongest.[11]

1. *Election gives greater weight to local demands.* All officials naturally prefer to do what is convenient to themselves and follow the routines that have served adequately in the past. It is much easier to brush aside the views of an appointed advisory committee than those of an elected representative who speaks with the authority given by those who voted for him. This is borne out by the entrenched position of the Heung Yee Kuk which was able in 1973 to obtain practically all its demands for modifications in government land policy. Conversely, Urban Councillors are well aware how much their credibility as spokesmen for the urban population is diminished by the small percentage of eligible electors who bother to turn out to vote. One Councillor has even advocated compulsory voting in order to remedy this.[12]

2. *Elections on a wide franchise give more adequate expression to the views of the poor and uneducated.* The rich who have time and energy to spare find it easy to organize committees to press their point of view and can argue articulately with officials without any feelings of inferiority. Without the counterweight of elections, which give each man only a single vote, it is easy for a civil servant to mistake the views he hears most frequently expressed as being the opinion of the majority, whereas in fact it is merely the opinion of those wealthy and successful men who find it easy to gain access to him.

3. *Elected representatives are more responsive to public opinion.* If they habitually ignore the views of their constituents they are unlikely to be

re-elected; whereas an official or an appointed adviser is only dependent on the good opinion of his superiors and may therefore suppress or belittle widely-held points of view which he thinks will be displeasing to them. This argument is generally, but not universally, true. It applies when the elective post is one which gives important powers or high status which the holder would be sorry to lose, or possibly large opportunities for peculation or corruption. But if this is not the case, and there is little competition for the post and the holder does not intend to stand for re-election, he can have little incentive to worry what his public thinks. In many countries such a situation tends to arise at the local level where election sometimes carries little prestige and candidates often have to be persuaded to stand for election and are then returned unopposed.

4. *The experience of working together on a local authority encourages the development of community spirit and a sense of belonging.* This may well be true, at least as far as the elected members are concerned. The population of Hong Kong is not homogeneous and groups often tend to be organized on the basis of clan or place of origin (Hakka, Chiu Chow, Fukienese etc.) rather than place of residence.[13] Joint activities of any sort may help to break down these barriers. However, the experience of active participation in decision-making cannot be extended very widely among the mass of the population. For the rest it seems doubtful how far the solitary act of voting would encourage a feeling of identification with others in the same neighbourhood, much less a sense of loyalty to Hong Kong as a whole.

5. *The experience of self-government liberates the creative energies of individuals,* whereas authoritarian rule, however benevolent, encourages the passive acceptance of things as they are. This is one of the 'classic' arguments for democracy.[14] The economic achievements of Hong Kong's entrepreneurs under colonial rule would seem to cast some doubt upon its universal validity.

6. *The people of Hong Kong demand their democratic right to vote.* This is the assertion of the Reform Club, of students and of other youth leaders. Since overt evidence of this is conspicuously lacking, an alternative claim is sometimes made that such demands are bound to arise in future and so government ought to take immediate steps to anticipate the first stirrings of the winds of change before they can grow into storms of violence. If these predictions were true then government might indeed be well-advised to try to deflect demands for self-government and participation into the potentially less damaging arena of local government. However, the author is sceptical whether such a widespread demand does in fact exist. If it does, it is unlikely that it can be diverted for long into the humdrum chores of local administration.

7. *Local government experience provides training for those who may go on to national offices.* In Britain many Members of Parliament have served an apprenticeship in local politics before being elected to the House of Commons. But this is totally irrelevant to Hong Kong where democracy at the central government level is permanently ruled out in deference to the wishes of China. This argument might even be turned upside down:

since self-government for the colony will never be possible, why whet the appetites of aspirant politicians by letting them nibble at fruit that they will never be permitted to enjoy?[15]

THE PRACTICAL DIFFICULTIES OF
SETTING UP LOCAL AUTHORITIES

There are thus a number of reasons (some good, some not so good) why elected local authorities are desirable. But these arguments must be balanced by considerations of the practical administrative difficulties involved. Though there are perhaps some who believe that the institution of responsible self-government should have overriding priority, most people would probably rate the efficient provision of services as being of equal or greater value. In general, and up to a certain point, larger administrative units allow operations to be organized more cheaply and efficiently than small ones, but give less scope for effective local participation in decision-making. It is little use to formulate plans by impeccably democratic methods if the authority lacks the resources to employ the specialized staff needed to carry them out. The alternative is to have the staff employed by an organization which jointly serves a number of small authorities. But then a problem of coordination arises: either each authority's decisions become purely consultative and have to be ratified by some larger council before they are carried out; or else the joint staff find themselves in the impossible position of receiving different and possibly conflicting orders from their divided political masters. Neither alternative is likely to promote operational efficiency or encourage the best-qualified local residents to offer themselves for election.

The difficulty of reconciling the conflicting requirements of participation and efficiency is acute in Hong Kong, because of the way the population is distributed. The colony has about 4 million people living in an area of 400 square miles, but over 3 million of them are crowded into the Kowloon peninsula and a narrow belt of land along the north coast of Hong Kong Island. These together total about 21 square miles—the most tightly packed agglomeration of humanity on the surface of the world. This whole area is treated by those who live there and by the departments concerned with it as a single unit. Schools serve the whole area, and children from a primary school in one district may go to secondary schools all over the metropolis, wherever they can gain admission. Hospitals are geared to serve the whole population on either side of the harbour, and not merely the residents of a single district. With the opening of the cross harbour tunnel in 1972 the operational plans of the Fire Services have been modified now that help can come quickly through the tunnel to deal with a major conflagration on either side.[16]

The ten city districts have an average population of 300,000 or more and each of them would be large enough, if people and not acreage is taken into account, to qualify as a major local authority in England.[17] But these divisions are too small in area and too recent in origin to be the focus of any sentiment of local pride or attachment for the mass of the population. No one has ever suggested that the departments serving this metropolis should be split up and reorganized into ten completely self-contained units. The furthest that either the *1966 Urban Council Report* or the *Dickinson Report* went was to propose that separate municipal councils might be set up on either side of the harbour. But it is difficult to see how the dislocations involved in such a split would bring much, or any, compensating gain either in making government less remote or increasing the possibility of democratic participation. Commonsense considerations of efficiency demand that the compact central urban area of Hong Kong should be treated as a single administrative whole.

Supposing for argument's sake that the possible international political repercussions could be ignored, would it then be sensible to devolve responsibility for such services as education, transport, housing and medical services from the present central government departments to the Urban Council, since these functions are normally performed by local authorities in Britain? The objection to this course is that the rump that was left of these departments would have hardly anything to do. Three-quarters of the problems of government in Hong Kong are the troubles, needs and conflicts of the urban areas, and the New Territories Administration deals with much of what is left. If the Urban Council's functions were enlarged in this way the colony would in effect have two governments of almost equal power who would spend much of their energy quarrelling over the co-ordination of their activities and the demarcation of their respective spheres of authority. A similar experiment was tried in Singapore between 1957 and 1959, but conflicts between the Singapore government and the City Council became so bitter and protracted that the abolition of the latter was the only solution.

These objections do not apply to the creation of local authorities in the new geographically distinct townships of the New Territories, having much the same restricted powers and functions as the present Urban Council. People get very annoyed when refuse is not collected or mosquitoes are left to breed undisturbed, so there is a lot to be said for having elected local councillors in Tsuen Wan or Sha Tin to chevy the staff of the Urban Services Department, and also to decide the number of recreation fields or reading rooms they want and are prepared to pay for. At present all such decisions are taken by the Director of Urban Services or the New Territories Administration. Once these new towns reach a reasonable size (200,000 perhaps, which Tsuen Wan has already attained), there appears to be no reason why the Urban Services Department should not form a self-contained division to provide all services needed, in the same way that the staff serving the Urban Council are now separately organized from those working in the New Territories. The main difficulty is likely to be a political one: the objections from the Heung Yee Kuk to any diminution of its area of influence.

There are two further factors which would make it difficult to extend the scope of local government beyond the supervision of public health and sanitation matters and the provision of cultural and recreational amenities. One of these is the substantial amount of devolution to voluntary agencies which already exists in the departments of Education,

Social Welfare and Health. In 1973 the Department of Education was directly responsible for the running of only 136 out of 903 schools which were financed by government.[18] In Britain education is the major responsibility of local government, but in Hong Kong the missionary societies and other bodies which run these schools would certainly object to being made subordinate to local authorities, and government is hardly likely to override their views, since it is so dependent on their help.[19] At most, any new local authorities might set up and run their own schools where there is a shortage of school places, receiving grants like any other voluntary agency, on the lines suggested in the *Dickinson Report*.[20] Similar difficulties would arise for any proposal to devolve Social Welfare or Health Services.

Another difficulty is said to be the reluctance of the best qualified and most widely accepted citizens to participate in local administration if they have to stand for election and risk the loss of face involved if they fail at the polls. This point was made by Mr. Tsui, Mr. Walden and Mr. Webb-Johnson (all senior government administrative officers) in their note of reservation to the *Dickinson Report*, and they suggested that as a consequence the standard of the candidates for election would be low and bring discredit on the whole idea of elected local authorities.[21] How far this fear is valid can be determined only by trying out the experiment. It might be suggested that it underrates the potentiality for leadership among those who are not already members of the local elite. However, if any more local authorities with elected members should ever be established—(which seems very doubtful)—government would presumably retain the power to appoint additional members as a safety precaution.

1. For a full account of the Young Plan see Endacott: *Government and People in Hong Kong*, pp. 182–95. For its final abandonment in 1952, see Sir Alexander Grantham, *Via Ports*, p. 112, and *H.K. Hansard 1952*, p. 252.

2. *H.K. Hansard 1949*, pp. 188–205. Six unofficial members spoke on a motion that the Legislative Council should consist of five official members and eleven unofficials, six of whom would be elected on a franchise narrowly confined to British subjects (i.e. Chinese and others born in the colony and expatriates from the Commonwealth). Mr. Watson (p. 197) made the point about the danger of clashes between the elected Municipal Councillors and the nominated Unofficials on the Legislative Council, if the original scheme went through. It was also argued that two Councils would be more expensive, and involve too many officials; also, that only British subjects could be trusted to have the interests of Hong Kong at heart. It is possible that the men of property on the Council were concerned about the danger to their interests of the wide franchise proposed for the new Municipal Council, but this was not mentioned in the debate.

3. *H.K. Hansard 1966*, p. 51–2.

4. Ibid. p. 111.

5. Urban Council, Hong Kong. *Report of the Ad Hoc Committee on the Future Scope and Operation of the Urban Council*, August 1966 (Government Printer).

6. *Report of the Working Party on Local Administration*, November 1966 (Government Printer).

7. Urban Council, *Report on the Reform of Local Government*, March 1969 (Government Printer). *White Paper, The Urban Council*, Oct. 1971 (Government Printer). The most pertinent comments on the ambiguities of the White Paper were made by Mr. Lo Kwee-seong. *H.K. Hansard 1971–72*, pp. 360–3.

8. An apt comment on the White Paper was made by an appointed member, Mr. Sales, who quoted Horace: 'The mountain went into labour and gave birth to a little mouse'.

(*Proceedings of the Urban Council*, 2 November 1971, p. 292.)

9. In other countries, for example France, similar functions are performed by provincial prefects who have executive authority over the staffs of central departments posted to their area.

10. *Report of the Ad Hoc Committee*, p. v.

11. This list of arguments is confined to those which are relevant to, and which have actually been used in, Hong Kong. For further discussion see L.J. Sharpe:Theories and Values of Local Government, *Political Studies,* Vol. XVIII, June 1970, pp. 153–74, and the references cited there.

12. Mr. Hilton Cheong-Leen, *Proceedings of the Urban Council*, 13 March 1973, p. 374. The Council's Chairman, Mr. Sales, agreed with him, (*ibid*).

13. *Report of the Working Party*, pp. 10–11 and p. 84. *Kowloon Disturbances 1966, Report of Commission of Enquiry*, 1967, p. 126, para. 462.

14. First found in the Funeral Oration of Pericles (Thucydides, Book 2) 430 B.C. Also, the main argument of John Stuart Mill, *Considerations on Representative Government*, Chapter 3 (first published 1861).

15. I have heard a public speaker advocate that Britain should introduce free elections so that when the inevitable Communist takeover occurs, those accustomed to democratic procedures in Hong Kong may help to mitigate the centralized authoritarian regime there, acting like a reforming leaven within the Chinese mass. This seems a little optimistic.

16. The Urban Services Department was until 1974 organized on a functional basis (the Cleansing Division, the Cultural Services Division, the Hygiene Division, etc.) and not on district lines. But in November 1973 a reorganization took place: fifteen U.S.D. District Officers were appointed to the ten City Districts and the five Districts in the New Territories. It is intended to organize the work of the department on territorial lines, with District U.S.D. Officers responsible for all services in their area. Specialist officers in the different functions of the U.S.D. will continue to work at headquarters and at three new regional offices overseeing Hong Kong Island, Kowloon and the New Territories to advise the new district 'general managers'.

17. The *Royal Commission on Local Government in England 1966–1969* Cmnd 4040 recommended a minimum population of 250,000 for a major local authority and a maximum of one million (H.M.S.O. 1969, Vol. I, p. 4). No minimum size in square miles was recommended, but the smallest metropolitan district proposed has an area of 41 square miles.

18. This is quite apart from 1982 private unsubsidized schools (*Education Department Statistical Summary*, March 1973, Table 1).

19. At present bureaucratic control by the Education Department largely insulates voluntary agency schools from any community pressures. The managers might be afraid of politically inspired attempts by elected local authorities to interfere in the running of their schools and influence admission policies.

20. *Report of the Working Party on Local Administration*, p. 38.

21. See Appendix 12, pp. 281–2.

PART III

Pressures and Influences

16 Not Democracy, but Politics

'Hong Kong has achieved the distinction as the show window of democracy
in the Far East'

Mr. Tse Yu-chuen (unofficial member)

'In Hong Kong we do not want politics of any kind'

Mr. Li Fook-shu (unofficial member)[1]

PRACTICALLY every country in the world claims to be a democracy. The
communist states of Eastern Europe style themselves 'People's Democracies', and authoritarian regimes in developing nations have dignified
themselves by such names as 'Basic Democracy' (Ayub Khan's Pakistan)
or 'Guided Democracy' (Sukarno's Indonesia). Since the meaning of
the term has been stretched to cover so many types of disparate regimes
it is not surprising that it is sometimes said that Hong Kong too is a
democracy.

If we assess this assertion by the standards of Western European
democracies—a government which is answerable to the people and liable
to be dismissed at a free election where all the adult population have the
right to vote—then the claim is clearly untrue. The Governor and the
senior decision-making officials are all in law responsible to Britain and
never have to submit themselves or their policies to the judgement of
an electorate. However, if we set a less exacting standard, it may be
admitted that there are certain democratic elements in the colony which
are found in few other developing countries: the courts are independent
of the executive and sometimes hand down decisions which the administration dislikes; the rule of law is observed; there is no censorship of the
press; there are no political prisoners detained without trial; groups and
individuals are free to protest against government decisions and to
organize agitation to have them changed.[2] These rights do not constitute
democracy in the fullest sense of the term, but they are preconditions
without which full democracy is not possible. They roughly correspond
to the position in Britain at the beginning of the nineteenth century before
the great reform bills which democratized the House of Commons.

It is sometimes argued that Hong Kong is a democracy in the sense
that government seeks the good of the people and attempts to maximize
popular consent for its policies. This may be true, provided we accept
the very doubtful proposition that government always knows what is

best for the people. But it is a very modest claim to make. All regimes proclaim that they are pursuing the common good, even when they are in fact acting in the interests of their own governing class; and every state seeks the widest measure of agreement that is compatible with the achievement of its policies, since such consent makes the task of administration so much easier. It would be an aid to clarity and precision if government spokesmen ceased to make dubious claims to democracy and concentrated on the real merits of Hong Kong, that it allows a greater measure of personal freedom than exists in all but a few of the countries of Asia.

However, if there is no democracy in Hong Kong in the strictest meaning of the term, there is certainly a great deal of political activity, though this is frequently denied or deplored by those holding official positions. 'Politics' is a very derogatory term in the colony and politicians are regarded as a very low species of life who go around stirring up conflict and disorder. Most leading Chinese would probably agree with Salazar, the former dictator of Portugal, when he said that he

> ...detested politics from the bottom of his heart; all those noisy and incoherent promises, the impossible demands, the hotchpotch of unfounded ideas and impractical plans...the opportunism that cares neither for truth nor justice, the inglorious chase after unmerited fame, the unleashing of uncontrollable passions, the exploitation of the lowest instincts, the distortion of facts...all that feverish and sterile fuss.[3]

Similar views of politics and politicians are expressed elsewhere, even in many democracies, particularly by those who are very comfortably situated in the present organization of society. Nevertheless, political activity is inevitable in all free countries where individuals and groups are at liberty to organize in order to press their demands against other groups or against the government. Every decision—whether to raise, lower or shift the burden of taxation, to spend money or to economize, to enforce obligations or to relax them, to build a reservoir or an oil refinery in one location rather than another—all these decisions bring advantages to some and impose hardships upon others. Unless the persons concerned are utterly abject and accept the government's decree without argument, they will be roused to organize themselves to seek a reversal or mitigation of the policy which is affecting them. For example, during 1973 teachers went on strike for higher pay, shop tenants in housing estates marched to Government House to petition the Governor over a newly revised tenancy agreement, the Hong Kong Chamber of Social Service demanded more aid for family planning, stock-brokers lobbied the unofficial members seeking amendments to the Securities Bill, residents of Kowloon protested against the airlines' proposal to resume night flights out of Kai Tak, and 575 organizations united to campaign against increased rents on the renewal of Crown Leases. Such politicking as this is normal in all free societies, and similar, though more covert, influences are exerted in authoritarian countries through different factions and subordinate leaders of the ruling party. The difference between Hong Kong and a 'Western' democracy is that there such operations supplement and run parallel to the electoral campaigning of political parties, while in Hong Kong they are almost the sole form of political activity. Everyone who wants to protect his own interests has to participate in this political process, otherwise he will find his demands pushed aside in favour of those who are more skilful at calling the attention of the public and the government to their plight. The political actors range from a remote group of villagers in the New Territories seeking increased compensation from the army, to the General Chamber of Commerce negotiating with the Financial Secretary over a rise in the water rate for industry. Many of those who are the first to deplore the intrusion of politics into the colony are themselves past masters at the game of influencing public policy in the direction they want—all done, of course, to promote the general good of Hong Kong!

Condemnation of politicking does not come only from the self-interest of those who already have easy access to government decision-makers and resent the rise of new groups to demand equivalent bargaining status. It can also spring from the rational fear that newly mobilized groups may adopt violent methods to secure public attention and the redress of their grievances, which in turn might deter much-needed foreign investment. Anti-political attitudes may also stem from a Confucian view of society as a naturally harmonious whole in which all classes and groups know their place and accept without argument the decisions of their betters.

Whether or not such a paradise ever actually existed before politicians appeared to sow the seeds of discord, it is clearly unrealistic to expect such harmony to be re-created at the present time. People are becoming more aware of the conditions of life elsewhere and less ready to accept the wisdom of their elders. Demands keep growing, the tactics for success- fully exerting pressure become more widely known, yet resources can never grow fast enough to satisfy everyone. This state of affairs is not created by politicians, though in some countries politicians may try to exploit it in order to gain power.

Paradoxically it is in this situation of escalating demands and limited resources that the skills of politicians are most needed. Politicians may sometimes exacerbate strife for their own ends, but if they are to gain more than limited success, they need far more to possess the talents for negotiation, bargaining and compromise in order to promote the peaceful resolution of conflicts. Politics has been defined as 'the activity by which differing interests within a given unit of rule are conciliated by giving them a share in power in proportion to their importance to the welfare and survival of the whole community'.[4] In Hong Kong, where inter- national factors preclude the settlement of differences through the ballot box, the alternative to politics is not harmony, but coercion. And in its delicate situation a policy of coercion is not feasible for any length of time. To ensure the stability and prosperity of the colony in the 1970s more, not fewer, practitioners of the art of politics as defined above are needed, both in government and in all positions of leadership within the community.

1. *H.K. Hansard 1967*, pp. 153 and 354.

2. Newspapers can be prosecuted for breaking the laws against sedition, libel or pornography, as in most countries, but there is no government censorship before publication. Marches and demonstrations in public places need permission from the police. This can hardly be considered unreasonable in view of Hong Kong's congestion.

3. Quoted in Bernard Crick, *In Defence of Politics* (Penguin, London, 1962), p. 15.

4. Ibid. p. 21.

17 Pressure Groups

'Essentially, the Hong Kong style is government by consultation and consent.'

(Mr. Haddon-Cave, Financial Secretary)[1]

ONE man by himself is rarely able to persuade government to modify its policy. Successful influence normally depends on the lobbying of an organized group which can mobilize the various resources of its members, such as money, information, numbers, or the strategic position which they hold in the economy. Political scientists refer to these groups as 'pressure groups', and they are normally defined as any groups which attempt to influence government decisions without themselves seeking to exercise the formal powers of government. (This last part of the definition serves to distinguish them from political parties.) Some groups in Hong Kong have a very long history: the General Chamber of Commerce goes back to 1861. Others are very recent: for example, a union of karate clubs formed in 1973 to fight a proposal that the police should regulate them. Some are permanent bodies, always alert to notice any government decision that may affect their members; others dissolve themselves as soon as they have gained their immediate object, such as the Campaign to make Chinese an Official Language.

Pressure groups may be classified in various ways. A distinction is commonly made between groups organized to protect an occupational or sectional interest (e.g. the Real Estate Developers Association, the Automobile Association), and groups which exist to promote a cause (e.g. the Society for the Prevention of Cruelty to Animals, the Conservancy Association). But this categorization is not entirely satisfactory since some groups might be classified under either heading, such as the Society for the Blind and various religious groups. Nor are all sectional groups entirely self-seeking. Some may occasionally take up a cause of no immediate benefit to their members, as when the Bar Association criticized the severity of government's proposals to deal with violent crime.[2] Some idea of the extent to which group organizations cover every aspect of life in Hong Kong may be gained from the following partial list. (To avoid repetition, 'Hong Kong' has been omitted from the titles of most of these associations, both here and elsewhere in the chapter.)

Business Groups—the Chinese Manufacturers Association, the Employers

Association, the Chinese Paper Merchants Association.

Professional Groups—the Law Society, the Magistrates Association, the Institute of Architects.

Trade Unions—the Motor Transport Workers Union, the Harbour Pilots Union, the Edible Birds' Nest Workers Union.

Sporting and Recreational Groups—the Lawn Tennis Association, the Jockey Club, the Dramatic Arts Association.

Religious and Charitable Groups—Caritas, Lutheran World Service, the Tung Wah Hospital Group, the Po Leung Kuk.

Local and Neighbourhood Groups—Kaifongs, clansmen's associations, rural committees, multi-storey buildings owners' incorporations.

Civic Groups—Rotary Clubs, the United Nations Association, the Reform Club.

Cause Groups—the Family Planning Association, the Christian Industrial Council, the Discharged Prisoners' Aid Society, the Education Action Group.

This is only a small selection of the number of groups in existence. A full list would run into thousands.[3] The majority of these groups were formed solely to cater for the needs of their members, without any thought of putting pressure on the administration; but if they find their activities impeded by government action or threatened by the moves of other groups they can soon mobilize their membership for action in the political arena.

By law any organized group is required to apply to the Registrar of Societies for registration within fourteen days of its founding. Societies established solely for religious, charitable, social or recreational purposes may be granted exemption from registration by the Registrar but all groups formed for other purposes must be approved and registered by him. (This does not apply to companies, trade unions, cooperative societies and certain other organizations which are covered by other ordinances.) A group whose application for registration is refused then becomes an unlawful society under the terms of the ordinance and its office bearers and members are liable to fines or imprisonment. This law was principally intended as a weapon against triads and other criminal or subversive societies. Any normal group will have no difficulty in securing registration.[4] Indeed, many of these groups have been set up with positive government encouragement (e.g. the Kaifongs in 1950, and the mutual aid societies organized in 1973 as part of the 'Fight Crime' campaign). Some have even been established by ordinance, such as the Tourist Association and the Federation of Hong Kong Industries.

WHY PRESSURE GROUPS
ARE ENCOURAGED BY GOVERNMENT

This government assistance may seem odd, since the existence of these groups to some extent puts limits on government's freedom of action. Four reasons may be suggested.

In the first place, consultation with pressure groups is the traditional way in which British administrators conduct their business. In the words of a former head of the British civil service:

It is a cardinal feature of British administration that no attempt should be made to formulate a new policy on any matter without the fullest consultation with those who have practical experience in that field, and with those who will be called upon to carry it out.[5]

Colonial administrators naturally followed the pattern which had been set at home. For instance, when introducing a *White Paper* on Educational Policy in 1965, the Director of Education pointed out: 'In certain cases the government has a moral if not a statutory obligation to consult interested parties before introducing changes in policy or practice which would affect them'.[6]

Secondly, government needs statistics and technical expertise from pressure groups in order to sort out the various options available and decide on the best policy. The Department of Commerce and Industry needs to be fully briefed by the Cotton Spinners Association and other groups represented on the Textile Advisory Board when entering into negotiations with foreign countries over tariffs and quotas on Hong Kong's exports, so as to obtain the best arrangements for the local industry. Delegates from the Textile Advisory Board even go overseas with official negotiating missions so that they can be immediately available for consultation. If the government wants to economize on fuel, it needs advice from the oil companies and the electricity undertakings as to which measures are likely to achieve the greatest savings. New laws to regulate the insurance industry for the protection of policy holders are likely to be effective and enforceable only if they are drafted after full consultation with the insurance associations and in the light of information which only they can supply.[7]

Thirdly, government needs cooperation in administration. Many of the jobs that government wants done in the social services are not carried out directly by government, but by voluntary agencies which staff and manage most of the schools and welfare agencies and many of the hospitals in the colony.[8] Government programmes in these fields would be impossible without their help. Professional associations such as the Medical Council and the Bar Association act on behalf of government to discipline their members, even forbidding them to practise if they are considered guilty of professional misconduct. From 1958 to 1965 public relations activities abroad to counteract propaganda campaigns against Hong Kong's exports were organized by a joint committee of the General Chamber of Commerce and the Federation of Hong Kong Industries. Government gave a subsidy to enable these activities to be expanded in 1962, but did not take over the task itself until 1965 when the Trade Development Council was set up.[9]

Finally, the colonial administration needs open consent for its policies. However benevolent and efficient the bureaucracy may be, it still remains in the eyes of the Chinese a government by foreigners whose motives are always regarded with some suspicion. Hong Kong's peculiar circumstances make democracy in the 'Western' sense impossible, yet government can only carry out its policies efficiently and cheaply with the willing cooperation of the population. Since it cannot assert its right to rule because it has won an election, government takes great pains to emphasize that changes in policy are not the arbitrary dictates of an imperial master, but are rather the outcome of the fullest possible discussion with the groups most likely to be affected. The people participate in decision-making, it is claimed, not by voting for the candidates of their choice, but through their group spokesmen who sit on the councils and advisory boards which government has established.[10] Thus the interests of the people are 'virtually represented' on these committees, and the policies agreed as a result of these consultations deserve popular support.[11] From this point of view, government achieves legitimacy, not through the ballot box, but by popular consent mediated by those group leaders who help to participate in the formulation of policy and then let their agreement to government's final proposals be made known.

HOW PRESSURE GROUPS INFLUENCE GOVERNMENT

The most common means of persuasion is not really a form of pressure at all. Group representatives explain their objections to government proposals and point to the likely difficulties, expense and undesirable consequences that may follow if government persists in this line of policy; alternative approaches are then suggested and their advantages stressed. The best arguments clearly and persuasively stated at a private meeting will often achieve all that a group wants, and well-established organizations hardly ever need to go further than this. Such points may be made formally at an advisory board meeting, or privately on the telephone or during a social gathering. The full-time officials of the General Chamber of Commerce are in daily contact with officers of the Commerce and Industry department and other government departments, and the same is true of other leading business and professional groups.[12]

Such groups which have easy access to departments and the secretariat are obviously in the strongest position to urge their case with top government decision-makers. Other groups which are not contacted by government before policy decisions are announced can put their objections to the unofficial members at the UMELCO office. These may either be groups whose interest in a bill was not anticipated by government, or groups to which government is unwilling to grant the privilege of consultative status. For example, after the second reading of the *Wild Birds and Wild Mammals Protection (Amendment) Bill 1971* officers of the Hong Kong Natural History Society, the Hong Kong Bird Watching Society and the Hong Kong Gun Club called on UMELCO to make representations. The first two organizations were concerned with the danger of rabies entering the colony as a result of the clause permitting the import of live civet cats from China; the Gun Club was protesting at the extension of the prohibition on shooting near a house or motor road from 100 to 200 yards, on the ground that the inclusion of further protected areas in the bill left very little of the New Territories where guns could legally be discharged. The unofficials agreed with government that the danger of rabies was minimal, but they supported the Gun Club's objection, and as a result the clause complained of was deleted in committee.[13] Since 1974 even a few 'leftist' groups have begun to make use of this avenue of approach to government: for example, a delegation from the Motor Transport Workers Union went to see a group of unofficials to urge their objections to the bill instituting fixed penalties for traffic offences.[14] Such lobbying can sometimes achieve substantial amendments to legislation. After publication of the Securities Bill 1973 the Financial Secretary received suggestions for nearly 300 amendments. These were subsequently reduced to 230, and government eventually accepted 115 of them.[15]

If a group is unable to obtain satisfaction by private contact the next step is usually to attempt to persuade government by a public campaign, which may take the form of letters to the newspapers, public speeches and posters. Attempts may be made to get press coverage by holding news conferences and providing reporters with press releases and angled stories. Support is sought from editorial writers, and perhaps a friendly unofficial may ask a question or a series of questions in the Legislative Council. The Joint Kaifong Association of Hong Kong and Kowloon or certain elected Urban Councillors may be persuaded to issue statements supporting the objectors' position.[16] The general aim of the organizing group is not so much to gain popular support (though this is welcome) as to foster the impression that their objections to government policy command widespread sympathy and that government is being unreasonable in not giving way. Senior government officers receive daily summaries and translations of all newspaper stories and comment relevant to their work, prepared by the Government Information Service, and the hope is that the cumulative effect of such adverse publicity may embarrass the administration and persuade officials to modify their stand. On any controversial decision there is likely to have been disagreement within government on the best course of action to adopt. Public objections may serve to alter the balance of forces within the bureaucracy or on the Executive Council. Government wants to be popular and such campaigns can be surprisingly successful, even when mounted by groups representing only a tiny minority: for example, the 1971 protests by European parents (less than one per cent of the population) led to the reversal of the decision to increase fees forthwith at the English schools.

Another method used by groups with more volunteers than money is to collect signatures for a petition either to the Governor or to the Secretary of State in Britain. With sufficient enthusiasts to pester innocent passers-by an impressive total of signatures can quickly be collected, though there is no guarantee that the signatories feel as deeply on the subject as the canvassers. Groups with connections in Britain can also request a friendly M.P. to ask a question in the House of Commons.[17] The hope is that the minister might be persuaded to put pressure on the colonial government to give the group a favourable hearing. One rural committee in the New Territories, dissatisfied with an offer of compensation, once threatened to petition Peking or send a delegation there. Such a tactic, if carried out, could prove embarrassing, but the announcement was probably only an astute publicity gimmick.[18]

The next escalation of pressure is to stage peaceful demonstrations. One of the most effective in recent years was the protest by blind workers against new pay scales at a factory run by the Hong Kong Society for the Blind. Marshalled by student supporters they formed a procession moving continuously around the Star Ferry concourse and along the Connaught Road underpass waving their sticks and carrying placards. Their plight attracted great public sympathy expressed in immediate cash donations from passers-by, and the sight of such a group demonstrating against government's callousness was hardly the image of Hong Kong which the Tourist Association wished to promote in front of visitors arriving at the Mandarin Hotel. Within 48 hours the administration caved in and gave the Society the additional funds needed to meet the blind workers' demands.[19] Other demonstrations have not achieved a similar success. Dispossessed hawkers sleeping outside Government House have been easily dispersed by the police when reporters or cameramen were not present, and students demanding drastic action against corruption in government were required by the police to hold their demonstration in an area where few casual passers-by would be found. Most demonstrations are mainly aiming at press publicity for their cause and incidents may be staged solely for this purpose, but normally the organizers hope the meeting will proceed in a peaceful and orderly manner so as to attract favourable newspaper comment. Open violence is usually counter-productive since it tends to mobilize public opinion against the cause advocated, and make it less likely that government will give way.

Groups which have easy access to government do not need to employ such methods. Their most potent weapon is the withdrawal of the cooperation which government needs, or even the mere suggestion that this might be contemplated. Such a threat would not need to be made publicly, so it is impossible to say how often it occurs. The Heung Yee Kuk has talked of using such tactics; and in the blind workers' demonstration described above Mr. Sales, the Chairman of the Society for the Blind, was reported as implying that he and the council of the society would resign if government did not provide additional funds.[20]

Withdrawal of cooperation by a pressure group which is in frequent and intimate contact with the administration is very similar to a trade union calling a strike. Since unions are very weak in Hong Kong—less than 15 per cent of the workers are unionized—strikes against government policy are rare. In 1973 non-graduate teachers were successful in extorting a higher pay award as a result of a series of one-day stoppages. Also in 1973 midwives threatened to stage a mass resignation from government service unless their pay scale was improved. In both cases the industrial action was directed against government which provided the money for salaries either directly or through a grant-in-aid. Rather different was a two-day stoppage by minibus drivers who took their vehicles off the road in protest against new government restrictions on their routes. They hoped that they would cause severe hardship to the travelling public and so persuade government to modify the restrictions. In fact, the absence of minibuses eased traffic congestion and helped the large bus companies, and so proved counter-productive for the striking drivers.

The grossest forms of political pressure—kidnappings, arson, bomb attacks and assassinations—were used in the colony during the 1967 confrontation, but have hardly been seen since then.[21] Such methods are most likely to be used by groups which know that they cannot hope to exercise influence within the present regime and instead seek to overthrow it. They are unlikely to secure any concessions unless the government is already close to the point of abdication, since such a surrender to brute force would cause a complete collapse of public confidence in the administration and encourage all other groups to press their demands to the limit.

In general, pressure groups are anxious to preserve their good reputation—which is an asset when bargaining with government—and so keep strictly within the law. It is improbable that corruption plays much part in their tactics. Normally they are seeking to secure changes in public policy which require the agreement of a number of officials acting under the spotlight of publicity. It is not impossible that money might change hands when a decision on a matter of detail which is important to a particular group is left to a single official or technical expert, but most controversial decisions are not of this kind. At most, generous hospitality might be offered, but this is not an offence under the *Prevention of Bribery Ordinance*.[22]

AN ASSESSMENT OF THE PRESSURE GROUP SYSTEM

The great advantage of the intimate contact and consultation between government and pressure groups is that it enables officials to find out at first hand the opinions and attitudes of the particular sections of society likely to be affected by any policy before the detailed drafting of a bill takes place. Difficulties are foreseen, problems are anticipated, and, it is to be hoped, solutions are found well before a proposal is enacted into law. Without the information and help which such groups provide, government decisions would be less rational, because they would be based on an inadequate knowledge of the relevant facts, and administration would be more expensive and less efficient since drawbacks would be discovered too late in the day for an easy remedy to be found. Above all, by consulting beforehand and making concessions on points of detail— and even sometimes on points of substance—government is more likely to obtain the willing consent which it needs to carry through its policies effectively.

However, there is a case to be made on the other side. All groups do not have equal access to government and officials are highly selective in choosing the groups with which they are willing to hold consultations. This system favours the richer business and employer groups, who are largely represented on advisory committees. Government needs their help, and so must pay attention to their views. Other groups, particularly the trade unions and those groups speaking for the poorer sections of society, can provide less positive assistance in administration to the bureaucracy and so are more easily ignored. Officials sometimes argue that such groups are not really representative and that if government consulted with them it would give them an exaggerated idea of their own importance. Unions in particular are regarded with suspicion because the majority of them are affiliated to communist or nationalist dominated organizations, and in consequence they have representation on only two advisory bodies, the Labour Advisory Board and the Industrial Training Advisory Committee.

Groups catering for the poor are bound to be at a disadvantage in any country. They cannot afford to hire officers with the skills needed to present their case adequately to government and so must rely on voluntary workers who may lack the time and competence to write to the press or lobby government officials effectively. In Hong Kong these difficulties are compounded by two factors: the main language of the government is English, a foreign tongue which only a small minority of the Chinese population can use fluently, and the absence of meaningful elections. Where every adult has a vote any government is forced to pay close attention to the complaints of the poor. Fear of losing seats at the next election often prevents the British government from giving way to a well-organized pressure group. The main political resource of the lower classes is their numbers, but in Hong Kong there is no way in which the majority can make this potential power effective, short of rioting in the streets. Those who are unable or unwilling to participate in the political process are too easily ignored by government. It is a justifiable complaint against the colonial administration in Hong Kong that it does little to encourage the weak to organize to protect their interests, and provides few accessible channels for such groups as have been formed to present their cases to it.

This, however, is not so much a complaint against the whole pressure group system as such, but rather a plea that its benefits, which are now mainly open to the more privileged groups, should be made more widely available. Moreover, the defects of the present system are in part mitigated by certain countervailing factors which on occasion set limits to the influence of powerful groups and increase the strength of weaker ones.

Pressure groups do not form a united front against government, but often spend as much or more effort in fighting against each other. Apart from the obvious conflict between employers' associations and trade unions, industrialists in the same sector of the economy can be ranged against each other: for example in 1972 the Hong Kong Cotton Spinners Association was bitterly critical of the decision that up to 36 per cent of garments exported to Britain under quota could be made from imported fabrics and need not be made from cloth spun in Hong Kong. Yet this same decision was welcomed by the garment manufacturers and workers.[23] Similarly in 1973 the President of the Chinese Manufacturers Association advocated government controls on rising commercial rents, while the President of the Real Estate Developers Association proposed instead that government should make more land available at reasonable prices, thus making rent controls unnecessary. Such conflicts between pressure groups give government considerable room for manoeuvre.

Secondly, the support of public opinion can give strength to the claims made by a group with few resources of its own. An example is the blind workers' demonstration described above (p. 190), where the choice of tactics served to maximize this advantage. On the other side, the teachers had to go to greater lengths than the nurses when asking for more pay because the Hong Kong public, most unfairly, regards teaching as a relatively easy job. Government is much more inclined to give way when it believes that a group has popular support, so any organization seeking to influence a government decision tries to show that its objects will serve the public interest of Hong Kong and seeks to present its case in terms which will be likely to attract public sympathy. That is why the successful campaign to get the terms of Crown Lease renewals revised concentrated on the plight of the poor widow with one room, rather than on the fat profits which the big property companies could expect to make as a result of government concessions.

A third factor which can work against a powerful pressure group is the extent to which its demands run counter to the ideology of government. The administration is not an inert mass of plasticine shaped by the pummelling inflicted on it by the blows of each group in turn—though there are times when this seems a very appropriate description! Senior government officials do still believe in the virtues of a free economy, even if their prostrations at the shrine of Adam Smith are no longer quite so devout as in the priesthood of Sir John Cowperthwaite. Any business group wanting subsidies or special protection is likely to get short shrift from the Governor's financial advisers. The absence of elections in Hong Kong means that, unlike the situation in Britain, the top decision-makers are permanent civil servants, not party politicians, and so they do not need to trim their policies to gain votes or to attract the financial contributions needed from industrialists or trade unions that are necessary to pay for party propaganda and electioneering.

So long as the civil service stands firm to guard the public interest as they see it—(which may not, of course, be the same thing as the majority of the Hong Kong people want)—the power of pressure groups need never become excessive, while their representations are an essential means for keeping the bureaucracy attuned to the needs and attitudes of the different groups which make up the colony's population.

1. Speech to the Hong Kong University Economics Society, *Sunday Post-Herald*, 27 January 1974.

2. See *Far Eastern Economic Review*, 29 January 1970, p. 16 and *Sunday Post-Herald*, 13 May 1973.

3. The Registrar of Societies (the Commissioner of Police) had 2,035 societies registered at the end of March 1973. This excludes 338 trade unions and all religious, charitable, social and recreational societies. (*Annual Report of the Commissioner of Police*, 1972–73, p. 29.)

4. Three societies were refused registration in 1970–1, one in 1971–2, and two in 1972–3. (*Commissioner of Police Annual Reports.*) For further details of exemptions and penalties see the *Societies Ordinance, Laws of Hong Kong*, cap. 151.

5. Sir Edward Bridges, *Portrait of a Profession* (Rede Lecture, 1952).

6. *H.K. Hansard 1965*, p. 271. For another example, see *H.K. Hansard 1971–72*, p. 441, when proposed tax changes on profits recommended by the Inland Revenue Ordinance Review Committee were held up because of opposition from several trade and accounting bodies.

7. 'The new laws are at present being drafted by the Assistant Principal Crown Counsel, Mr. E. Corbally, in close consultation with the insurance industry here.' (*South China Morning Post*, 26 June 1973.)

8. 'Next year no less than 25 per cent of total recurrent expenditure will go to assist non-Government bodies to provide services of various kinds.', the Financial Secretary, Budget Speech, 27 February 1974. *H.K. Hansard 1973–74*, p. 572.

9. *Report of the Hong Kong General Chamber of Commerce 1962*, p. 8; and *Report 1965*, p. 7.

10. For example, when introducing certain regulations made under the *Factories and Industrial Undertakings Ordinance*, the Commissioner of Labour assured the Legislative Council, 'The Labour Advisory Board endorses the proposals unanimously. The Federation of Hong Kong Industries, the Employers Federation of Hong Kong, the Hong Kong General Chamber of Commerce, and the Chinese Manufacturers Association whom I have also consulted all informed me that they had no objection to the new regulations.' (*H.K. Hansard 1969*, p. 527.)

11. The concept of 'virtual representation' was used in eighteenth century England to defend the unreformed House of Commons. It was claimed that the views of those who did not have the franchise were virtually represented by the member for their area, or by a member from another part of the country who belonged to the same interest. Thus, for example, the member for the port of Bristol could voice the opinions of shipowners elsewhere who did not participate directly by electing their own member. See A.H. Birch, *Representative and Responsible Government* (Allen & Unwin 1964), p. 28.

12. Interview with Mr. J.B. Kite, Director of the General Chamber of Commerce.

13. See *H.K. Hansard 1970–71*, pp. 859–62.

14. Interview with Mr. R.W. Primrose, Administrative Secretary of UMELCO and *UMELCO Annual Report 1973–4*, p. 28.

15. *H.K. Hansard 1973–74*, p. 268.

16. For examples of statements by the Joint Kaifong Research Council see Aline K. Wong, *The Kaifong Associations and the Society of Hong Kong*, pp. 65–7.

17. e.g. *House of Commons Debates*, 8 Nov. 1966, written question. col. 244. (European civil servants' pay), 16 November 1970 oral question col. 832. (Chinese as official language). On 12 Dec. 1967 (cols. 178–9), Mr. Rankin presented a petition against the Public Order Ordinance organized by the Reform Club and signed by 30,000 people, asking the Secretary of State to advise the Queen to exercise her powers of disallowance against the ordinance.

18. Motion passed at a rally held by the Ha Tsuen Rural Committee (*South China Morning Post*, 7 April 1972). No such delegation has yet been sent.

19. *South China Morning Post*, 11, 12 and 13 November 1971.

20. 'Mr. Sales said he would ask the Government for the money. Asked if Government refuses, Mr. Sales retorted that without the necessary finance, a new chairman and council would have to be found for the society.' (*South China Morning Post*, 11 November 1971.)

21. An isolated incident occurred on 27 March 1971 when a suspicious object was found at night outside the Central Government Offices beside posters protesting against an increase in the water rates and demanding the use of Chinese as an official language. While this object was being investigated by the police ballistics officer it exploded causing serious injuries to his right arm. There were also a number of hoax bomb warnings in the next few days, but nothing more.

22. An amendment was moved in committee by the Attorney General to permit this, 'because of the widespread fears of the business community, of the Kaifongs and of the Heung Yee Kuk, that to make the acceptance of entertainment into a criminal offence is to interfere unreasonably with the normal conduct of business life' (*H.K. Hansard 1970–71*, pp. 278ff).

23. On this matter the Department of Commerce and Industry accepted the 64 per cent: 36 per cent split recommended by the Textile Advisory Board. This is an example of the way government can sometimes use advisory committees to take a difficult decision on its behalf. (*South China Morning Post*, 27 and 31 January, 8 March 1972.)

18 Public Opinion

'A constitution such as Hong Kong's has as a matter of plain commonsense
to be as sensitive as possible to the state of public opinion.'

Sir David Trench[1]

ALL democratic governments claim that they pay close attention to
public opinion. This professed deference is dictated by the need for self-
preservation, since if the views of the voters are disregarded they may turn
out the government at the next election. The colonial administration of
Hong Kong is not responsible to the local population and so it could,
in theory, pay little heed to popular views since, however much the Chinese
may dislike their British masters, they are unlikely to seek to overthrow
them in order to put themselves under communist rule. However, in
practice government is 'painfully sensitive'[2] to public opinion and rarely
takes any step which it fears may arouse widespread opposition. Rather
than defy public opinion it prefers to delay or find an excuse to put off
action indefinitely. But this is not always possible; its long procrastination
in 1966 before it sanctioned the fare increases requested by the Star Ferry
Company gave time for popular resentment to build up, culminating in
three nights of street rioting. The danger of a similar outburst in future
is a strong reason to avoid antagonizing the public. Such crises make bad
publicity for the colony, frighten away investment and stimulate unwelcome ministerial and parliamentary interest in the colony's affairs. More
positively British officials feel obliged to emphasize that the administration
is carried on in the interests of the people and that the views of the public
are taken into account. This helps to justify the continuance of colonial
rule at the bar of world opinion, and also serves to bridge the gulf between
the democratic principles that officials profess at home and their place in
the authoritarian structure of the colonial regime. Thus they can freely
admit that government is not 'by the people' while at the same time they
are able to claim that it is 'for the people' and so really satisfies the basic
object of democracy.[3]

However, it is not easy to gauge public opinion. On many, if not most,
policy proposals the majority of the population have no views, and the
only relevant 'public' as far as the government is concerned are a few
pressure groups, or perhaps only one. The bulk of legislation falls into
this category: for instance, the *Nurses Registration (Amendment) Bill*, the

Gasholders Examination (Amendment) Bill, and the *Merchandise Marks (Amendment) Bill*, all of which were passed through the Legislative Council with hardly any formal debate in 1972.

On other matters public interest may be aroused, but government finds itself faced with a wide spectrum of opinions, with no view obviously commanding majority support. For example, on the question of legalized abortion, some may be utterly opposed to this measure on principle, others would permit it only when the life of the mother is endangered, others would also agree to it in the case of rape, or on strictly defined social grounds, while yet another group advocates that facilities for abortion should be freely available.[4] Such a case makes it clear that the term 'public opinion' is an abstraction. Opinions are held by individuals and there is no reason to suppose that on any issue the opinions of the majority will be found clustered round a particular point. Normally, the most that government can hope to do is to find the compromise that will give least offence, even if it is a course that is positively desired by only a minority.

Another difficulty is that the opinions of the public often rest on misunderstandings or ignorance of the relevant facts. Some decisions that government must take are appallingly complex and are based on the assessment of a vast amount of technical data and future projections, many of which are in dispute between the experts themselves. How can any individual who is not professionally involved spare the time and energy to master the arguments for and against the Mass Transit Underground Railway or the proposed refinery and petro-chemical complex on Lamma island? The latter problem involves guesses about the likelihood of a world glut or shortage of oil in three years' time, the relative costs then of imported or home-produced plastics, the dangers of pollution and the feasibility of effective controls, and many other factors. The opinions expressed by the man in the street are unlikely to be influenced by more than one or two points which seem salient to him, such as sympathy with the fishermen who will be dispossessed or a dislike of the smell of oil near his home. No responsible government would willingly leave such a decision to the ill-informed prejudices of the masses—though if passions were sufficiently aroused this might be found to be the easiest course to follow.*

Furthermore, public opinion is often inconsistent and determined by short-range considerations. Most people find no difficulty in advocating at the same time both increased government expenditure and lower taxation. Even unofficial members of the Legislative Council sometimes fall into this trap. Similarly it is frequently suggested that Hong Kong's reserves should be drawn on to finance current expenditure, ignoring the fact that they may be needed if the colony's export earnings were to be sharply cut back by a world slump—an eventuality which actually occurred in 1974—and also that these reserves help to maintain the Hong Kong dollar as one of the most stable of the world's currencies.

*This is not an argument against democracy. Democracy (modern Western style) is not a system where people take the decisions, but where the people choose, and dismiss, the decision-makers. (The 1975 British referendum on E.E.C. membership was exceptional.)

All these difficulties ensure that in many government decisions 'sensitivity to public opinion' is more an ideal to be aimed at rather than a practical guide for policy-making.

THE SOURCES OF PUBLIC OPINION

Government gathers the views of the public in a number of different ways, which include the following:

Opinions encountered in the course of official business, particularly by officers in frequent contact with the public, such as District Officers, City District Officers, Labour Officers, Housing Managers etc.

Surveys carried out by CDOs or the Government Information Services.

Letters to government departments and petitions to the Governor.

Letters to newspapers, editorials, and reports of meetings.

Discussion programmes on radio and television, and comments phoned in by the public.

Remarks made to government officials at social gatherings.

Official contacts with leaders of pressure groups, kaifongs and rural committees. Delegations to government departments.

Formal meetings of advisory committees and boards.

Speeches made at meetings of the Legislative Council, the Urban Council and the Heung Yee Kuk.

Personal representations and complaints received by the UMELCO office, ward offices of the Urban Council, and at enquiry counters of CDOs.

Demonstrations, strikes and riots.

This may seem a long list, but each of these sources has its own characteristic distortions or inadequacies. For example, government officials like to assume that those they talk to on advisory boards can be trusted to represent correctly the views of the groups they come from. But it is always possible that those who have been selected may be more concerned to ingratiate themselves by agreeing with the officials than risk their displeasure by bluntly disagreeing with them.[5] There is also the opposite danger that spokesmen for a pressure group may take up an extreme position against government in order to gain publicity, impress their members and show that they are getting value for their subscriptions, whereas in fact many of the members would be quite prepared to accept that the policy complained of is reasonable.[6]

Surveys run by City District Officers might seem a better means of ascertaining public opinion. But the technical safeguards and checks needed to ensure that a scientifically valid sample of the population has been interviewed are very complex, and it seems unlikely that hard-pressed CDOs have either the time or the training needed to set this up. Even if this difficulty were to be surmounted, surveys fail to discriminate between the reply of a concerned citizen who has given some thought to the matter and the casual off-the-cuff response of the man who had no ideas on the subject until he was approached by the interviewer. In such cases the way in which the question is put, or even the emphasis given by the questioner can easily bias the answer.

For such reasons as these government does not give great weight to the occasional surveys which it sponsors, or to the weekly digest of popular opinions, 'Town Talk', which is submitted to the Home Affairs Department from the city district offices. When a survey supports what government wants to do, the result is produced to show that government policy is in accordance with public opinion. When it does not, government stresses the dangers and difficulties of relying on such tests. For example, in December 1970, when Dr. Chung was pressing for the discontinuance of the summer-time alteration of the clocks, the Colonial Secretary cited the views of the public collected by the Home Affairs Secretariat in support of government's view that there was no demand for any change. However, six months later, the Secretary for Home Affairs was asked to consider banning the attendance of children at unsuitable films. He admitted that a survey of 600 people had in fact found that a majority were in favour of prohibiting children from seeing films containing scenes of a violent or sexual nature. But since this survey result was contrary to government's policy of non-interference he went on to belittle the finding, pointing out that the question posed in the survey did not indicate that there would be practical difficulties and the possibility of rising prices. So government took no action, though the Secretary did promise to keep the subject under review.[7]

All these methods of ascertaining public opinion have their deficiences, but when government finds that the speeches of the unofficial members of the Legislative and Urban Councils, the views expressed by the spokesmen of pressure groups and kaifongs, and the soundings taken by district officers all coincide, then it normally gives way. In the words of Sir Alexander Grantham, referring to a proposal to raise rents in 1953, 'When the public is strongly opposed to a certain course of action, one does not pursue it unless a matter of fundamental importance is involved. None was in this case, and government bowed to the public will.'[8] Government similarly reversed its policy in the face of demands for tougher laws against criminals in 1971 and over Crown Lease Renewals in 1973.

Government is in a more difficult position when the unofficial members of the Legislative Council take up an attitude which is at variance with the opinions gathered by government from other sources. In such a situation officials prefer, if at all possible, to do nothing rather than risk giving offence. Consequently the reform of Chinese marriage law and the abolition of concubinage was delayed for nearly twenty years in spite of intermittent pressures for action by the unofficial members, because government was afraid that any change would scandalize the less sophisticated and more traditionally-minded people in the rural areas.[9] Similarly the widespread popularity of all forms of gambling among the Chinese in Hong Kong suggests that the public would have no great objections to greater legalization of this pastime, but government was unwilling to make any move in this direction until opinion in the Legislative Council had unanimously moved in its favour. In both cases government deferred any action until it judged that the views of the unofficials and general Chinese opinion had converged.

But procrastination of this sort is not always possible. Sometimes government cannot avoid taking a decision which will give offence to one party or another. In these cases the views of the unofficials on the Legislative Council will normally be decisive, especially if they are united in their stand. For example in 1969 it is a fair guess that most Chinese, if asked, would have supported the idea of an independent 'Ombudsman' to investigate complaints against government.[10] But the unofficials (with one dissentient) were strongly opposed to this proposal, so government accepted their view that nothing more than a strengthening of the UMELCO office was necessary.[11]

When the unofficials are divided or not very interested in the matter government has greater freedom to do what it thinks is best in the public interest. Public opinion is then largely a negative check on government: it can sometimes restrain it from taking action, but is not often successful in persuading government to initiate a change. The imposition of rent controls in 1963 and 1970 were exceptional cases in this respect. There had been little pressure in the Legislative Council for the imposition of controls before government introduced legislation (one unofficial had spoken in favour in 1962, and two in 1970), but government nevertheless acted, contrary to its own *laissez-faire* principles, in deference to widespread anxieties about rising rents.[12] It may be suggested that the reason in this case was that government is particularly concerned to keep middle-class Chinese opinion on its side, and it was largely this sector of the population which was vulnerable to rising rents.[13] The poorer classes were less affected since many were accommodated in low-cost and resettlement housing estates.

Normally, however, when government is unwilling to act it has no difficulty in finding pretexts for delay or excuses for doubting the extent of public support. In face of this inertia agitation needs to be spearheaded by a resourceful promotional pressure group which can keep the issue alive for weeks or months until government feels obliged to take some positive action. But such a campaign is only likely to succeed if there is genuinely widespread support for its aims, and if such 'authorized' spokesmen of public opinion as the unofficials on the Legislative Council and the Heung Yee Kuk are favourably disposed towards the agitation or at least neutral. These conditions were fulfilled in 1971 when the students' campaign for Chinese to be made an Official Language succeeded in forcing government to appoint a committee which conceded most of their demands, culminating in the *Official Languages Bill 1974*. It is a reasonable assumption that the Chinese population has always wanted the maximum use of their own language in administration, but this passive preference had little effect on government policy until a popular demand was whipped up by the student leaders. But such successful agitations are very rare.

The power of public opinion must not be assessed solely on the results of particular campaigns, since this might lead one to underestimate its importance. The views held by officials and among the general population tend to change gradually over time, and this subtle modification in the climate of opinion works its effect on government policy decisions almost unnoticed. For example, in 1953 an allocation of 24 square feet per person in resettlement estates appeared reasonable in comparison with the hovels that the occupants had previously lived in; but by 1969 it was generally agreed that the standard should be raised to 35 square feet. Four years later it was decided, almost without argument, that all new estates from 1974 should be designed to a standard of 50 square feet per person. Similarly, in 1947 Princess Elizabeth was given a wedding gift of HK$50,000,[14] and Princess Margaret received the same sum on her marriage in 1960, although the colony was then much richer. But in 1973 a gift of carpets to Princess Anne on her marriage cost only HK$5,000. Possibly the size of the gift was prompted by fears that anything larger might lead to an unseemly public protest. It might also be argued that one reason for government's more accommodating attitude to China in the past few years has been the gradual decay of pro-Kuomintang sentiments among the general population since the 1950s.

GOVERNMENT'S EFFORTS
TO INFLUENCE PUBLIC OPINION

Officials are not merely passive recipients of the views of the public. They also seek to mould the attitudes of the people and induce them to want the things that government thinks are good for them.[15] This is partly attempted by district officers, CDOs and other officers in frequent contact with the public in the course of their duties, but the main effort is in the hands of the Government Information Services and Radio Hong Kong. Unlike the British Broadcasting Corporation, which is an independent body, Radio Hong Kong is a government department. Its basic function, according to government spokesmen, is 'to inform, to educate, and to act as a bridge between Government and the people'.[16] All local news bulletins, both for Radio Hong Kong and for the commercial stations, are prepared by the Government Information Services and must be transmitted without alteration.

This does not mean that there is no criticism of government on radio and television. Those who object to particular policies are allowed to state their case in discussion programmes. But every attempt is made to create favourable attitudes to government by giving full coverage to its successes and glossing over its mistakes. Since Hong Kong has no 'loyal opposition' in the British sense, critics have no automatic right of reply to official broadcasts and the colonial regime itself cannot be called into question.[17]

Government has paid great attention to its public relations efforts in recent years. After the 1967 confrontation the expenditure on this increased from HK$9.9 million in 1967–8 to HK$16 million the following year. In August 1972 the new Governor created the post of Secretary for

Information to enable Mr. Cater to coordinate Radio Hong Kong, the information services and all other government activities in this area. Since the McKinsey reorganization this has become part of the portfolio of the Secretary for Home Affairs.

How much value government gets for its money must remain doubtful. Successful persuasion depends on the absence of competing information, and the prestige and credibility of the source. Even in China after a sustained barrage of propaganda for twenty years under the most favourable conditions pre-Communist attitudes remain deeply entrenched, as Chairman Mao Tse-tung has frequently complained. The Hong Kong government comes nowhere near to obtaining such saturation coverage. In 1971 the Information Services budgeted $100,000 for a campaign to persuade qualified residents to enrol as Urban Council voters. Ten thousand posters, 500,000 leaflets and 50,000 car stickers were produced, Radio Hong Kong Television provided six short films, and there were constant radio slogans on all channels.[18] The final result was that out of some hundreds of thousands who were eligible only 5,438 new voters bothered to enrol and the number of electors on the register went down from 37,788 to 31,284 (see above Chapter 14, p. 158).

A more successful attempt to encourage public participation has been the new system of publishing 'Green Papers' outlining proposed changes and new programmes in various policy areas. The first of them was the draft paper on Social Welfare published in October 1972 and this was followed by proposed plans for Education and for Medical Services in 1973. The intention is that comments and criticisms from all sources will be collated and assessed before the Governor in Council takes the final decisions. In fact few changes were made in the Social Welfare proposals, which were generally welcomed. But the Education Green Paper was severely criticized and extensive alterations were made in the definitive White Paper which was produced in 1974. However these changes failed to satisfy the Education Action Group and other critics who are continuing to agitate for further modifications, particularly the increased use of Chinese as a medium of instruction.

This is a danger that government faces in stimulating the public to put forward their views more freely. If the opinions expressed go beyond the limits imposed on government by the colony's peculiar political and economic situation, those who have been encouraged to speak up and then find that nothing comes of it may feel more frustrated and alienated than if they had never been asked. This poses a dilemma for the administration. The ambitious programmes on which it has now embarked, and the higher taxes that will be needed to pay for them, require a greater measure of popular consent for their successful implementation than government needed to elicit in the past when it concerned itself less with people's social conditions. One way of gaining this consent is to encourage participation, but such attempts cannot be allowed to go too far, lest they endanger the whole basis of the colonial regime.

1. *H.K. Hansard 1971–72*, p. 11.

2. *The City District Officer Scheme, A Report by the Secretary for Chinese Affairs* (January 1969), p. 35: 'The picture that some people paint of the Government as an inhuman machine which would react only to inquisitors armed with statutory powers is a strange one to arrive at about a Government which is almost painfully sensitive to public opinion, but it nevertheless seems to be quite widely held.'

3. This is the argument used for example by S.W. Rainbird, *Oxford Progressive Economics and Public Affairs*.

4. This example is adapted from the speech by the Attorney General on the *Offences Against the Person (Amendment) Bill, H.K. Hansard 1971–72*, p. 512.

5. This point is made about Kaifong leaders in the report quoted in note 2 above, p. 12. 'Some associations make extravagant claims of active membership and influence, and the mechanism by which leaders represent the views of members cannot always be relied on.... They have perhaps an undue regard for Government officials with whom they are in regular contact.'

6. A possible example of this might be the vehement campaign of the Hong Kong Automobile Association in early 1974 against the *Fixed Penalty (Criminal Proceedings) Bill* and the increased taxation on motor vehicles. Only about twenty members attended the annual general meeting on 11 March 1974 where bitter attacks on government's 'greedy bullying' were made.

7. *H.K. Hansard 1970–71*, pp. 213f and pp. 665f.

8. Grantham, *Via Ports*, p. 109.

9. The original proposal for reform was made in the *Strickland Report* of 1950. A further report by McDougall and Heenan was produced in 1965. Government defended its delays in a debate in 1967, when Mrs. Ellen Li Shu-pui was pressing for immediate action, *H.K. Hansard 1967*, p. 259. The law was finally amended in 1970.

10. There is no survey evidence to prove this, but the Urban Council voted in favour of establishing an Ombudsman by 14 to none (officials and some appointed unofficials abstaining) on 23 Dec. 1969, pp. 391–6.

11. See Chapter 10, note 10 for references to Legislative Council speeches.

12. Once government had decided to legislate, the unofficials on both occasions, supported the bill. Mr. Dhun Ruttonjee was in favour of controls in 1962 (*H.K. Hansard 1962*, p. 80). Mr. Wilfred Wong Sien-bing spoke in favour (*H.K. Hansard 1969–70*, p. 36) and Mr. Fung Hon-chu asked a question (ibid. p. 227) before government acted in 1970.

13. On an unscripted radio discussion in 1970, the Attorney General said, 'Of course government pays attention to public opinion—I mean educated middle-class opinion' (noted at the time).

14. Princess Elizabeth asked that most of the gift should be retained in Hong Kong to help young people. (*H.K. Hansard 1947*, pp. 293f.)

15. The most forthright expression of this point of view is to be found in the *Report by the Interdepartmental Working Party on Social Security, 1967*. The nine civil servants on this committee (including four Chinese) proposed to institute a comprehensive social security programme, but they recognized that this was likely to be unpopular, so they recommended:

'If social insurance is to be introduced in Hong Kong we are sure that the success thereof will largely depend upon conditioning the public, in the sectors concerned, to acceptance beforehand. We believe that with skilful publicity through all the available media, such as television, radio and films, it should be possible to to 'sell' the idea to a significant proportion of those likely to be affected. This preparatory action must not be left until too late. It should be the aim of such publicity to create an actual desire for the programme which is contemplated before any announcement of definite intention to introduce is made.' (p. 96)

Government did not in fact accept this report, primarily for financial reasons.

16. From a speech by the Financial Secretary, *H.K. Hansard 1967*, p. 91.

17. Similarly in Britain, fascists, communists and Welsh Nationalists are only rarely allowed to put their case on the air. See also p. 225, note 6.

18. *Proceedings of the Hong Kong Urban Council*, 9th May 1972, pp. 47f. See R. Rose, *Influencing Voters* (Faber, London, 1967), pp. 180ff, for a sceptical discussion of the effectiveness of most political propaganda.

19 The Role of the British Government

'The interference from London was really quite intolerable.'
Sir Alastair Blair-Kerr, Judge of the Hong Kong Supreme Court.[1]

IN constitutional law the administration of Hong Kong is completely subordinate to the Crown—that is, to the government at present holding office in Britain; but in practice the colony is very largely autonomous, particularly in internal matters, and discussions between London and Hong Kong are sometimes much more like diplomatic negotiations between two sovereign states than the compliant obedience by an inferior to orders from above. The rights and obligations set out in the constitutional documents give a very misleading picture of the relationship, since the British government is in fact inhibited from exercising most of its ample legal powers by long-established conventions and by the practical difficulties and risks involved.

THE FRAMEWORK OF POWERS AND CONVENTIONS

Parliament is entitled to pass laws applicable in Hong Kong, or alternatively the Crown can legislate for the colony by issuing Orders in Council; but by convention Parliament rarely legislates except

i. where legislation is beyond the power of the local legislature, e.g. where it is of extra-territorial operation;
ii. where the subject is of concern to more than one country and uniformity is desirable, e.g. fugitive offenders; and
iii. where the subject is an important one of Commonwealth or United Kingdom concern and therefore not merely of a domestic nature, e.g. matters such as defence, air navigation and treaties.[2]

In similar fashion, Orders in Council are almost entirely confined to the detailed application of such acts of parliament, to minor textual amendments to the *Letters Patent* and *Royal Instructions*, and to certain ceremonial matters such as the issuing of medals or the striking of new coinage.

The Crown has the right to disallow ordinances passed by the Legislative Council, but this has not been done since 1913. Instead a convention has grown up that any controversial bill will be submitted to London beforehand, so that any objections raised in Whitehall can be taken into account and compromises negotiated before the bill is introduced into the Legislative Council. (See pp. 99–100 above.)

The Governor is required to obey all instructions from the Secretary of State. Such directives are occasionally sent, particularly when international relations are involved. For example, Sir Alexander Grantham records that in 1953 the Colonial Office insisted over his protests that an oil tanker owned by the Chinese government, which was then undergoing repairs in a Hong Kong dockyard, should be requisitioned. The reason in this case was that Britain was under pressure from the United States and, in Grantham's words, 'was more scared of what the United States might do to Britain than of what China might do to Hong Kong'.[3] But on most internal matters messages from Whitehall to the Governor are framed in much less peremptory terms. It is a long-established principle of British government that the man in charge on the spot is in the best position to judge what is practicable. The Governor's despatches are the main source of information available in London about local conditions, and ministers have generally been very reluctant to override such advice, particularly since the Governor would have the responsibility for dealing with any trouble or rioting which might follow if a minister's decision proved to be mistaken. In the words of a very senior civil servant in the Colonial Office in 1956, 'To overrule the considered and maintained advice of a Governor is a thing which no Secretary of State would do lightly or unless he was convinced that his action was right and could be publicly defended'.[4]

This reluctance is reinforced by the effect of two conventions that have become established in Hong Kong: that the official majority in the Legislative Council is never used to override the views of the Finance Committee on expenditure, nor to force through legislation to which the unofficials are unanimously opposed. Most policy changes involve either money or legislation to carry them into effect; so if the unofficials stood firm against a ministerial proposal London would have the choice of giving way or provoking an unprecedented confrontation by mobilizing the official majority. It is difficult to think of any internal matter so vital that the Secretary of State would choose to order the latter course to be taken.[5]

The power to select the next Governor is potentially the most important control over Hong Kong which Britain possesses, since the work of the whole government machine turns on his decisions. But this too has its limitations. Any man who is considered capable of directing the affairs of a complex colony such as Hong Kong is not likely to be very amenable to advice sent from 8,000 miles away. Once ensconced in Government House any Governor will find that he is under pressure from the expectation of his subordinates that he will resist guidance from Whitehall, and he will suffer a loss of authority if he fails to do so. There are plenty of examples of men who have been put in charge of an organization in order to bring it to heel who have instead turned out to be the staunchest defenders of its autonomy; perhaps particularly so when they arrive saddled with the former reputation. The governorship of Hong Kong is no longer a stepping stone to higher things, and so once appointed he is not beholden to the British government for anything, not even for his pension.[6]

All the most senior officials are formally appointed by the Secretary of State, as are also the unofficial members of the Executive and Legislative Councils. But it is very difficult for the Foreign and Commonwealth Office in London to dispute the Governor's assessment of the merits of local officers for promotion; moreover it would be contrary to the practice of the British government to deny him the right to choose his own subordinates when a vacancy occurs, provided he kept within the established rules of the civil service; nor would an officer be transferred to Hong Kong from another colony without his consent. Similar considerations apply to appointments to the Executive and Legislative Councils. All members of the Public Service (except Judges of the Supreme Court) hold their offices during the pleasure of the Crown and are in theory liable to be dismissed at any time. But by convention this would only be done on the advice of the Public Service Commission and in accordance with the procedure laid down in *Colonial Regulations* and the *Establishment Regulations* of the Hong Kong government.

Governors can be recalled and replaced before their term is completed, and this power has occasionally been exercised in other colonies in recent years. In 1962 the Governor of Kenya, Sir Patrick Renison, was recalled when London saw fit to reverse its previous policy of refusing to negotiate with Jomo Kenyatta, the leading nationalist figure; and in 1967 the Governor of Aden, Sir Richard Turnbull, was replaced when Britain decided that arrangements for the territory's independence must be worked out with the National Liberation Front, which Sir Richard had banned two years previously. In both these cases British troops were being used, or had recently been used, on internal security operations and the interests of the British government—and the British taxpayer—in a swift end to colonial rule had to take priority. But these were exceptional cases, and such a protracted terminal crisis of colonialism is unlikely in Hong Kong. All Governors since the war have had their appointments extended beyond their official five-year term and one, Sir Alexander Grantham, served for ten years.

All the rights of the Crown mentioned so far might be described as the exercise of positive powers; they are instances where the British government can take the initiative and intervene directly in the colony's affairs. But there are also times when the Hong Kong government requests permission to be allowed to do something itself, or asks Britain to take some action on its behalf. On such occasions Britain can exercise a negative power by refusing permission or by declining to bestir itself very energetically on Hong Kong's behalf. The first kind of positive power may appear more important, but, as can be seen, it is in fact seldom exercised; the second, negative, power is less obvious, but is probably now the more significant factor in the relationship between the metropolis and her colony.

The most important permission which Hong Kong repeatedly requested in the past few years was to be allowed to reduce the sterling content of her external reserves while retaining the guarantee of their value. The colony's case was that no other country covered by the guarantee was required to keep so high a proportion of its external reserves in sterling as Hong Kong. Until 1971 this proportion was 99 per cent; then a token reduction to 89 per cent was permitted by Britain, but no further diversification was permitted without loss of the guarantee until 1974 when the guarantee was ended and Hong Kong was at last able to manage its reserves as it pleased (see above, pp. 9–11). A similar case, where Britain is able to further her own interests and obstruct Hong Kong's merely by doing nothing, occurred in 1974 over a proposal to set up a Hong Kong shipping register. Talks on this matter had been going on between the Hong Kong government and the Department of Trade and Industry since 1972, but the proposal now appears to have been rejected by the new Labour government in deference to the views of various seamen's unions in Britain.[7]

Over the last twenty years the list of matters on which Hong Kong must seek London's permission has been considerably shortened. In 1958 the colony was freed from the obligation to submit the annual estimates and certain supplementary estimates to London before their introduction into the Legislative Council, and the agreement of the Secretary of State was no longer required before a loan could be raised (see above p. 115). Since 1959 the Hong Kong authorities have been entirely free to keep budget surpluses on deposit in local banks or invest them in London, whereas previously all such investment had been the responsibility of the Crown Agents.[8] When Britain devalued sterling in 1949 the colony was instructed from London, without any consultations, that the exchange rate of the Hong Kong dollar was to be adjusted by an identical amount; but when Britain devalued again in 1967 Hong Kong was left free to decide her own exchange rate.[9] Subsequently, when the pound was allowed to 'float' in 1972, Hong Kong decided to peg its rate to that of the U.S. dollar.

These relaxations were welcome, but a number of important matters still require Britain's consent, giving her a certain leverage over the Hong Kong administration. In addition, Hong Kong is largely dependent on Britain's assistance in external affairs. Because it is a colony, Hong Kong has no independent foreign relations, and many international negotiations are conducted on its behalf by Britain. When tariff or quota barriers are raised against its exports it has to rely on British diplomats to make its protest (see p. 41 above). Hong Kong has set up offices in London, Washington, Geneva and Brussels to foster its commercial relations, and the Department of Commerce and Industry sends many missions abroad; but at international economic conferences and in negotiations within the European Economic Community its officials sit as part of the British delegation and are dependent on British diplomats as to how vigorously Hong Kong's case is pressed in the complex bargaining that takes place before final agreement is reached. Similarly, the locally based airline, Cathay Pacific, has to use Britain's good offices to negotiate any extension of its route network, and is unable to use landing rights at Kai Tak as a bargaining factor, since the right to fly into Hong Kong is controlled by Britain in the interests of British Airways.

Hong Kong also needs British goodwill to counter threats to her trade in the United Kingdom market. Since the late 1950s British textile manufacturers have been actively lobbying for curbs on Hong Kong imports, and the case for restrictive quotas and tariffs is strongly voiced in Parliament by the members for Lancashire. The willingness of the Cabinet to resist such pressures will turn to a large extent on how considerate Hong Kong has been to British interests in other respects.

Since Hong Kong is dependent on the British government's cooperation on all these matters, the colony cannot afford to alienate it by any excessively blatant display of independence, for fear that Britain may do nothing when Hong Kong next asks for help. This is no doubt one reason why the Hong Kong government acceded, though very reluctantly, to British pressure for the accelerated release of communists convicted for criminal offences in the 1967 riots. Britain wished to improve its relations with Peking and secure the release of a newspaper reporter imprisoned in China; the Hong Kong authorities were more concerned about the bad effects on local opinion of any grant of clemency, but did in fact free the prisoners on various pretexts before they had served their full sentences.[10]

The presence of China is a further complicating factor. China has a large stake in Hong Kong's continued commercial prosperity and naturally takes an interest in the affairs of what is, in her view, Chinese territory. Any attempt by Britain to wave the big stick at her colony might well incur China's displeasure. No doubt officials are ready to remind London of this fact.

THE ACTORS: MINISTERS VERSUS THE HONG KONG ADMINISTRATION

Within this framework of legal powers, well-established conventions, practical difficulties and considerations of advantage, the outcome of any disagreement between London and Hong Kong will also depend on the interest felt in the issue and the determination to get their way shown by Her Majesty's ministers—and ministers rarely stay in the same post for more than a couple of years—and also, from Hong Kong's side, on the obstinacy or tractability of local officials.

During the period from the end of the war up to 1967 the Colonial Office showed little desire to concern itself overmuch with the internal affairs of the colony. Ministers and civil servants were kept far too busy with the problems of guiding the rest of the colonial empire to independence to worry much about what was happening in Hong Kong, except when under pressure from America about trading with China, or from Lancashire about textile exports. One noble Lord described the position rather colourfully in a parliamentary debate as,

The old Colonial Office dying on its feet, merging with the Commonwealth Office, seeing those remnants of countries overseas finishing up in disorder and disintegration, and costing money: Administrations here in this country saying to themselves over past years, 'Hong Kong is a shining example. Leave it alone. Let it get on with it. Let them do what they like.'[11]

For its part, the Hong Kong administration was happy to exploit this benign neglect. Many Chinese suspect expatriate officials of servile truckling to Whitehall,[12] but there is plenty of evidence that Sir John Cowperthwaite for one always put the colony's interests first. During most of the 1960s he took full advantage of Hong Kong's newly acquired financial autonomy by declining to transfer the colony's budget surpluses to London, where they would have been a very welcome addition to the reserves of the sterling area. Instead, he kept the money on deposit in Hong Kong banks and only resumed transfers in 1969 after the conclusion of the sterling guarantee agreement.[13] But for this, Hong Kong's losses at the time of the 1967 sterling devaluation would have been far greater. This independent attitude of Hong Kong officialdom was noted with displeasure by at least one visiting member of parliament, who said on his return,

The word 'unique' is rather overworked in this House, but I think that it applies to two colonies in their attitude towards Her Majesty's Government and Whitehall. One is Southern Rhodesia and the other is Hong Kong. Ian Smith has cocked a snook at Her Majesty's Government, and over the years it has been my impression that Hong Kong has been equally autonomous, despite not having self-government, like Rhodesia, since 1922. I say that because of the acts of her officials, who believe that they can do all manner of things which I have not found happening in other Colonial Territories, particularly in Africa. I do not believe that these officials care very much about Whitehall.[14]

During the 1950s this stand of the Hong Kong administration did not receive much open support from the unofficial members of the Executive and Legislative Councils. When British interests are involved ministers may be ready on occasions to overrule protests from the Governor and his officers, but they are much more wary of going against public opinion as voiced by the unofficials, whose strength they are unable to judge from afar. Sir Alexander Grantham was keenly conscious of the need for this reinforcement in his battles with Whitehall, and at the end of his governorship in 1957 he felt it necessary to gently chide the unofficials for their supine attitude:

One thought concerning Legislative Council, however, remains, and that is this. Would the authorities in London pay greater heed to Hong Kong and its just claims if the Council, which in this connexion means the unofficial members thereof, were to be more vocal in pressing those claims than has been the tradition in the past? I leave the thought with honourable members.[15]

During the 1960s the attitude among the unofficials began to change. There was much more readiness to voice open criticism of the British government and in 1967 Mr. Kan Yuet-keung even forced a division in his protest against the amount of the defence contribution. Such public demonstrations may make it easier for officials to negotiate more favourable terms when the Defence Costs Agreement next comes up for renewal, and also enable them to rebuff pressures from London for policy changes on the ground that it would be politically impossible to carry them through the Legislative Council.

The complacent attitude of Whitehall towards Hong Kong ended with the 1967 riots. Additional troops had to be sent to the colony, correspondents covering the confrontation sent back stories on working conditions in factories, and the Labour government found itself under pressure from its own backbenchers to take firm action. The Minister of State at the Foreign and Commonwealth Office, Lord Shepherd, visited Hong Kong and insisted that the legally permitted working hours for women and juveniles must be reduced from 60 to 48 a week, though this reform was only to take effect over a four-year period.[16] At the beginning of 1968 the Commissioner of Labour, Mr. Hetherington, announced a programme of thirty-three measures to improve workers' rights, and two labour advisers were sent out from England to assist in the preparation of the necessary ordinances and regulations.[17]

The need for British support to deal with the confrontation weakened the colony's position in its relations with London, and gave the British government the opportunity and the authority to insist that certain reforms must be carried through. At the same time, in the aftermath of the riots, the need for changes was recognized within the administration and also among the unofficials. But it seems that this shift in the balance of power was only a temporary one. Hong Kong made a remarkably swift recovery from the troubles: by 1969 the garrison had been run down to its normal strength and capital was coming back into the economy and inflating the reserves. In 1970 British interference in labour matters was bitterly criticized by Dr. Chung in the Legislative Council.[18] The following year the last of the Labour Advisers went home, and in 1972 only one new piece of labour legislation was brought forward.[19] At the beginning of 1974 about three-quarters of the labour reforms promised six years previously had been enacted into law, but bills on severance pay for redundant workers, apprenticeship, industrial training, the establishment of compulsory machinery for consultation between management and workers, and the setting of a minimum age for employment in the catering trades and in hawking had still not seen the light of day.

The actions of the Hong Kong government in 1973 in encouraging the banks to sell their sterling assets after Britain had refused to negotiate any diversification of Hong Kong's reserves, and in choosing a Japanese consortium to build the underground railway in preference to rival groupings which included British firms, show that the colony's effective autonomy in internal affairs remains unimpaired. The banks were fully within their legal rights in disposing of their sterling holdings and forgoing the guarantee, but the Hong Kong government could have stopped them from doing so, if it had wanted to be helpful to Britain, just as it could have found a reason to prefer a British group for constructing the railway.[20] But in both cases Hong Kong was determined to put its own interests first, and Britain, in accordance with past precedents, allowed her colony to do so. She still possesses the constitutional powers to act, but the political will to exercise them has atrophied from long disuse.

CHANNELS OF COMMUNICATION:
THE FOREIGN AND COMMONWEALTH OFFICE
AND THE HONG KONG LONDON OFFICE

The main channel of communication between the British government and Hong Kong is the Hong Kong Department of the Foreign and Commonwealth Office, which took over the functions of the former Commonwealth Office and Colonial Office in 1968. Its activities may be broadly described under three headings:

1. To convey and explain to the colonial administration the decisions of Her Majesty's government and those policies which may affect it.
2. To represent and safeguard the interests of Hong Kong in negotiations with foreign governments, with international organizations and —most important—with other departments in Whitehall.
3. To provide assistance to the colony through the visits of the Secretary of State's advisers (on police, education, etc.), by providing staff for specialized duties on secondment, and by offering guidance on the framing of legislation and internal policies by drawing attention to the solutions found elsewhere.[21]

In the past the Colonial Office recruited staff for the colonies, but this is now arranged by the Crown Agents,[22] and increasingly by the Appointments Section of the London Office.

The Hong Kong Department is headed by an Assistant Secretary who will normally hold the post for three years. He is unlikely to have had previous knowledge of the colony and so will begin his duties with an extended visit. Thereafter his information comes from the Governor's despatches, contacts with the London Office, local newspapers and magazines, and calls made by officials on leave, by unofficial members of the Executive and Legislative Councils visiting London, by businessmen and by the spokesmen of British pressure groups. He deals with all routine matters referred to London by the local administration, drafts replies to parliamentary questions and briefs ministers. How much is personally decided by ministers will depend on how much interest they choose to take, and the pressure of other business. The Secretary of State himself will only rarely be involved; most matters requiring ministerial attention will be dealt with by one of the ministers of state. For the last three years of the 1964–70 Labour government this was Lord Shepherd, who has lived in Singapore. Under the 1970–4 Conservative government the ministers responsible were Mr. Royle and (briefly) Mr. Blaker, both of whom were formerly prominent in the Anglo-Hong Kong Parliamentary group. In the new Labour government of March 1974 the minister charged with special responsibility for South-East Asia and the Far East is Lord Goronwy-Roberts, the Parliamentary Under-Secretary of State. He had never visited Asia before his appointment.

Hong Kong has maintained an office in London since the end of the last war, when it evolved from the planning unit which was established within the Colonial Office after the fall of Hong Kong to make plans for the colony's post-war rehabilitation.[23] As it is now organized, it forms part of the Colonial Secretariat, with its Commissioner directly responsible to the Colonial Secretary. Its primary purpose is to provide a focus and point of contact between the Hong Kong government, British government departments and commercial and trading interests in Britain. The Foreign and Commonwealth Office normally communicates directly with Hong Kong and not through the London Office, and it is not involved in direct negotiations with Britain. For example, when the quota agreement on textiles is to be revised, the Hong Kong delegation at the talks is led by the Director or Deputy Director of Commerce and Industry who comes to London for that purpose, assisted by a team of businessmen from the Textiles Advisory Board. On such occasions the delegation uses the London Office as a base and is provided with secretarial facilities and other assistance.

The main activities of the London Office are to keep a close watch on commercial and economic developments in Britain which may affect the colony's interests; to provide assistance with their problems for Hong Kong residents in Britain, particularly those studying there, for whom a Students Centre is maintained; and to provide information on Hong Kong and coordinate its public relations effort in Britain. This last activity was greatly expanded in 1967 and the London Office now conducts a vigorous campaign to present Hong Kong's case to the British public. Press releases and photographs are sent to newspapers; articles are written for specialized magazines; a panel of speakers is maintained to lecture to clubs and societies; films are made available and complimentary copies of the *Hong Kong Yearbook* and other publicity material are distributed.

There are also other organizations in Britain which look after Hong Kong's interests. In order to counter the influence of the Lancashire Textile lobby in the House of Commons an Anglo-Hong Kong parliamentary group has been set up of M.P.s who have connections with the colony or an interest in it. These members are active in putting Hong Kong's case in the House and in rebutting accusations made by other speakers. The Governor invariably addresses this group on his visits to London. There is also the Hong Kong Association, a society supported by firms and individuals who have commercial links with Hong Kong. This pressure group represents the colony's interests on various trade and export councils and chambers of commerce in Britain, and formerly arranged for visits to the colony by M.P.s.[24]

The suggestion has been made that the present channels of communication between Hong Kong and London need to be supplemented by the granting of life peerages to prominent Hong Kong people who could speak up for the colony in the House of Lords.[25] There is a precedent for this: Sir Leary Constantine, the famous West Indies cricketer from Trinidad, was created a life peer (a baron) in 1969. But possibly this idea overestimates the attention which British governments pay to what is said in the House of Lords and underestimates the many other means by which the views of Hong Kong are communicated to London. Any such representation could do nothing to alter the colony's irremediable weakness in its dealings with the Secretary of State: the fact that its 4 million inhabitants have no votes in British general elections.

Sources

The communications that pass between ministers, British civil servants and the Hong Kong administration are strictly confidential, and the possibility of disagreement between any of these three is never openly admitted. It is only on rare occasions that the veil of secrecy is lifted; one such example can be found in Appendix 6, Document B(ii), pp. 255–6. Consequently, any discussion of the relationship between Hong Kong and London must be based primarily on the memoirs of Sir Alexander Grantham, general accounts of the work of the Colonial Office, and deductions from publicly available material. I have sampled the files of correspondence between Whitehall and Hong Kong which are open up to 1941 in the Public Record Office in London—(the copies in Hong Kong were destroyed during the Japanese occupation)—but these are not necessarily indicative of the post-war relationship. They show that the Colonial Office officials at that time were very reluctant to dissent from any case put up by the Governor, even though their minutes on his despatch showed that they may have had their private doubts about his proposals. The following comment, on a request for permission to pay compensation to the Yacht Club, is typical: 'I do not like this very much, but the buildings are presumably worth the money to the government and I doubt if it is worth interfering in such a minor local affair,? approve'.

1. As quoted in the *Sunday Post-Herald*, 3 June 1973. The comment refers to the intervention by the Secretary of State, Sir Alec Douglas-Hume, to reprieve a murderer in spite of the fact that the Governor, having heard the advice of the Executive Council, had decided that he should be hanged. The judge had good reason to object to this decision: the authoritative legal textbook by Sir Kenneth Roberts-Wray, *Commonwealth and Colonial Law* (Stevens, London, 1966) p. 342, gives six cogent reasons why the Secretary of State should never advise the Queen to exercise this overriding power. The Governor made a similar but more subdued protest in his speech to the Legislative Council on 17 Oct. 1973, referring to 'the reprieve, on the advice of Her Majesty's Government, of a convicted murderer against the express advice of the Governor in Council and the wishes of the overwhelming majority of the population'. *H.K. Hansard 1973–4*, p. 3.

The Governor was particularly unlucky in his timing. After the decision to refuse a reprieve had been taken in the Executive Council the House of Commons twice voted against the death penalty: on 11 April, when it rejected a bill for the reintroduction of capital punishment by 320 to 178; and on 14 May when, on the advice of the Conservative Government, it abolished capital punishment in Northern Ireland by 253 to 94. Both these were free votes, and so were not influenced by party discipline. The day after the Northern Ireland vote (15 May) the Secretary of State granted Tsoi Kwok-cheung's petition to the Queen for mercy. Later it was stated by certain British M.P.s who were visiting Hong Kong (*South China Morning Post*, 2 June 1973) that the Leader of the Opposition had threatened to put down a motion of censure on the government for countenancing lower standards of justice in Hong Kong than in the United Kingdom, if a reprieve were not granted. This would have been highly embarrassing for the Conservatives in the eyes of public opinion, even though it was hardly a matter on which the government might have been forced to resign if defeated. So the considered views of the authorities in Hong Kong were on this occasion subordinated to humanitarian sentiments and political manoeuvrings in Britain.

2. This is the formulation of the present convention by Roberts-Wray, op.cit. p. 142. Acts of Parliament applicable to Hong Kong are listed in Volume 19, Appendix II of the *Laws of Hong Kong*. Those passed since the war include five acts successively redefining British Nationality, eight relating to the conduct, discipline and trials of British servicemen, four regulating Civil Aviation, an act extending diplomatic privileges, and a Fugitive Offenders Act regulating extradition procedures within the Commonwealth.

3. *Via Ports*, p. 163. For another example in a dispute over the ownership of aircraft between China and Taiwan see W.M. Leary, 'Aircraft and Anti-Communists: CAT in Action 1949–52', *China Quarterly* no. 52, 1972, pp. 654–69 and Grantham, op. cit. pp. 162–3.

4. Sir Charles Jeffries, *The Colonial Office* (Allen and Unwin, London, 1956), p. 36. Sir Charles was then Deputy Under-Secretary, that is the second most senior civil servant.

5. Martin Wight, *The Development of the Legislative Council* (Faber, London, 1946), p. 160: 'The Secretary of State may prefer to sanction measures which he considers unwise rather than to adopt the invidious position of opposing both the local government and local public opinion. These difficulties are increased when, as in Kenya and Ceylon under the 1923 constitution, a finance committee of the council composed of all the unofficials with only two officials in addition, has gained control not only over finance, but over policy as well.' Hong Kong is now also in this position. See Chapter 9, pp. 115–16.

6. The last five governors retired after leaving Hong Kong. Before that Sir Andrew Caldecott (1935–7) went on to govern Ceylon, and Sir Cecil Clementi (1925–30) to govern the Straits Settlements (Malaya).

7. In November 1973 the Conservative government introduced a *Merchant Shipping Act* which included provisions to allow the testing of safety equipment to be delegated from surveyors at the Department of Trade and Industry to outside organizations. This part of the bill was believed to be connected with the proposal to set up a separate Hong Kong register of shipping, and so was bitterly attacked by M.P.s speaking on behalf of the Mercantile Marine Service Association, the Merchant Navy and Airline Officers Association and the National Union of Seamen. (*House of Commons Debates*, 29 Nov. 1973, cols. 625–6, 673–4, 679.) This bill had not completed its passage through parliament when the House of Commons was dissolved for the general election of February 1974. It was then reintroduced by the Labour government in May 1974, but without the hiving off provisions to which the unions had objected. (*House of Lords Debates*, 20 May 1974, cols. 1250f.) See also on this subject *H.K. Hansard 1973–74*, pp. 362f, and reports in the *China Mail*, 18 April 1974 and the *South China Morning Post*, 19 April 1974.

8. *H.K. Hansard 1969*, p. 207.

9. *H.K. Hansard 1967*, pp. 499f.

10. The sentences of the first thirteen criminals were reduced in May 1969, apparently to secure the freedom of the Reuters' correspondent in Peking. Further releases were made over the next four years and the last of those convicted for their part in the 1967 riots were released in 1973. Even with full remission for good conduct the last of them should have remained in prison until 1977 (government statement in *South China Morning Post*, 5 July 1972). *The Times* correspondent in Hong Kong reported that these releases were being made under pressure from London against the wishes of the local administration (23 October 1970 and 20 January 1972). So also the *Far Eastern Economic Review*, 3 April 1971, p. 19.

11. Lord Rhodes, *House of Lords Debates*, 9 Nov. 1967, col. 564.

12. For example, Dr. Chung Sze-yuen: 'Occasionally there are cases in which there are conflicting interests between Her Majesty's Government and the Hong Kong Government. Since Hong Kong is a colony officials in the Hong Kong Government, with greatest respect, are basically members of the U.K. civil service and, strictly speaking, are under directives of Whitehall. Despite all their good efforts, the voices of Hong Kong people are seldom heard within the U.K. Government.' *H.K. Hansard 1973–74*, p. 63. This view was indignantly repudiated by later official speakers.

13. See *H.K. Hansard 1967*, p. 83, the Financial Secretary, 'I have even heard it alleged that as a Colony we are compelled to hand over our surpluses and reserves to Britain, as if it were some form of tribute. This is very far from the truth. . . . We have not in fact remitted any funds to Britain since 1959; but we *have* left there all interest received on the existing reserves and, as this interest has exceeded our expenditure in Britain on stores, equipment and so on, our balances there have continued to grow.'

For the resumption of remissions in 1969 because of the influx of funds see *H.K. Hansard 1969–70*, pp. 363 and 439.

14. Mr. J. Johnson, *Commons Debates*, 27 Feb. 1967, col. 51.

15. *H.K. Hansard 1957*, p. 292. Sir Alexander puts the point much more strongly in his memoirs: 'Another disadvantage of the deferential politeness of the unofficial members becomes apparent when the Colonial Office wants to do something that the unofficials regard as being detrimental to the interests of the colony. Instead of supinely accepting the 'diktat' of the Colonial Office they should protest in the loudest possible terms, if necessary sending a delegation to London with the maximum publicity.' (*Via Ports*, p. 110.)

16. Lord Shepherd described his activities in Hong Kong as follows: 'Following discussions which I had with Government and employers' representatives agreement was reached for the weekly working hours of all women and young persons in industry to be reduced from 60 to 48 hours. . . . I also had discussions on the hours of work for men. I should like to see, and I think this is now possible, men given a statutory day off each week. . . . Proposals for strengthening the staff of the Labour department are now being actively pursued—and I do not mean 'actively pursued' merely in the parliamentary sense.' *House of Lords Debates*, 9 November 1967, col. 580.

See Chapter 6, p. 69, note 28 for his remarks on the death penalty in Hong Kong, which were made at the same time.

17. *H.K. Hansard 1968*, pp. 33–8. Eleven of these measures concerned improved standards of health and safety in employment; six gave workers increased entitlement to rest-days, sickness benefit and compensation for industrial accidents; three were concerned with contracts of service and protection of wages, employment agencies and workers going

overseas; and there were also bills to set up Labour Tribunals and to alter the law on Trade Unions. The last bill in fact tightened up the law against picketing, though it made other changes which were of some help to the unions. All the above measures had been enacted into law by the end of 1973.

On Labour Advisers, see *H.K. Hansard 1968*, pp. 28 and 47.

18. *H.K. Hansard 1969–70*, pp. 343f.

19. This was a set of regulations for the safety of workers engaged in chromium plating. In 1973 six new pieces of legislation were introduced; this might perhaps be connected with the arrival of the new Governor a year earlier.

A Bill to provide for compulsory severance pay for redundant workers was passed by the Legislative Council in August 1974.

20. Certain commentators connected the choice of a Japanese consortium with the Hong Kong government's annoyance at the refusal of Britain to entertain any diversification of the reserves (*South China Morning Post*, 18 December 1973). (The Japanese withdrew from the project in January 1975.)

On the reserves and negotiations see pp. 9–10 and articles cited in the notes there.

21. Jeffries, op.cit. p. 35.

22. This is a purchasing and procurement agency used by overseas governments and administrations. It is owned by the British government, but run as a commercial enterprise.

23. For fuller details of the activities of the London Office, see the *Annual Departmental Report by the Hong Kong Commissioner in London*. The *1971–2 Report* gives a full history of the office.

24. Arrangements are now made by the Hong Kong government.

25. Suggestion by Dr. Chung Sze-yuen, *H.K. Hansard 1973–74*, p. 64. Previously the *Sunday Post-Herald*, 3 June 1973, had proposed that all ex-Governors should be given life peerages.

20 Pressures from China

'Hong Kong does not do anything silly and against China's legitimate interests, but at the same time does not allow herself to be pushed around unreasonably.'

Sir David Trench[1]

THE Hong Kong government is ultimately responsible through the Secretary of State to the British Parliament, but on most practical matters it is much more important for the Governor to know the attitudes and likely future actions of the Chinese authorities than the views held in Westminister and Whitehall. This was most dramatically demonstrated at the time of the 1967 devaluation of sterling. The rate of exchange between the pound and the U.S. dollar dropped by 14.3 per cent, and, like a dutiful daughter, the Hong Kong dollar was promptly devalued by the same percentage, in order to keep to the former rate of exchange of sixteen dollars to the pound. Unfortunately it was then discovered that Peking intended to raise the price of her exports to the colony by a similar percentage, in order to keep up their value in U.S. dollar terms. So the Hong Kong government was obliged to reverse its decision and revalue its dollar upwards by 10 per cent, in order to minimize the effect on the colony's cost of living of Peking's decision.[2]

This is an example of Hong Kong's economic dependence on China; but the same relationship holds in other areas. Like any small country beside a powerful neighbour which could easily put an end to its separate existence, Hong Kong has always followed the policy of avoiding unnecessary provocations and seeking to be as accommodating as possible to all China's reasonable requests both great and small; in particular this means seeing that China has every legitimate opportunity to increase her off-take of foreign exchange. Obviously, the more profit China makes out of Hong Kong, the less incentive there is to alter the *status quo* by force. During the time when the colony was bound by the exchange regulations of the Sterling Area from 1941 to 1972, Chinese-owned enterprises were given a special dispensation to remit their locally earned profits back to Peking. In 1971 an amendment to the *Wild Birds and Wild Mammals Protection Ordinance* legalized the import of live civet cats, pangolins and otters; these rare species are protected in the colony where trapping, hunting and killing them are punishable offences, but government apparently ceases to worry about the conservation of endangered species when China wants to earn a little more foreign exchange by exporting them to be eaten in the colony's restaurants.[3]

Similar toleration is extended in other matters. Communists are free to set up schools, organize trade unions, publish newspapers and distribute propaganda; so long as they keep within the law, the authorities have no objection. But officials of the Taiwan government are not permitted to enter the colony; and in 1973, Kuomintang supporters were forbidden to fly Nationalist flags on the Lion Rock on the 'Double Tenth'—10th October, the Republic of China's national day—though this had been permitted in previous years. Requests by the Soviet Union for permission to establish a consulate have been refused, and Russian ships are discouraged from calling at the port; on previous occasions soviet agents among the crews have used the opportunity to distribute anti-Maoist propaganda leaflets or attempted to recruit spies.[4] On some of these matters China may have conveyed a specific request to the Governor; but in many cases no such approach would be necessary. Senior officials will always take China's possible reaction into account when making any important policy decision and try, as far as they can, to avoid giving her any reasonable grounds for complaint. China thus exercises a pervasive influence over government policy-making merely by the fact that she is there and potentially capable of causing difficulties, without the need for her to take any positive action at all.

How far the British authorities would be prepared to go to oblige Peking is a matter for speculation. In view of the criticisms made in Britain about Portugal's policy of handing over to China any refugees found in Macau, it might have been thought that this would never happen in Hong Kong, particularly as China has never made a public demand for their return. But in December 1974 the Hong Kong government decided to send back any 'freedom swimmers' apprehended by the police in the New Territories. This astonishing reversal of policy was apparently motivated by the hope that China would reciprocate by cutting down the flow of legal emigrants, who are mainly the old and infirm that China has no use for. It will be interesting to see if the intended result occurs, or whether this will merely encourage China to put further pressure on the colony. In Macau, as a result of the humiliations heaped on the Portuguese governor by the local 'Red Guards' in December 1966 and January 1967, all the decisions of the Portuguese administration are now taken at the behest of the local communists and their supporters are free to act as they please without interference from the police. Probably a similar process of 'Macanization' is Peking's ultimate objective for Hong Kong. It is possible, but by no means certain, that Britain would prefer to withdraw rather than submit to such dictation.

If China felt that her legitimate interests were being disregarded, there are many methods of applying pressure open to her. These include:

The cutting off or restriction of water supplies;

The cutting off of food exports, or the drastic raising of prices;

The creating of incidents on the frontier, for example, kidnapping policemen on patrol;

The harrassing of local fishermen by Chinese gunboats in international waters;

The fomenting of strikes and industrial unrest, especially in key sectors such as the docks, transportation and electricity supply;

The use of local communist newspapers and broadcasts from Canton to exacerbate any dispute between local groups and government;

The revival of agitation over the status of the old walled city of Kowloon;

The staging of demonstrations and riots;

The permitting of large numbers of useless elderly people to cross the border so as to overstrain the colony's welfare services.[5]

It is surprising to see what little use China has made of these weapons in the five years up to 1974. The flow of legal emigrants increased dramatically in the last months of 1973, reaching 7,000 in October. But this upsurge did not seem to have been related to any particular political objective, and the number permitted to leave was later restricted to 2,000 a month after British representations to Peking. This figure was still larger than the quota of 50 a day which had previously been informally agreed with the Chinese authorities, but the reduction did show some willingness to take account of the colony's difficulties. However, numbers were allowed to increase again at the end of 1974.

Why has Peking been so reluctant to make trouble for Hong Kong when there are so many means available? One reason may have been the wish of the Chinese leadership to present a smiling face to the world during the era of 'ping pong diplomacy'. But there are more pertinent reasons why the use of such pressures, even in combination, would be unlikely to be effective and might even be counter-productive.

Serious disruption of the colony's life would drive away foreign capital and tourists, and deter local industrialists from investing. At the same time local Chinese disapproval of such tactics would lead to a loss of the goodwill which Peking has been sedulously cultivating since 1968. This could take concrete expression in the withdrawal of deposits from communist banks and boycotts of communist goods and stores. All this would diminish Peking's offtake of foreign exchange, which is its main reason for tolerating the colony's existence.

Moreover the administration has taken steps to minimize the inconvenience which the colony might suffer from the use of such tactics, quite apart from the obvious precaution of strengthening the police. The building of the Plover Cove and High Island reservoirs and the future operation of a desalination plant will reduce the colony's need for water supplies from China. In 1967–8 37 per cent of its water came from China; in 1972–3 this was down to 25 per cent.[6] The loss of Chinese supplies would be uncomfortable, and involve water rationing, but it would not be unbearable except possibly if the colony were suffering from a prolonged drought. Similarly, the colony imports 35 per cent of its foodstuffs from China, but its sources of supply for most commodities are diversified and the wholesalers who participate in the Rice Control Scheme are required to keep three months supply in reserve. This would be time enough to buy rice from elsewhere to make up for the shortfall from China, though the price might be higher.

But the most effective bulwark to resist external pressures is the support of the colony's inhabitants for its administration. The events of 1967 showed that most of the population were prepared to put up with considerable inconvenience rather than give in to communist pressure and government can probably hope that similar determination will also be shown in future. But such support is crucially dependent on two factors: the confidence of the people that government will not give way to threats, and their belief that they have a lot to lose if the communists were to win. Obviously no one is going to risk reprisals against himself or his family for refusing to go on strike or join a riot if he suspects that government is half-hearted and will give way if pushed hard enough. This was the reason why government was most unwilling to release prematurely those leftists convicted of criminal activities in 1967, since this would be interpreted as a sign of weakness and an encouragement to rioters in any future confrontation. It is equally important that the mass of the workers should feel that they are getting their fair share of the fruits of economic growth and that government is taking adequate steps to meet their aspirations for better living conditions and wider educational opportunities for their children. There was considerable disquiet in high quarters in 1967 at the number of young people who were prepared to join the demonstrations, and after the troubles were over the unofficial members begged government to launch imaginative social programmes to win back their allegiance. Unfortunately nothing very much was done in this direction until 1972 (see above p. 106 and note 5, p. 116).

Thus it appears that, though government is generally willing to do what it can to accommodate China's reasonable requests, Peking would face considerable difficulties if it should seek to get its way by threats or open pressures against the colony. Hong Kong's greatest advantage is that it wants very little from China except to be left alone, whereas China's industrial progress is critically dependent on the colony's foreign exchange earnings. By contrast Britain is much more concerned to cultivate good relations with China, principally to secure trading advantages in what is potentially the world's largest market. It would be surprising if China's diplomats did not seek to take advantage of this when her favours are being courted by so many Western nations. In 1971–2 Britain was eager to raise her diplomatic mission in Peking to ambassadorial level, but China delayed agreement until Britain accepted her views on the status of Taiwan. In 1973 hints were dropped that British Airways would not be granted landing rights until the issue of China's representation in the colony was satisfactorily settled.[7]

In early 1974 discussions had been in progress for a year on China's suggestion that she should appoint an official representative in Hong Kong. Though the previous Nationalist government had had a commissioner in the colony until Britain recognized the People's Republic in 1950, the Hong Kong authorities have never been very happy about such a proposal. A communist commissioner could easily abuse his diplomatic immunity[8] by openly taking a partisan stand on current issues, thereby encouraging communist and other opposition groups, and embarrassing government by turning domestic disputes into international confrontations. This was the reason why Sir Alexander Grantham blocked a similar Chinese proposal made in 1956, allegedly remarking, 'There's no room for two governors in Hong Kong'.[9] On the other hand, it is possible that there might be some advantage for the colony in this proposal. China has been careful to stand aloof from its domestic affairs since 1969, and the presence of a Chinese consular official could be taken as a public acknowledgement of British sovereignty, signifying that China had no immediate intention to alter the *status quo*. It is for this reason that the official title of the proposed representative is of some diplomatic importance, and it was rumoured in March 1974 that the talks were deadlocked on this issue.[10] Meanwhile China is apparently content to wait, as she did over the issue of Taiwan, in the expectation that Britain's eagerness to advance her commercial interests will eventually overcome the objections of the colonial administration.

At present China's senior representative in Hong Kong is the Director of the New China News Agency, who has his office in the Bank of China building. Though officially he has no diplomatic status, he and his predecessors have served as a channel of communication to and from the Hong Kong authorities since 1949.

On such questions involving the triangular relationship Peking-London-Hong Kong it is important for the Governor to know exactly what is going on in Peking and also to see that Hong Kong's viewpoint is fully appreciated and given its proper weight in Foreign Office policy discussions. In this area Governors since the war have been assisted by a Political Adviser seconded from the Foreign Service. The holder of this post has normally served previously in the British mission in China and keeps in close touch with the British embassy in Peking. Former Governors were very glad of this assistance, since they had all risen through the colonial administration.[11] Sir Murray MacLehose (who was himself Political Adviser from 1959 to 1962) is better situated in this respect, though it may have been easier for his predecessors to impress upon the British government that the particular interests of Hong Kong should not take second place to the betterment of Sino-British relations when China was more preoccupied with her internal troubles and her diplomacy less outward-looking.

1. *Hong Kong and its Position in the Southeast Asian Region* (The Dillingham Lecture, Oct. 1971, East-West Centre, Hawaii), p. 6.

2. Similarly the decision to tie the value of the Hong Kong dollar to the U.S. dollar in July 1972 was determined by Peking's successive revaluations of the renminbi as the pound floated downwards; see *Far Eastern Economic Review*, 15 July 1972, p. 38.

3. *H.K. Hansard 1970–71*, p. 793. The government spokesman, Mr. Haddon-Cave, argued that the imported civet cats were bred in captivity in China, so the species would not be further endangered by this change.

4. KMT flags, *South China Morning Post*, 15 Oct. 1973; Russian whaling fleet, ibid. 9

June 1972; alleged Russian spies, ibid. 2 April 1974. On the returning of refugees, see *Far Eastern Economic Review*, 13 Dec. 1974, p. 21 & 20 Dec. 1974, p. 21.

5. In 1974 during the oil crisis land was made available for China to construct oil storage tanks at Shatin and Tsing Yi. The quantities to be imported represented only about 7 per cent of Hong Kong's total oil requirements, but if supplies ran short, this could become a further means of exerting pressure. *South China Morning Post*, 5 Feb. and 8 May 1974.

6. Even in 1967 Peking did not cut off water supplies. The agreement then in operation provided that China would supply 15,000 million gallons every year between 1 October and 30 June. This was done; but the Chinese authorities did not accede to a further request for additional supplies that year in July and August. See the *Annual Reports of the Director of Public Works*, section on Water Supply.

7. The correspondent of the London *Financial Times*, 13 April 1973, reported: 'I was assured in Peking recently that the lack of a representative office in Hong Kong poses a number of practical problems, particularly in the communications field.... Officials in Peking have also indicated that there will be difficulties about agreeing on the establishment of a direct rail link between Hong Kong and Canton while what they regard as the principal issue in Hong Kong remains outstanding. There is less precision in Peking about the question of an air service agreement and the start of a BOAC scheduled service to China, but the view is taken that this matter is connected "to a considerable extent" with the question of a representative.'

8. Strictly speaking, foreign representatives in Hong Kong are of consular status while diplomatic functions are the task of the country's embassy in London; but in practice both they and the Hong Kong government enjoy a degree of independence which makes the term 'diplomat' appropriate.

9. As related by Hughes, *Hong Kong, Borrowed Place, Borrowed Time*, p. 30. Sir Alexander Grantham alleges (*Via Ports*, p. 131) that the Special Commissioner of the Nationalist Government encouraged the agitators in the Kowloon Walled City dispute of 1947.

10. According to a report in the Chinese newspaper *Fai Po* (Express) London thought that the appropriate title would be 'Hong Kong Office of the Embassy of the People's Republic of China in Britain'; but Peking proposed 'Hong Kong Office of the Kwangtung Province of the People's Republic of China'. (Quoted by *South China Morning Post*, 30 March 1974.) By the end of 1974 talks on this issue had apparently been suspended with no decision reached.

11. Sir Alexander Grantham states that as far back as 1928 he had advocated that the colony should be placed under the Foreign Office and not the Colonial Office, since its fundamental political problem was its relations with China and not preparations for self-government. The first Political Adviser was appointed in 1947, just before his return as Governor (op. cit. p. 105).

Conclusion

'Living in Hong Kong is like farming on the slopes of a volcano: the crops are lush, and after a while you get used to the periodic rumblings from inside.'

A long-time resident

THE Hong Kong system of government is difficult to classify. If we focus our attention on the structure of government decision-making, it appears closely to resemble the authoritarian system of its mighty neighbour, the People's Republic of China: in both countries power is concentrated in the hands of a small elite—the party cadres in China and the expatriate bureaucrats in Hong Kong; neither group stands in any danger of being ejected from office by free elections. But there the similarity ends. The Communist Party is determined to enforce total control over all aspects of social and economic life and is engaged in a perpetual struggle to remould every Chinese into a new type of man in accordance with the Maoist blueprint; whereas in Hong Kong individuals are largely left free to run their own lives and pollute their environment as they please under minimal restrictions, and even these not very effectively enforced. Government may feebly try to foster a community spirit and talk of building up a sense of 'Hong Kong belonging', but this bears no comparison even with Lee Kwan Yew's strident rhetoric about creating a 'rugged society' in Singapore,[1] much less the excesses of totalitarian rule in China.

Yet this relative freedom in daily life from party or police interference which the Hong Kong population enjoys does not bring with it the institutional forms of 'Western' democracy which Britain has exported to her other colonies. The administration may be responsive to public opinion, particularly to the views of business and commercial pressure groups, but it is adamantly opposed to any suggestions that it should set up meaningful free elections or to the idea that government should submit to being responsible to the people it rules.

Can this unique political system, where a tiny expatriate elite exercises power by consent over 4 million Chinese, continue to survive in this modern age? This depends less on the effectiveness of government than in almost any other country in the world. It is far more likely to be destroyed by decisions taken in Peking or London, or by the impersonal operations of the world economy, than by any actions or omissions of the colonial administration. Unlike most governments in the developing world it has very little to fear from internal revolt. A coup d'etat by the British troops here or the British-officered Gurkha battalions is out of the question. The police, with the help of the army if necessary, are strong enough to contain any normal urban riot provided it does not attract active and sustained communist support, backed by Peking. And if that occurred, turmoil in the streets would be unnecessary; Mao could take over Hong Kong, as the saying goes, merely by lifting the telephone and putting a call through to London. It is just possible to imagine a revolt provoked by the hardship of local conditions, whether this was due to government oppressiveness or incompetence or to conditions beyond its control, which China might feel obliged to support against its own better judgement, to avoid the opprobrium of allowing its compatriots to suffer unaided; but there is no sign of this occurring at present. The population has stoically endured a substantial drop in its standard of living as a result of the world commodity price inflation in 1973–4 without any outward sign of complaint except a few ill-attended rallies and some fly-by-night slogan painting.

The risk of internal disorder is much less than the danger that the British government might one day decide to cast off the colony, as part of a complete abandonment of its commitments in Asia. But the profits made by British-owned firms and the benefits to British Airways from the control of landing rights at Kai Tak, together with the ultimate legal power to prevent the liquidation of Hong Kong's sterling balances still seem to be powerful enough arguments against any such withdrawal. Similarly, a takeover by Peking seems to be ruled out, so long as the People's Republic is in urgent need of foreign exchange earned through the colony; though if China happened to discover extensive gold deposits or vast new oilfields which could be quickly and cheaply brought into production, Hong Kong would have to fear for its future. China's official line is that the problem of Taiwan must be settled before there is any question of altering the status of Hong Kong and Macau. But this attitude could well alter if Hong Kong's value to China suffered a decline. In any case all these calculations depend on the supposition that politicians in London and Peking will behave rationally in following their economic interests. This is perhaps a dangerously optimistic assumption to make, particularly if a struggle for power develops after Mao's death.

The fact that the Lease of the New Territories legally terminates in 1997 does not make much difference to this position. China does not publicly acknowledge the 1898 Convention of Peking (though she has not officially abrogated it either—see Chou En-lai's ambiguous remarks quoted on p. 226) and if the communist leaders find that they have no further use for Hong Kong before 1997 the existence of this Convention, and the earlier treaties of Nanking and Peking, will not prevent the People's Liberation Army from marching in. On the other hand, if economic considerations still take precedence over nationalism in the 1990s and China wishes the colony's independent existence to continue, Peking will have to make its intentions known well in advance to encourage capital and skilled manpower to remain, since Britain recognizes the terminal date as still valid and will start making preparations to withdraw well beforehand if nothing is agreed. The rump of the colony would not be economically viable with the loss of its airport and most of its water supply and manufacturing capacity, and it is unrealistic to imagine that an international frontier could be re-established along Boundary Street in Kowloon.

If then we assume that Hong Kong will survive and prosper as a separate entity for a further span of years, are there likely to be any changes in its system of government? Or will its nineteenth century constitution still continue without any concession to 'democracy'?

Moves for change could be instituted from China, from Britain, by local agitation, or within the administration itself. It seems highly unlikely that Peking would press for any changes which would give a greater say in the colony's government to the local Chinese who have fled from or rejected their motherland and who are suspected of pro-Taiwanese sentiments. In other colonies the initiative for constitutional change has sometimes come from the metropolitan government before any serious local pressures developed;[2] but the British government appears to have ruled out any such move here, in deference to the wishes of China.

There is little sign of local agitation for changes in a democratic direction. The demands of the Reform Club and the Civic Association seem so far to have attracted little public support. It is arguable whether this apathy is the result of lingering Confucianism, alienation, or (as officials maintain) a rational appreciation of the risks involved.[3] But whatever the reason, the colonial administration is unlikely to make any such move except under pressure. There is, of course, no guarantee that this apathy will continue. It is always possible that the people may become obsessed by the fond delusion of Hong Kong as an independent Cantonese Republic, may demand their 'inalienable' democratic rights and rush blindly like the Gadarene swine over the edge of the precipice. However, the pragmatic Chinese seem singularly unlikely to succumb to any such lemming-like tendencies.

Judging by past precedents, the most likely future source of change is the Governor himself. The Young Plan of 1946 and the initiative for local government reform in 1966 were both excogitated in Government House. Both were, however, subsequently squashed, the Young Plan by the opposition of the unofficial members and the reform of local government by the bureaucracy. A new Governor is always an unknown quantity and some such similar plans cannot be ruled out in future. But whether they would get any further is quite another matter.

A different possible future for the colony is what might be termed 'creeping Macanization'—the progressive reduction of the administration to a position of total subservience to Peking's wishes. This might even take place with the connivance of the British government. Such a situation could have certain advantages. The question of 1997 would then become irrelevant. Macau is flourishing under such a regime; investment is booming and the communists can guarantee good labour discipline to foreign firms. It may perhaps be said that Britain would not be prepared to tolerate such a demeaning position. But Britain has been humiliated so much in the past twenty-five years that no indignity is impossible.

However, the greatest danger at present is official complacency.[4] All large bureaucracies are slow to change. As they grow older it becomes increasingly more uncomfortable to alter established procedures and responses, and, with no market test of their efficiency, they tend to become more concerned with their own growth and prerogatives than in serving any social function. Those organizations which fill all their top posts by internal promotion are particularly liable to such conservatism since all those who do not subscribe to the established orthodoxy are liable to be passed over or frozen out. In the 1950s and 1960s the bad effects of this inbreeding were somewhat reduced by the intake of officials who had retired from other colonies on independence. But this source has now almost dried up and the only future external recruitment at the top is likely to be civil servants on temporary secondment from Britain.

In a democracy bureaucratic inertia is offset by the presence of politicians at the top of the departmental pyramid who are more sensitive to the needs of the electorate, which can dismiss them from office, than to the convenience of officials. A minister does not generally stay in a department long enough to be smothered by it, and while he is there he should be able to goad civil servants into introducing the innovations needed to keep the department responsive to changes in its environment, which may be either shifts in public attitudes, or new methods and systems developed elsewhere.[5]

In Hong Kong there is no such prodding from ministers. There is also an absence of a lively public opinion, and so the main stimulus on government to improve its performance comes from the pressure groups. In some cases this can be extremely effective: by common repute Commerce and Industry is one of the most efficient departments since it has to satisfy the insistent demands of its powerful clients, the business and commercial interests. Other departments can more easily become self-satisfied, and at least until 1971, officials tended to react to criticism more often by seeking to muzzle it than by reassessing their own performance.[6] When the unofficial members of the Legislative Council also failed to give adequate voice to the grievances of the public, as was largely true in the 1950s and early 1960s, officialdom developed such a thick crust of complacency that it needed the riots of 1966 and 1967 to stir it into energetic innovation. These outbursts produced the City District Officer scheme, a rush of labour legislation and a 59 per cent increase in the number of Chinese administrative officers (from 22 in 1967 to 35 in 1969).

It is to be hoped that a similar upheaval will not be necessary again before further changes are put in hand. There are some promising signs. Government is now encouraging widespread discussion before final policy decisions are taken by the publication of 'Green Papers' for public comment. The unofficial members are now more actively critical than ever before. Student agitation was largely responsible for the increased use of Chinese in official business and it also helped to press for the establishment of the Independent Commission Against Corruption. The Chinese-run Education Action Group is effectively needling the Education Department. Meanwhile the internal workings of the bureaucracy are now apparently to be submitted to an annual efficiency audit by a visitation of the McKinsey firm of management consultants.[7] One trusts that this momentum will be kept up and that the administration will be supple enough to make an adequate response, within the constraints imposed by Hong Kong's economy and its international position, to the changing values and new demands of its citizens in the latter half of the 1970s.

1. See T.S. George, *Lee Kwan Yew's Singapore* (Deutsch, London, 1973), esp. pp. 132–9 and 182–94.

2. From 1945 onwards Labour Party Colonial Secretaries actively encouraged the setting up of elected local governments in the colonial territories. The rapid decolonization of the Belgian Congo largely stemmed from political initiatives taken by ministers in Brussels against the advice of officials on the spot, particularly the visit to the Congo of the 'working group' in 1958.

3. The argument that Hong Kong's political apathy is the result of alienation is put by Aline K. Wong, 'Political Apathy and the Political System in Hong Kong', *United College Journal* (Hong Kong), Vol. 8 (1970–71), pp. 1–20. According to Mr. D.C. Bray, now the Secretary for Home Affairs, in a speech at the United College, 12 Nov. 1971: 'Hong Kong's stability rests on a tripod of consents, each one of which is essential for the continuation of anything like the present way of life. These three consents are the consent of Hong Kong people, the consent of China and the consent of Britain. The withdrawal of any one of these consents will endanger the whole structure. Extreme measures aimed at bolstering any one of these consents run the risk of destroying one or both of the others. The necessity to retain the stability of this tripod of consents sets quite severe limits on what is practical in the way of political reform and this is generally known and appreciated throughout the colony.'

4. See for example Sir Alexander Grantham: 'To plan is easy, but quickly to implement those plans, or to modify them in the light of experience, is not easy, especially for government organizations which tend to suffer from the ponderous slowness of the bureaucratic machine.' (*Via Ports*, p. 102.) See also p. 110 on the need for officials to be needled by the unofficial members.

For a recent academic study see Anthony Downs, *Inside Bureaucracy* (Little Brown, Boston, 1967), esp. pp. 19–20, 158–66 (The Rigidity Cycle), 193–7, 228–31 (Selective Recruitment).

5. See the remarks by a senior British Cabinet minister, R. Crossman, *Inside View* (Cape, London, 1972) p. 76: 'For about three years he (the minister) remains an active foreign body and there can be creative friction—a battle out of which something comes. But sooner or later a point is reached where he gets too close to the department.'

6. See for example, p. 34 above (deportation of student activists); p. 163 (attempt to restrict the operation of the Urban Council ward system); p. 161 (curbing of Urban Council debates). In 1970, after certain church leaders had ventured to comment on social reform and labour matters, Sir David Trench warned them not to allow their Christian works 'to degenerate into something like political polemics.... Your cloth gives you no special expertise in the detailed solution of governmental problems.' (*Far Eastern Economic Review*, 29 Jan. 1970, p. 16.)

Accounts of the censorship of discussions and interviews on Radio Hong Kong critical of government policy are given in the *Far Eastern Economic Review*, 16 January 1971, p. 5; 29 July 1972, pp. 19f; 14 May 1973, p. 17. For instance, in 1970 the following Radio Hong Kong staff instruction was issued: 'H.E. the Governor has directed that Radio Hong Kong will give no further broadcast coverage to the situation arising from the University Grants Commission's quadrennial budget for the Universities. (signed) Director of Broadcasting.' (*Far Eastern Economic Review*, 28 May 1970, p. 6).

7. The McKinsey consultants originally visited Hong Kong in 1972–3. They returned in 1974 to take a particular look at the departments dealing with law and order and the information services. (*South China Morning Post*, 18 May 1974.)

Appendix 1
Document to Chapter 2

THE CHINESE GOVERNMENT AND HONG KONG

Louis Heren, foreign correspondent of *The Times*, gave the following account of the views of Chou En-lai after a private interview:

'Few problems were seen to exist between Britain and China, although the future of Hong Kong would have to be decided. A state must enter into negotiations when a treaty expired. Now that full diplomatic relations existed between the two countries Britain naturally would have to negotiate at the appropriate time.

Territories taken from China were bound to be returned. This was not a new procedure, but unlike India over Goa, it was not Chinese policy to embark upon such matters with undue haste. China has territory known as Macau. The Soviet Union has tried to provoke China into taking it back by force, but China would not be provoked over Macau or Hong Kong. It would eventually call for negotiations. In a changing world this matter would have to be settled, but it did not have to be considered now. The treaty expires in 1997.'

(The Times, 23 October 1972)

(The interview was 'off the record' and so Mr. Heren was not able to quote Chou's words directly.)

Appendix 2
Documents to Chapter 4

A. THE GOVERNMENT'S REJECTION OF PLANNING

The Financial Secretary, Sir John Cowperthwaite, dissects a suggestion by an unofficial member that an Industrial Development Council should be set up:

'... It is not so much the idea of such a Council that dismays me but the attitude adverse to freedom of private enterprise which is implicit in its suggested functions. These are "to establish priorities on development, to provide inducements for new industries and to discourage over-expansion of existing ones"—a complete blueprint for government regulation of industry, negative as well as positive, even if my honourable Friend shies away from the word "planning". I am afraid that I do not believe that any body of men can have enough knowledge of the past, the present and the future to establish "development priorities"—which presumably means procuring some developments as being good and prohibiting others as being bad. The second purpose—special inducements to new industries—must inevitably mean distortion and stunting of the growth of industry as policies of granting protection and privilege to so-called "pioneer" industries elsewhere have shown clearly.

Presumably these two first functions should be read in conjunction with another passage where Dr. CHUNG suggests that Government should provide loans at attractive interest rates, say 5 per cent, to, and I quote, "specific priorities of development for desirable industries" (which privilege he argues, rather obscurely, should not be regarded as a subsidy). What mystifies me is how he or any one else can determine what is a desirable type of industry such as should qualify for special assistance of this kind. In my own simple way I should have thought that a desirable industry was, almost by definition, one which could establish itself and thrive without special assistance in ordinary market conditions. Anything else suggests a degree of omniscience which I, at least, am not prepared to credit even the most expert with. I trust the commercial judgment only of those who are themselves taking the risks....

But it is the Council's third suggested function which dismays me most—discouragement of over-expansion of existing industries. By what standard can one possibly measure over-expansion? On what basis can one forecast it? On whose judgement can we rely? Who is to decide who is to have the good fortune to reap what I have heard called "the spoils of economic planning"? Do we no longer put our faith in the judgement of free private enterprise? I can myself recall being told repeatedly, in the early post-war years and at intervals thereafter, that the cotton spinning industry was over-expanding. It has expanded many times since then and still thrives. I recall even more vividly a prominent and influential businessman telling me in 1956 that Government must take early steps to restrict the further growth of the garment industry because it was already too large; since then it has expanded its exports by ten times or $2,000 million a year. I, for one, will not forget that lesson.

One of the things that most surprises me about my honourable Friend's remarks is that he characterizes his proposal for state intervention in, and control of, industry as "innovation and a spirit of adventure" and condemns free private enterprise as "prosaic precedent". This is a strange paradox. I would put it precisely the other way round. What he advocates is based on the 'prosaic precedent' of many of our rivals who have to resort to wooing industry with artificial aids and have had remarkably little success at it. Recent events have shown that enterprising spirits still prefer our economic freedom to the restrictive swaddling clothes offered elsewhere. Possibly I am a romantic in this but I, for one, do not believe that our spirit of adventure is in need of artificial stimulation— nor do I believe that we can afford the wasteful application of our scarce resources which they would entail—we are neither desperate enough, nor rich enough, for such expedients to make economic sense. It is, of course, all the fashion today to cry in any commercial difficulty, "why doesn't the Government do something about it". But I would rather go back to the old days when even the most modest attempt by Government to intervene in commerce and industry was rudely rebuffed than contemplate the kind of guided and protected economy Dr. CHUNG appears to propose.'

(H.K. Hansard 1968, pp. 211–13)

B. GROWING AND DECLINING INDUSTRIES

(i) *THE STEEL INDUSTRY 1968*

The Director of Commerce and Industry, Mr. T.D. Sorby: 'In this Council on the second of August, 1967, I said that the steel industry in Hong Kong was then facing a number of difficulties, but special treatment for a particular industry would run counter to Government's well tested economic policies and would have to be justified by quite special circumstances. I said that the evidence of such circumstances was less than complete, but I proposed to pursue the matter with the industry. I have done so.

My department has also considered, sympathetically and exhaustively in conjunction with other departments, in particular with the Director of Public Works, the methods of assistance available to the Government. We reached the conclusion that none of them are likely to have more than a temporarily palliative effect, and that the advantages to be gained by the steel rolling industry would be more than offset by the possible consequential disadvantages to the economy as a whole. This was the consensus of opinion of the Trade and Industry Advisory Board, which I consulted; and of the Executive Council whose advice you, Sir, have accepted.

I believe that all who have been concerned with these matters are satisfied that the capacity of the industry as a whole considerably exceeds existing and fore-seeable future demand, both domestic and overseas and that the industry must contract substantially as a prerequisite to economic viability.'

(H.K. Hansard 1968, p. 431)

(ii) *ENAMELWARE AND WIGS 1970*

Sir John Cowperthwaite: 'I was particularly struck by my honourable Friend, Mr. K.S. Lo's concern at the decline in the enamelware industry as an example of the effect of lost advantages, as if this decline were a loss rather than a gain to the community. It has declined, I believe, because we have learned to use our resources of enterprise, capital and labour in other more profitable directions. That is progress. We would be in a sorry way if enamelware was still our fourth biggest industry.

In a rather similar vein my honourable Friend, Mr. ANN takes the wig industry to task for offering inducements to labour. In my view it is best that labour should be employed by the employers who can pay it most, even if it has adverse effects on employers who cannot match their terms. That, too, is the way of progress.'

(*H.K. Hansard 1970–71*, pp. 114f)

(iii) *NO SUBSIDIES FOR TOURISM, 1971*

In a debate on the tourist industry Mr. BROWNE had asked for special assistance. The new Financial Secretary, Mr. HADDON-CAVE, replied:

'...I am afraid that, in pursuit of diversity, there can be no question of public funds being committed to the provision of specialized facilities for one sector of the economy for the purpose of expanding the volume and range of its activities even in the hope of raising its level of profitability. Public funds cannot be used to embark on a policy of what my honourable Friend, Mr. BROWNE has described as "positive help" because it would put that sector in an artificially favourable position (thereby distorting the labour market in particular). I would not rule out action to correct disabilities flowing from the imperfect operation of the market mechanism but, even then, only in very special circumstances.'

(*H.K. Hansard 1970–71*, p. 765)

(iv) *TEXTILES, 1972*

'In 1972, production of cotton yarn was 250 million pounds, compared with 308 million pounds in 1971. This figure would have been higher but for substantial quantities of cotton yarn imported from Pakistan at prices lower than those at which Hong Kong mills could obtain raw cotton. Although this led to an appeal for protection from the industry, the government did not feel that the circumstances warranted a departure from the existing free trade policy.'

(*H.K. Annual Report 1973*, pp. 13f)

C. SIR JOHN COWPERTHWAITE DERIDES GOVERNMENT LOANS FOR SMALL INDUSTRIES

I must confess my distaste for any proposal to use public funds for the support of selected, and thereby, privileged, industrialists, the more particularly if this is to be based on bureaucratic views of what is good and what is bad by way of industrial development, but I have been studying the report referred to with some interest.

In the light of our rapid industrial expansion of recent years, I was not surprised to find that, after two special sample surveys, the committee concluded that there was no real evidence that industrial development was being hindered by lack of finance; indeed, the evidence suggested on the whole that sources of finance were adequate. My honourable Friend, Mr. Lo, has himself pointed out the unusual strength of our medium industry, for which there is nothing comparable in the region. I was surprised, however, that the Committee then went on to make proposals for a scheme to provide a special source of finance.

But even were it to be accepted that, in spite of the the findings of the surveys, some scheme should be introduced for some reason, such as a feeling that the surveys' conclusions are not well-founded, speaking for myself, I find the actual scheme proposed substantially defective in a number of its main features. Basically it suggests that, when a bank receives an application for a loan for industrial development which it is not prepared to grant at its own risk in the normal course of business, then it refers it to an official organization, which might be the Productivity Centre, for a report on its 'technical and financial viability'. If that report were favourable *and* the bank agreed, then a Government guarantee would be made available for a part of the risk at a charge of some kind. Unlike the banks, Governments would not have the right to reject a loan on which a favourable finding has been made. . . .

. . . The present proposal would allow the banks to select their worst risks for guarantee, automatic guarantee, while keeping all the profit on their better risks. In underwriting terms this is wholly unacceptable. . . .

. . . I find the latter proposition rather alarming—that we should be prepared to take greater *commercial* risks with public funds than banks are prepared to take with commercial funds in the course of their business. . . .

Thirdly, I find odd the view that a Government institution is better placed to evaluate 'the technical and financial viability' of a project than a commercial bank. It may well be that our banks are deficient in the kind of expertise required for assessing projects but then what we should be doing is encouraging banks to acquire such expertise or to make use of outside, commercial, expertise. I do not believe in any case that a Government machine can provide a reliable judgement on such matters, an opinion the banking members of the committee appear to have shared, for they have prudently refused to commit themselves to accepting its advice. I myself tend to mistrust the judgement of anyone not involved in the actual process of risk-taking.

(*H.K. Hansard 1970–71*, pp. 116f)

However, after Sir John's departure, the new Financial Secretary did set up such a scheme (*H.K. Hansard 1971–72*, p. 432). It was not a success and very few loans were taken up by industrialists (*H.K. Hansard 1973–74*, pp. 916–18).

D. ATTRACTING NEW INDUSTRIES TO HONG KONG

The Director of Commerce and Industry: 'My honourable Friend has asked what are the major factors discouraging foreign investors from establishing technologically advanced industries here. Basically they are just two: land and labour; the former being the more important obstacle.

The attraction of foreign technology to Hong Kong is itself a competitive exercise. Overseas industrial companies and, indeed to an increasing degree, local industrialists don't consider Hong Kong in isolation when they wish to establish an industrial operation in Asia. They compare us with other possible locations and many countries are competing for their investment. In comparison with almost any other possible site in Asia for a manufacturing plant, the price of industrial land is very high here. Some relatively sophisticated industries can reduce the land cost element in their costings by operating in multi-storey building but, as honourable Members know, this is not possible for all industries. And some of those for which it *is* possible cannot, or will not, set up here unless there is a nucleus of supporting industries which must operate in single storey buildings.

The Government has recognized the effect which this situation can have on our industrial—and therefore economic—development. As Your Excellency said at the opening of the 1972 Chinese Manufacturers' Association Exhibition:

'Government has for some time been aware of the benefits which could accrue to Hong Kong if certain types of engineering industry, and perhaps other industries of an advanced technological character, could be established here. Consideration is now being given to making certain areas of land available for sale on a restricted user basis confined to these industries; and it is hoped that one lot in Tsing Yi Island will be sold on this basis in the near future.'

That particular lot was advertised internationally last month.

There are for the industrialist other difficulties with industrial land apart from its price. These are, principally, its general scarcity and the methods of sale which, although fair, can be so time consuming as to deter overseas companies. Once they have come to a decision to pursue a project they frequently expect to be able to take immediate action on it. And they can do this in most countries with little difficulty.

The overall supply of labour is not too great a problem for the technologically advanced industries in which we are interested for they are, of course, less labour intensive than our older industries. Skilled labour, technicians, technologists and engineers are, however, still in relatively short supply. Some other countries can at present do better. My honourable Friend is aware of the steps being taken to overcome this difficulty.

The question of labour cost has also to be taken into account. In comparison to the majority of developing countries in Asia, to which potential investors will look, our labour costs are high. While we all hope that the real wages of our work force can continue to increase, this does mean that we must rely increasingly on the more sophisticated industries—and in this field we are in competition with other developing countries in the region.'

(*H.K. Hansard 1972–73*, pp. 675f)

Appendix 3
Documents to Chapter 5

LETTERS PATENT & ROYAL INSTRUCTIONS
TO THE GOVERNOR OF HONG KONG

LETTERS PATENT
Passed under the Great Seal of the United Kingdom, constituting the Office of Governor and Commander-in-Chief of the Colony of Hong Kong and its Dependencies.

Dated 14th February, 1917.
Amended 30th April, 1938.
        "   29th June, 1939.
        "   16th March, 1950.
        "   1st March, 1955.
        "   26th August, 1960.
        "   17th November, 1967.
        "   5th February, 1971.

I. There shall be a Governor and Commander-in-Chief in and over Our Colony of Hong Kong and its Dependencies (hereinafter called the Colony), and appointments to the said Office shall be made by Commission under Our Sign Manual and Signet.

II. We do hereby authorize, empower, and command Our said Governor and Commander-in-Chief (hereinafter called the Governor) to do and execute all things that belong to his said office, according to the tenour of these Our Letters Patent and of any Commission issued to him under Our Sign Manual and Signet, and according to such Instructions as may from time to time be given to him, under Our Sign Manual and Signet, or by Order in Our Privy Council, or by Us through one of Our Principal Secretaries of State, and to such laws as are new or shall hereafter be in force in the Colony.

III. Every person appointed to fill the office of Governor shall, with all due solemnity, before entering upon any of the duties of his office, cause the Commission appointing him to be Governor to be read and published in the presence of the Chief Justice or other Judge of the Supreme Court, and of such Members of the Executive Council of the Colony as can conveniently attend; which being done he shall then and there take before them the Oath of Allegiance, in the form provided by an Act passed in the Session holden in the Thirty-first and Thirty-second years of the reign of Her Majesty Queen Victoria, intituled "An Act to amend the Law relating to Promissory Oaths"; and likewise the usual Oath for the due execution of the office of Governor and for the due and impartial administration of justice; which Oaths the said Chief Justice or Judge, or if they be unavoidably absent, the senior Member of the Executive Council then present, is hereby required to administer.

IV. The Governor shall keep and use the Public Seal of the Colony for sealing all things whatsoever that shall pass the said Public Seal.

V. There shall be an Executive Council in and for the Colony, and the said Council shall consist of such persons as We shall direct by Instructions under Our Sign Manual and Signet, and all such persons shall hold their places in the said Council during Our pleasure. The Governor may upon sufficient cause to him appearing suspend from the exercise of his functions in the Council any Member thereof pending the signification of Our pleasure, giving immediate notice to Us through one of Our Principal Secretaries of State. If the suspension is confirmed by Us through one of Our Principal Secretaries of State the Governor shall forthwith by an instrument under the Public Seal of the Colony revoke the appointment of such Member, and thereupon his seat in the Council shall become vacant.

VI. There shall be a Legislative Council in and for the Colony, and the said Council shall consist of the Governor and such persons as We shall direct by any Instructions under Our Sign Manual and Signet, and all such persons shall hold their places in the said Council during Our pleasure. The Governor may upon sufficient cause to him appearing suspend from the exercise of his functions in the Council any Member thereof pending the signification of Our pleasure, giving immediate notice to Us through one of Our Principal Secretaries of State. If the suspension is confirmed by Us through one of Our Principal Secretaries of State the Governor shall forthwith by an instrument under the Public Seal of the Colony revoke the appointment of such Member, and thereupon his seat in the Council shall become vacant.

VII. The Governor, by and with the advice and consent of the Legislative Council, may make laws for the peace, order, and good government of the Colony.

VIII. We do hereby reserve to Ourselves, Our heirs and successors, full power and authority to disallow, through one of Our Principal Secretaries of State, any such law as aforesaid. Every such disallowance shall take effect from the time when the same shall be promulgated by the Governor in the Colony.

IX. We do also reserve to Ourselves, Our heirs and successors, Our and their undoubted right, with the advice of Our or their Privy Council, to make all such laws as may appear necessary for the peace, order, and good government of the Colony.

X. When a Bill passed by the Legislative Council is presented to the Governor for his assent he shall, according to his discretion, but subject to any Instructions addressed to him under Our Sign Manual and Signet or through one of Our Principal Secretaries of State, declare that he assents thereto, or refuses his assent to the same, or that he reserves the same for the signification of Our pleasure.

XI. A Bill reserved for the signification of Our pleasure shall take effect so soon as We shall have given Our assent to the same by Order in Council, or through one of Our Principal Secretaries of State, and the Governor shall have signified such assent by message to the Legislative Council or by proclamation: Provided that no such message shall be issued after two years from the day on which the Bill was presented to the Governor for his assent.

XII. In the making of any laws the Governor and the Legislative Council shall conform to and observe all rules, regulations, and directions in that behalf contained in any Instructions under Our Sign Manual and Signet.

XIII. (1) The Governor, in Our name and on Our behalf, may make and execute grants and dispositions of any lands within the Colony that may be lawfully granted or disposed of by Us.

(2) The powers conferred on the Governor by this Article may be exercised on behalf of the Governor by any person authorized, whether by name or by reference to an office, to exercise those powers by the Governor and such authorization shall be notified in the *Hong Kong Government Gazette.*

(3) Any such authority shall be subject to such conditions and restrictions (if any) as the Governor may specify, and may be varied or revoked by the Governor, and such conditions, restrictions, variation or revocation shall be notified in the *Hong Kong Government Gazette.*

(4) Grants and dispositions of land under this Article shall be made in conformity with the provisions of such Instructions as may from time to time be given to the Governor under Our Royal Sign Manual and Signet or through a Secretary of State and such laws as may for the time being be in force in the Colony.

XIV. The Governor may constitute and appoint such Judges, Justices of the Peace and other public officers as may be lawfully appointed, all of whom shall, unless otherwise provided by law, hold their offices during Our pleasure.

XIVA. (1) When the holder of the Office of Governor or of any office constituted under Article XIV of these Letters Patent is on leave of absence pending relinquishment of his office, it shall be lawful for another person to be appointed substantively to the same office.

(2) When two or more persons are holding the same office by reason of an appointment made pursuant to paragraph (1) of this Article, then for the purposes of Articles XVII and XVIIA of these Letters Patent and for the purpose of any function conferred upon the holder of that office, the person last appointed to the office shall be deemed to be the holder of the office.

XV. When any crime or offence has been committed within the Colony, or for which the offender may be tried therein, the Governor may, as he shall see occasion, in Our name and on Our behalf, grant a pardon to any accomplice in such crime or offence who shall give such information as shall lead to the conviction of the principal offender, or of any one of such offenders, if more than one; and further, may grant to any offender convicted of any crime or offence by any court of law in the Colony (other than a court martial established under any Act of Parliament), either free or subject to such conditions as the Governor may think fit to impose, a pardon or any remission of the sentence passed on such offender, or any respite of the execution of such sentence for such period as the Governor thinks fit, and may remit any fines, penalties, or forfeitures due or accrued to Us. Provided always that the Governor shall in no case, except where the offence has been of a political nature unaccompanied by any other grave crime, make it a condition of any pardon or remission of sentence that the offender shall be banished from or shall absent himself or be removed from the Colony.

XVI. Subject to the provisions of Article XVIA, the Governor may, subject to such instructions as may from time to time be given to him by Us through one of

Our Principal Secretaries of State, upon sufficient cause to him appearing, dismiss or suspend from the exercise of his office any person holding any public office within the Colony, or, subject as aforesaid, may take such other disciplinary action as may seem to him desirable.

XVIA. (1) Subject to the provisions of the following paragraphs of this Article a judge of the Supreme Court shall hold office until he attains the age of sixty-two years:

Provided that notwithstanding that he has attained the age of sixty-two years, a person holding the office of a judge of the Supreme Court may continue in office for so long after attaining that age as may be necessary to enable him to deliver judgment or to do any other thing in relation to proceedings that were commenced before him before he attained that age.

(2) A judge of the Supreme Court may at any time resign his office by writing under his hand addressed to the Governor.

(3) Notwithstanding anything in paragraph (1) of this Article or in any other enactment, a judge of the Supreme Court may be removed from office only for inability to discharge the functions of his office (whether arising from infirmity of body or mind or from any other cause) or for misbehaviour, and shall not be so removed except in accordance with the provisions of paragraph (4) of this Article.

(4) A judge of the Supreme Court shall be removed from office by the Governor by instrument under the Public Seal if the question of his removal from office has, at the request of the Governor made in pursuance of paragraph (5) of this Article, been referred by Us to the Judicial Committee of the Privy Council under section 4 of the Judicial Committee Act.1833 or any other enactment enabling Us in that behalf, and the Judicial Committee has advised Us that the judge concerned ought to be removed from office for inability as aforesaid or for misbehaviour.

(5) If the Governor considers that the question of removing a judge of the Supreme Court from office for inability as aforesaid or for misbehaviour ought to be investigated, then—

(a) the Governor shall, by instrument under the Public Seal (which he may vary or revoke by another such instrument), appoint a tribunal, which shall consist of a Chairman and not less than two other members selected by the Governor from among judges who hold or have held office as judge of a court having unlimited jurisdiction in any part of the Commonwealth or a court having jurisdiction in appeals from any such court;

(b) the tribunal shall enquire into the matter and report on the facts thereof to the Governor and recommend to the Governor whether he should request that the question of the removal of the judge concerned should be referred by Us to the Judicial Committee; and

(c) if the tribunal so recommends, the Governor shall request that the question should be referred accordingly.

(6) If the question of removing a judge of the Supreme Court from office has been referred to a tribunal appointed under paragraph (5) of this Article, the Governor may suspend the judge concerned from performing the functions of his office.

(7) Any such suspension may at any time be revoked by the Governor and shall in any case cease to have effect—

(a) if the tribunal recommends to the Governor that he should not request that the question of the removal from office of the judge concerned should be referred by Us to the Judicial Committee; or

(b) if the Judicial Committee advises Us that the judge concerned ought not to be removed from office.

XVII. (1) During any period when the office of Governor is vacant or the holder thereof is absent from the Colony or is for any other reason unable to perform the functions of his office, those functions shall, during Our pleasure, be assumed and performed by—

(a) such person as may be designated under Our Sign Manual and Signet or by instructions given by Us through one of Our Principal Secretaries of State; or

(b) if there is no person in the Colony so designated and able to perform those functions, the person lawfully discharging the functions of Colonial Secretary.

(2) Before assuming the functions of the office of Governor for the first time, any person as aforesaid shall make the oaths directed by Article III of these Our Letters to be made by the holder thereof.

(3) Any such person as aforesaid shall not continue to perform the functions of the office of Governor after the holder thereof, or some other person having a prior right to perform those functions, has notified him that he is about to resume, or assume, those functions.

(4) The holder of the office of Governor or any other person as aforesaid shall not, for the purposes of this Article, be regarded as absent from the Colony or as unable to perform the functions of that office at any time when there is a subsisting appointment of a Deputy under Article XVIIA of these Our Letters.

XVIIA. (1) Whenever the Governor—

(a) has occasion to be absent from the Colony for a period which he has reason to believe will be of short duration; or

(b) is suffering from any illness which he has reason to believe will be of short duration; or

(c) considers for any reason that the public interest so requires, he may by instrument under the Public Seal appoint a person to be his Deputy and in that capacity to perform on his behalf such of the functions of the office of Governor as may be specified in such instrument.

(2) The powers and authority of the Governor shall not be abridged, altered or in any way affected by the appointment of a Deputy under this Article and a Deputy shall comply with all instructions which the Governor may address to him, but the question whether a Deputy has in any matter complied with such instructions shall not be enquired into by any court.

(3) Any appointment under this Article may be revoked at any time by Us by instructions given by Us through one of Our Principal Secretaries of State or by the Governor by instrument under the Public Seal, and subject thereto a person appointed under this Article shall hold that appointment for such period as may be specified in the instrument by which he is appointed.

XVIII. And We do hereby require and command all Our officers and ministers, civil and military, and all other the inhabitants of the Colony, to be obedient, aiding and assisting unto the Governor and to any person for the time being administering the Government of the Colony.

XIX. In these Our Letters Patent the term "the Governor" shall include every person for the time being administering the Government of the Colony.

XX. And We do hereby reserve to Ourselves, Our heirs and successors, full power and authority, from time to time, to revoke, alter, or amend these Our Letters Patent as to Us or them shall seem meet.

XXI. And We do further direct and enjoin that these Our Letters Patent shall be read and proclaimed at such place or places within the Colony as the Governor shall think fit, and shall come into operation on a day to be fixed by the Governor by Proclamation.

ROYAL INSTRUCTIONS

Passed under the Royal Sign Manual and Signet to the Governor and Commander-in-Chief of the Colony of Hong Kong and its Dependencies.

Dated 14th February, 1917.
Amended 30th April, 1938.
" 1st March, 1955.
" 1st July, 1964.
" 6th January, 1966.
" 17th November, 1967.
" 28th February, 1969.
" 5th February, 1971.
" 28th June, 1972.

I. The Governor may, whenever he thinks fit, require any person in the public service of the Colony to take the Oath of Allegiance, in the form prescribed by the Act mentioned in Our said recited Letters Patent, together with such other Oath or Oaths as may from time to time be prescribed by any laws in force in the Colony. The Governor is to administer such Oaths, or to cause them to be administered by some public officer of the Colony.

II. The Executive Council of the Colony shall consist of the Officer for the time being in a command of Our regular forces within the Colony (hereinafter called the Commander British Forces), the persons for the time being lawfully discharging the functions of Colonial Secretary, of Attorney General, of Secretary for Home Affairs, and of Financial Secretary of the Colony, who are hereinafter referred to as *ex officio* Members, and of such other persons as We may from time to time appoint by any Instructions or Warrant under Our Sign Manual and Signet, or as the Governor in pursuance of Instructions from Us through one of Our Principal Secretaries of State may from time to time appoint by an Instrument under the Public Seal of the Colony. Persons so appointed are hereinafter referred to as Official Members or Unofficial Members according as they hold, or do not hold, office under the Crown in the Colony at the time of appointment.

Every Unofficial Member shall vacate his seat at the end of five years from the date of the Instrument by which he is appointed or of such other period as may be specified in that Instrument, but shall be eligible to be re-appointed in the manner aforesaid for a further period or periods, each period not exceeding five years:

Provided that if any such Member is provisionally appointed to fill a vacant seat in the Council and his provisional appointment is immediately followed by his definitive appointment, the said period of five years shall be reckoned from the date of the Instrument provisionally appointing him.

If any Official Member cease to hold office under the Crown in the Colony his seat in the Council shall thereupon become vacant:

III. Whenever any Member, other than an *ex officio* Member, of the Executive Council of the Colony shall, by writing under his hand, resign his seat in the Council, or shall die, or be declared by the Governor by an Instrument under the Public Seal of the Colony to be incapable of exercising his functions as a Member of the Council, or be absent from the Colony, or shall be acting in an office the holder of which is an *ex officio* Member of the Council, or shall be suspended from the exercise of his functions as a Member of the Council, or whenever the seat of any such Member shall otherwise become vacant, the Governor may, by an Instrument under the Public Seal of the Colony, pro-visionally appoint any public officer to be temporarily an Official or temporarily an Unofficial Member of the Council, and any person not a public officer to be temporarily an Unofficial Member of the Council in the place of the Member so resigning, or dying, or being suspended, or declared incapable, or being absent, or sitting as an *ex officio* Member.

Such person shall forthwith cease to be a Member of the Council if his appointment is disallowed by Us, or if the Member in whose place he was appointed shall be released from suspension, or, as the case may be, shall be declared by the Governor by an Instrument under the Public Seal capable of again discharging his functions in the Council, or shall return to the Colony, or shall cease to sit in the Council as an *ex officio* Member.

IV. The Governor shall, without delay, report to Us, for Our confirmation or disallowance, through one of Our Principal Secretaries of State, every provisional appointment of any person as a Member of the said Executive Council. Every such person shall hold his place in the Council during Our pleasure, and the Governor may by an Instrument under the Public Seal revoke any such appoint-ment.

V. *Revoked 1.3.55.*

VI. The Governor shall forthwith communicate these Our Instructions to the Executive Council, and likewise all such others, from time to time, as We may direct, or as he shall find convenient for Our service to impart to them.

VII. The Executive Council shall not be summoned except by the authority of the Governor.

VIII. (1) The Governor shall, so far as is practicable, preside at meetings of the Executive Council.

(2) In the absence of the Governor there shall preside at any meeting of the Council—
    (*a*) such Member of the Council as the Governor may appoint; or
    (*b*) in the absence of a Member so appointed, the senior *ex officio* Member present; or
    (*c*) in the absence of a Member so appointed or of an *ex officio* Member, the senior Official Member present.

(3) For the purposes of sub-paragraphs (*b*) and (*c*) of paragraph (2) of this clause—

- (*a*) the Commander British Forces shall not be regarded as an *ex officio* Member of the Council;
- (*b*) the remaining *ex officio* Members of the Council shall have seniority in the order in which their offices are mentioned in clause II of these Instructions; and
- (*c*) the Official Members of the Council shall have seniority according to the priority of their respective appointments to the Council:

    Provided that Members appointed by the same Instrument shall have seniority among themselves according to the order in which they are named therein.

IX. (1) No business except that of adjournment shall be transacted in the Executive Council if objection is taken by any Member present that there are less than four Members present besides the Governor or the Member presiding.

(2) Subject to the provisions of paragraph (1) of this clause, the Executive Council shall not be disqualified for the transaction of business by reason of any vacancy in the membership of the Council, and any proceedings in the Council shall be valid notwithstanding that some person who was not entitled to do so took part in those proceedings.

(3) The Governor or the Member presiding, when in his opinion the business before the Executive Council makes it desirable, may summon any person to a meeting of the Council, notwithstanding that that person is not a Member of the Council.

X. In the execution of the powers and authorities granted to the Governor by Our said recited Letters Patent, he shall in all cases consult with the Executive Council, excepting only in cases relating to the appointment, disciplinary control or removal from office of a public officer or in cases which may be of such a nature that, in his judgment, Our service would sustain material prejudice by consulting the Council thereupon, or when the matters to be decided shall be too unimportant to require their advice, or too urgent to admit of their advice being given by the time within which it may be necessary for him to act in respect of any such matters. In all such urgent cases he shall, at the earliest practicable period, communicate to the Executive Council the measures which he may so have adopted, with the reasons therefor.

XI. The Governor shall alone be entitled to submit questions to the Executive Council for their advice or decision; but if the Governor decline to submit any question to the Council when requested in writing by any Member so to do, it shall be competent to such Member to require that there be recorded upon the minutes his written application, together with the answer returned by the Governor to the same.

XII. The Governor may, in the exercise of the powers and authorities granted to him by Our said recited Letters Patent, act in opposition to the advice given to him by the Members of the Executive Council, if he shall in any case deem it right to do so; but in any such case he shall fully report the matter to Us by the first convenient opportunity, with the grounds and reasons of his action. In every such case it shall be competent to any Member of the said Council to require that there be recorded at length on the Minutes the grounds of any advice or opinion he may give upon the question.

XIII. The Legislative Council of the Colony shall consist of the Governor, the persons for the time being lawfully discharging the functions of Colonial Secretary, Attorney General, Secretary for Home Affairs, and Financial Secretary of the Colony, who are hereinafter referred to as *ex officio* Members, and such other persons holding office under the Crown in the Colony, and not exceeding ten in number at any one time, as We may from time to time appoint by any Instructions or Warrants under Our Sign Manual and Signet, or as the Governor, in pursuance of Instructions from Us through one of Our Principal Secretaries of State, may from time to time appoint by an Instrument under the Public Seal of the Colony, and all such persons shall be styled Official Members of the Legislative Council; and further of such persons, not exceeding fifteen in number at any one time, as the Governor, in pursuance of Instructions from Us through one of Our Principal Secretaries of State, may from time to time appoint by an Instrument under the Public Seal of the Colony, and all such persons shall be styled Unofficial Members of the Legislative Council.

If any Official Member of the Legislative Council cease to hold office under the Crown in the Colony, his seat in the Council shall thereupon become vacant.

XIV. Whenever any Member of the Legislative Council, other than an *ex officio* Member, shall, in the manner hereinafter provided, have resigned his seat in the Council or shall die, or whenever the seat of any such Member shall otherwise become vacant, or whenever any such Member shall be suspended from the exercise of his functions as a Member of the Council, or be declared by the Governor by an Instrument under the Public Seal to be incapable of exercising his functions as a Member of the Council, or be absent from the Colony, or shall be acting in an office the holder of which is an *ex officio* Member of the Council, the Governor may, by an Instrument under the Public Seal, appoint some person to be provisionally a Member of the Council in the place of such Member.

Such person shall hold his place in the Council during Our pleasure and shall forthwith cease to be a Member of the Council if his appointment is disallowed by Us, or revoked by the Governor or superseded by the definitive appointment of a Member of the Council, or if the Member in whose place he was appointed shall be released from suspension, or, as the case may be, shall be declared by the Governor capable of again exercising his functions in the Council, or shall return to the Colony, or shall cease to sit in the Council as an *ex officio* Member.

When any person shall be lawfully discharging the functions of more than one of the offices the holders of which are *ex officio* Members of the said Council, the Governor may, by an Instrument under the Public Seal, appoint any fit person to be provisionally a Member of the Council so long as the said offices shall continued to be so discharged by one person but any such appointment may be disallowed or revoked as aforesaid.

The Governor shall, without delay, report to Us, through one of Our Principal Secretaries of State, every provisional appointment of any person as a Member of the Legislative Council.

XV. *Revoked 15.11.28.*

XVI. Every Unofficial Member of the Legislative Council shall vacate his seat at the end of four years from the date of the Instrument by which he is appointed or of such other period as may be specified in that Instrument, but shall be eligible to be re-appointed in the manner hereinbefore provided for a further period or periods, each period not exceeding four years:

Provided that if any such Member is provisionally appointed to fill a vacant seat in the Council and his provisional appointment is immediately followed by his definitive appointment, the aforesaid period of four years shall be reckoned from the date of the Instrument provisionally appointing him.

XVII. If any Unofficial Member of the Legislative Council shall become bankrupt or insolvent, or shall be convicted of any criminal offence, or shall absent himself from the Colony for more than three months without leave from the Governor, the Governor may declare in writing that the seat of such Member at the Council is vacant, and immediately on the publication of such declaration he shall cease to be a Member of the Council.

XVIII. Any Member of the Legislative Council, other than an *ex officio* Member, may resign his seat in the Council by writing under his hand, but no such resignation shall take effect until it be accepted by the Governor in writing, or by Us through one of Our Principal Secretaries of State.

XIX. The Legislative Council shall not be disqualified from the transaction of business on account of any vacancies among the Members thereof; but the said Council shall not be competent to act in any case unless (including the Governor or the Member presiding) there be present at and throughout the meetings of the Council ten Members at the least.

XX. *Revoked 1.3.55.*

XXI. (1) The Governor shall, so far as is practicable, preside at meetings of the Legislative Council.

(2) In the absence of the Governor there shall preside at any meeting of the Council—
   (a) such Member of the Council as the Governor may appoint; or
   (b) in the absence of a Member so appointed, the senior Official Member present.

(3) For the purposes of sub-paragraph (b) of paragraph (2) of this clause the Official Members of the Council shall have seniority as follows:
   (i) first, the persons discharging the functions of the offices specified in clause XIII of these Instructions, in the order in which those offices are mentioned therein;
   (ii) second, the other Members according to the priority of their respective appointments to the Council:

Provided that Members appointed by the same Instrument shall have seniority among themselves according to the order in which they are named therein.

XXII. All questions proposed for debate in the Legislative Council shall be decided by the majority of votes, and the Governor or the Member presiding shall have an original vote in common with the other Members of the Council, and also a casting vote, if upon any question the votes shall be equal.

XXIII. The Legislative Council may from time to time make standing rules and orders for the regulation of their own proceedings; provided such rules and orders be not repugnant to Our said recited Letters Patent, or to these Our Instructions, or to any other Instructions from Us under Our Sign Manual and Signet.

XXIV. It shall be competent for any Member of the Legislative Council to propose any question for debate therein; and such question shall be debated and disposed of according to the standing rules and orders:

Provided always that every ordinance, vote, resolution, or question, the object or effect of which may be to dispose of or charge any part of Our revenue arising within the Colony, shall be proposed by the Governor, unless the proposal of the same shall have been expressly allowed or directed by him.

XXV. In the passing of Ordinances the Governor and the Council shall observe, as far as practicable, the following Rules:

1. All laws shall be styled 'Ordinances', and the enacting words shall be, 'enacted by the Governor of Hong Kong, with the advice and consent of the Legislative Council thereof'.

2. All Ordinances shall be distinguished by titles, and shall be divided into successive clauses or paragraphs, numbered consecutively, and to every such clause there shall be annexed in the margin a short summary of its contents. The Ordinances of each year shall be distinguished by consecutive numbers, commencing in each year with the number one.

Except in the case of Bills reserved for the signification of Our pleasure, all Ordinances passed by the Legislative Council in any one year shall, if assented to by the Governor, be assented to by him in that year, and shall be dated as of the day on which the assent of the Governor is given, and shall be numbered as of the year in which they are passed. Bills not so assented to by the Governor, but reserved by him for the signification of Our pleasure, shall be dated as of the day and numbered as of the year on and in which they are brought into operation.

3. Each different matter shall be provided for by a different Ordinance, without intermixing in one and the same Ordinance such things as have no proper relation to each other; and no clause is to be inserted in or annexed to any Ordinance which shall be foreign to what the title of such Ordinance imports, and no perpetual clause shall be part of any temporary Ordinance.

XXVI. The Governor shall not, except in the cases hereunder mentioned, assent in Our name to any Bill of any of the following classes:

1. Any Bill for the divorce of persons joined together in holy matrimony:

2. Any Bill whereby any grant of land or money, or other donation or gratuity, may be made to himself:

3. Any Bill affecting the Currency of the Colony or relating to the issue of Bank notes:

4. Any Bill establishing any Banking Association, or amending or altering the constitution, powers, or privileges of any Banking Association:

5. Any Bill imposing differential duties:

6. Any Bill the provisions of which shall appear inconsistent with obligations imposed upon Us by Treaty:

7. Any Bill interfering with the discipline or control of Our forces by land, sea, or air:

8. Any Bill of an extraordinary nature and importance, whereby Our preroga-

tive, or the rights and property of Our subjects not residing in the Colony, or the trade and shipping of Our United Kingdom and its Dependencies, may be prejudiced:

9. Any Bill whereby persons not of European birth or descent may be subjected or made liable to any disabilities or restrictions to which persons of European birth or descent are not also subjected or made liable:

10. Any Bill containing provisions to which Our assent has been once refused, or which have been disallowed by Us:

Unless in the case of any such Bill as aforesaid the Governor shall have previously obtained Our instructions upon such Bill through one of Our Principal Secretaries of State, or unless such Bill shall contain a clause suspending the operation of such Bill until the signification of Our pleasure thereupon, or unless the Governor shall have satisfied himself that an urgent necessity exists requiring that such Bill be brought into immediate operation, in which case he is authorized to assent in Our name to such Bill, unless the same shall be repugnant to the law of England, or inconsistent with any obligations imposed on Us by Treaty. But he is to Transmit to Us, by the earliest opportunity, the Bill so assented to, together with his reasons for assenting thereto.

XXVII. Every Bill, not being a Government measure, intended to affect or benefit some particular person, association or corporate body shall contain a section saving the rights of Us, Our heirs and successors, all bodies politic and corporate, and all others except such as are mentioned in the Bill and those claiming by, from, and under them. No such Bill shall be introduced into the Legislative Council until due notice has been given by not less than two successive publications of the Bill in the *Hong Kong Government Gazette*, and in such other manner as may be required by the Standing Rules and Orders for the time being in force; and the Governor shall not assent thereto in Our name until it has been so published. A certificate under the hand of the Governor shall be transmitted to Us with the Bill signifying that such publication has been made.

XXVIII. When any Ordinance shall have been passed or when any Bill shall have been reserved for the signification of Our pleasure, the Governor shall transmit to Us, through one of Our Principal Secretaries of State, for Our final approval, disallowance or other direction thereupon, a full and exact copy in duplicate of the same, and of the marginal summary thereof, duly authenticated under the Public Seal of the Colony, and by his own signature. Such copy shall be accompanied by such explanatory observations as may be required to exhibit the reasons and occasion for passing such Ordinance or Bill.

XXIX. *Revoked 5.2.71.*

XXX. *Revoked 17.11.67.*

XXXI. Before disposing of any vacant or waste land to Us belonging, the Governor shall cause the same to be surveyed, and such reservations to be made thereout as he may think necessary for roads or other public purposes. The Governor shall not, directly or indirectly, purchase for himself any of such lands without Our special permission given through one of Our Principal Secretaries of State.

XXXII. *Revoked 5.2.71.*

XXXIII. *Revoked 30.4.38.*

XXXIV. Whenever any offender shall have been condemned by the sentence of any Court in the Colony to suffer death, the Governor shall call upon the Judge who presided at the trial to make to him a written report of the case of such offender, and shall cause such report to be taken into consideration at a meeting of the Executive Council, and he may cause the said Judge to be specially summoned to attend at such meeting and to produce his notes thereat. The Governor shall not pardon or reprieve any such offender unless it shall appear to him expedient so to do, upon receiving the advice of the Executive Council thereon; but in all such cases he is to decide either to extend or to withhold a pardon or reprieve, according to his own deliberate judgment, whether the Members of the Executive Council concur therein or otherwise, entering, nevertheless, on the Minutes of the Executive Council a Minute of his reasons at length, in case he should decide any such question in opposition to the judgment of the majority of the Members thereof.

XXXV. *Revoked 17.11.67.*

XXXVI. The Governor shall not upon any pretence whatever quit the Colony without having first obtained leave from Us for so doing under Our Sign Manual and Signet, or through one of Our Principal Secretaries of State.

XXXVII. In these Our Instructions the term 'the Governor' shall, unless inconsistent with the context, include every person for the time being administering the Government of the Colony.

Appendix 4
Documents to Chapter 6

A. ON BEING A GOVERNOR

(i) Sir Alexander Grantham, Governor 1947–1957:

In a crown colony the Governor is next to the Almighty. Everyone stands up when he enters a room. He is deferred to on all occasions. It is always 'Yes, Sir'; 'Certainly, Your Excellency'; heady wine that is bad for the constitution if taken too long at a time. That is why it is good for a governor when on leave to have to take his place in a queue and to have his toes trodden on in a crowded railway carriage. It brings home to him that he is but an ordinary mortal like anyone else, and that the dignity attaches to the office and not to the individual. As the Queen's representative, the Governor has to behave and be treated as such. He should be dignified without being pompous, approachable and friendly without being intimate, because if he is intimate with any one individual or any particular group, he will be accused, rightly or wrongly, of favouritism. He should not confine his associations to the 'upper crust' for he belongs to everyone in the colony, from the highest to the lowest. He must be discriminating, but not exclusive, in the social entertainment that he offers and accepts. Many governors, and I was one of them, made it a rule not to accept private invitations of hospitality, but to confine himself to members of Councils, heads of the Services, the Consular Corps and so on. If he were to accept an invitation to dinner from Mr. and Mrs. A who held no particular position in the colony, he would then have to accept invitations from Mr. and Mrs. B and the whole way through the alphabet. This social aloofness of a governor by no means implies that he should be aloof in other ways, or that he should have no contacts with anyone except his officials and advisers. It is essential, I consider, that in seeking opinions he should cast his net as widely as possible and be available to people of all degrees. After a time, he gets to know who is worth seeing and who will merely waste his time. Thus he manages to keep his finger on the pulse of public opinion, and to know what is going on in the colony.

(*Via Ports*, p. 107)

(ii) I was keenly interested in social welfare work, and decided that the best way in which I could help was by giving public encouragement and showing that the Governor was in favour of it; for though many of the Chinese themselves did welfare work in one form or another, or subscribed to charitable funds, many did not. I was always irritated by Chinese socialites, particularly of the female species, who said they did not care or could not be bothered. Just as I had no patience with European housewives who boasted that they never went into their kitchens. At any rate, I think I was successful in making social welfare socially acceptable, and the legislature more willing to loosen the purse strings for welfare projects than it had been in the past.

(*Via Ports*, p. 119)

B. A GOVERNOR'S RELATIONS WITH LONDON

(i) A suggestion was made that the Commissioner General at Singapore should have executive authority over the Governor of Hong Kong in all matters appertaining to defence—a wide definition—as he had over the Governor of Singapore and the High Commissioner of Malaya, though he had never used those powers. On the face of it the arrangement was logical. The service commanders in Hong Kong were under the authority of their respective commanders-in-chief in Singapore, *ergo* the civilian governor of Hong Kong should be in the same relationship to the civilian Commissioner General; a nice tidy set-up. I thought it a bad idea, and gave my objections to the Colonial Office. In reply I was told that the matter had been decided by 'ministers'—that magic formula that is supposed to crush all argument—and that nothing more remained to be said. I persisted in saying more.

Malcolm MacDonald, the Commissioner General, held a conference with the commanders-in-chief and myself. He sided with me—he was no empire builder. Also, the matter being of considerable importance to Hong Kong, I informed the unofficial members of the Executive Council. They objected in the strongest terms. 'Malcolm MacDonald would be all right', they said: 'we know and trust him, but he is not going to remain as Commissioner General for ever. In principle we are completely opposed'. I duly reported to the Colonial Office, which sent out an official for discussions. I was not present when he and the members of the Executive Council had their meeting, but the proposal was dropped.

(Via Ports, pp. 142–3)

(ii) The Royal Naval Dockyard had been in existence almost as long as had the Colony. It was the symbol of Britain's presence in Hong Kong and, until the construction of the naval base at Singapore in the thirties, was the Navy's only base of any size in the Far East. Since then it had taken second place, and soon after the end of the Pacific War the Commander-in-Chief had moved his headquarters from Hong Kong to Singapore. Although the Hong Kong yard was efficient, to have two dockyards within the same area was clearly uneconomic. Moreover, the Singapore yard was both larger and more modern. Consequently the Treasury in London was constantly pressing for the closure of the Hong Kong yard. Just as constantly, I resisted the pressure with all my might and main. In this I had the firm support of successive commanders-in-chief and the Admiralty. The reasons for my resistance were twofold. In the first place, the dockyard was a large employer of labour, and if it were closed the unemployment situation would be aggravated, at a time too, when it was already serious because of the influx of refugees. In the second place—and this was a more fundamental objection —the hauling down of the white ensign would be taken by the people of the Colony as a sign that Britain was going to withdraw altogether from Hong Kong. That this was not so, but was solely for financial reasons, was beside the point. It just would not have been believed, and confidence would have been severely shaken.

When, however, in 1957 the British government published a White Paper which stated that a number of other dockyards, including some in the United Kingdom, were going to be closed down, my objection to the closure fell to the ground, for it would now be seen that the closure of the Hong Kong yard was part of an overall policy, and had nothing to do with the question of Britain remaining in the Colony.

(Via Ports, p. 193)

C. EXTRACTS FROM THE MINUTES OF THE
EXECUTIVE COUNCIL 1937–1939

26 MAY 1937   CRIME

The Governor-in-Council considered the sentence of death passed upon Chiu Yuk Fai for the murder of Cheung Yuk Ching. Council advised by a majority of six votes to three that the clemency of the Crown should not be exercised in this case. His Excellency accepted the advice and ordered that the sentence of death should be carried into effect on 11 June 1937.

28 APRIL 1938   RENTS

The matter of increasing rents was raised by Sir Henry Pollock* and it was agreed that Government should appoint an officer to register reports by tenants of increases of their rents from a date subsequently to be determined by the Council in order that data should be available, should restrictive action become necessary, and to facilitate a watch being kept on the rental situation. The Colonial Secretary was requested to submit to the Council at its next meeting his detailed proposals for the conduct of such registration.

*The senior unofficial member at this time. Member of the Executive Council 1921–1941.

28 SEPT. 1938   HONG KONG VOLUNTEER DEFENCE-CORPS

The Governor-in-Council discussed the question of rates of pay for volunteers.

It was agreed that there should be no discrimination between the European and non-European members of the H.K. Volunteer Defence Corps on mobilization and that this view should be represented strongly to the Secretary of Security for the Colonies for communication to the War Office.

23 NOV. 1938   NEWSPAPERS: SEDITION ORDINANCE 1938

The Governor-in-Council discussed an article in the Hong Kong Daily Press entitled 'China Break Up Move'. It was agreed that steps should be taken to amend the Sedition Ordinance 1938 to include under the definition of 'seditious intentions' the bringing into hatred or contempt or the exciting of disaffection against the Government established by law in the United Kingdom, so as to enable a charge to be brought in the courts in the case of such articles.

29 MARCH 1939   BILLS

The Governor-in-Council considered the question as to whether the Betting Duty Amendment Bill, 1939 on approval for introduction into Legislative Council by the Governor-in-Council on 31 January, 1939 should be withdrawn or postponed for further consideration of the points raised by the Honourable Unofficial Members. It was agreed that the second reading of the bill should be postponed and that before a reply is sent to the representations of the Honourable the Unofficial members, the Hon. the Colonial Secretary, the Hon. the Attorney General, the Hon. Sir H.E. Pollock and the Hon. Sir R.H. Kotewall should discuss the matter further with the Hon. Mr. T.E. Pearce and one other representative of the Jockey Club.

13 DEC. 1939   CHINESE LABOUR CORPS

His Excellency the Governor recounted to members the details of a proposal by Her Majesty's Government to recruit Chinese labourers through Hong Kong for service in France during the present war and gave the gist of the correspondence which had passed between the Secretary of State for the Colonies and the Government on this subject.

Council approved in principle the terms of a telegram to the Secretary of State for the Colonies dealing with the question whether the labourers should be despatched direct from the depot in Hong Kong or through an intermediate depot in the Straits Settlements. Sir H.E. Pollock indicated his dissent from the whole scheme of recruitment in Hong Kong of Chinese labour for service in France.

(Taken from the files of the Public Record Office, London (C.O. 131 97; C.O. 131 98; C.O. 131 103) by permission.)

Appendix 5
Documents to Chapter 7

A. GOVERNMENT ADMINISTRATION AND
COMMERCIAL MANAGEMENT CONTRASTED

1. Measured in terms either of its population or of its economy, Hong Kong has one of the highest growth rates in the world—a situation that imposes heavy pressure on Government to expand the scale and scope of the services it provides. It must respond to the demand to increase the volume of existing services. It must satisfy the rising expectations of the population by improving the quality of these services and by introducing new ones. And because the services are becoming increasingly complex in themselves, Government may require increasingly sophisticated methods of providing them.

2. In addition to meeting the requirements of growth Government must continue to satisfy the normal criteria of public sector activities, both legislative and executive. In its legislative and policy-making roles, for example, it must provide Hong Kong with a stable legal environment, it must ensure that all the implications of proposed Government action are considered and that all interests receive an equitable hearing, it must be seen to be fair and honest. In its executive role—for example, in building roads, educating children or running hospitals—it must satisfy in addition criteria that are more akin to those of a commercial undertaking, namely to respond rapidly to changing needs, to provide goods and services to the required standard at minimum cost, and to achieve increasing standards of efficiency and effectiveness.

3. Whether or not the Government satisfies the first set of criteria to a sufficient degree involves a qualitative judgement that is beyond our competence to make. However, on the question of whether or not the Government satisfies the criteria for its executive role, we were able to apply more factual measures.

9. . . . Successful management in Government is considerably more difficult than in a company in the private sector. First, Government controls a comparatively large organisation: in Hong Kong it employs about 100,000 people. Second, unlike senior management in most businesses, top-level Government staff in Hong Kong have to cope with a wide diversity of operations, ranging across every field of activity in the Colony. Third, whereas in business most decisions can be based on agreed, quantifiable criteria such as profitability, in Government they depend frequently on value judgements on questions to which there is no wholly right or wrong answer, and very often no answer that will satisfy all interested sectors of the community. Is it better to spend money on housing or on education? What should be the overall standards of medical care, and what should Government's contribution be to meeting these standards? Fourth, despite these difficulties, the public expects Government to get all its

decisions right. Public pressure, via the Press and other media, focuses on mistakes and gives little offsetting credit for successes. In contrast, the shareholders in a business tend not to concern themselves with individual decisions so long as overall results are satisfactory.

(McKinsey & Company, *The Machinery of Government*)

B. RECRUITMENT TO THE ADMINISTRATIVE CLASS

Mr. WANG: 'What are the academic qualifications and other qualities required of a candidate for appointment as an administrative officer in Government service? How many vacancies for this post have there been for this year? How many of this year's graduates from our Universities have applied and how many have been accepted?'

The COLONIAL SECRETARY (ACTING) (Mr. S.T. KIDD):—Sir, the academic qualification for appointment as an Administrative Officer is a First or Second Class Honours degree from a Hong Kong or British university, or equivalent. In addition, an Administrative Officer requires qualities of character and intelligence which are difficult to define, but which were described in the Annexe to the 1971 Salaries Commission Report on Administrative and Professional Salary Scales as being 'plus something'.

Vacancies for Administrative Officers were advertised locally in November 1971. Altogether, 250 applications were received, including 114 from final-year university students, who, along with other qualified candidates, were invited to sit a written examination. Of the 98 final-year students who actually sat the written examination, 14 passed and were invited for interview, but none was found suitable for appointment. I might add here that only two appointments have been made this year in connection with the November 1971 advertisement, leaving a number of vacancies unfilled.

This result is clearly unsatisfactory and a thorough review of the selection procedures for Administrative Officers has been undertaken with the co-operation of the University authorities in order to see whether the procedures are too rigorous or whether there is any way in which the Universities can assist in preparing candidates of the requisite calibre at the pre-graduate stage. If any changes are to be made, these will be introduced before direct University recruitment takes place next year.

MR. WANG:—Sir, can my honourable Friend give an account of what is that something which is not generally found as a plus among the graduates who apply?

The COLONIAL SECRETARY (ACTING) (Mr. KIDD):—Sir, the selection board which participated in the 1971 recruitment reported that, generally speaking, the candidates seemed somewhat limited in their outlook, able usually to express themselves on their particular field of study but showing little knowledge of, or interest in, public affairs either in Hong Kong or internationally. The board considered that some candidates might be recruited as Executive Officers in the first instance and, after acquiring some maturity, confidence and poise through some working experience, re-apply to become Administrative Officers. It was with this in mind that the very recent advertisement for Administrative Officers stated that preference would be given to candidates with at least two years working experience.

As part of the current review of the selection procedure, the views of university authorities have been sought as to how to promote better understanding about the job of an Administrative Officer by university students.

(*H.K. Hansard 1971–72*, pp. 1038f)

C. IN PRAISE OF ADVISORY COMMITTEES

Heads of departments do not get their fat salaries and their ulcers sitting about waiting to be told what to do. They are responsible for Government activity in various fields—not just doing what they did yesterday but constantly on the look-out for changes to suit the times, answers for new problems and for problems that have not even occurred. If they believe some major change in policy is required, or more taxpayers money is needed, or that the law should be changed they make proposals to the central government organization but for the rest they are responsible. They do not, however, act alone and unfettered. In Social Welfare and Transport, two fields I have discussed, the heads of departments receive advice from an advisory committee. Anybody who thinks advisory committees have no power has no understanding of human processes. It is, for instance, a fact that it is the central government which must constitutionally propose expenditure on social welfare subventions to the Legislature who alone can approve it but it is quite wrong to conclude that the Social Welfare Advisory Committee has no say in the matter. The detailed examination of applications for these subventions is done in the Social Welfare Advisory Committee and their recommendations have for years been embodied in the budget. The facts of life are that this Committee, without any statutory powers, does in practice, influence to the point of control all decisions on this important aspect of public expenditure. Similarly the Advisory Committee on Public Transport, largely because of the energy of its Chairman, (Mr. Y.K. Kan) exerted considerable influence over the formation of public transport policy in very difficult times.

In the case of the Secretariat for Home Affairs and the New Territories Administration the advisory bodies which range in formality from the statutory New Territories Heung Yee Kuk to the informal groups consulted by C.D.O.s are not confined to any particular field of administration but are bound by geographical limits only. Our Rural Committees in the New Territories have no statutory powers. They control no tax revenue beyond a small subvention for office expenses and can enact no legislation. But any functional organization—be it civil servant or functional board or advisory committee—which attempts any matter of importance without consulting the Rural Committee is liable to find itself in trouble. This is not a matter of law but of political reality.

(From a speech by Mr. D.C. Bray, Commissioner for the New Territories, at United College, 12 November 1971.)

D. DIFFICULTIES OF THE TRAFFIC ADVISORY BOARD AND THE TRANSPORT ADVISORY COMMITTEE

(i) Mr. W.C.G. KNOWLES: Would Government please state whether, under the terms of reference of the Traffic Advisory Board, unofficial members of that Board can initiate subjects for discussion and, if not, whether consideration will be given to changing the terms of reference so as to allow them to do so?

The COLONIAL SECRETARY: Sir, there are no fixed standing orders of procedure of general application to all boards and committees, and it is probable that practice varies considerably. Some boards and some committees draw up their own standing orders or rules of procedure, and in some cases procedural principles can be deduced from the Terms of Reference themselves; but other boards and committees which work more informally do not adhere to any fixed principles of procedure, nor do I think it necessary or desirable that they should be asked or required to do so.

My honourable Friend has referred specifically to the Traffic Advisory Committee. The Terms of Reference of that Committee are 'to consider and advise on any matters connected with traffic in the Colony of Hong Kong which are referred to it by Government or by the Commissioner of Police'. Thus only the Chairman on the instructions of Government, or the Commissioner of Police, has the *right* to initiate subjects for discussion. I am advised, however, that in practice if a member wishes a particular subject to be discussed, and indicates his wish to the Commissioner in sufficient time, arrangements can almost invariably be made for the subject to be referred to the Committee, so long of course as it lies within the Committee's Terms of Reference. So far as I am aware the arrangements work reasonably well and I see no necessity to consider amending the Terms of Reference. If, however, the Committee itself should, after due consideration, feel that the public interest would be better served by some amendment of its Terms of Reference, Government will of course be very ready to consider any representations that the Committee may wish to make to that effect.

(Question in *H.K. Hansard 1961*, p. 331f)

(ii) The COLONIAL SECRETARY (speaking in a debate on transport and traffic policy): The Transport Advisory Committee was appointed 'to advise the Governor on the coordination, improvement and development of internal transport facilities'. A Guidance Note attached to the terms of reference set out the Committee's responsibilities in more detail and referred in particular to the position of statutory authorities. It was made clear that, while the committee may *advise* a statutory authority (for example the Commissioner for Transport) the final decision must remain with him. This is important, first because the statutory authority bears full responsibility for the decision, and second because the authority's decision might be successfully challenged in the Courts if it could be established that he was accepting instructions from the Committee. It is very helpful to the Commissioner for Transport to receive advice from this experienced body. Naturally he will give great weight to the advice of the committee, and one would expect that in most cases there would be no divergence of opinion on the policy to be adopted. But in rare cases, and I know only of the one case which Mr. WATSON mentioned, the Commissioner may not feel able to accept the Committee's advice. Like Mr. WATSON, I would then expect the Commissioner to explain his reasons to the Committee, and it may be that, after further discussion, the Committee may succeed in convincing him. If not, the statutory authority's decision must prevail.

This is the relationship between any statutory authority and an advisory committee. As Mr. WATSON says, there is nothing new in it, and the system normally works satisfactorily.

(*H.K. Hansard 1968*, p. 586)

(iii) Mr. SZETO WAI (Chairman of the Transport Advisory Committee):
'... Because of the urgency in the present case, for reasons given by my honourable Friend, the Financial Secretary, this Council is being asked to make a decision on it today though between last April and now there was ample time for the matter to have been studied in great detail, and it is regrettable that the Transport Advisory Committee was not asked for its views.'

(*H. K. Hansard 1970–71*, 16 Dec. 1970, p. 273)

(iv) The Financial Secretary: 'In accordance with normal practice, the Transport Advisory Committee was consulted on how the affairs of the Kowloon Motor

Bus Company should be put in order. The Committee examined the Company's affairs with great care and came to the conclusion that the Company's financial position was critical and that the fare structure needed to be revised upwards. But I am bound to inform honourable Members that the Committee did not recommend the retention of the flat fare structure and, in particular, did not recommend that the fare on the main urban routes should be increased from 20 cents to 30 cents. In Government's considered view, however, the Committee's proposals, which involved the charging of fares by distance, would have undesirable social consequences and would involve difficulties of collection, particularly when the sections are so short.

Government welcomes, however, the Committee's proposal to establish a standing sub-committee under the chairmanship of Mr. Lo Tak-shing to keep under constant review KMB's services and operations and to process complaints and suggestions from the travelling public. The Company will also, I am sure, welcome such constructive and helpful advice as the sub-committee can offer.'

(H.K. Hansard 1970–71, p. 883)

Appendix 6
Documents to Chapter 8

A. THE ORIGINS OF LEGISLATION

(i) Mr. R.M. HETHERINGTON (Commissioner of Labour) moved the second reading of the *Factories and Industrial Undertakings (Amendment) Bill 1969.*

'Sir, several deficiencies and defects in the Factories and Industrial Undertakings Ordinance have come to light in recent years. This situation is neither surprising nor unwelcome. It arises from wider experience in enforcing the provisions of the Ordinance and from continuous developments in the field in which this Ordinance operates. Indeed, there would be some reason for concern if the question of amending this Ordinance did not arise from time to time. In common with other heads of department who are responsible for enforcing similar legislation, I keep a record of desirable amendments which come to my attention. This is a continuous process. A problem which arises periodically is to decide when an opportune moment has arrived to incorporate them in an amending bill. This involves balancing the inconvenience of delaying several desirable amendments until there are sufficient of them to include in one larger bill against the inconvenience of introducing a series of small amending bills. For other reasons, which I will shortly mention, it is necessary to amend the Factories and Industrial Undertakings Ordinance and a convenient opportunity is consequently presented to make several small but important changes in the existing provisions.'

(H.K. Hansard 1969, p. 15)

(ii) The Attorney General moved the second reading of the *Prevention of Bribery Bill.*

'Those whose task it is to prevent, investigate, or prosecute cases of corruption have long considered that the present law is inadequate in that it confers insufficient powers of investigation and makes the proof of offences too difficult and technical. Accordingly, in 1968, the Government instituted a detailed study of the present law. As the legislation of Singapore and Ceylon (both of which have had to face serious corruption problems) contained provisions which might, it was thought, be of value to us, visits were made to these countries, to find out exactly how their anti-bribery laws worked in practice.

Thereafter, a Working Party was established to consider amendments to the present Prevention of Corruption Ordinance (which I will refer to as Chapter 215) in the light of the knowledge which was gained from these visits. The Working Party expressed the opinion that, if corruption was to be successfully countered here, new legislation was imperative and put forward a draft bill, which was referred to the Advisory Committee on Corruption (under the chairmanship of

Sir Cho-yiu Kwan). This Committee, which has great experience of the problem in Hong Kong, endorsed the bill, with a number of suggestions for amendment, which were embodied in it, and this bill (which I will call the 1969 bill) was published last year, with an invitation to members of the public to comment on its provisions.

At the same time, it was circulated to the Hong Kong Bar Association, the Law Society of Hong Kong, the Exchange Banks Association and those Civil Service Staff Associations represented on the Senior Civil Service Council. Comments from these bodies, opinions expressed in the press, the views of heads of departments and the reactions of the public, as these became available particularly through the City District Offices, were all carefully studied and a number of changes have been made in consequence of them, mainly to provide safeguards against the possible abuse of some of the provisions of the bill, though the bill before Council today does not differ greatly in matters of substance from the 1969 bill.

(*H.K. Hansard 1970–71*, p. 132–3)

B. THE DRAFTING OF LEGISLATION

(i) The Attorney General: 'During 1962 48 Ordinances were enacted together with some 63 pieces of subsidiary legislation, and this does not take account of the various Orders and Proclamations which required the attention of the draftsman. Altogether this totals to the sum of 900 printed pages representing the draftsman's endeavours. Invariably there is considerable jostling in the queue of Bills and subsidiary legislation for which drafting instructions have actually been given. Equally, there always seems to be some special piece of legislation which is required as a matter of the greatest urgency, for example, when a spiral of rent increases or a flood of illegal immigrants calls for immediate action, and appropriate legislation has to be produced at the expense of agreed priorities and often is produced at a speed which scarcely gives the draftsman a chance. Further, disregarding immediately urgent legislation and assuming that a piece of legislation is in Category I as we call our top priority rating, that does not mean that its appearance as a Bill depends solely on the speed with which the draftsman works. In the course of the preparation of a Bill the draftsman may have to seek further instructions time and time again and in so doing may raise matters requiring important policy decisions which in turn may be made only after reference to other departments and perhaps after consultation with various public bodies. There are inevitable delays before the draftsman receives the relevant policy decision, and cases have occurred where for these reasons a Bill has been in draft for years before being introduced into this Council. Nevertheless, we continue to be inundated with demands for legislation: there are at present over 80 pieces of prospective legislation on the priority list which have been approved in consultation with the Colonial Secretary every 6 months. Thus, at present, any Category III legislation has, I fear, only the slimmest chance of ever being drafted.'

(*H.K. Hansard 1963*, pp. 142–3)

(ii) Sir Alastair Blair-Kerr's report on the disappearance of Chief Superintendent Godber while under investigation for suspected corruption gave details of the drafting of the *Prevention of Bribery Ordinance:*

'It was agreed that there should be a new Ordinance; and the draftsman of what is now the Prevention of Bribery Ordinance Cap. 201 began his labours. In his first draft, he prepared a provision which was basically what was recommended by the Working Party. This met with a certain amount of mild opposition locally; but that was nothing to what emanated from the Legal Advisers to the Secretary of State who were quite unable to see why the law of Hong Kong should be made to differ from the law of England as regards corruption. One argument was that there may be many Chinese civil servants who come from well-to-do families and whose standard of living reflects (and perfectly legitimately) the financial standing of the family rather than their own salaries. It was argued that there may be many reasons why an officer would not wish to explain in public how he had acquired, or had access to, means other than his official emoluments, although he might have no objection to giving an explanation to the head of his department. A local critic came up with this suggestion. He said:

'...it should be made absolutely clear in the clause that before giving his consent to a prosecution under this clause, the Attorney General personally must be dissatisfied with the public servant's explanation.'

And so, in a subsequent attempt to make section 10 more palatable to the critics, the draftsman inserted what is now sub-section (2) of section 10, namely:

'No prosecution for an offence under sub-section (1) shall be instituted without the consent in writing of the Attorney General, who shall, before consenting to the institution of a prosecution against a person for such an offence, inform that person that a prosecution against him for such an offence is under consideration and give him an opportunity of making representations in writing to the Attorney General.'

(First Report, p. 12f)

C. A BILL WITHDRAWN AND REDRAFTED

The Director of Medical and Health Services moved the *Pharmacy and Poisons Bill, 1966*:

'The main purpose of the Bill is to consolidate and clarify legislation that has become confusing through frequent amendment since it was first enacted in 1938. In fact with a few important exceptions, which I shall explain in detail, the Bill makes little significant change in the legislative position....'

'The Bill was drafted by a sub-committee of the Pharmacy Board and one of the three representatives of the trade who are members of the Board sat on this sub-committee. The Hong Kong General Chamber of Commerce and the Pharmaceutical Trade Federation were also invited to comment and have signified their approval of the draft Bill.'

(H.K. Hansard 1966, p. 269 and p. 270)

The Bill was not completed for three years, as the Director explained when moving the *Pharmacy and Poisons Bill, 1969*:

'Honourable Members will recall that on 20th April 1966 I moved a similar bill to amend the Pharmacy and Poisons Ordinance. The second and third readings of that bill were postponed following representations by certain professional bodies and others interested with regard to the provisions of the bill. These objections were mainly concerned with the composition of the Pharmacy Board, the effect of the bill on the Chinese herbalists and the question of control of the manufacture, import and export of poisons and pharmaceuticals. In order to consider these objections, a Committee was set up under the Chairmanship of my honourable Friend, Sir Albert RODRIGUES. The terms of reference of this

Committee are "to study the proposed Pharmacy and Poisons Bill having regard to representations and suggestions which have been made or which may be made concerning the provisions and to make recommendations and amendments to the bill if such are considered necessary". The Committee submitted its report in February 1967 and with one slight modification all its proposals were accepted and incorporated into the present bill. Because of the substantial nature of the consequential amendments to incorporate the proposals of the "Rodrigues Committee" and because of further changes which were made and which Members have not had the opportunity to examine, it was decided that instead of proceeding with the Committee stage amendments a fresh bill agreed to by the Pharmacy Board, the Pharmaceutical Society of Hong Kong, the Professional Associations, the relevant Government Departments and as far as practicable in conformity with the wishes of those interested should be laid before the Council.'

(*H.K. Hansard 1969*, p. 450)

D. PUBLIC REACTION AND THE UNOFFICIAL MEMBERS

(The second reading of the *Immigration Bill 1971*)
Mr. Woo Pak Chuen: Sir, since the first reading of this bill on the 21st July last there have been many adverse comments and criticisms in the press and by local organizations. Some of these comments and criticisms arose from misunderstanding of the explanatory memorandum of the bill. The vast majority of local residents know no more of the bill than what has been published in the Chinese press based on the Chinese version of the explanatory memorandum. This memorandum refers to Hong Kong belongers but the phrase is nowhere defined in the bill itself. . . .

A very different public reaction to this bill might have resulted if, instead of drawing distinction between those who are and those who are not—in the strict immigration sense of the word—"belongers", the explanatory memorandum had contained the aforesaid assurance now given by the Director of Immigration.

This matter is very important in the sphere of "closing the gap" between the Government and the people and demonstrating Government's real concern for the *de facto* Chinese residents of Hong Kong. It is the opinion of my Unofficial colleagues, as a matter of great importance and principle, that their status should be clearly defined. We therefore suggest that the following categories of persons should be given statutory recognition in this bill. . . .

The Unofficial Members have had a number of discussions on this bill with my honourable Friend. They have been informed that Government will accept their recommendations on these four categories and that the bill will be amended accordingly at the committee stage. On this understanding, Sir, the Unofficials will vote "Aye" on the motion for the second reading of the bill.'

(*H.K. Hansard 1971–72*, pp. 101–3)

THE ATTORNEY GENERAL (Mr. ROBERTS): 'Sir, as has been indicated, there has been a number of consultations between myself and Unofficial Members since the second reading of this bill was moved in July. During these meetings we took into account various representations which had been received from public bodies and comments which had been contained in editorials and in the correspondence columns of newspapers.

The Government fully realizes that the right to enter and live in Hong Kong is a matter which is of the greatest importance to the individual. Therefore, we have re-examined the bill with great care to see whether it can be improved and I shall move a number of substantial amendments at the committee stage, to achieve the objects which have been referred to by the honourable Mr. P.C. Woo and the honourable Mr. Oswald Cheung.'

(*H.K. Hansard 1971–72*, p. 108)

E. THE GOVERNMENT GIVES WAY UNDER PRESSURE

On 10th May 1972 the unofficial members moved a motion asking Government to undertake a thorough review of its policy of assessing Crown rents on renewable Crown Leases. The Financial Secretary (Mr. Haddon Cave) replied to the debate:

'Honourable Members have stressed the problems which they feel will arise from adherence to Government's policy concerning renewal of leases. This policy has been applied since the first lease was renewed (in 1948) and has been the subject of particular consideration over the past ten years because of the number of leases falling due for renewal in 1973. This consideration has been largely concerned with working out ways and means whereby the straightforward application of the policy can be varied to meet the particular circumstances of particular groups of land owners (or, more correctly, owners of leases). I think it would be fair to say that honourable Members have stressed the problems of these owners, and rightly so, for honourable Members are watchdogs of the private as well as of the public interest. But I must say, here and now, Sir, that it is not part of Government policy to diminish those rights or to confiscate them in any way. Honourable Members have argued for a change in the level of payment for the renewal of the right to hold and use land to a figure below that provided for in the lease contract. It is because the problems referred to by honourable Members have already been recognised that various methods are available to land owners for renewal of their leases. The fact is, however, that land owners generally form a comparatively wealthy segment of the community and have, by and large, done very well in Hong Kong in recent years. It is this segment of the community, which includes the large property companies, which stands to gain most if the present policy on renewal is changed in the way proposed by honourable Members. And it is the public interest, the wider interest of the community as a whole, which would be prejudiced by such a change. . . .

This brings me, Sir, finally to the financial consequences of a change of policy. The anticipated revenue from the renewal of Crown leases has been allowed for since the year 1973–74 first came within the scope of the annual five year forecasts of revenue and expenditure back in 1969–70. If the sums involved, amounting to some $150 million in 1973–74 rising to $200 million a year by 1975–76 and staying at roughly that figure thereafter, are to be diminished in any way, then the fiscal or expenditure implications or both will have to be faced. Yet it would be quite unrealistic to suppose that any necessary adjustments to the revenue earning power of other levies or to expenditure plans could be arranged in a way which was equitable in terms of the general public interest. The fact is that lease owners would be, by any change in long standing policy, beneficially treated. And let us not imagine that those lease owners, who are also landlords, will pass the benefits of any such change on to their tenants. Landlords will, in general, continue—and understandably so—to charge their tenants the highest rents the tenants are willing to pay and, in some cases, the law permits, regardless of the rents that the landlords are paying to the Crown.'

(*H.K. Hansard 1971–72*, pp. 754–9)

After the debate Government announced a number of concessions, and these were further extended by a bill introduced in March 1973 by the Attorney General, who concluded his speech as follows:

'It is, I think, appropriate that I should remind honourable Members, lest they should be unduly influenced by a misplaced sympathy for lessees, that this bill represents only one in a long series of concessions to them. Indeed, it might well be argued that the Government has been too generous in its treatment of one small, and generally prosperous, sector of the community at the expense of the ordinary taxpayers in Hong Kong.

In this Council, in May last year, the Colonial Secretary announced a number of important modifications to Government policy on the assessment of Crown rents. Firstly, the general level of all renewal rents assessed in accordance with Crown leases was to be effectively reduced by 20%. Secondly, the increased renewal rents would be introduced by gradual stages over a period of 5 years from 1973. This is being effected by charging only 50% of the reduced' rent in 1973 and thereafter increasing the percentage by annual stages of 10% until the full annual amount of the reduced rent is charged in 1978 and thereafter.

Thirdly, the existing Crown rent will continue to be paid on any lot which contains pre-war rent-controlled property, until that property ceases to be controlled under the Landlord and Tenant Ordinance. Fourthly, a lessee with under-developed property has been given an option to renew his lease, at a rent assessed on the basis of existing use and development.

These very significant reductions, combined with those which are contained in the bill before honourable Members should, I suggest, satisfy all but the most fervent partisan that the Government has been fair, indeed many might argue that it has been over-generous, in its treatment of Crown lessees.'

(*H.K. Hansard 1972–73*, pp. 611–12)

However the Unofficial members and the landlords were still dissatisfied, as the senior Unofficial member Mr. Woo Pak-chuen explained when the second reading debate was resumed a month later:

'Sir, this bill incorporates by implication in clause 9 the present formula used by Government for fixing of the re-assessed Crown rents upon expiry of renewable Crown leases. Furthermore it fixes a specific date upon which the value of the land is to be computed. I am sure that Government is aware that the Chinese Manufacturers Association of Hong Kong and 575 Colony-wide associations have joined together to oppose what they regard as the unjust and unreasonable formula. At their request the Unofficial Members have listened to their further representations against proceeding on the present basis. Since then my colleagues and I have given earnest consideration as to whether that formula, even after the concessions announced by Government in this Council on 24th May last year, can be supported. Sir, the Unofficials have reached the conclusion that they cannot support the formula as it stands and in consequence we are unable to vote in favour of this bill as at present drafted. In saying this, I have taken due account of the views of those Unofficial Members who are not present here today. Our strength on the ground is rather weak, but the strength of our views is not diminished thereby. We feel bound to advocate on behalf of the community at large that Government should think again before going ahead on the present basis of renewal.'

(*H.K. Hansard 1972–73*, pp. 744–5)

In the face of this implied threat of a unanimous vote against the bill by the unofficials, government retreated yet again. Further concessions were announced in a statement made by the acting Attorney General twelve weeks later:

'On 28th March several honourable Members spoke against the motion and urged reconsideration of the basis proposed in the bill for assessing the Crown rent payable under renewed Crown leases. They drew attention to the hardship that would be experienced by the owners of smaller properties; to the great number of associations which had united in opposition to the policy; to the effect high land prices would have on the level of the reassessed Crown rent; and to the fundamentally opposed views which are held with respect to the legal interpretation of the proviso for renewal contained in renewable leases.

'Sir, the Government had by then already modified earlier proposals in a number of respects in order to meet objections.... Since then, the policy has again been re-examined, particularly with a view to meeting the case of the many thousands of owners of smaller flats, and I must say right away that it has not been possible to achieve this principal aim without benefitting all property owners equally; nor without foregoing the major part of the revenue which would have accrued from the reassessed Crown rents....

'The basis of assessment now proposed is one which some honourable Members have advocated. It will be a percentage of rateable value, a method which has the merit of simplicity and might enable Crown rent to be collected along with the rates payable under the Rating Ordinance. The percentage to be taken has itself been the subject of very careful consideration, with the needs of owners of small properties particularly in mind....'

(*H.K. Hansard 1972–73*, p. 881)

The cost of these concessions was revealed by the Financial Secretary in the 1974 Budget Debate. After announcing various taxation increases he pointed out:

'If members think this proposal is a little harsh, may I remind them that the revised terms for renewing renewable Crown Leases (three per cent of rateable values) will yield about $8 million a year only, whereas under the previous proposal (five per cent of market values) we expected to collect $300 million in 1974–75, and $1,200 million over the three years of the forecast period.'

(*H.K. Hansard 1973–74*, p. 600)

F. DIVISIONS IN THE LEGISLATIVE COUNCIL AND REVOLTS BY THE UNOFFICIAL MEMBERS 1946–1975

1947 *Hansard p. 132–56*. Bill introduced to impose income tax and profits tax on a permanent basis for the first time in peace time. All officials plus four unofficials (three Europeans and one Chinese) voted in favour, three unofficials against (two Chinese, one Portuguese).

Hansard pp. 190–210 and 217–47. Motion proposed by unofficials calling for a vigorous attack on the housing problem and noting with grave concern government's refusal to modify 'its present unfair and repressive policy in regard to the renewal of 75 year Crown Leases'. Motion defeated by 8 votes (all officials) to 7 votes (all unofficials).

1949 *Hansard pp. 188–205*. Resolutions proposed by Sir Man Kam Lo rejecting Sir Mark Young's plan for constitutional reform and proposing an alternative. Resolutions carried unanimously by the votes of the unofficials; officials abstained from voting. (There is a full summary of this debate in Endacott: *Government and People in Hong Kong* pp. 189–94.)

1952 *Hansard pp. 31–51.* Government proposed that the Public Works Department should construct the new city hall in association with Professor Gordon Brown. Mr. Watson (unofficial member) wanted an open competition for the design. His views were rejected by 16 votes to one.

1953 *Hansard pp. 172–6, 194–225 and 229–45.* Government proposed a bill to allow increases in controlled rents. This was attacked by all but one of the unofficials. After an adjournment government cut all proposed increases by half. This satisfied all but one of the unofficials, who divided the Council on an amendment to allow no increases at all for domestic premises. The amendment was defeated (p. 238, votes not recorded).

1953 *Hansard pp. 339–44.* Government proposed to amend the royalty paid by the Yaumati Ferry Company to bring it into line with that paid by the Star Ferry. Unofficials wished to make this amendment conditional on the directors of the Yaumati Ferry Company altering their Articles of Association to make their shares freely transferable and not only at the discretion of the directors, as was the case with the Star Ferry Company. Government took the view that the promise made to the Yaumati Ferry Company to keep the terms of its franchise equal with those of the Star Ferry Company was unconditional and binding; and that in any case other monopoly franchise holders had similar restrictions in their articles. Officials 9–Unofficials 8.

1955 *Hansard pp. 280–307.* Mr. Blackword, speaking on behalf of the General Chamber of Commerce, protested against two new amendments to the Inland Revenue Bill designed to close loopholes in the assessment of profits tax. He claimed a division and lost by 16 votes to one.

1956 *Hansard pp. 3–29.* Following disagreement in the Finance Committee, government asked the Council to vote an additional $1,000,000 subvention to Hong Kong University as recommended by an independent committee. Four unofficials wished to reduce the sum to $700,000. This amendment was defeated 13–4. Four unofficials voted with the officials, four voted against.

1960 *Hansard pp. 222–31.* Most unofficials objected to a government bill to legalize betting on football pools. On the second reading vote 7 unofficials voted against, one unofficial abstained, together with all the officials.

1965 *Hansard pp. 490–520.* Mr. Dhun Ruttonjee protested against the terms granted to the company constructing the cross harbour tunnel. Defeated by 20 votes to one, with one other unofficial abstaining, (Dr. Chung).

1967 *Hansard pp. 124–6 and 273.* Mr. Kan Yuet-keung protested against the increase in the contribution to pay for the British forces in Hong Kong. Defeated by 24 votes to one, (Mr. Watson abstained).

Since the revision of the standing orders in 1968 there have been no further divisions, but on the following occasions government clearly overruled the majority view of the unofficials.

1969 *Hansard 1969 pp. 413–24* and *1971–72, pp. 819–21.* Government proposed to legalize minibuses as public transport operators and to make an *ex gratia* payment to the Motor Bus Companies for the loss of their statutory monopoly. The Attorney General believed they had a moral right to compensation. The unofficials 'with one or two exceptions' (p. 420) argued that the bus companies had forfeited any claim to compensation because of their poor and inadequate service. Nevertheless the unofficials subsequently voted the sum that had been agreed in negotiations between officials and the companies.

1970 *Hansard 1969–70 pp. 517–31*. Government proposed to withdraw the concessionary rate of diesel fuel duty previously granted to the Motor Bus Companies in consequence of the abolition of its requirement to pay royalty. Some unofficials felt that the motion was being rushed through the Council and that this concealed subsidy should continue to keep down fares. Mr. Watson (unofficial) wished to postpone a decision on the government motion pending more information, 'I understand, however, that the Official Members will vote against any motion to adjourn this debate. In spite therefore of the fact that most of the Unofficials would have supported such a motion. I will refrain from proposing it.' (pp. 528f.)

The question was put and agreed to without a division. Mr. Fung Hon-chu stated that he abstained.

1973 The Financial Secretary proposed to withdraw the allowance granted to income taxpayers to deduct the sums paid as life insurance premiums from their taxable income. All the unofficials except one who spoke about this in the budget debate condemned the change, and he only gave it very tepid support (*Hansard 1972–73*, p. 788). However there was no division against the bill, perhaps as a result of a threat by the Financial Secretary that he would withdraw certain new concessions if this change were not accepted (*Hansard 1972–73*, p. 660).

1975 *H.K. Hansard, 23 April*. During the second reading debate on the *Mass Transit Corporation Bill*, Mr. Lo Tak-shing vigorously attacked the whole proposal to build an underground railway. When the President proposed to adjourn the debate Mr. Lo called out 'No' on a voice vote. No other unofficial joined him in this protest. This was said by the *South China Morning Post*, 24 April 1975, to have been the first 'No' vote for many years.

Appendix 7
Documents to Chapter 9

A. THE POWERS OF A FINANCIAL SECRETARY

SIR JOHN COWPERTHWAITE: 'I should like next to take my opportunity to-day to try to dispel some misconceptions which seem to be prevalent about the powers and purposes of a Financial Secretary in the making of our budgets. It appears that many people are under the impression that he sits at his desk and with dictatorial ruthlessness slashes away at requests by Departments for the funds they consider necessary for the carrying out of their policies and purposes, and so, fashions the shape of the year's public services to his own conservative view of the prudent extent of public expenditure. It does not happen at all like that. I doubt if I can influence the amount of the year's estimate of expenditure by more than a very few million dollars. The estimates, year by year, flow, not from my arbitrary judgement, but from a multiplicity of decisions continuously being taken by Government as a whole on the desirable, and possible, rate of priorities of expansion of our public services, mostly in the shape of long-term programmes or objectives. I do not say that I am not without influence—for good or ill—on these decisions but mine is only one voice among many; and not always, I like to think, on the illiberal side. These programmes and objectives are always under review and are constantly changing. For example, we have just recently laid down new programmes and targets for resettlement housing and have for some time been going through a rather painful process of producing a new policy of educational expansion.

What I *do* attempt to do is to ensure that, while agreed policies are put into effect efficiently, this is done with all due economy; to ensure that the estimated expenditure for the year is realistic in relation to a department's ability to spend (but without thereby imposing a brake on its planned activities); and, particularly but not only for the longer term, to ensure, so far as one can foresee these things, that we do not pitch our aim so high, in terms either of quantity or quality, that we are unlikely to be able to reach our goal without imposing excessive strains on the economy or killing those geese which have been such prolific layers of golden eggs in recent years, and which it must also be the aim of financial policy to foster.'

(*H.K. Hansard 1965* pp. 74f)

'...I have for years tried to explain that Government's plans must not be judged by one year's estimates of expenditure but by the, in the short term, largely irreversible plans of expansion in nearly all fields of Government activity. It is true, all the same, I think, that our present economic prosperity and financial strength have led both Government departments and subvented organizations to think more largely. Financial restraints do tend to loosen in such circumstances and it becomes more difficult for a Financial Secretary to say about any single relatively modest increase in expenditure, and some not so modest, that we cannot afford it.'

(*H.K. Hansard 1970–71*, p. 415)

B. THE FUNCTIONS AND ACTIVITIES OF THE FINANCE COMMITTEE

(i) *A PLEA FOR MORE WORK*

Mr. KAN Yuet-keung: '. . . I have for a long time felt that not nearly sufficient use has been made by Government of the Finance Committee and its two important Sub-Committees—the Establishment Sub-Committee and the Public Works Sub-Committee. . . . The practice at present seems to be to refer to Finance Committee for approval all proposals by Heads of Departments only if they are accepted by the Secretariat. What is not accepted seldom, if ever, goes any further. I suggest that it is in the public interest that all Departmental requests and proposals which have financial implications should go to the Finance Committee or its appropriate Sub-Committee for consideration irrespective of whether they are accepted by the Secretariat or not. Whilst we the unofficial members have never regarded ourselves as "the Opposition Party"—although having heard some of my Unofficial colleagues just now, I am not so sure—at least do not let us be treated as government back-benchers tied to the party machine. For my part, I shall not be content to be one.'

(*H.K. Hansard 1965*, pp. 118f)

(ii) *THE OFFICIAL REPLY*

The Colonial Secretary: 'The principal function of the Finance Committee and its two Sub-Committees is to advise the Legislature on proposals for public expenditure put to them—speaking in a strictly constitutional sense—by Your Excellency, although proposals arise initially in many ways, often from one of our advisory bodies or from suggestions in this Council. In any event such proposals are marshalled and presented by the Secretariat, as in Britain by the Treasury. This work is continuous throughout the year and continuously expanding. But if, as Mr. KAN suggested, each department's proposals for expenditure went direct to the Finance Committee, with or without further official scrutiny or support, this would not only derogate from Your Excellency's constitutional powers, but would quickly lead, I think, to a situation of considerable confusion.'

(*H.K. Hansard 1965*, p. 233)

(iii) *THE CHECKS AGAINST EXCESSIVE STAFF INCREASES*

The Colonial Secretary: 'Members have referred to the expansion which has taken place in the Service and have made understandable enquiries on the methods we employ to ensure that new posts are really necessary and whether existing staff are used to the best advantage and with the optimum efficiency. At the moment, mainly because of the astonishing expansion which has been necessary, the Civil Service is going through a very difficult period, where experience is at a premium. It is easy to recruit men and women—it is very much more difficult to recruit experience. We are a very young Service, and particularly in the middle grades we are over-stretched.

As regards the methods we employ to ensure that new posts are really necessary, I can reassure honourable Members. Indeed I sometimes think that we make Heads of Departments go through too many hoops in acquiring necessary additions to their staff. Once the Head of Department is himself convinced he makes a case to the Finance Branch of the Secretariat, and it is then examined by the Complements and Grading Division who may or may not find it necessary to consult the Organizational Surveys Unit, the Cost Control Unit and the Establishment Branch. Having passed that obstacle, and it is no ordinary one (indeed there is an apocryphal story of a Head of a Department who applied for an Assistant Director and got a messenger), (laughter) it then has to pass the eagle eye of the Deputy Financial Secretary and the Establishment Secretary.

His request then goes through the Establishment Committee of Finance Committee and Finance Committee itself. Finally, if the post in question is of a relevant grade, the actual selection of the person to be appointed is made by the Public Services Commission.'

(*H.K. Hansard 1970–71*, p. 529)

(iv) *WHY THE FINANCE COMMITTEE SITS IN PRIVATE*

The Colonial Secretary: 'I would refer to the suggestion made by my honourable Friend, Mr. Y.K. KAN, that the Finance Committee of this Council should sit in public....

It is true that at least from 1893 until the occupation, Finance Committee meetings were held in public, and that the minutes of the Committee are recorded in the prewar Hansards.

But a study of those minutes is not altogether reassuring. In the earlier years they do indicate a fair measure of discussion, but not on the unfettered scale which we now enjoy. But by 1941 the exchanges largely took the form of few and very short questions and answers. The proceedings had become formalized and stereotyped—I have, Sir, a genuine fear that the same thing might happen again.

There is no clear record of why this practice was not resumed in 1946 but it seems likely that it was felt to be incompatible with the greatly expanded volume of business in those postwar years.

The problems of volume of business, and the great amount of detail presented to Finance Committee in its agenda items still remain, and it would seem that if Finance Committee meetings are to be held in public, then the Committee will have to be relieved of the less weighty issues that now have to go to it. This would involve greater delegation of authority to the Financial Secretary to approve supplementary provision. Furthermore, it would, as Mr. KAN has recognized, inevitably mean that agenda items presented to Finance Committee would in some cases be less informative, since the protection afforded by the present restricted grading for documents would be removed....

...My main doubt centres round one consideration—the Committee at present works—in both senses of the word—and is an indispensable part of the Government machine. I would not like to see its operation become so formalized—or inhibited under the public gaze—that it lost efficiency.

One last, but important point I would make and that is this. There is nothing clandestine nor covert about the recommendations of the Finance Committee. It is a Committee of this Council, enjoying delegated powers, but its decisions all come up to this Council, in public, for ratification. They are embodied in a series of motions, moved by the Honourable Financial Secretary, and it is open to any member who doubts the wisdom of a provision, or who wishes to explain or associate himself with any provision, to speak to that motion, and draw the attention of this Council and the public to any appropriation on which he feels strongly or on which he feels more should be said.

(*H.K. Hansard 1970–71*, pp. 121–3)

C. THE REPORT OF THE DIRECTOR OF AUDIT

(i) *EXTRACTS FROM THE REPORT ON THE YEAR ENDING 31 MARCH 1972*

28. *Excessive, Dormant and Obsolete Stocks.* Further cases were noted during the year of departments holding excessive, dormant and obsolete stocks, to which reference was made in paragraph 35 of my previous report. In one case stocks of 485 different items of motor vehicle spare parts, originally costing over $20,000, held in the Government Supplies depots at Caroline Hill and Sung Wong Toi Road, which were found to be obsolete, were disposed of by auction for $300.00, the vehicles for which a number of these spare parts were stocked, having been disposed of several years ago. In addition, at the same depots stocks of 150 different items of stores were found to be obsolete, and 420 other items in excess of recently determined reordering levels, were also noted....

31. *Under-utilization of Departmental Transport Services.* Audit reviews of three departmental transport services provided to convey staff morning and evening from Kowloon to and from locations in the New Territories revealed that they have been substantially under-utilized. In the case of Agriculture and Fisheries, operating between departmental Headquarters and Tai Lung Farm, and in the case of the District Office Yuen Long, operating between South Kowloon Magistracy and the District Office Yuen Long, the vehicles had a passenger capacity of ten but passengers carried have been averaging less than four and two respectively. The other service between South Kowloon Magistracy and the District Office Tai Po was operated by a 3-ton lorry with a seating capacity of twenty-two but was only used, according to the 'Passenger Book', by less than three persons per trip. This latter service has now been suspended following on the audit observation; the possibility that officers may have used this transport but not paid the required fare is being pursued separately....

34. *Social Welfare Department Transport.* In yet a further case the attention of the Director of Social Welfare was invited in November 1969, to the free use of departmental transport for private journeys by the staff of the Castle Peak Boys' Home and their families, at which time the practice had been in force for a year. A departmental circular was subsequently issued in April 1970, drawing the attention of officers to the limitations placed on the use of Government transport for private purposes as laid down in General Regulations, but despite this, the unauthorized and free use of departmental transport continued and the position was not regularized until some two years after my observation was first raised. In his original submission to the Financial Secretary the Director of Social Welfare proposed that the charges involved up to October 1971, be written off, but according to the latest correspondence copied to me, he now maintains that after further investigation the majority of the journeys which were recorded in the vehicle log books as private were in effect official ones, being for despatch of mails to the nearby Post Office. This case again illustrates the point made in paragraph 37 of my previous report that I am often unable to establish misuse as I must rely on the description of the journeys shown in the vehicle log books, the supervision of departmental officers in ensuring that the descriptions are correct, and on their integrity in investigating and replying to observations I may raise. The matter is still under correspondence with the Director of Social Welfare and the Colonial Secretariat.

(ii) *EXTRACTS FROM THE GOVERNOR'S DESPATCH TO THE SECRE-
TARY OF STATE*
*PARA. 31: UNDER-UTILIZATION OF DEPARTMENT TRANSPORT
SERVICES*

The Director of Agriculture and Fisheries reports that the under-utilization of
the vehicle operating between Headquarters and Tai Lung Farm was due to
frequent breakdowns. This vehicle has now been replaced, and the average
number of passengers carried has risen to seven per trip.

The District Commissioner, New Territories, reports that the under-utilization
of the vehicle operating between South Kowloon Magistracy and District Office,
Yuen Long, was due to its being unsuitable for the purpose. It has been replaced
by a mini-bus and the number of passengers carried has increased to an average
of five per trip.

*PARAS. 32 AND 33: POLICE AND PRISONS DEPARTMENTS TRANS-
PORT*

The question of charging is under consideration with the Commissioners of
Police and of Prisons.

PARA. 34: SOCIAL WELFARE DEPARTMENT TRANSPORT
Disciplinary action against those responsible has been proposed.

(Legislative Council Sessional Paper 10 January 1973)

Appendix 8
Documents to Chapter 10

A. QUESTIONS

(i) *AN ADVERTISEMENT CRITICIZED*

Mr. KAN Yuet-keung: The recent advertisement by Government for the post of Director of Protocol lays down the following qualifications:
'Candidate should
(i)   preferably be over 40 years and under 57 years of age;
(ii) have a good general education, with preferably a British or Hong Kong University degree, or equivalent;
(iii) have previous experience in a position of authority, together with proven organizational ability, and
(iv) be able to speak fluent English and preferably have a good knowledge of other languages, including French.
It is also stated that previous experience in the armed forces may be an advantage.
(1) Why is French singled out as a preferable foreign language?
(2) Why is knowledge of Chinese not a specific requirement or preference?
(3) Why is previous experience in the armed forces an advantage?

THE COLONIAL SECRETARY:—Sir, the answer to the first part of the question is that French is still the language of diplomacy. The Director of Protocol is responsible for liaison with the Consular Corps and for meeting and assisting important visitors from overseas. When these are not fluent in English, French is the most likely alternative.

The answer to the second part of the question is that a knowledge of Chinese is of no special advantage in the efficient performance of the duties of this particular post. The Director of Protocol has few, if any, dealings with those who speak only Chinese.

The answer to the third part of the question is that almost all ceremonial functions involve the participation of the Armed Services and are based on military ceremonial.

Mr. KAN:—Sir, the qualifications laid down give me the impression that they are thought up with someone in mind. Would that impression be a correct one?

THE COLONIAL SECRETARY:—Sir, that is not the case.

Mr. KAN:—Sir, is there in fact someone in mind for the job, such as a retired expatriate civil servant?

THE COLONIAL SECRETARY:—Sir, there is no one in mind. That is why we are advertising.

Mr. KAN:—Thank you.

(*H.K. Hansard 1969*,pp.25–6)

(ii) *A COMPLAINT QUICKLY RECTIFIED*

Mr. WONG Sien-bing: Is the Director of Urban Services aware of the appalling conditions at Repulse Bay where rocks line the beach both above and under water at low tide making it hazardous for swimmers? Could the Director indicate what positive measures he proposes to take to restore Repulse Bay as a beach for swimmers?

Mr. D.R.W. ALEXANDER:—Sir, this is a hardy annual which invariably promotes questions in the press and in the Urban Council. The situation is therefore not unknown to me. Unfortunately, there is no easy solution to the problem.

Much of the sea bed at Repulse Bay is covered with large rocks. The majority of these are below the low water mark and normally do not impede swimming. As for removing smaller rocks and stones from above the low water mark, the advice we have received is that this might lead to an unacceptable degree of sand erosion while, in any case, past experience has shown that fresh stones are very quickly washed up in place of those removed. Consideration is being given to covering at least some of the rocks with a layer of sand, and I hope that it will be possible to try this out soon even though there may be more than a fair chance of this sand again being washed away.

In the meantime, however, since last year we have been clearly marking two 'safe passages', each about 20 feet wide, down to the normal low water mark so as to allow swimmers unimpeded access to the sea, and I have asked my staff to consider providing more such passages—not only at Repulse Bay but wherever they may be needed at other gazetted beaches.

Mr. WONG:—Sir, as surprisingly the rocks at Repulse Bay beach above the waterline almost disappeared a few days after the question was sent in... (*laughter*)...would the Director of Urban Services keep up the pressure on the beach staff to continue the good work and also keep on solving the problem of rocks below the waterline?

Mr. ALEXANDER:—Certainly I give this assurance, Sir, but I must make it quite clear that over the past off-season my staff have removed enough stones to build a wall 120 feet long by 6 feet by 5 feet, so there is no question of this being a last minute show in response to the question. (*Laughter*).

(*H.K. Hansard 1971–72*, p. 682)

(iii) *A BUFFALO AT KAI TAK AIRPORT*

Mrs. LI Shu-pui: What precautionary measures are there to prevent stray animals and unauthorized persons from getting into the restricted areas in the airport?

THE ACTING COLONIAL SECRETARY:—Sir, unauthorized access to the Airport is prevented generally by a perimeter fence. During the past year an additional coiled barbed wire fence has been constructed inside the perimeter fence as an added precaution.

Within the Airport there are various restricted areas which only authorized persons may enter, on production of a pass. In recent months several improvements have been made to the entrances, fences and other physical security arrangements in these areas.

My honourable Friend's reference to stray animals is perhaps prompted by the recent unauthorized entry of a buffalo into the Airport. This large animal presented itself at the entrance to the Fire Services airport establishment on Sung Wong Toi Road, and insisted on gaining admission through the gate provided for fire appliances. The fireman on duty at the gate was understandably unable to frustrate the animal's designs. But immediate action was taken by the Fire Services staff who sent vehicles to head the buffalo away from the runway. They were successful and the animal was killed near the Far East Flying Training School without having caused damage to people or property.

(*H.K. Hansard 1968*, pp 571f)

B. CASES DEALT WITH BY UMELCO

(i) *REGISTRATION OF SCHOOL IN A DOMESTIC BUILDING* (Type A)

The UMELCO Office received an appeal from the proprietor of a private school concerning the refusal by the Director of Education to register a school on the second floor of a domestic building in Kowloon on the grounds that there would be danger to those using the proposed school premises. He had previously obtained a fire safety certificate for the school and had spent money on preparing the premises for use as a school. Subsequently four illegal factories had begun operation in the same building, and the Director of Fire Services had withdrawn his agreement to the operation of the school since this change in the use of the premises had so increased the risk of fire in the building or the danger from panic in the event of fire that there was an undue risk of danger to those using the proposed school premises. The Commissioner of Labour advised UMELCO that the illegal factories had been prosecuted successfully on several occasions but the fines imposed did not prevent the proprietors from continuing their operations. Members of UMELCO felt that this position was quite unacceptable and therefore consulted the Attorney General. Following their discussion a Crown Counsel was instructed to prosecute again and to ensure that the magistrate was informed of all the relevant circumstances, including the effect on the school of the operation of these factories. Each of the illegal factory operators was conditionally discharged on agreeing to enter into a recognizance in a sum of money not to operate a factory in the premises for a period of 6 months. One operator failed to comply with his undertaking, was prosecuted again and heavily fined. As a result, all four illegal factories ceased operation. Therefore the way was finally cleared for the Director of Fire Services to drop his objection and so enable the appellant's school to be registered by the Director of Education.

(Case 11—*1970–71 Annual Report*)

(ii) *APPEAL AGAINST REFUSAL TO ALLOCATE A RESETTLEMENT ESTATE PRIMARY SCHOOL* (Type C)

An appeal was received by UMELCO against the refusal of the Director of Education to allocate to a missionary organization a subsidized primary school in a resettlement estate. The Administrative Secretary requested access to the Education Department's files on the subject to see what the reasons for refusal were. The Director of Education released the pertinent files and it was ascertained that there were several factors against such an allocation:

(i) the organization concerned already had a small private school with four classrooms which was not well run.

(ii) the organization itself was not substantial.

(iii) to run a 24-classroom resettlement estate primary school requires a considerable amount of expertise not possessed by the appellant. Furthermore many substantial and experienced sponsors for such schools were available.

The Administrative Secretary was therefore fully satisfied with the reasons for the decision of the Director of Education. A full explanation was given to the Superintendent of the missionary organization concerned.

(Case 56—*1971–72 Annual Report*)

(iii) *PARDON FOR TRAFFIC OFFENCE* (Type A)

A taxi-driver, who was convicted of an offence of jumping a set of traffic lights, complained to the UMELCO that there were, in fact, no traffic lights at the street junction purported to be the scene of the offence in question. The taxi-driver had been convicted in the Magistrates Court on sworn evidence given by a prosecution witness whereas he, the taxi-driver, called no witness and gave no sworn evidence but merely elected to make an unsworn statement from the dock. UMELCO called for a report from the Principal Government Highway Engineer who confirmed that there were, in fact, no traffic lights at the street concerned. It transpired that the discrepancy was the result of a mistake by the Police constable concerned, who had mistaken the street for another. There was reason to believe that the taxi had driven through a red traffic signal at a nearby junction. After due enquiry the Commissioner of Police was satisfied that the officer's action had not been malicious, but was the result of a genuine mistake. The constable has since then been disciplined for his carelessness in this case. The matter was then referred to the Chief Justice who, in turn, referred it to the Attorney General with a request that he should take such action as he considered proper. The Attorney General felt that the need to maintain the reputation for high standards in the administration of justice warranted the granting of a pardon and remission of the fine imposed. The Attorney General tendered advice to this effect to His Excellency the Governor who accepted it and granted a pardon and remission of the fine. In this case an error of fact came to light after the conclusion of the Court case, which was rectified by invoking the Crown's prerogative of pardon.

(Case 12—*1971–72 Annual Report*)

(Note: In such a case, the Swedish Ombudsman might have instituted a prosecution for perjury.)

(iv) *DELAY IN A PASSPORT APPLICATION* (Type B)

The UMELCO Duty Roster Member interviewed a client who was having difficulty in obtaining a British passport. It transpired that he had adopted a name different from the one shown in his local birth certificate, although he was able to produce other documents as evidence of his basic identity. He was therefore aggrieved that the Immigration Department was not prepared to issue him with a passport in time for him to travel abroad with his employers. On the instructions of the Duty Roster Member, the case was drawn to the personal attention of the Director of Immigration. In his reply the Director advised that a passport could not be issued to the complainant until it had been established beyond reasonable doubt that he was in fact the rightful owner of the birth certificate in question. This involved making certain checks and he was still awaiting certain information. However, since the complainant was required to accompany his employers abroad, he would in the meantime be issued with a certificate of identity to enable him to travel whilst his claim to a British passport was being sorted out.

(Case 74—*1972–73 Annual Report*)

(v) *REFUND OF EX-GRATIA COMPENSATION* (Type A)

The complainant, a squatter running a Chinese medicine shop, received a demolition notice in November 1970 stating that his structure would have to be demolished because the area was required as a borrow area for the Kai Tak Airport Runway Extension. He was paid an *ex-gratia* cash allowance by way of compensation. Later, in May 1971, he was informed that it was not, after all, necessary to clear the structure in which he carried on his business as the contractor for the Kai Tak Airport Runway Extension had decided at a late stage that the part of the proposed clearance area in which his structure was located would not be required. He was also informed that he was required to refund the cash allowance. The complainant then claimed to the Resettlement Department that he had already spent most of the money in preparation for the move and asked to be allowed to repay the sum by instalments. The Resettlement Department intimated that this could only be agreed on the basis of interest charged at 10% per annum on the reducing balance. In January 1972, the Resettlement Department, not having heard further from the complainant, wrote asking him to indicate within two weeks whether he was going to refund the compensation in one lump sum or by 36 equal monthly instalments including 10% interest on the reducing balance. At this point the complainant approached UMELCO. He said he was quite prepared to pay by instalments but objected to the interest payment since he had already suffered inconvenience in preparation for the move. The matter was brought up for discussion at a meeting of UMELCO when the Administrative Secretary was directed to draw the complaint to the attention of the Deputy Financial Secretary, adding that in the opinion of UMELCO it was inappropriate in these circumstances to add interest to the amount to be repaid by the complainant. The outcome was that Government agreed to accept the offer to repay by instalments over the period suggested and to drop any claim for interest. It has also been agreed that interest will not be charged in future cases of this nature.

(Case 99—*1971–72 Annual Report*)

Appendix 9
Documents to Chapter 11

Mr. Woo Pak-chuen gives the unofficial members' view of their activities.

'This is the first occasion on which I myself speak in an opening debate as the Senior Unofficial Member of the Council. I am conscious of the responsibility which this places upon me. But I hasten to say that this is not a formal position embracing, for example, the duties of the Leader of the Opposition in Britain. I regard myself as being no more than the Unofficial who by seniority has the privilege of speaking for the Unofficials on matters which concern them as a whole. I also have the pleasant duty to preside at the meetings of the Unofficials which are regularly held to consider, prior to each meeting of this Council, the business to be transacted and the stand which the Unofficial Members intend to take.

We do not regard ourselves, Sir, as being an opposition to the Government. Indeed we consider it our duty to help the Government in every possible way to devise the most suitable laws, policies and methods of administration for this unique twentieth century Crown Colony. The Unofficials do, also, take note of public opinion on new legislation and matters of topical public concern and, where appropriate, make representations in this Council. In doing so it is from time to time necessary for us to comment upon and where necessary to criticize both draft legislation and Government policies and administration. It falls to us to prod the Official Members of this Council by means of questions and through other forms of parliamentary procedure which have been devised over the centuries to keep the Government on its toes....

...This is part of the Unofficials' contribution to closing what has been called the gap between the Government and the people. It is one of the steps which the Unofficials have taken to put themselves more closely in touch with the ordinary people of Hong Kong....

...I would mention in particular the setting up of a study group of Members to consider draft legislation or particular topics of public concern such as, during the year that has just ended, the new Immigration Bill, the White Paper on the Urban Council's reform and the question of Crown rents for renewable leases. In April 1972 we set up a group to discuss with various Heads of Departments their views on what steps should be taken to deal with the increase in crime. More recently, we have formed a group to study the "green" paper on Social Welfare tabled at the last meeting of this Council. Some Members will express their individual views on various aspects of that paper today or tomorrow. It is too early as yet for us to express any comprehensive overall view but we consider it to be a most useful and comprehensive blueprint for the future, and we think it is generally on the right lines.

Apart from serving on the study groups, Unofficial Members pay periodical visits to all districts in the Colony so as to keep in touch with new developments and current problems. The Public Relations Group also meets regularly twice a month with the same purpose in mind.

(H.K. Hansard 1972–73, pp. 51–3)

Appendix 10
Documents to Chapter 12

THE TROUBLES OF DISTRICT OFFICERS

(i) *MINES, FUNG SHUI AND RABIES*

15. A rise in the price of minerals, especially wolfram, stimulated a vivid interest in mining. Besides written application from many quarters for mining rights, illicit mining by small groups, and individuals, started on a big scale, particularly in the area known as Fa Shan, the south-western spur of Taimoshan, where serious damage was done by hundreds of illicit miners, who were beyond the ability of the small outdoor staff of the Department to deal with. The Police moreover found considerable difficulty in coping with them under the law as it stood. The result was the formation of a small mining sub-department of the Labour Department headed by a Superintendent of Mines, responsible to the Hon. Commissioner of Labour. The Law was also amended. Temporary mining licences then started to be granted, and by the end of the year the situation was more orderly.

19. Questions of fung shui (geomancy) were occasionally prominent, mostly in the Yuen Long District, where the District Officer handling them is the only Chinese in the Administrative Service in Hong Kong, Mr. Tsui Ka-cheung. In the first of two cases handled by this officer, he found himself obliged, against the dictates of good planning, to support a fung shui objection to building development at the northeast foot of the hill on which his District Office is situated. When, soon afterwards, he found himself faced with objections by one of the most litigious villages in the New Territories to proposals by a man from town to obtain white clay under permit from a hill near the coast, he felt he was on his mettle, and at the week-end went back to his old university, the University of Hong Kong, and borrowed from the library there several books on fung shui. When the hearing of the case continued after the week-end, he severely grilled the village's chief witness, their geomancer, who broke down under his examination. The outcome was that the objection by the village was overruled, and the village requested the District Officer to become their geomancer in the place of a discredited adviser. On Cheung Chau the D.O. South rejected local fung shui objections to the sinking of an unusually deep well on ten and a half acres of Crown land bought by a gentleman from Hong Kong.

28. In the course of the year the Agricultural Department took over from the District Administration the responsibility for inoculating dogs against rabies. This is carried out as part of the general inoculation programme including cattle, pigs, and chickens.

(New Territories Annual Report 1951–52)

(ii) *A VILLAGE FEUD*

77. In October 1955, a serious dispute arose between the villages of Nam Pin Wai and Shan Pui in the Yuen Long District. Shan Pui is hemmed in between a hill, a marsh and a deep river and its only access is through or round Nam Pin Wai. Nam Pin Wai is surrounded on three sides by fishponds belonging to Shan Pui. These two villages have been at loggerheads for so long (at least 300 years) that both have forgotten how it all started. But the feud has been kept alive and the physical location of the villages—a form of double encirclement unknown to European politics—has meant that tempers are always short and violence never far round the corner.

78. The dangerous time is in the autumn; the harvest is in and hands are idle and pockets full. The actual incident was trivial enough: a Nam Pin Wai child picked a dead fish from a Shan Pui fish pond. 'Stealing fish', said the owner. 'Leave my young brother alone', said another man. And so a chain reaction of words, blows, ambushes, arrests. . . and that night the chief representative of Shan Pui was in hospital, gravely injured. Further acts of violence occurred and by 1st November both villages were prepared for war. The Police acted promptly; a strong force of Pakistanis was stationed between the two villages and an informal curfew was imposed. War could not begin, but peace was not yet in sight.

79. Attempts at reconciliation were at first coldly received; representatives of each village were invited to drink tea together but the atmosphere was stiff and progress was slow. Visits were made to the villages by the Chairman of the Heung Yee Kuk, the Magistrate, the Senior Superintendent of Police, New Territories, the District Officer and myself and we listened to the remembered tales of past iniquities. The chairmen of adjoining districts and the committee of the Heung Yee Kuk also took a hand and the whole story of petty hatred was slowly unrolled. Tempers cooled gradually and by December the villagers were ashamed and ready to talk peace terms. A treaty was drafted and approved, and signed by every male over 16 in both villages; there was a feast of reconciliation and the hatchet was finally buried.

(New Territories Annual Report 1955–56)

(iii) *MODERN DEVELOPMENT*

My honourable Friend, Mr. BROWNE mentioned the development of resorts in the New Territories. This has been discussed in the Advisory Committee on Recreational Development and Nature Conservation for the New Territories. Our consideration of this matter has barely started but we are looking again at the report prepared in 1965 for the Tourist Association on 'Hong Kong as a Holiday Resort'. The proposals for the Sai Kung Peninsula in that report will become much more attractive than they were once the High Island Water Scheme is completed.

My honourable Friend, Mr. CHEUNG wondered whether we had sufficient staff for forward planning. We do not and I believe it is the staff we need most. Accordingly I have proposed last December that a Special Duties Division should be established in my headquarters to keep our current operations under review and make sure we are not overtaken by events. In the last year our organization, already stretched, has had to accommodate decisions to go ahead with the High Island Water Scheme and build a race course at Sha Tin. We have had to consider how to react to the possibility of a refinery at Lamma, the extension of Government housing to the rural areas, the building of the medium sized desalter and the much bigger one later, two reports on land requirements for refuse disposal, the increasing demands for recreational use of the countryside, the improvement of means to ensure that in new towns all the facilities thoughtfully provided in the plans come on stream when they should do, and the revision of procedures on small houses and squatter control. I am afraid honourable Members will have noticed that our staff increases exceeded the average for the public service this year and I fear this will probably be the case for some years yet. These are increases to cope with work already arising. They do not enable us to get ahead of events. As for the planning and thinking, as my honourable Friend so rightly says we should do more of that: the establishment of a Special Duties Division will shortly be proposed to honourable Members on the Establishment Sub-Committee.

In conclusion I should like to take this chance to pay tribute to the District Officers and their staff. I think few realize the demands that have been made on them in the recent boom years by the thrusting of the city into the country and by a prospering countryside. District Officers are accessible and deal with an articulate and enterprising public. It is not only dealing with the land applications and other papers but also the meetings, official functions, travelling time, social functions, and receiving callers and so forth that require a full and long working day. Their only executive authority lies in the field of land administration but the task of co-ordinating all Government activities in the Districts with only the power of reason and persuasion requires just as much ingenuity and industry.

(H.K. Hansard 1971–72, pp. 572f)

Appendix 11
Documents to Chapter 13

A. THE GAP BETWEEN GOVERNMENT AND PUBLIC

After the 1966 riots a commission was set up to investigate what had happened and probe into the underlying causes.

462. We feel that the majority of the population have accepted Hong Kong as a home because of the lack of a satisfactory alternative and despite the traditional mainland pull of culture, language and clan or the more recent ties with other countries through relatives and friends who have emigrated. Lack of homogeneity in the population tends to inhibit the development of a widespread and strong civic feeling as illustrated by the vigour of the clan and neighbourhood associations. . . .

469. The emergence or existence of a gap between the Government and the people is a continual danger and anxiety for any form of administration, whilst a colonial or bureaucratic government tends to be at a disadvantage in evoking or securing the support of its people, even though it may provide the most efficient administration and offer the best chances for their economic and social progress. But, the evidence before us did not indicate that the vast majority of the population would welcome any fundamental change in the constitutional form of the Government or that this was a material factor in causing the riots. We were left with the impression that those who complain are seeking not so much a change in Government, as readier access to the Government.

470. In this connection, however, two matters emerged as tending to create a gap between Government and the people which might well merit closer attention in the future: (a) difficulties arising from the fact that the language of the law and of much of the administration is not understood by the bulk of the population; and (b) the centralization, both physical and organizational, of the Government which has been conducive in the past to efficiency and economy in the provision of services but which has tended to create an image of detachment from the actual problems of the man in the street. . . .

474. . . . We do not believe that the Government deliberately ignores public opinion and there are a number of instances where constructive proposals have been readily accepted. However, the degree of misunderstanding of Government's aims exposed by our Inquiry emphasizes the importance of ensuring that its policies and problems are clearly explained and the public's co-operation in their implementation actively pursued. Possible means of achieving this are by a greater degree of decentralization of administration with a view to providing a range of simple services at the local level in order to build up local community spirit and improve the public's access to Government: by developing local representation

on advisory, consultative or executive bodies at a local level: and by a greater consciousness of the need for public relations at all levels. . . .

479. The comparative absence of a decentralized administration, particularly in the densely populated area of Kowloon, and the slow growth of an effective system of leadership at the local level has, we believe, thrown a heavy burden on the police. This may indeed have contributed to an impression which we were told exists in some quarters that 'the Government does not care and gives all power to the police': a misconception which it is clearly desirable to remove.

(*Kowloon Disturbances 1966—Report of Commission of Inquiry, pp. 126–31*)

B. AN EARLIER PROPOSAL FOR REGIONAL ADMINISTRATION IN THE URBAN AREA

Hong Kong society is accustomed to organize itself into groups based not upon identity of community interest in a given area but upon traditionally accepted charitable objectives, language, place of origin, occupation, business, profession, etc. It is largely within groupings based upon such common ideals and interests that individual citizens give community service. Members of these groups generally choose for their leaders persons who they know personally and believe to be shrewd, able, resourceful and effective organizers for action.

The complexity of these groupings is such that they do not provide a practicable organizational basis for regional local administration as recommended in this report. However, the members feel that until such time as the public has gained confidence in a system of election by popular vote it is essential to draw upon this valuable reserve of respected, able and public-spirited community leaders by tapping it for participation in the administration of the Colony at the local level as well as at the central level.

The members consider that most of the functions recommended earlier in this report for transfer to local authorities should first be operated on a regional basis by Government departments and achieved by a process of departmental decentralization. This would ensure continuity in the provision of efficient services throughout the transitional phase.

At the same time the members consider it essential that there should be effective co-ordination and control of Government operations within the locality by a Regional Administrator operating on lines comparable with the District Officers of the New Territories Administration. The holders of these offices on the one hand personalize the 'authorities' working in the area and on the other, with the assistance of their unofficial advisory councils ensure that the total Government effort is guided in the direction which seems to provide the best compromise between the wishes of the people of the locality and the overall public interest.

There should be a statutory obligation for the Regional Administrator to consult the Regional Council on all matters scheduled for adoption by the future local authority and non-statutory arrangements for consulting the council on all matters of concern to citizens, excluding defence, foreign affairs and other reserved subjects. The feed-in of the Regional Councils' views into the Government organization would be effected through the Regional Administrator either direct to the departments working within his area of control or to Central Government. . . .

There is some feeling amongst people living in the Urban areas that they are too much out of touch with authority and lacking sufficient access to it to ensure that their points of view are sufficiently considered. A number of grave misconceptions also exist such as, for example, that taxes or at least a substantial portion of the taxes levied are drained off to the United Kingdom. They question whether Chinese views are properly represented on the councils of government, and they seek improvements over a wide range of public services without much thought as to how this is to be achieved.

These feelings are not surprising in a dependent territory, where many senior civil servants are expatriates and the language of administration and the Courts of law is foreign to the majority of the population. As one result, the extent of the actual separation in such matters as finance and administration between the Hong Kong Government and the United Kingdom Government is not well understood. Nor is it to be supposed that in other countries, where elected representation is a long-standing tradition and all speak the same language, these same feelings do not exist. Nevertheless, the difficulties arising from the nature and political status of Hong Kong are greater than elsewhere and greater efforts to overcome them are in consequence demanded. Moreover, in a political situation as is presented by the present social circumstances of Hong Kong the dangers arise less from the actual shortcomings of the system than from what the public believe those shortcomings to be. It is for this reason that the members feel that their views on the attitude of the man in the street towards the Government however unreasonable, unpalatable or unjust need to be stated. . . .

The interim proposals for Regional Councils recommended here should do much to improve understanding between the Government and the people. It should also help to remedy the inadequacies which often arise from lack of departmental co-ordination and the unwillingness of Civil Servants, who in all other respects are dedicated to their work, to seek the advice of the public they are supposed to be serving.

(*Report of the Working Party on Local Administration*, Nov. 1966 Note of reservation by Mr. Tsui, Mr. Walden and Mr. Webb-Johnson, pp. 84ff)

Appendix 12
Document to Chapter 15

Three members of the Dickinson commission (Mr. Tsui, Mr. Walden and Mr. Webb-Johnson) argued in a minority report against the applicability of democratic local government to Hong Kong.

'The system proposed, based as it is, on the principle of popular representation, as determined by ballot box elections on a very wide franchise, is not well understood by the great majority of Hong Kong people and is unlikely to command public support and confidence.

In most Western democracies election from amongst candidates nominated by political parties by majority vote is the accepted way of selecting representatives of the people. Fear of loss of face by failure at the polls does not normally deter a candidate from standing for election and the general acceptance by the public of the elective principle is a natural corrective to abuse of the system. In Hong Kong the position is entirely different and it is doubtful whether popular representation at the present time will be successful in bringing forward the best qualified and most widely accepted citizens to participate in local administration. There is indeed a definite risk that a system based on popular representation as determined by ballot box elections could quickly become controlled by unscrupulous or corrupt power seekers.

The small turn out of voters at Urban Council elections and the poor public response to the recent registration of voters under the enlarged franchise is evidence of lack of popular support for an elective system, and indicates either lack of understanding or distrust. This is not in any way to under-rate the valuable work done by present and past elected members of the Urban Council. It is sincerely believed that these public-spirited people provide a very healthy stimulus for the bureaucracy. But notwithstanding none of them could claim to have any substantial numerical following amongst the ordinary citizens of Hong Kong.

Another factor which has an important bearing on the applicability of the system of local administration recommended in the report, which borrows much from British local government, is that in the United Kingdom the singular local government system is generally acknowledged to be unsatisfactory. It is now under investigation by a Royal Commission and in a submission to the Commission, the National Association of Local Government officers recommend the abolition of County, Borough, Urban and Rural Councils and the establishment of regional councils and authorities which would concern themselves with policy whilst the executive was given increased authority and power in relation to the implementation of those policies. This, of course, is only one viewpoint and a Civil Servants' viewpoint at that, but it does suggest that caution should be exercised in imposing upon Hong Kong a system which has not proved satisfactory and which has been evolved in a society with a totally different political, economic, social, cultural and historical background.

It must also be borne in mind when considering the reactions of a Chinese community to matters relating to Government and administration that the familiar pattern is that of strong bureaucratic control by scholars disciplined by strict moral principles . . . .'

(*Report of the Working Party on Local Administration*, November 1966, pp. 82f.)

Bibliography

A. HONG KONG GOVERNMENT PUBLICATIONS

(i) *SERIALS*

Annual Report: *Hong Kong 1973, Hong Kong 1974* etc.

Annual Departmental Reports (1946 onwards) e.g. *The Commissioner of Labour 1971–72.*

Annual Report of the UMELCO Office (1970–71 onwards)

Report of the Public Works Sub-Committee of Finance Committee (annually).

Report of the Establishment Sub-Committee of Finance Committee (annually).

A Report on the Public Service (annually).

Estimates of Revenue and Expenditure (annually).

The 1973–74 Budget: Economic Background (and subsequent years).

Hong Kong Trade Statistics (monthly).

Hong Kong Review of Overseas Trade (annually).

Hong Kong Government Staff List (1947 onwards).

Civil and Miscellaneous Lists (six monthly; 1967 onwards; previously bound with Staff List).

Hong Kong Hansard, Reports of the Sittings of the Legislative Council of Hong Kong.

Proceedings of the Urban Council.

(ii) *REPORTS OF COMMISSIONS ETC.*

Report on the Riots in Kowloon and Tsuen Wan 1956 (1957).

The Report of the Advisory Committee on Gambling Policy, June 1965.

Report of the Working Party on the Urban Council Franchise and Electoral Registration Procedure, August 1965.

Report of the Ad Hoc Committee on the Future Scope and Operation of the Urban Council, August 1966.

Kowloon Disturbances 1966, Report of Commission of Enquiry (1967).

Report of the Working Party on Local Administration, Nov. 1966 (the Dickinson Report, published 1967).

Background Information on the Hong Kong Rice Trade, together with a Statement by the Hon. T.D. Sorby in the Legislative Council on 1st February 1967.

Report of the Interdepartmental Working Party to consider certain aspects of Social Security, April 1967.

White Paper on Chinese Marriages in Hong Kong, May 1967.

The McDonall-Heenan Report 1965 (on Chinese Marriages, published in 1967).

The City District Officer Scheme, A Report by the Secretary for Chinese Affairs, January 1969.

Urban Council: Report on the Reform of Local Government, March 1969.

Report of the Committee to Review the Doctor Problem in the Hong Kong Government, May 1969.

Reports of the Chinese Language Committee, Feb., April, May and July 1971.

Hong Kong Salaries Commission Report 1971 (the Mallaby Report).

White Paper: The Urban Council, October 1971.

Hong Kong Population and Housing Census 1971, Main Report (Census and Statistics Department, 1972).

Social Welfare in Hong Kong: The Way Ahead—Draft (the Social Welfare 'Green Paper') October 1972

The Machinery of Government, A New Framework for Expanding Services (The McKinsey Report), June 1973.

First Report of the Commission of Inquiry under Sir Alastair Blair-Kerr (into the disappearance from Hong Kong of Superintendent Godber while on a corruption charge), July 1973.

Second Report of the Commission of Inquiry under Sir Alastair Blair-Kerr (into the working of the Prevention of Bribery Ordinance), Sept., 1973.

Report of the Board of Education on the Proposed Expansion of Secondary School Education in Hong Kong in the next decade (the Education 'Green Paper') August 1973.

B. BOOKS

ALMOND, GABRIEL and VERBA, SIDNEY, *The Civic Culture* (Princeton University Press, New Jersey, 1963).

BAGEHOT, WALTER, *The English Constitution* (Collins, Fontana Library, London, 1963).

BIRCH, A.H., *Representative and Responsible Government* (Allen & Unwin, London, 1964).

BROWN, R.G.S., *The Administrative Process in Britain* (Methuen, London, 1971).

CHURCHILL, Sir WINSTON S., *The Second World War, Vol. 1 The Gathering Storm* (Cassell, London, 1948).

COLLINS, Sir CHARLES, *Public Administration in Hong Kong* (Royal Institute of International Affairs, London, 1952).

COOPER, J., *Colony in Conflict: The Hong Kong Disturbances May 1967– January 1968* (Swindon Book Company, Hong Kong, 1970).

CRICK, BERNARD, *In Defence of Politics* (Penguin Books, London, 1962).

CROSSMAN, RICHARD, *Inside View* (Cape, London, 1972).

DAHL, ROBERT A., *Modern Political Analysis* (Prentice-Hall, New Jersey, 1963).

DOWNS, ANTHONY, *Inside Bureaucracy* (Little Brown, Boston, 1967).

ECKSTEIN, ALEXANDER, *Communist China's Economic Growth and Foreign Trade* (McGraw-Hill, New York, 1966).

ENDACOTT, G.B., *Government and People in Hong Kong 1841–1962. A Constitutional History* (Hong Kong University Press, Hong Kong, 1964).

ENDACOTT, G.B., *A History of Hong Kong* (O.U.P., London, 1958).

FRIEDRICH, CARL J., *Man and his Government, An Empirical Theory of Politics* (McGraw-Hill, New York, 1963).

FURSE, Sir RALPH, *Aucuparius: Recollections of a Recruiting Officer* (O.U.P., London, 1962).

GEORGE, T.S., *Lee Kwan Yew's Singapore* (Deutsch, London, 1973).

GRANTHAM, Sir ALEXANDER, *Via Ports, from Hong Kong to Hong Kong*, (Hong Kong University Press, Hong Kong, 1965).

HAMBRO, E.I., *The Problem of Chinese Refugees in Hong Kong* (A.W. Sijthoff, Leyden, 1955).

HOPKINS, KEITH (ed.), *Hong Kong: The Industrial Colony* (Oxford University Press, Hong Kong, 1971).

HUGHES, RICHARD, *Hong Kong: Borrowed Place, Borrowed Time* (Deutsch, London, 1968).

INGRAMS, H., *Hong Kong* (H.M.S.O., London, 1952).

JARVIE, I.C. and AGASSI, JOSEPH (eds.), *Hong Kong: A Society in Transition* (Routledge & Kegan Paul, London, 1969).

JEFFRIES, Sir CHARLES, *The Colonial Office* (Allen & Unwin, London, 1956).

KORNBERG, A. and MUSOLF, L.D. (eds.), *Legislatures in Developmental Perspective* (Duke University Press, Durham, N.C., 1970).

LIN YU-TANG, *My Country and My People* (Heinemann, London, 1938).

MAO TSE-TUNG, *Selected Words of Mao Tse-tung* (Foreign Languages Press, Peking, 1967).

MITCHELL, R.E., *Pupil, Parent and School, A Hong Kong Study* (Asian Folklore and Social Life Monographs, 26), (Orient Cultural Service, Taipei, 1972).

MORRISON, HERBERT (LORD MORRISON OF LAMBETH), *Government and Parliament*, 3rd edition (O.U.P., London, 1964).

NEUSTADT, R.E., *Presidential Power, The Politics of Leadership*, (Wiley, New York, 1960).

NORTON-KYSHE, J.W., *History of the Laws and Courts of Hong Kong* (original edition London, 1898, reprinted Vetch and Lee, Hong Kong, 1971).

O'CONNELL, D.P., *International Law*, 2nd edition (Stevens, London, 1970).

PERHAM, M., *Lugard: the Years of Authority* (Collins, London, 1960).

PUNNETT, R.M., *British Government and Politics* (Heinemann, London, 1968).

Report of the Committee on the Civil Service, Cmnd. 3638 (H.M.S.O. London, 1968).

RIDLEY, F. and BLONDEL, J., *Public Administration in France* (Routledge & Kegan Paul, London, 1969).

ROBERTS-WRAY, Sir KENNETH, *Commonwealth and Colonial Law* (Stevens, London, 1966).

ROSE, R., *Influencing Voters* (Faber, London, 1967).

Royal Commission on Local Government in England 1966–1969, Cmnd. 4040 (H.M.S.O., London, 1969).

WALKLAND, G.A., *The Legistative Process in Britain* (Allen & Unwin, London, 1969).

WIGHT, M., *The Development of the Legislative Council* (Faber, London, 1946).

WILKINSON, R., *The Prefects* (O.U.P., London, 1964).

WONG, ALINE K., *The Kaifong Associations and the Society of Hong Kong* (Asian Folklore and Social Life Monographs, 43), (Orient Cultural Service, Taipei, Taiwan, 1972).

C. ARTICLES AND SHORT MONOGRAPHS

BRIDGES, SIR EDWARD, *Portrait of a Profession* (Rede Lecture, London, 1952).

CATRON, GARY, 'Hong Kong and Chinese Foreign Policy, 1955–60', *China Quarterly* no. 51, July/Sept. 1972, pp. 405–24.

CHANEY, D.C., and PODMORE, D.B.L., *Young Adults in Hong Kong: Attitudes in a Modernizing Society* (Centre of Asian Studies, Hong Kong University, 1973).

CLARKE, SIR RICHARD, 'Parliament and Public Expenditure', *Political Quarterly*, Vol. 44 (1973), pp. 137–53.

DAVIES, J.C., 'Towards a Theory of Revolution', *American Sociological Review*, Vol. 27(1962), pp. 5–19.

ELLIOTT, ELSIE, *The Avarice, Bureaucracy and Corruption of Hong Kong* (Friends Commercial Printing Factory, Hong Kong, 1971).

ENGLAND, JOE, 'Industrial Relations in Hong Kong', in Hopkins, K. (ed.), *Hong Kong: The Industrial Colony* (O.U.P., London, 1971), pp. 207–59.

HARRIS, P.B., 'The International Future of Hong Kong', *International Affairs*, Vol. 48, 1972, pp. 60–71.

————'The Frozen Politics of Hong Kong', *The World Today*, Vol. 30 (1974) pp. 259–67.

HOADLEY, J. STEPHEN, 'Hong Kong is the Lifeboat: Notes on Political Culture and Socialization', *Journal of Oriental Studies*, Vol. 8 (1970), pp. 206–18.

KING, YEO-CHI AMBROSE, *The Political Culture of Kwun Tong: a Chinese Community in Hong Kong* (Social Research Centre, the Chinese University of Hong Kong, Hong Kong, June 1972).

LETHBRIDGE, H.J., 'Hong Kong Cadets, 1862–1941', *Journal of the Hong Kong Branch of the Royal Asiatic Society*, Vol. 10, 1970, pp. 36–56.

————'Hong Kong under Japanese Occupation: Changes in Social Structure', in JARVIE, I.C. and AGASSI, J., *Hong Kong: A Society in Transition* (Routledge, London, 1969), pp. 77–127.

LEARY, WILLIAM M., 'Aircraft and Anti-Communists: CAT in Action, 1949–52', *China Quarterly,* no. 52, Oct/Dec 1972, pp. 654–69.

PODMORE, DAVID, 'Localization in the Hong Kong Government Service', *Journal of Commonwealth Political Studies* IX, (1971), pp. 36–51.

RABUSHKA, ALVIN, *The Changing Face of Hong Kong, New Departures in Public Policy* (A.E.I. Hoover policy studies, Washington, D.C., 1973).

REAR, JOHN, 'One Brand of Politics', in Hopkins, K. (ed.), *Hong Kong: The Industrial Colony* (O.U.P., London, 1971), pp. 55–139.

———'The Law of the Constitution', in Hopkins, K. (ed.), *Hong Kong: The Industrial Colony* (O.U.P., London, 1971), pp. 339–415.

RUTTONJEE, DHUN, BERNACCHI, BROOK and CHEUNG WING-IN, *Report on the Feasibility of instituting the Office of Ombudsman in Hong Kong* (Hong Kong Branch of Justice, 1969).

SHIVELEY, STAN, *Political Orientations in Hong Kong, a Socio-Psychological Approach* (Social Research Centre, The Chinese University of Hong Kong, Hong Kong, 1972).

SHIVELEY, ALIZA, M., and SHIVELEY, STAN, *Value Changes During A Period of Modernization—the case of Hong Kong* (Social Research Centre, the Chinese University of Hong Kong, Hong Kong, 1972).

SHARPE, L.J., 'Theories and Values of Local Government', *Political Studies*, XVIII (1970), pp. 153–74.

TRENCH, SIR DAVID, *Hong Kong and its Position in the Southeast Asian Region* (The Dillingham Lecture, East-West Centre, University of Hawaii, Oct. 1971)

WESLEY-SMITH, P., 'The Kowloon Walled City', *Hong Kong Law Journal*, Vol. 3, Pt. 1 (1973), pp. 67–96.

WONG, ALINE K., *The Study of Higher Non-Expatriate Civil Servants in Hong Kong* (Social Research Centre, Chinese University of Hong Kong, Hong Kong, June 1972).

———'Political Apathy and the Political System in Hong Kong', *United College Journal* (Hong Kong), Vol. 8 (1970–71), pp. 1–20.

Index

(Hong Kong is omitted from the names of many groups and institutions.)

ABATTOIRS, 160, 163.
Abortion, 66, 93, 95, 130, 196.
Accountant General, 114.
Accountants, Society of, 97.
Acts of Parliament, 13n, 53, 66, 96, 203, 212n, 213n.
Aden, 6, 205.
Adjournment debates, 120–1.
Administrative officers, 72, 74, 76–8, 79–80, 82–4, 124, 136, 150, 152, 155, 250; *see also* District Officers; City District Officers.
Advisory Committees, 59, 84–7, 95, 172, 197, 251–2, 278–9; classification, 84–6; composition, 84–6, 88n, 143–5; criticism, 86–7, 191, 197, 251–3; influence, 85–6, 92, 112, 145, 187, 211, 251–2; and legislation, 92–3, 96, 100, 130, 146, 256–7; as substitute for democracy, 86, 171, 188, 251.
Africa, 5, 208.
Agriculture Department, 77, 140, 142, 266–7, 275.
Air Force, Royal, 6, 13n.
Airport Facilitation Committee, 85.
Airport Operations Committee, 85.
Aldrich Bay, 150.
Anglo-Hong Kong Parliamentary Group, 210–11.
Angus, H.A., 77.
Anne, Princess, 200.
'Anticipated reaction', 110, 112, 216.
Apathy in Hong Kong, 31–6, 43, 106, 134, 158–9, 169, 173, 199, 201, 223, 281.
Appropriation Bill, *see* Finance.
Argentina, 6.
Army, *see* British Army; Hong Kong Regiment; People's Liberation Army.
Art gallery, 160.
Asian Development Bank, 52.
Attitudes of Hong Kong Chinese, vii, 29–39, 134, 148; to administration, xiv, 3, 11, 30–1, 34–6, 53, 67, 126–7, 149, 183, 187, 195, 197, 199, 201, 207, 218, 222, 278–80; to China, 22, 32, 195, 200, 207, 218; 'Confucianism', 24n, 34–6, 66, 133–5, 172, 183, 198, 223, 282; to elections, 31, 158–9, 169, 172–3, 176, 201, 223, 281–2; to trade unions, 28; to unofficials, 126, 182; *see also* Apathy in Hong Kong.
Attorney General, 54, 63, 66, 78, 90, 93, 96, 98, 109, 121, 146, 202n, 256–60, 270.
Audit Department, 69, 78, 79, 114–15, 162, 266–7.
Australia, 19, 97.
Automobile Association, 185, 202n.
Aviation, 11–12, 85, 203, 206, 218; *see also* Kai Tak.
Aviation Advisory Board, 85.
Ayub Khan, 181.

BANK OF ENGLAND, *see* Sterling Reserves.
Bank of China, 18, 219.
Banking, Banks, 10, 18, 21, 33, 41, 99, 128, 132, 206, 209, 229–30, 255.
Bar Association, 185, 187, 255.
Basle Agreement (currency), 9.
Bernacchi, Brook (Elected member, Urban Council, 1952–), 101n, 157, 161, 165, 166n, 167n.
Bhutan, xiii.
Bills, *see* Ordinances.
Bird Watching Society, 188.
Black, Sir Robert (Governor, 1958–64), 62, 65.
Blake, Sir Henry (Governor, 1898–1903), 140.
Blaker, Peter (Minister of State, 1974), 210.
Board of Education, 85, 89n.
Boards, *see* Advisory Committees.
Boxer rebellion, 36.
Bray, Dennis, vii; (quoted), 225n, 251.
Bribery, *see* Corruption.
Britain: Attitudes to Hong Kong, 5–6; trade with China, 7–8, 18, 21,

218; trade with Hong Kong, 7, 20, 41, 192, 206–7, 211.
British Airways, 11–12, 206, 218, 222.
British Army, 4–5, 6–7, 12, 22, 58, 79, 90, 99, 139, 142–3, 151, 157, 169, 183, 205, 209, 222, 246.
British Cinematograph Films Ordinance, 99.
British government, 3–14, 203–14; and China, xiv, 3, 4, 8, 11–12, 15, 18, 23–4, 26, 80, 139–40, 204, 207, 212n, 215–19, 222–3, 226; choice of governor, 62, 204–5; and Hong Kong foreign relations, 12, 41, 54, 99, 203, 206–7, 210; and Hong Kong internal policy, 8, 9–10, 54, 59, 67, 79, 115–16, 136, 203–14, 222, 246; and Hong Kong legislation, 53, 94, 99–100, 102n, 103n, 204, 210; powers of, 11, 50–1, 53–4, 63, 64, 72, 78, 90, 114, 203–7; reasons for retaining Hong Kong, xiv, 3–14, 26, 221–2; and U.S.A., 4, 204, 207; *see also* Colonial Policy; Foreign and Commonwealth Office; Parliament; Sterling Reserves.
British Textile Confederation, 7.
Broadcasting, 36, 93, 97, 109, 126, 197, 180–1, 217.
Browne, H.J.C. (Unofficial, Legislative Council, 1968–73), 55, 229.
Brunei, 4, 13n, 147n.
Budget, *see* Finance.
Buildings Ordinance, 140.
Bureaucracy, *see* Public Service.
By-laws of Urban Council, 100–1, 161, 162.

CABINET (U.K.): and finance, 70n, 104, 106; compared with Executive Council, 64–5; and Prime Minister, 64–5, 76.
Cadres in China, 153, 221.
Campaign for Chinese as Official Language, 85–6, 156, 185, 194n, 199, 224.
Candidates, *see* Urban Council.
Canton, 16, 28n, 30.
Capital punishment, 51, 56n, 66–7, 212n.
Car parks, 44, 121, 156.
Caritas, 186.
Castle Peak, 141, 146, 170.
Cater, Jack, 77, 78, 200.
Cathay Pacific Airline, 206.
Censorship, 181, 200, 224, 225n.
Census and Statistics Department, 77.
Ceylon (Sri Lanka), 3, 27, 212n, 213n.
Chairmen, *see* Heung Yee Kuk; Urban Council.
Chambers of Commerce, 54–5, 91, 136n, 146, 183, 185, 187–8, 256.
Chamber of Social Service, 182.
Chan Chi-kwan, Peter (Elected member, Urban Council, 1969–), 165.

Chan Po-fun, Peter (Appointed member, Urban Council, 1968–), 165.
Chancellor of the Exchequer (U.K.), 10, 70n, 106, 117n.
Charitable gifts and taxation, 111.
Charles I, 104.
Charter of 1843, 49.
Cheong-Leen, Hilton (Elected member, Urban Council, 1957–, Unofficial, Legislative Council, 1973–), 55, 91, 101n, 135, 153n, 157, 161, 165, 167n, 177n.
Cheung, Oswald (Unofficial, Legislative Council, 1970–, Executive Council, 1974–), 63, 100, 109, 111, 258.
Chiang Kai-shek, 22, 23, 25.
China, 15–28, 215–20; benefits from Hong Kong, 17–22, 23–4, 26, 215–16, 217, 218, 222; and Britain, xiv, 3, 4, 8, 11–12, 15, 18, 23–4, 26, 80, 139–40, 204, 207, 212n, 215–19, 222, 226; Cultural Revolution in, 4, 22, 26, 30, 32, 137n; and democracy in Hong Kong, xiv, 19, 24–6, 134, 177n, 201, 223; and European Economic Community, 24; and Hong Kong's internal policy, 8, 29, 34, 60, 80, 169, 173, 189, 215–19; immigrants from, 32, 37n, 216, 217; and Macau, 16, 24, 216, 223, 226; and New Territories lease, 16, 139–40, 222–3, 226; and Taiwan, 17, 22–4, 218–19, 222, 223; trade with Hong Kong, 7, 15, 17, 20, 44, 60, 169, 188, 207, 215–18; refugees from, 4, 5, 17, 27n, 31–2, 38n, 40, 140, 169, 216, 223; representation in Hong Kong, 156, 218–19, 220n; and Soviet Union, 16, 23–4, 28n, 216, 226; and United Nations, 16, 24; water supplies from 15, 17, 60, 216, 217, 220n; *see also* People's Liberation Army; 'Walled City' of Kowloon.
China Motor Bus Company, 7, 94, 262.
Chinese Affairs, Secretariat for, *see* Home Affairs Department.
Chinese attitudes, *see* Attitudes of Hong Kong Chinese; *and* China.
Chinese language in government, 29, 36n, 85–6, 92, 97, 156, 185, 192, 199, 201, 224, 257, 278, 280.
Chinese Manufacturers Association, 185, 192, 194n, 259.
Chinese Paper Merchants Association, 186.
Ching dynasty, 15, 35, 83, 143.
Chiu Chau, 173.
Choa, Dr. G.H. (Official member, Executive Council, 1972–), 63, 123.
Chou En-lai, 41, 222, 226.
Chung Sze-yuen (Unofficial, Legislative Council, 1968–, Executive

Council, 1972–), 57n, 63, 121, 131, 209, 213n, 214n, 227–8, 261.
Cinemas, 99, 198.
City District Officers, 76, 148–54, 158, 197, 200, 251, 255; criticism, 152–3; functions, 150–1, 172, 200; origins, 149–50, 224, 278–80.
City Hall, 156, 160, 261.
Civic Association, 157, 158–9, 161.
Civil Service, see Public Service.
Clague, Sir Douglas (Unofficial, Legislative Council, 1958–60, Executive Council, 1961–74), 57n, 63.
Clan associations, 31, 148, 173, 278, 279.
'Clean Hong Kong' campaign, 151.
Colonial Office, 45, 50, 53, 155, 169, 204, 207, 210, 212n.
Colonial Policy, British, 3, 5, 6, 45, 79, 83, 100, 114, 168, 187, 195, 204–5, 208, 210, 212n, 225n, 246, 256.
Colonial Regulations, 52–3, 58, 62, 65, 79, 115, 205.
Colonial Secretariat, 51, 59, 65, 77, 84, 112, 162, 210, 278; committees in, 65, 72, 76, 84, 149, 170; functions of, 61, 71–6, 106, 130; McKinsey reorganization, 73–6, 86, 91, 141, 200, 225, 249–50; see also Public Service.
Colonial Secretary (H.K.), 63, 72, 73, 76, 78, 90, 106, 108, 109, 198, 211, 247, 264–5, 269.
Colonial Service, British, 35, 55, 58, 62, 82, 83, 114, 223, 224.
Commander British Forces, 58, 63, 90, 246.
Commander in Chief, Hong Kong, 58, 246.
Commerce and Industry Department, 77, 91, 187, 188, 206, 224.
Commissions of Enquiry: of 1908 (Sanitary Board), 155; of 1967 (Kowloon Disturbances), 149, 278–9; of 1973 (Godber, corruption), 127n, 255–6.
Commissioner of Registration of Persons, 157–8.
Committees, see Advisory Committees; Colonial Secretariat; Legislative Council; Urban Council.
Common Market, see European Economic Community.
Commonwealth, 3, 8, 33, 203.
Commonwealth immigrants to Britain, 5, 13n, 147n.
Commonwealth Preference, 7, 20.
Commonwealth Relations Office, 50, 207, 210.
Community Relief Trust, 143.
Compensation for criminal injuries, 109.
Concorde airliner, 21.

Confederation of British Industry, 132.
Confucius, 34.
'Confucian' attitudes in Hong Kong, 24n, 34–6, 66, 133–5, 172, 183, 198, 223, 282.
Conseil d'Etat (France), 126.
Conservancy Association, 31, 185.
Conservative Party (U.K.), 6, 67, 76, 104, 210, 212n, 213n.
Constantine, Sir Leary, 211.
Consular representatives, 218–19, 220n, 245.
Constitutions, general, 49–50; of Hong Kong, xiii, 49–57, 58, 64, 181, 203–7; see also Conventions; Letters Patent, Royal Instructions.
Consultation in government, see Advisory Committees; Executive Council; Legislative Council; Pressure groups; Unofficials.
Consumers Council, 88n.
Consumer Price Index, 33.
Conventions of the constitution, in Britain, 49–50, 64, 116; in Hong Kong, 53–5, 58, 79, 94, 108, 115, 119, 140, 203–7.
Convention of Peking (1860), 15, 140, 222.
Convention of Peking (1898), 15, 139, 222, 226.
Coordination of government services, 72–6, 142, 150, 171–2, 174.
Corruption, 96, 129, 135, 146, 155, 156, 173, 190, 191, 255–6.
Corruption, Advisory Committee on, 85.
Cotton Spinners Association, 187, 192.
Coup d'état, xiii, 222.
Courts of Law, 52, 181.
Cowperthwaite, Sir John (Financial Secretary, 1961–71), 44, 45, 64–5, 106, 111–12, 115, 193, 207, 227–30, 263.
Crick, Bernard (quoted), 183.
Crime, 33, 38n, 73, 131, 134–5, 186, 198, 207, 218; see also Corruption.
Cross-harbour tunnel, 61, 85, 93.
Crown Agents, 206, 210, 214n.
Crown Leases: renewal, 69n, 94, 117n, 120, 136, 182, 193, 198, 258–60, 273; resumption, 142, 147n, 151–2; sales, 42, 192, 230–1.
Crown, powers of, see British Government; Colonial Office; Letters Patent, Royal Instructions.
Cultural Revolution in China, 4, 22, 26, 30, 32, 137n.
Currency, 19, 99, 196; parity of Hong Kong dollar, 9, 66, 196, 206, 215, 219n.

DANGEROUS GOODS STANDING COMMITTEE, 84.

Death Penalty, see Capital punishment.

Debates, see Legislative Council; Urban Council.

Defence, see British Army.

Defence Contribution, 6, 58, 93, 136, 208, 261.

Delegated Legislation, 52, 100–1; drafting of, 100; Executive Council and, 66; Legislative Council and, 51, 100–1, 120, 161; pressure groups and, 100–1, 194n; reasons for, 100–1; Urban Council and, 101, 161, 162.

Democracy: arguments in favour, 172–4, 196n; in Hong Kong, 24–6, 30, 158, 172, 181–4, 188, 192, 195, 221, 223, 278–82; and China, 19, 24–6, 134, 177n, 201, 223; types, 181–2; see also Elections; Politics.

Demonstrations, 31, 33–4, 146, 190, 197, 217, 222.

Department heads, 60, 63, 66, 71–3, 75, 77–8, 79, 86, 90, 96, 106, 113, 115, 164, 251, 264; see also Names of departments.

Departments, relations with Secretariat, 69–75.

Deportation, 17, 33, 38–9n.

Deputy Colonial Secretary, 73, 76, 79.

Devaluation: revaluation of Hong Kong dollar, 9, 196, 206, 215; of sterling, 9–11, 206, 215.

Disallowance, 53, 59, 99–100, 194n, 203.

Dickinson Report on Local Administration, 1966, 39n, 146, 149, 170–1, 175, 176, 279–82.

Diplomats, 18, 24, 62, 218–19, 220n, 245.

Director of Urban Services, 77, 89, 96, 160–2, 163, 175, 269.

Discharged Prisoners Aid Society, 186.

District Commissioner for New Territories, see Secretary for New Territories.

District Officers in New Territories, 35, 76, 140–3, 145–6, 151–2, 172, 197, 200, 275–7, 279.

Divisions; in Legislative Council, 25, 54, 66, 92–5, 98–9, 102n, 107, 169, 204, 259, 260–2; in Urban Council, 157, 163, 202n.

Divorce, 95, 99.

Dockyard, 3, 4, 33, 58, 148, 168, 204, 217, 246.

Doctors, 81–2.

Drafting of Legislation, 65, 97, 100, 191, 255–7.

Dramatic Arts Association, 186.

Drug addiction, 148.

Dulles, Foster, 23.

EASTERN CITY DISTRICT, 151, 165.

Economic Growth of Hong Kong, xiii, 12, 32–3, 40, 44, 173, 218, 221.

Economic Policy, see Finance; Foreign investment, Laissez-faire; Taxation.

Edible Birds' Nests Workers Union, 186.

Education Action Group, 186, 201, 225.

Education Department, 77–8, 91, 143, 151, 174, 175–6, 225, 270; policy, 36, 60, 78, 106, 110–11, 116, 161, 170, 187, 189, 201, 218.

Eisenhower, President, 23.

Elections, 43, 93, 106, 126, 128, 168, 172–3, 192, 281–2; in Britain, 5, 60, 129, 133, 159, 166n, 173, 192, 195, 211, 281; for Legislative Council, 24–6, 123, 134, 168–9, 176n; in New Territories, 143–4, 159, 172; for Urban Council, 31, 34, 129, 155, 158–60, 172, 281.

Electoral Register, Urban Council, 31, 157–8, 166n, 201.

Electricity supply, 33, 105, 187, 217.

Electronics firms, 19, 42.

Elizabeth II, Queen, 117n, 200, 202n.

Elliot's proclamation of 1841, 52–3, 140.

Elliott, Mrs. Elsie (Elected member, Urban Council, 1963–), 85, 101n, 126, 129, 157, 158, 165.

Emergency Regulations Ordinance, 49, 51

Emergency relief, 33, 143, 151.

Emigration from Hong Kong, 34, 82, 83, 88n.

Employers Association, 60, 186, 192, 194n.

Entrepot trade, 18–20, 40, 41, 169.

Environmental Pollution, Advisory Committee on, 142.

Establishment Branch, see Secretary for the Civil Service.

Establishment Regulations, 78, 161, 205.

Establishment Sub-committee, see Legislative Council.

Estonia, 11.

European Economic Community, 20, 24, 41, 206.

Europeans in Hong Kong, 5, 31, 91, 110–11, 134, 189; see also Public Service; Expatriate officers.

Ex officio members, see Executive Council; Legislative Council; composition.

Exchange Fund, 8, 99.

Exchange Fund Ordinance, 14n, 99, 103n.

Exchange Fund Advisory Committee, 84.

Executive Council, 7, 51, 62–70, 72, 75–6, 79, 119, 144, 201, 246, 247–8; agenda, 65–6, 247–8; composition,

63, 65, 90, 133; finance and, 63, 66, 112; Governor and, 59, 63–5, 67; legislation and, 63, 65–6, 93, 98, 100, 130, 133, 247; prerogative of mercy, 66–7, 212n, 247; voting in, 64.

Expatriate officers, *see* Public Service.

Exports, *see* Britain, China, etc.; trade with.

Factories and Industrial Undertakings Ordinance, 100, 131, 194n, 254.

Falkland Islands, 6.

Family Planning Association, 69n, 182, 186.

Federation of Hong Kong Industries, 186, 187, 194n.

'Fight Violent Crime' campaign, 186.

Films, 99, 198.

Finance, 104–18, 162–3; Appropriation Bill, 66, 75, 96, 98, 105, 107, 108, 111, 112–14, 120; budget-making, 42, 66, 106, 108, 111–12, 162, 196, 208, 251, 258–60, 262, 263–4; British government control over, 52, 115–16, 206; loans, 52, 115, 162–3; parliamentary control in Britain, 104–5, 107; scrutiny of departments' spending, 73, 75, 106, 108, 113, 115; supplementary appropriations, 75, 108, 114, 115; unofficials' pressure and, 44, 106, 107, 110–12; *see also* Audit Department; Legislative Council; Reserves; Sterling Area.

Finance Committee, *see* Legislative Council.

Financial Secretary, 63, 66, 73, 74, 78, 90, 106, 108, 112–13, 162, 183, 260, 262; *see also* Cowperthwaite; Haddon-Cave.

Fire Services, 73, 77, 86, 96, 142, 170, 174, 270.

Fish Marketing Organization, 44–5.

Fixed Penalty (Traffic Contraventions) Ordinance, 100, 189, 202n.

Football Pools Betting Bill, 66, 137n, 261.

Foreign and Commonwealth Office, 50, 58, 62, 209, 210–11, 219.

Foreign investment, inducements and deterrents to, 19, 20, 30, 42, 60, 183, 195, 217, 227–8, 230–1.

Forsgate, H.M.G. (Appointed member, Urban Council, 1965–), 165.

France, 7, 83, 126, 177n.

Fukien, 173.

Fung Shui in New Territories, 142, 275.

GAMBLING, 66, 130, 135, 198.

Garrison, *see* British Army.

Gasholders' Examination Ordinance, 194.

General Chamber of Commerce, 54–

5, 91, 136n, 183, 185, 187, 188, 194n, 256.

Germany, 9; trade with Hong Kong, 41.

Gibraltar, 6.

Goa, 16, 226.

Gordon, Sir Sidney (Unofficial, Legislative Council, 1962–6, Executive Council, 1965–), 57n, 63.

Goronwy-Roberts, Lord (Parliamentary Undersecretary of State, 1974-), 210.

Governor, 58–70, 245–6; appointments made by, 54, 61–2, 90–2, 108, 129, 162, 205; ceremonial duties, 61, 245; choice of, 62, 204–5; and honours list, 61, 128; powers of, 51–3, 58–9, 63–5, 106, 113, 163, 223; as President of Legislative Council, 59, 90, 92, 93, 120, 169; and Public Service, 51, 53, 54, 59–60, 76, 78, 79, 124; relations with Britain, 53, 58–9, 115, 204–5, 208, 210–11, 215, 246; tenure, 59, 62, 205; and Urban Council, 162, 163, 190.

Governor in Council, *see* Executive Council.

Government Gazette, 97, 98, 100, 102n, 112, 113.

Government Information Service, *see* Information Services.

Grantham, Sir Alexander (Governor, 1947–57), 4, 58, 62, 68n, 69n, 88n, 198, 204, 205, 208, 212n, 219, 220n, 225n, 245–6.

'Great Leap Forward' in China, 23.

Green Papers, 201, 224, 273.

Grey, Anthony (Reuter's correspondent), 207.

Grievance procedures, 119, 123–7, 143, 151, 153, 159, 163–5, 197; *see also* UMELCO; Urban Council Ward Offices.

Gross Domestic Product of Hong Kong, xiii, 32.

Gun Club, 188.

Gurkha soldiers, 4, 6, 13n, 222.

HADDON-CAVE, C.P. (Financial Secretary 1971–), 76, 105, 185, 219, 229.

Hakka, 173.

Harbour Pilots Union, 186.

Hawaii, 4,

Hawker Commultative Committee, 150.

Hawkers, 150, 159, 160, 190.

Heligoland, 27n.

Henessey, Sir John Pope (Governor, 1877–82), 68n.

Hetherington, R.M., 209, 254.

Heung Yee Kuk, 31, 74, 84, 143–7, 170, 172, 175, 190, 197, 199, 251, 276.

Hire purchase controls, 135.
Ho Chi Min, 28n.
Home Affairs Department, 71, 74n, 140, 148–54, 198, 251; see also City District Officers.
Hong Kong Association, 211.
'Hong Kong belonging', 34, 173, 218, 221, 257, 278.
Hong Kong Regiment, Royal, 4, 13n.
Hongkong and Shanghai Bank, 44.
Hongkong and Yaumati Ferry Company, 94, 261.
Honours List, 61, 128.
House of Commons, 181; behaviour of members, 133–4; and cabinet, 64, 87n, 104, 132, 133; and finance, 104–5, 107; and Hong Kong, 60, 116, 169, 189, 194n, 195, 207, 211, 212n; Standing Orders of, 107; see also Members of Parliament Opposition.
House of Lords, 87n, 116, 207, 211.
Housing: Authority, 77, 142, 156, 166n; Department, 74n, 151, 197; policy, 33, 43, 44, 140, 150, 156, 170, 182, 200; see also New Towns; Rent Control; Resettlement; Squatters.
Hu Hung-lick, Henry (Elected member, Urban Council, 1967–), 165, 166n.
Huang Mong-hwa, Dr. Denny (Elected member, Urban Council, 1967–), 165.

IDEOLOGY OF GOVERNMENT, see laissez-faire.
Immigration: Department, 71, 86, 271; Ordinance, 17, 96, 98, 256, 257–8, 273; see also Refugees.
Imports, see under Britain, China, etc.; trade with—.
Independence, for Hong Kong, 3, 13n, 16, 80, 169, 174, 208, 223; for other colonies, 3, 5–6, 168, 207.
Independent Commission Against Corruption (ICAC), 77, 225.
India, 5, 16, 46n, 53, 226; trade of, xiii.
Indian Chamber of Commerce, 91.
Indians in Hong Kong, 91–2.
Indirect Rule, 5.
Industrial Training Advisory Committee, 192.
Information Services Department, 92, 142, 163, 189, 197, 200–1, 211.
Inland Revenue Ordinance, 96.
Institute of Architects, 186.
Insurance companies, 46n, 187, 262.
Interest groups, see Pressure groups.
International Labour Office, 42, 45n.
International Monetary Fund, 9.
Interpretation and General Clauses Ordinance, 100, 109.

JAPAN, xiii, 9, 32, 45n, 139, 209; trade with Hong Kong, 19, 41.
Japanese occupation 1941–5, 4, 31, 40, 55, 139, 155, 210, 212n, 265.
Jardine, Matheson and Co., 43.
Jockey Club, Royal Hong Kong, 43, 138n, 186.
Judges, 51, 52, 66, 78, 79, 181.
Judicial review, 52.
Jurors, 155, 157, 166n.
Justices of the Peace, 54–5, 91, 144, 151.

KAI TAK AIRPORT, 12, 14n, 20, 43, 136, 139, 182, 206, 222, 223, 269–70, 272; see also Aviation.
Kaifong associations, 31, 148, 151, 186, 189, 197, 202, 278, 279.
Kan, Sir Yuet-keung (Unofficial, Legislative Council, 1961–72, Executive Council, 1966–), 54, 57n, 93, 110, 133, 167n, 170, 208, 251, 261, 264–5, 269.
Kan Yat-kum (Elected member, Urban Council, 1969–73), 165.
Kenya, 205, 212n.
Kenyatta, Jomo, 205.
Korea, South, 4, 42.
Korean War, 4, 23, 40.
Kowloon, 122, 140, 150, 160, 223; see also 'Walled City'.
Kowloon City ward, 165.
Kowloon Motor Bus Company, 7, 94, 253, 262.
Khruschev, Nikita, 23.
Kuomintang party, 25, 30, 32, 139, 169, 192, 200, 216, 218, 223.
Kwan Ko Siu-wah, Mrs. (Appointed Member, Urban Council, 1972–4, Unofficial, Legislative Council, 1974–), 92.
Kwantung province, 16, 32.
Kwun Tong, 31, 165.

LABOUR: Advisory Board, 192, 194n; Department, 77, 101, 132, 141, 197, 209, 254, 275; legislation, 43, 60, 69n, 100, 131, 136, 194n, 209, 213n, 214n, 224, 254; relations, see Trade Unions; Tribunals, 102n, 214n.
Labour Party (U.K.), 5, 6, 67, 104, 129, 206, 209, 210, 212n, 213n, 225n.
Laissez-faire ideology, 21, 30, 40, 42, 43–5, 93, 94, 105, 129, 193, 199, 227–30.
Lancashire textiles, 7, 12, 207, 211.
Lamma Island, 196, 276.
Land sales, see Crown Leases.
Landlord and Tenant Ordinance, 140, 148, 259.
Latvia, 11.
Law Society, 186, 255.
Lawn Tennis Association, 186.
Lee Kwan Yew, 221.

Lee, Dr. Raymond (Elected member, Urban Council, 1953–67), 163.
Legal Aid Department, 125, 151.
Legal system, see Constitution; Courts of Law; Judges.
Legislation, see Delegated legislation; Ordinances.
Legislative Council, 51, 52, 90–138, 197; adjournment debates, 120–1; composition, 54–5, 90–1, 133; debates, 120–1, 132–4, 169, 170; Establishment Sub-committee, 108, 110, 112, 264–5, 277; Finance Committee, 54, 63, 64, 66, 72, 75–6, 85, 107–15, 119, 162, 204, 212n, 264–5; functions, 95, 119–20, 131, 134; Governor as President, 59, 90, 92, 93, 120, 169; Public Works Sub-committee, 108, 112, 117n; questions in, 115, 120, 121–3, 132, 133, 134, 155, 268–70; reforms proposed, 24–6, 123, 134, 168–9; Standing Orders, 93–4, 102n, 106, 107, 108, 111, 120, 121, 123, 127n; select committees, 98, 117n; Urban Council and, 91, 161, 162–3, 166–7n; voting in, 25, 54, 66, 92–5, 98–9, 107, 169, 204, 259, 260–2; see also Ordinances; Unofficials.
Legitimacy of Hong Kong government, 29–30, 35, 65, 119, 129, 136, 187–8, 191, 200, 201, 221, 278–80.
Lenin, 26.
Letters Patent, 50–1, 53–4, 58, 62, 78, 107, 203, 232–7.
Libraries, 148, 156, 160.
Li Fook-kow, 77.
Li Fook-shu (Unofficial, Legislative Council, 1962–8, Executive Council, 1966–8), 111, 181.
Li Shu-pui, Mrs. Ellen (Unofficial, Legislative Council, 1966–73), 53, 92, 138n, 202n, 269.
Liao Poon-huai, 78.
Lin Yu-tang (quoted), 35.
Liquor licensing, 156, 160.
Lithuania, 11.
Lo, Sir Man Kam (Unofficial, Legislative Council, 1935–41 and 1946–50, Executive Council, 1946–59), 120, 260.
Lo Tak-cheung (Appointed member, Urban Council, 1966–), 165.
Lo Tak-shing (Appointed member, Urban Council, 1970–74, Unofficial, Legislative Council, 1974–), 165, 167n, 253, 262.
Lo Wu, 32.
Lobo, R.H. (Appointed member, Urban Council, 1965–75, Unofficial, Legislative Council, 1972–), 165.
Local government, 139–77; arguments in favour, 171–4; in Britain, 104, 173, 177n; in France, 177n; in Hong Kong, difficulties, 169, 174–

6; proposed reform of, 60, 146–7, 152–3, 155, 168–77, 223, 278–80; see also City District Officers; Heung Yee Kuk; Urban Council.
Localization of Public Service, see Public Service.
London Office of Hong Kong Government, 210–11.
Lutheran World Service, 186.

'MACANIZATION' OF HONG KONG, 216, 223.
Macau, xiii, 16, 24, 216, 223, 226.
MacKenzie, John (Appointed member, Urban Council, 1971–), 165, 167n.
MacLehose, Sir Murray (Governor, 1971–), 45, 62, 68n, 69n, 214n, 219.
Magistrates, 96, 140, 141, 271.
Magistrates Association, 186.
Malaysia, Federation of, 27, 45n.
Management Unit in Colonial Secretariat, 76.
Manila, 20.
Mao Tse-tung, xiv, 15, 23, 25, 26, 36, 41, 201, 222.
Margaret, Princess, 117n, 200.
Marriage: gifts to royalty, 117n, 200; problems, 143, 151; reform, 53, 130, 137n, 198.
Mass Transit Scheme, 45, 61, 66, 196, 209, 262.
'May 4th Movement', 36.
'May 30th Incident', 31.
McKinsey Report on Public Service, 73–6, 86, 87n, 88n, 91, 141, 200, 225, 249–50.
Media, see Broadcasting; Information Services; Newspapers; Radio Hong Kong; Television.
Medical Advisory Board, 85.
Medical and Health Department, 91, 92, 142, 163, 170, 174, 176, 201, 256–7.
Medical Council, 95, 187.
Members of Parliament, 95, 104, 107, 116, 123, 129, 132, 173, 189, 207, 209, 211.
Merchant Shipping Act (U.K.), 206, 213n.
Merchandise Marks Ordinance, 196.
Metrication Committee, 85.
Middle class, xiv, 148, 159, 199, 202n.
Midwives, 190.
Military governments, 44, 181.
Minibuses, 190, 261–2.
Ministers and civil service in U.K., 50, 78, 131, 204, 210, 224, 246; and Hong Kong, see British Government.
Mining Ordinance, 100, 275.
Ministry of Defence, 4, 58.
Missionary societies, see Voluntary agencies.
Mong Kok, 165.

Motor Transport Workers Union, 186, 189.
Multi-national companies, 19, 20, 41, 42, 82.
Multi-storey buildings owners' incorporations, 151, 186.
Museum, 160.
Mutual Aid Committees, 186.

NARCOTICS, see Drug addiction.
Nationalism, xiv, 15, 30, 222.
Nationalists, see Kuomintang, Taiwan.
Natural History Society, 188.
Navy, Royal, 3, 4, 6, 13n, 246.
New China News Agency, 219.
New Grant Lots, 140.
New Territories, 139–7, 159, 188, 198; Administration, 75, 77, 140–3, 145–7, 149, 151–2, 160, 266–7, 275–7, 282; China and lease of, 16, 139–40, 222–3, 226; local government reform in, 146–7, 170, 175–6; see also District Officers; Heung Yee Kuk; New Towns; Rural Committees.
New Towns, 74, 75, 140, 142, 146, 277.
New Zealand, 20, 123.
Newspapers, 36, 96, 97, 102n, 109, 113, 115, 120, 125, 126, 135, 146, 189–90, 197, 210, 216, 217, 247, 255, 257.
Ng Ping-kin, Peter (Appointed member, Urban Council, 1966–), 165.
Ngan Shing-kwan (Unofficial, Legislative Council, 1951–61, Executive Council, 1959–61), 66, 137n.
Nien rebellion, 36.
Northern Ireland, 6, 212n.
Nurses, 76, 193, 195.
Nurses Registration Ordinance, 195.

OFFICIAL LANGUAGES ORDINANCE, 36n, 199.
Official members, see Executive Council; Legislative Council, composition of.
Oil prices, 10, 40, 196, 220n, 222.
Old Schedule Lots, 140.
Ombudsman, 93, 123–4, 126, 130, 143, 151, 199; see also UMELCO.
Opposition in Britain, 5, 6, 29, 107, 130–1, 133, 200, 212n, 273; in Hong Kong, see Unofficials.
Orders in Council (U.K.), 50, 139, 140, 203.
Ordinances, 49, 95–101, 254–60; advisory committees and, 92–3, 96, 100, 130, 146, 256–7; amendments, 54, 93, 97, 98, 106, 113, 189, 257; assent by Governor, 52, 98–9, 113; classification, 95–6; consultation with Britain on, 53, 99–100, 102n, 103n, 203, 255–6; disallowance, 53, 59, 99–100, 194n, 203; drafting, 65,

97, 100, 191, 255–7; Executive Council and, 63, 65–6, 93, 97; finance bills, see Finance; initiation, 92, 96, 133, 199; pressure groups and, 92, 96–7, 102n, 130, 146, 189, 195–6, 199, 255–60; private members' bills, 95; procedure in Legislative Council, 51, 97–9, 130; repeal, 95, 102n; reserved subjects, 52, 99; UMELCO and, 97, 188–9.
Overlords in British government, 76, 87n.

PALESTINE, 6.
Palmerston, Lord, 53.
Parks, 156, 160.
Parliament: Acts of, 53, 66, 96, 203, 212n, 213n; and cabinet, 64; legislates for Hong Kong, 53, 203, 212n; see also House of Commons; House of Lords; Members of Parliament; Opposition.
Parliamentary Commissioner for Administration, 123, 126, 127n.
Parties in Britain, see Conservative Party; Labour Party.
Parties in Hong Kong, see Civic Association; Reform Club.
People's Liberation Army, 4, 17, 18, 22, 23, 169, 222.
Permanent secretaries (U.K.), 78.
Petitions, 53, 189, 194n, 197.
Pharmacy and Poisons Board, 84, 101, 256.
Philippines, 4, 42, 45n.
Planning, 44, 45, 59, 61, 73–4, 76, 131, 170, 227, 276–7.
Po Leung Kuk, 31, 148, 186.
Police, 4, 17, 22, 33, 56n, 60, 71, 77, 78, 79–80, 101, 120–1, 135, 136, 140, 142, 145, 150–1, 185, 190, 216, 217, 221, 222, 271, 276.
Political Adviser to Governor on Foreign Affairs, 62, 76, 219.
Political culture of Hong Kong, see Apathy; Attitudes of Hong Kong Chinese.
Politics, politicians, 5, 24, 25, 62, 133, 158–9, 168, 173–4, 193; rejection of, in Hong Kong, 170, 181–3.
Pollution, 121, 142, 196, 221.
Polytechnic, 96.
Population, 141, 146, 147n, 149, 174.
Port Committee, 85.
Port Executive Committee, 85.
Portugal, 216.
Portuguese in Hong Kong, 63, 91.
Post Office, 44, 77, 86.
Pottinger, Sir Henry (Governor, 1843–4), xiii, 49.
Pressure groups, 148, 181–3, 185–94, 224; access to government, 97, 98, 130, 172, 183, 188, 190, 191–2, 256, 278–80; classification, 185–6, 279;

consultation with, 60, 92, 96, 97, 100, 102n, 112, 135, 148, 150, 152, 186–93, 197, 221, 255–7; countervailing forces to, 172, 192–3, 199; dangers, 110, 148, 183, 191–2, 197; leadership, 34, 132, 144, 148, 171, 188, 197, 279; methods used by, 146, 188–91; and ordinances, 92, 96–7, 102n, 130, 146, 189, 195–6, 199, 255–60; reasons for government contact with, 60, 150–1, 176, 186–8; and UMELCO, 97.
Prevention of Bribery Ordinance, 146, 191, 194n, 255–6.
Price, I.R., 77.
Prime Minister, 61, 64–5, 76, 106, 117n.
Primrose, R.W., 124, 126–7, 194n.
Printing Department, 69.
Prisons Department, 86, 131.
Privy Council, 50, 55n.
Productivity Council, 85.
Public Enquiry Centres, 149, 150.
Public health, 155, 159, 160, 175.
Public Health Bill (1886), 53, 155.
Public interest, 181–2, 183, 193, 199, 258, 279.
Public opinion, 62, 125–6, 144, 183, 195–202; in Britain, 5–6, 29, 60, 104, 131, 171–2, 211; difficulty in assessing, 195–9; government attitude to, 60, 67, 96, 98, 119, 136, 155, 164, 170, 189, 193, 195, 198–200, 221, 278–80; government influence on, 59, 92, 142, 149, 150–1, 200–1, 211; ignorance, 35, 39n, 196, 280; inconsistency, 196; sources, 197–8, 255; unofficials and, 198–9.
Public Revenue Protection Ordinance, 113.
Public Service, 44, 71–89; classes, 76–8, 80; criticism of, 35, 101n, 119, 124, 126, 133, 152–3, 166n, 278–80; complacency in, 59, 149, 172, 224; confirmation of officers, 79, 84; departmental heads, 60, 63, 66, 71–3, 75, 77–8, 79, 86, 90, 96, 106, 113, 115, 164, 251, 264; discipline, 51, 53, 79, 114, 162, 205; education allowances, 82, 111; expatriate officers, 11, 29, 79–83, 111, 131, 136, 187, 221, 268; localization, 3, 79–84, 111, 131, 149, 224, 250, 268; McKinsey Report, 73–6, 86, 87n, 88n, 91, 141, 200, 225, 249–50; promotion of officers, 59, 69, 74, 77, 79, 82–3, 205, 224; recruitment, 78–84, 152, 210, 250, 268; relations with Britain, 78, 83, 114, 205, 207–9, 264; salaries, 82, 84, 112, 161–2; size, 80–2, 110, 264–5; suspicion of, 35, 83, 125–7, 187; *see also* Administrative Officers; Executive Officers.

Public Service Commission, 54, 59, 65, 78–9, 85, 162, 265.
Public Works Department, 71, 74, 91, 108, 142, 150–1, 163, 170, 205, 261.
Public Works Sub-committee, *see* Legislative Council.
Public relations, *see* Information Services; Public opinion; Government influence on.

QUEEN, *see* British Government.
Questions: in House of Commons, 56n, 60, 118n, 123, 127n, 134, 189, 194n, 210; in Legislative Council, 56n, 115, 120, 121–3, 132, 133, 134, 137n, 155, 189, 268–70; supplementaries, 121, 122, 133; in Urban Council, 161.
Quotas against exports, 7, 21, 41, 206–7, 211.

RABIES, 188–9, 275.
Radiation Board, 84.
Radio Hong Kong, 93, 109, 126, 197, 200–1.
Railway, 43, 86.
Rates, 140, 155, 157, 162–3, 183, 260.
Real Estate Developers Association, 185, 192.
Recreation, 30, 143, 148, 151, 175, 276–7.
Recreational Development, Advisory Committee on, 143, 276.
Re-exports from Hong Kong, 18, 19, 20, 40, 41, 169.
Reform Bill of 1832, 181.
Reform Club, 157, 158–9, 161, 173, 186, 194n.
Refugees, 4, 5, 17, 27n, 31–2, 38n, 140, 169, 216, 223.
Registrar General, 148n; *see* Home Affairs Department.
Registrar of Births, 141.
Registrar of Societies, 186.
Regulations, *see* Delegated legislation.
Renison, Sir Patrick, 205.
Rent control, 21, 44, 56n, 130, 136, 192, 198, 199, 247, 258, 261.
Representation, 54–5, 58–9, 91–2, 128–9, 132, 143, 158, 168, 172–3, 188, 192, 197, 211, 281; virtual, 188, 194n; *see also* Democracy.
Republic of China, *see* Taiwan.
Reserves of Hong Kong government, 8–11, 12, 19, 99, 103n, 116, 196, 205–6, 208, 209, 222.
Reserved bills, 52, 99.
Reservoirs, 40, 142, 145, 217, 276.
Resettlement areas, estates, 156, 161, 164, 200; Department, 74n, 77, 78, 150, 272.
Rhodesia, 208.
Rice Control Scheme, 44, 46n, 217.

Rights of the individual, 49, 52, 56n, 134–5, 181–2, 184n, 221.
Riots, 12, 15, 29, 106, 192, 197, 204, 217, 218, 222; of 1956, 4, 30; of 1966, 4, 30, 33, 60, 85, 149, 195, 224; of 1967, 4, 30, 31, 60, 67, 149, 171, 191, 207, 209, 218, 224; see also Violence.
Robson, J.J., 76.
Rodrigues, Sir Albert (Unofficial, Legislative Council, 1953–9, Executive Council, 1959–74), 63, 256.
Rotary clubs, 186.
Royal Instructions, 50–2, 53–4, 58, 63, 64, 65, 66–7, 90, 91, 99, 106, 107, 203, 237–44.
Royal Navy, 3, 4, 6, 13n.
Royle, Anthony (Minister of State, 1970–4), 210.
Rural Committees, 31, 84, 143–5, 152, 186, 189, 197, 251.
Russia, see Soviet Union.
Ruttonjee, Dhun (Unofficial, Legislative Council, 1953–8 and 1959–68), 69n, 76, 88n, 91, 93, 101n, 116n, 202n, 261.

Sai Kung, 141, 152, 276.
Salaries Commission, 84, 112, 118n.
Salazar (quoted) 182.
Sales, Arnaldo de Oliveira (Appointed member, Urban Council, 1957–), 157, 161, 165, 167n, 176n, 177n, 190, 194n.
Salmon, G.M.B. (Unofficial, Legislative Council, 1970–2), 76.
Sanitary Board, 155.
Saunders, J.A.H. (Unofficial, Executive Council, 1966–72), 132.
Schools, 36, 60, 83, 110–11, 142, 143, 170, 174, 176, 189, 216, 270.
Secrecy of Finance Committee, 109, 265.
Secretariat, see Colonial Secretariat.
Secretariat, Secretary for Chinese Affairs, 148n; see also Home Affairs Departments.
Secretary for the Civil Service, 74, 75, 79, 108, 109, 265; Colonial, see Colonial Secretary; for Economic Affairs, 74n, 74; for Environment, 74, 91; Financial, see Financial Secretary; for Home Affairs, 63, 74, 77, 78, 90, 198, 201; for Housing, 74, 75, 91; for Information, 77, 200–1; for the New Territories, 75, 91, 141–5, 160, 175; for Security, 74, 91; for Social Services, 74, 77, 91.
Secretary of State, see British Government.
Seychelles, 6.
Sha Tau Kok, 4, 68n.
Sha Tin, 141, 146, 170, 175, 276.
Sham Shui Po, 153n, 165.

Shanghai, 19, 22, 31, 41, 169.
Shepherd, Lord (Minister of State, 1967–70), 67, 68n, 116, 209, 210, 213n.
Sin Cho-chiu (Elected member, Urban Council, 1971–5), 165.
Singapore, xiii, xiv, 4, 20, 32, 42, 45n, 58, 152, 175, 210, 221, 246.
Sinkiang, 22.
Sino-Japanese War, 1894–5, 139.
Smith, Adam, 193.
Smith, Ian, 208.
Social Security, 202n.
Social Welfare Advisory Committee, 85, 251; Department, 71, 77, 125, 141, 143, 149, 151, 176, 266–7; Policy, 60, 106, 116n, 170, 201, 218, 245, 251.
Societies Ordinance, 144, 186.
Society for the Blind, 185, 190, 193.
Society for the Prevention of Cruelty to Animals, 185.
South Korea, 4, 41, 42.
Southern District, New Territories, 144.
Soviet Union, 11, 16, 17, 21, 23, 24, 26, 216, 226.
Special Branch of Hong Kong Police, 17, 22, 33.
Spies, 17, 216.
Sports Grounds, 160, 162.
Squatters, 139, 141, 142, 146, 156.
Sri Lanka (Ceylon), 3, 27, 212n, 213n.
Stadium, 156, 160, 163.
Stalin, 26.
Standing Orders, Legislative Council, 93–4, 102n, 106, 107, 108, 111, 120, 121, 123, 127n.
Star Ferry Company, 30, 85, 94, 261; riots, see Riots, of 1966.
Sterling Area, 8–9, 215; guarantee, 8–10, 205–6, 208; reserves, 8–11, 12, 19, 99, 103n, 116, 196, 205–7, 208, 209, 222.
Stock Exchanges, xiv, 45, 122, 189.
Street naming, 156, 163.
Strikes, 30–1, 37n, 190, 197, 217–8.
Students, 31, 34, 36, 86, 151, 173, 190, 199, 211, 224.
Subsidiary legislation, see Delegated legislation.
Subsidies, 43–4, 45, 94, 105, 110–11, 187, 193, 227, 229.
Sugar Convention Ordinance (1913), 100, 203.
Sukarno, President, viii, 181.
Sun Yat-sen, 36.
Superscale Salaries, Standing Committee on, 85.
Surveys, 37n, 38n, 39n, 150, 159, 197–8.
Swimming pools and beaches, 160, 162, 269.
Switzerland, 9.
Szechuan, 35.

Symons, Mrs. C.J. (Appointed member, Urban Council, 1969–72, Unofficial, Legislative Council, 1972–), 92, 136n, 165.

Szeto Wai (Unofficial, Legislative Council, 1965–74, Executive Council, 1972–), 138n, 252.

TAI LAM CHUNG RESERVOIR, 145.

Taiping rebellion, 36.

Tai Po, 141, 144.

Taiwan, 4, 17, 19, 20, 22, 23, 24, 42, 156, 216, 218–19, 223.

Tang Ping-yuan (Unofficial, Legislative Council, 1964–8, Executive Council, 1968–71), 63.

Tariffs, 7, 41, 206–7, 229.

Taxation, 20, 42, 43, 66, 93, 95, 96, 105, 107, 111–12, 113–14, 115, 118n, 129, 136, 137n, 157, 182, 194n, 196, 201, 260, 261, 262, 280.

Teachers, 39n, 76, 166, 182, 190, 193; see also Education; Schools.

Telecommunications Ordinance, 100.

Telephones, 89n, 105, 142.

Television, 126, 197, 200.

Tenders, 66.

Teng Pin-hui, Dr. (Official member, Executive Council, 1966–70), 63.

Textile Advisory Board, 187, 211.

Thailand, 45n.

Tibet, xiv, 22.

Topley, K.W.J., 78.

Trade and Industry Advisory Board, 85.

Trade balance, see Britain, China, etc.

Trade Development Council, 12, 43, 77, 187.

Trade Unions, 30, 60, 96, 186, 190, 191–2, 216, 255.

Trade Union Registration Ordinance, 96, 102n.

Trade Union Congress (U.K.), 132.

Transport Advisory Committee, 85, 92, 142, 251–3; Department, 71, 77, 149, 151, 170.

Treasury control in Britain, 105–6.

Treaty of Nanking (1842), 15, 49.

Trench, Sir David (Governor, 1964–71), 40, 60, 62, 65, 127n, 169, 171, 195, 225n.

Triad gangs, 186.

Tourism, 12, 20, 41, 135, 217, 229, 276.

Tourist Association, 12, 135, 186, 190, 276.

Town Planning Board, 142.

'Town Talk', 150, 200.

Tse Yu-chuen (Unofficial, Legislative Council, 1964–70), 181.

Tsing Yi island, 231.

Tsuen Wan, 141, 146, 152, 170, 175.

Tsui Ka-cheung, Paul, 82, 149, 176, 275, 279–82.

Tuen Mun new town (Castle Peak), 141, 146, 170.

Tung Wah Hospital Group, 31, 85, 148, 186.

Turnbull, Sir Richard, 205.

Typhoons, 33, 143, 148, 151.

ULTRA VIRES, 52.

UMELCO office, 92, 97, 117n, 123–7, 143, 164, 167, 188–9, 197, 199, 270–3.

Underground railway, see Mass Transit Scheme.

Unemployment, 15, 39n, 40, 141, 147n, 246.

Unions, see Trade Unions.

United Kingdom, see Britain; British.

United Nations, 4, 12, 16, 24, 40.

United Nations Association, 186.

United States: Congress, 43, 97, 133; and defence of Hong Kong, 4, 23; relations with China, 4, 23, 204, 207, 212n; Fleet, 4, 23; trade with Hong Kong, 19, 20, 41.

Universities, 34, 54, 80, 82, 95, 108, 261.

Unofficial members: and advisory committees, 86, 92, 101n, 112, 130; attitudes, 25, 66, 106, 111, 124, 129, 133, 168–9, 198–9; and British government, 58–9, 94, 115–16, 204, 208–9, 210, 246, 264; business connections, 44, 54–5, 92, 112, 128, 131–2, 260; cohesion, 66, 129, 130–1, 136, 137n, 259; comparison with British M.P.s, 107, 130–2, 133–4, 136–7n, 137n, 273; expertise, 129–30, 131–2; facilities for, 92, 112, 124, 130; functions, 95, 119–20, 131, 132, 224, 273–4; government consultation with, 93, 95, 97, 124, 132, 257–8, 264, 273; illiberality, 52, 134–5; not professional politicians, 25, 123, 129–32; office of, see UMELCO; power of, 106, 108–12, 119, 128, 135–6, 198–9, 257–60, 270–2; prestige, 129, 131–2, 136, 168, 173; Senior Unofficial, 54, 63, 66, 102n, 110, 273; silence in 1950s, 132, 208, 213n, 224; tameness, 107, 109–11, 126, 128, 132–4, 208, 224; unrepresentativeness, 91–2, 128–9, 198–9; wealth, 92, 128–9.

Urban Council, 51, 155–67; by laws, 100–1, 161, 162; candidates, 129, 157, 158–9, 189; Chairman, 161, 162, 164; committees, 157, 160–1, 166n; composition, 31, 156–7; controls over, 161, 162, 163; debates, 161, 163, 164, 197; divisions, 157, 163, 202n; elections, 31, 34, 129, 155, 158–60, 172, 281; expenses for members, 130, 157, 167n; finance, 162–3; functions, 156, 160, 172; meetings, 157, 161; promotion to

Legislative Council, 55, 91, 164–5; questions in, 161; reforms proposed, 156, 157–8, 169–71, 174–5; registration of electors, 31, 157–8, 201; *Standing Orders,* 161, 164; Statement of Aims, 164; Ward offices, 125, 126, 152–3, 157, 163–5, 197.

Urban Services Department, 77, 91, 96, 141, 150–1, 153, 160, 161–2, 163, 169, 175, 177n.

VEGETABLE MARKETING ORGANIZATION, 44–5.

Village representatives, 143–4, 146.

Violence, 6, 15, 36, 141, 159, 173, 183, 190, 191; *see also* Riots.

'Virtual representation', 188, 194n.

Voluntary agencies, 60, 85, 95, 112, 176, 186–7, 194n, 270; *see also* Pressure groups.

Voting, *see* Elections; Heung Yee Kuk; Legislative Council; Urban Council.

WAGES, 33, 42.

Walden, J.C.C., 176, 279–82.

'Walled City' of Kowloon, 139–40, 217.

Wanchai, 165.

Water supplies, 40, 43, 73, 140, 142, 145, 183, 217, 223; from China, 15, 17, 60, 216, 217, 220n.

Ward offices, *see* Urban Council.

Watson, K.A. (Unofficial, Legislative Council, 1964–70), 116n, 121, 252, 261, 262.

Webb-Johnson, S.A., 176, 279–82.

Western City District, 151, 165.

White Papers, 93, 120, 187, 201; on

Urban Council (1971), 86, 158, 166n, 171, 273.

Wild Birds and Wild Mammals Protection Ordinance, 188–9, 215–16.

Williams, P.G. (Unofficial, Legislative Council, 1972–), 55, 57n.

Women in Legislative Council, 92.

Wong, Henry (Elected member, Urban Council, 1969–73), 165.

Wong Sien-bing, Wilfred (Unofficial, Legislative Council, 1965–74), 120, 127n, 137n, 202, 269.

Wong Wing-cheung, Mrs. Mary (Unofficial, Legislative Council, 1972–3), 92, 136n.

Wong Tai Sin, 165.

Woo Pak-chuen (Elected member, Urban Council, 1953–7, Unofficial, Legislative Council, 1964–74, Executive Council, 1972–), 56n, 89n, 102n, 111, 120–1, 134, 137n, 138n, 165, 257, 259.

Working Party on Local Administration, *see* Local government, proposed reform.

Wu Man-hon (Appointed member, Urban Council, 1968–73, Unofficial, Legislative Council, 1972–), 165.

YAU MA TEI, 165.

Yaumati Ferry Company, 94, 261.

Yeung Lai-yin, Miss Cecilia (Elected member, Urban Council, 1971–), 165.

Young, Sir Mark (Governor, 1941–7), 168.

Young Plan (1946), 31, 120, 155, 156, 168–9, 170, 223, 260.

Youth camps, 143, 151.

Yuan dynasty, 35.

Yuen Long, 141, 144, 276.